The Women and War Re

The
Women and War
Reader

EDITED BY

Lois Ann Lorentzen

AND

Jennifer Turpin

New York University Press

NEW YORK AND LONDON

NEW YORK UNIVERSITY PRESS
New York and London

© 1998 by New York University

A previous version of chapter 1 appeared in *The Encyclopedia of Violence, Peace, and Conflict,* Academic Press, San Diego, 1998; chapters 2, 3, 4, 8, 12, 13, 17, 22, 24, 25, 29, 30, 31, 33, 35, and 36 appeared previously in *Peace Review,* 8:3, September 1996, Lois Ann Lorentzen and Jennifer Turpin, eds. CARFAX Publishing Company, P.O. Box 25, Abingdon, Oxfordshire OX14 3UE, UK; chapter 5 appeared previously as "Politics of Identity and Gendered Nationalism," in *Foreign Policy Analysis,* Neak/Haney eds. © 1995, 177–184, reprinted by permission of Prentice Hall, Inc., Upper Saddle River, NJ; chapter 7 is reprinted from *Mass Rape: The War against Women in Bosnia-Herzegovina,* ed. Alexandra Stiglmayer, by permission of the University of Nebraska Press, © 1993 Kore Verlag GmbH and © 1994 by the University of Nebraska Press; chapter 15 is reprinted here by permission of *Der Überblick;* chapter 21 is reprinted from *Liberation Theologies, Postmodernity, and the Americas,* edited by David Batstone et al., by permission of Routledge; an earlier version of chapter 23 was published in *Filozofska Istrazivanja,* no. 64, 1997 (Croatian) and in *Synthesis Philosophica,* no. 23, 1/1997 (English).

Library of Congress Cataloging-in-Publication Data
The women and war reader / edited by Lois Ann Lorentzen and Jennifer Turpin.
p. cm.
Includes bibliographical references and index.
ISBN 0-8147-5144-X (hardcover : alk. paper). — ISBN 0-8147-5145-8 (pbk. : alk. paper)
1. World War, 1939–1945—Women. I. Lorentzen, Lois Ann, 1952– .
II. Turpin, Jennifer E.
D810.W7W656 1998
940.53'082—dc21   98-18165
                         CIP

New York University Press books are printed on acid-free paper, and their binding materials are chosen for strength and durability.

Manufactured in the United States of America

10 9 8 7 6 5 4 3 2 1

For our sisters, mothers, and daughter
Ruth Ann Lorentzen
Nelia Lorentzen
Rachel Smith
Solveig Turpin
Madeleine Elias
Strong women, our inspiration

Contents

Preface

Lois Ann Lorentzen and Jennifer Turpin

From Rwanda to the former Yugoslavia, wars continue to rage in our post-Cold War world. Each war affects women in profoundly different ways than men. Women play many roles during wartime: they are "gendered" as mothers, as soldiers, as munitions makers, as caretakers, as sex workers. Ironically, while war making relies on women's participation, women are also most often at the forefront of peacemaking efforts. How is it that womanhood in the context of war may mean, for one woman, tearfully sending her son off to war, and for another, engaging in civil disobedience against the state? How might war's social and economic consequences send some women into military prostitution and others into soldiering? And why do we think of war as "men's business" when women as civilians are more likely to be killed and to become war refugees than men?

These questions have emerged for us through our combined experience as activists and educators. Lois first encountered the many ways women suffer during war while working in refugee resettlement programs in the state of Minnesota. The stories told her by Hmong, Vietnamese, Vietnamese Chinese, Lao, and Cambodian women deeply moved her and convinced her that women experience war in ways that often differ from men. Solidarity work in the United States and in El Salvador further forced her to examine the connections between gender, militarization, and peace activism.

Jennifer worked with rape survivors for seven years, while at the same time studying the effects of Cold War militarization on civilians. Her studies and travels introduced her to women peace activists in the United States and the former Soviet Union as well as in the countries where the superpowers fought the Cold War. These experiences forced her to confront the connections between micro and macro violence as well as between militarism and violence against women.

Since our early studies, feminist scholarship on women and war has gone beyond simplistic gender dichotomies. More and more we recognize that claiming inherent differences between women and men contradicts the real life actions of men and women. Simply arguing that men are militarists and women are antimilitarists belies the facts. History has demonstrated that many men resist war through refusal to participate, draft evasion, and outright protest. In addition, many women express their citizenship or even nationalism by proudly sending sons to war or fighting those wars themselves. Other women constitute the backbone of the military economy, working in defense-related production. Feminist scholarship is gradually abandoning its early dichotomies, while still recognizing that *something* is different—we do observe patterns in men's and women's relationships to war, and more often men are war's makers, while women are war's resisters. If we reject essentialism, how do we account for this?

Feminist scholarship on war has also broadened these debates by integrating questions of class, race, and ethnicity. It is too simple, for example, to say that women form the bedrock of military-industrial production. We need to probe deeper. While some women may do defense work to express patriotic values, economic factors must also be weighed. Poor people tend to "volunteer" for military service in disproportionate numbers, with large numbers of people of color sent to the battle lines. A whole body of scholarship addresses how poor women and girls are forced or coerced into sex work in times of war, from the Korean "comfort women" to military brothels to prostitution around military bases. Other works have emerged focusing on wars in specific regions. These works have challenged us to look at women and war comparatively, demonstrating that some previously documented patterns persist while others must be challenged.

Perhaps most contentious in the debates around women and war is the role of motherhood. Women around the world cite motherhood as one of the pivotal components of their war resistance. Witness the many women's peace groups organized and named after motherhood: The Madres de la Plaza de Mayo, Las Comadres of El Salvador, Another Mother for Peace, and many others. However, other scholars have challenged the view that motherhood produces a peace perspective, emphasizing that women as *mothers* also play central roles in supporting wars. What can we conclude about the role of motherhood in war? How can we understand the many twists and turns that womanhood takes in the various wartime contexts in which it is expressed?

In *The Women and War Reader* we examine many questions—to complicate our understandings of women and war while also clarifying them. The contributions from numerous scholars address women's wartime experiences from a wide range of disciplines and perspectives and from many of the world's regions.

From its early stages, *The Women and War Reader* was a collective effort. We first must thank our contributors. We have benefited from their fine scholarship, activism, stories, strength, and generosity of spirit. Their enthusiasm for the project made working on the reader a privilege. Our editorial assistant, Jodi York, spent long hours and late nights helping us bring the reader to press. Her competence, professionalism, and calm in the midst of chaos made her indispensable. We also thank Brianna Leavitt for her heroic efforts in the final stages of manuscript preparation. We couldn't have done it without her.

We have been fortunate to enjoy support from our colleagues at the University of San Francisco. Support from Dean Stanley Nel and the Faculty Development Committee of the College of Arts and Sciences at the University of San Francisco made research for this book possible. Several of *The Women and War Reader*'s essays first appeared in a special issue of *Peace Review*. Robert Elias, editor of *Peace Review*, merits special thanks.

We also thank New York University Press, especially Associate Editor Jennifer Hammer, for professionalism and enthusiasm for the project. Finally, we thank our partners Gerardo Marín and Robert Elias for their loving support and feminist sensibilities.

Part I

Theoretical Debates

Chapter One

Many Faces
Women Confronting War

Jennifer Turpin

War has profound and unique effects on women. Rather than being separate from women's lives, war making relies on women's participation. However, conventional views of the relationship between gender and war suggest that men make war, women make peace. Men, representing their nations or social groups, combat men of another group, while women remain outside the fighting, protected by "their" men. Women do remain invisible in military policy-making, reflecting taken-for-granted international assumptions about the maleness of war. But both feminist scholarship and empirical reality challenge the prevailing assumptions about war's relationship to men and women.

It is important to examine the many faces of women confronting war: the distinct impact that war has on women due to their gender and the various ways that women respond. We should consider the major debates within this field of study and explore gender inequality as a cause of war.

The Impact of War on Women

Women suffer from war in many ways, including dying, experiencing sexual abuse and torture, and losing loved ones, homes, and communities. Many people assume that women are unlikely to die in wars, since so few women serve in the armed forces worldwide. But women, as civilians, are more likely to be killed in war than are soldiers.

Women as Direct Casualties

War's impact on women has changed with the development of increasingly efficient war-making technologies that make war and militarism more and more deadly. The past century has witnessed the killing of about 104 million people in wars—more than three quarters of all war dead recorded since the year 1500. Most people killed in war are civilians. The advent of high-altitude bombing, more powerful bombs, and a strategy of "total war" in practice has ended the distinction between combatants and civilians as targets of war. While 50 percent of World War II's casualties were civilians, in the 1980s this figure rose to 80 percent, and by 1990 it was a staggering 90 percent. Women and their children constitute the vast majority of these civilian casualties (Hauchler and Kennedy 1994; Vickers 1993).

These deaths are not randomly distributed throughout the world—most of the wars since the 1960s have taken place in the less-developed countries, particularly in Asia and sub-Saharan Africa. Military intervention, on the other hand, is perpetrated primarily by the former colonial powers, mostly by the United States, followed by Britain and then the USSR/Russia, Belgium, South Africa, and India. In addition to their direct intervention, the United States and former Soviet Union have also exported the most arms to the developing world (Hauchler and Kennedy 1994).

Besides analyzing war through the lens of gender, we must also explore the global intersections between gender and class, race, nation, and ethnicity. Women may be more or less vulnerable to the effects of war and militarization depending on their home society, their economic status, and their racial/ethnic identity. Women in developing countries are most likely to experience war, and most likely to be driven from their homelands (Forbes Martin 1992; Hauchler and Kennedy 1994; Sivard 1996).

Women as War Refugees

Women are also most likely to be uprooted by war. More than four-fifths of war refugees are women and young girls, who also experience additional and often sexualized violence during their flight. By the end of 1992 more than 46 million people had lost their homes; about 36 million of these were women and girls. In Africa there were more than 23.6 million external and internal refugees; more than 12.6 million people fled their homes in the Middle East and in South and Central Asia. There are two million displaced persons in Latin America, and about six million refugees in Europe. About two million people fled the former Yugoslavia (Hauchler and Kennedy 1994).

Refugee women often serve as their children's sole caretakers, as many of them are widows or separated from their spouses and other extended family. They must seek food and safety not only for themselves, but also for their children, who also need health care, housing, and an education. Refugee women in exile are often the supporters of an extended family network, playing a central economic role yet still lacking decision-making power in their societies (Forbes Martin 1992; Collett, this volume).

Wartime Sexual Violence against Women

The United Nations High Commissioner on Refugees (UNHCR) cites sexual attacks on women and girls by camp guards as a major problem (Vickers 1993). Even those women and girls stationed in camps and refugee settlements, as well as in new societies of residence, frequently suffer sexual abuse, abduction, and forced prostitution. History has demonstrated the link between war and control of women's sexuality and reproduction through rape, sexual harassment, and militarized prostitution.

Rape. John Tenhula relates the stories of women and children who fled Vietnam by boat and were the subjects of attacks by pirates during their flight. He quotes eyewitnesses of these attacks: "Two of the young and pretty girls were taken to the front of the boat and raped. Everyone heard everything, all of the screams. That is what I remember, the screams. After a while the screams stopped, the crying stopped, and there was silence" (1991:69).

But being young and pretty has very little to do with becoming a victim of wartime rape. There are numerous accounts of very old women being brutally raped and murdered. These women, who often have limited mobility and live alone, are especially vulnerable to attack by soldiers.

The torture of political prisoners is also gendered. Women imprisoned for their political activities are commonly raped repeatedly by multiple rapists (Lorentzen, this volume). In the former Yugoslavia, thousands of Muslim women have been forced into camps and raped by Serbian soldiers, and Muslim and Croat soldiers have also committed mass rapes (Stiglmayer 1994). Rape has been used as a weapon for ethnic cleansing, using attacks on women to humiliate and attempt to exterminate another ethnic group.

The idea that genocide could be accomplished by the mass rape of the women of the enemy's ethnic group derives from a patriarchal definition of ethnicity. The child is thought to inherit the ethnicity of her/his father, implying, for example, that if a Serb soldier rapes a Muslim woman and she becomes pregnant, her child would be a Serb. And because women are viewed as symbols of the family, and the family as the basis of society, the humiliation for women of giving birth to the enemy's children symbolizes the destruction of the community (Nikolić-Ristanović, this volume; see also Copelon, this volume).

Vesna Nikolić-Ristanović has interviewed many refugee women from different ethnic groups in the former Yugoslavia. Those women who became pregnant because of wartime rape expressed anguish over carrying a child who was both their own and the enemy's. This form of psychological torture is incomparable to other forms of wartime torture. In addition, raped women are often stigmatized. Women may be shunned by their own families and communities, viewed as tainted, worthless "property."

The horrifying reports of mass, ethnically defined rape have attracted widespread public attention, but they are not unique to the war in the former Yugoslavia (see Rejali, this volume). Soviet soldiers raped approximately two million women in eastern Germany in 1945. In 1971 Pakistani soldiers raped more than 200,000 Bengali women in the Bangladesh war of independence (Hauchler and Kennedy 1994). One estimate claims that during the war against Kuwait, Iraqi troops raped as many as 3,200 women between August 1990 and February 1991 (Enloe 1993). The link between rape and war has been ignored by many policymakers and scholars, but feminists have identified wartime rape as symptomatic of war's gendered nature (cf. Enloe 1993; Stiglmayer 1994; Brownmiller 1994; MacKinnon 1994; Reardon 1985).

Even the United Nations peacekeepers—the multilateral forces sent to protect civilian human rights in war-torn areas—have committed rape and sexual abuse against women and young girls. Such cases have been documented in Mozambique, Somalia, Cambodia, and other regions (Nordstrom, this volume). This suggests that those trained to fight wars are not best suited to protect the human rights of women and children, and that sexual violence is endemic to military culture.

Attitudes of military personnel often support the sexual abuse of women and girls. When the head of the U.N. mission in Cambodia was questioned about the sexual abuse of women and girls by U.N. troops, he responded that he was "not a puritan: eighteen-year-old, hot-blooded soldiers had a right to drink a few beers and chase after young beautiful things of the opposite sex" (Fetherston 1995:22). And in 1995, when three United States Marines were charged with assaulting and raping a twelve-year-old girl on the Japanese island of Okinawa, the commander of the United States Pacific Command told reporters: "I think it was absolutely stupid, as I've said several times. For the price they paid to rent the car, they could have had a girl" (Enloe 1996:15). In addition to implicitly accepting rape as a part of military life, militaries around the world also support and may even enforce prostitution attached to their military installations.

Prostitution. Wartime prostitution may be either physically forced or economically coerced. During World War II the Japanese military set up brothels in eastern and southern Asia, forcing between 100,000 and 200,000 women into prostitution. Cynthia Enloe has pointed out that prostitution relies not only on the "sex worker" and the "client," but rather involves a whole host of characters, mainly men, who contribute to the creation and maintenance of prostitution as an institution around any military base in the world. It includes husbands and lovers, bar and brothel owners, local public health officials, local police and mayors, national and foreign finance ministry and defense officials, male soldiers in the national, local, and foreign forces, and local civilian male prostitution customers.

Militaries may manage and control the lives of women working as prostitutes by implementing curfews, demanding regular checkups for sexually transmitted diseases, and even regulating which customers they have sex with. During World War II, brothels linked to United States military bases generally had two separate entrances: one for men of color and another for whites (Enloe 1993; Riley 1997). Because militaries may provide huge infusions of capital into the societies where they establish bases, the local government has an incentive to cooperate with demands for women to have sex with the soldiers, and poor women may have little other choice in order to support themselves and their families.

The prostitutes are often young girls endeavoring to support their families, or women who need to support their children. Stories are told of young girls coming down from the mountains around Subic Bay (the recently closed United States military base in the Philippines) when American military ships pull into the harbor. The girls, from poor rural families, come to serve as prostitutes for American servicemen (Kirk and Okazawa-Rey, this volume). And girls who are orphaned by war may be sold into domestic and sexual slavery. In societies where women are valued for their virginity, these girls may be permanent outcasts, trapped in a life of prostitution, and if they live to old age, of poverty (Nordstrom, this volume).

Wartime Domestic Violence

While battering of women is common in most societies in peacetime, recent research indicates that domestic violence increases in wartime. This suggests a link between gendered violence at the micro and macro levels, and calls for an inquiry into the gendered dynamics of power from the household to the international arena. Among the findings of research conducted through a Belgrade agency for domestic violence are the following: an increase in the number of sons who commit violence against their mothers in wartime; an increase in the number of assaults involving weapons, including pistols, grenades, and other weapons from the war; an increase in violence in marriages where the husband and wife's ethnicity differ; an increase in alcohol consumption among men returning from combat; and a link between economic decline, especially refugee status, and wife battering and rape (Nikolić-Ristanović, this volume).

What wartime conditions would lead to an increase in woman battering and rape within the household? Several factors have been postulated. First, in wartime there is an influx of weapons into societies, and those weapons are often not controlled or limited to battlefield use. Research from both criminology and security studies demonstrates that the presence of weapons increases both the likelihood and lethality of violence. Second, former soldiers or soldiers who have contact with their families have been affected by their experiences in combat. They may be frustrated, nervous, intolerant, and aggressive.

State-produced media propaganda that endorses violence as an acceptable means of conflict resolution, combined with hate propaganda against members of other ethnic groups, may also be related to the escalation of domestic violence in wartime. All of these factors, along with a cultural acceptance of violence against women, even at peacetime, put women at greater risk.

Loss of Family

Loss of family members inflicts suffering on women and men alike, but women are affected in particular ways because of their family roles. Women may lose husbands and sons on the battlefield, and they may lose their girls and young children as civilian casualties, or witness their suffering as victims of assault and rape. As the primary caregivers to children in most societies, women arguably suffer the loss of their children in gender-specific ways. Although the relationship of motherhood to women's stance toward war is debated (cf. Ruddick 1990; Scheper-Hughes 1992; Nikolić-Ristanović, this volume; Mazali, this volume; de Alwis, this volume), women in many different historical and cultural contexts have argued that a mother's suffering is unique. Nationalist propaganda often calls on women to give up their sons in wartime and to take pride in a son's military service. Clearly, many women do respond to this call, and not every mother responds to the loss in the same way; women living in conditions of scarcity and violence may more readily surrender their sons and husbands to death (Scheper-Hughes 1992).

Losing husbands and sons may mean not only emotional loss but also lost economic support and social legitimacy. Women's lack of economic power and opportunity may force them to rely on their male family members for economic survival. These women may become poor and homeless when they lose their husbands and sons. In some societies, women with no male family members lose all rights to protection, employment, benefits, or guarantees of security (Collett, this volume).

Loss of Work, Community, and Social Structure

Those women who are able to work outside the home may lose their jobs when war destroys the economic infrastructure. Indeed, with total war as the strategy of contemporary militaries, factories, hospitals, office buildings, agricultural fields, and civilian communities all become targets. Destruction of the economy, whether it be industrial or agriculturally based, affects women in unique ways because of their caretaking roles in the family and community. In conditions of food scarcity, women are more likely than men to give up their food so that children can eat (Oniang'o 1996). Women's caretaking roles become increasingly burdensome as they struggle to feed their children in adverse conditions created by war and to nurse wounded survivors when hospitals, medicine, and clean water are scarce.

War, Environmental Destruction, and Women

In addition to destroying the social and economic infrastructure, war destroys the natural environment. This has devastating consequences for women, again due to their roles as food providers and as caretakers. In most of the world, women grow the food—for example, in Africa, women produce 80 percent of it (Vickers 1991). Women also gather most of the fuel and water and prepare the meals. When war destroys the vegetation, these tasks become difficult, if not impossible. For example, in El Salvador, which has been devastated by war, 80 percent of the natural vegetation has been eliminated, and 77 percent of the soil has eroded or lost its fertility. The militaries employed "scorched earth" tactics similar to those used by the United States in Vietnam, destroying huge tracts of land and forest. Peasant women there find it harder and harder to gather firewood and grow food (Lorentzen and Turpin 1996).

Water pollution becomes a major problem for women, as they need it not only for themselves and their families to drink, but also to clean wounds. Illnesses caused by lack of potable water account for 34.6 percent of all child deaths in the developing world. And women, who often walk for hours to find water, must walk farther and farther in their search (Lorentzen and Turpin 1996).

In the Gulf War, both the Iraqis and the Allies (primarily the United States) deliberately destroyed the natural environment of the region as a part of their war strategy. Iraq pumped oil into the sea, causing an oil slick about 80 miles long and 10 miles wide. About six hundred oil wells were set afire in Kuwait. The United States deliberately bombed chemical and nuclear facilities, causing black rain to fall throughout the region. Hospitals and clinics were destroyed, and the water supply became contaminated. Basic health and sanitation levels dropped in the region, and the impact on the local economy made food prices soar. Women suffered in gender-specific ways as they struggled to provide for their children (Hauchler and Kennedy 1994).

The Impact of Military Spending on Women

In spite of war's increasing destructiveness, huge amounts of resources continue to be spent on arms while displacing social spending. Military expenditures account for 5 percent of goods and services produced in the world, five times more than that allocated before World War II, representing three times the government expenditures for education and fifteen times those for housing worldwide. Governments are spending thirty times the amount of money allocated to each child in school on each member of the armed forces (Sivard 1996; Vickers 1993).

While governments are constantly decrying their lack of available funds to meet social needs, there seems to be an unending supply of capital for military spending, and many have observed a direct trade-off between the two (Peterson and Runyan 1993). For every dollar spent on research and development in the United States, 64 cents goes to the military while only 1 percent goes to protecting the environment (Sivard 1996).

The huge military expenditures of the last few decades have produced social service cuts, where women worldwide are most likely to be employed (Peterson and Runyan 1993). Although military spending does provide jobs for some women, they tend to be low-paying, assembly-line work in defense factories. Women provide cheap labor for defense contractors, which in the United States rely primarily on the labor of Asian, Black, and Latina women (Enloe 1993).

Women's Responses to War

Joining

Although women are stereotyped as pacifists or war resisters, they have fought in wars and now often seek equal treatment in the militaries of many countries. Other women support the war effort through their work in munitions factories or defense firms. Women tend to occupy the lowest ranks and to perform "women's roles" within those settings, although those roles are being challenged and debated.

Soldiers

Although women have reportedly fought in wars for centuries, they have routinely been relegated to second-class status in the military. Public resistance to women as warriors is rooted in traditional ideas about femininity and masculinity. These ideas become more flexible in certain political contexts. Women have been known to fight in wars of liberation and civil wars, including with the Chinese Communists in the 1930s and 1940s, the African National Congress in South Africa in the 1970s and 1980s, in Vietnam in the 1960s and 1970s, and in El Salvador in the 1980s. But once the context changes and the war ends, women tend to return to their traditional roles. In recent decades, however, we have witnessed a shift toward increasing, although not equal, numbers of women in the military along with expanded roles for them (Segal 1995).

While some restrictions on women in combat have been removed, women are still excluded from ground combat by the United States military as well as ground, naval, and air combat by most other militaries. Almost no women have served in the U.N. military peacekeeping operations. Only 5 of the 6,250 troops who served in military peacekeeping missions between 1957 and 1979 were women, and from 1957 to 1989, only 20 of the roughly 20,000 troops were women. Most of these women served in traditional roles as nurses in medical units. Women still comprise less than 2 percent of the troops in U.N. peacekeeping missions (Beilstein 1995).

This trend is evident in national militaries as well: while a small percentage of women hold high-ranking positions, most women are relegated to traditionally feminine roles within the military as secretaries, nurses, and technicians. Militaries often emphasize differences between men and women rather than their equal abilities; for example, the Israeli military teaches women how to apply their makeup (D'Amico, this volume). These military roles are not only gendered, they are also race and class based, as poor and working-class women from minority groups are disproportionately recruited.

Some feminists have argued for women's greater access to military jobs and benefits (Stiehm 1989; Holm 1992). This argument is based on a militarized notion of citizenship, wherein citizenship derives in part from one's capacity to fight for one's country. Equal-rights feminists have argued that political power has in part been elusive for women because in many countries, military service is a prerequisite for high political office. Western feminists have argued that increased military participation can emancipate women from their status as the weak and defended (Stiehm 1989).

Critics of this approach charge that the military is not good for women, or that women should reject the military because of its sexism. They point out that military indoctrination for men generally includes the systematic denigration of all that is "feminine." Male recruits are often called "girls" as a form of humiliation, and they often chant sexist lyrics as part of training. Women recruits report being sexually harassed and even raped by their fellow soldiers (Feinman, this volume; Riley 1997).

Military Production Workers

Another way women can support militarization is to work in the defense industry. During both world wars, there was a huge influx of women into munitions factories. Recruitment propaganda called on women to do munitions work previously done by men. A British recruitment poster proclaimed, for example, that "These Women Are Doing Their Part: Learn to Make Munitions." About a million British women worked in munitions factories during the First World War, making guns, shells, explosives, and aircraft. Women munitions makers in both world wars achieved more economic independence than before, and many expressed pride in contributing to the war effort (Woollacott 1994).

In contrast, today's women defense workers are some of the worst paid women in the labor force. As noted earlier, most women working in the defense industry occupy low-paying jobs as assembly workers, with few if any benefits (Enloe 1993). It is not clear that these women feel linked to success in any particular war.

Sending, Supporting, and Reproducing Men

Militaries have not only conducted campaigns to bring women into munitions work; they have also generated propaganda that links motherhood, nationalism, and militarism.

Women and girls have been enlisted to urge their husbands and boyfriends to war. A British leaflet issued to "the young women of England" in 1917 asked:

> Is your "best boy" wearing khaki? If not, don't you think he should be? If he does not think that you and your country are worth fighting for, do you think he is worthy of you? If your young man neglects his duty to his king and country, the time will come when he will neglect YOU. Think it over—then ask him to JOIN THE ARMY. (Peace Pledge Union 1997:9)

Women and girls were told to "show a white feather," used as a symbol of cowardice, to any man they saw whom they suspected of having failed to enlist.

Mothers have been targeted by war propaganda in very different countries. Governments attempt to educate women as to what constitutes a "good mother" during wartime; their propaganda strategies are remarkably similar, drawing on representations of the good (patriotic) mother as one who is willing to sacrifice her sons to war (Bayard de Volo, this volume).

During the American Civil War, as well as during both world wars, the United States government established organizations whose aims were to stimulate feelings of motherly patriotism among women. Similar organizations, such as the Mothers of Heroes and Martyrs, were developed in Nicaragua during the war against the Contras (Bayard de Volo, this volume). State propaganda has also been directed at mothers in Israel to prevent dissent against their sons' involvement in the Israeli Defense Forces. Women who protest the war are portrayed as disloyal to their children (Mazali, this volume). Women are even called upon by many states to produce more sons for the military, and some states, such as Croatia in the former Yugoslavia, have outlawed abortion in wartime (Nikolić-Ristanović 1996; Enloe 1993). Despite governments' efforts to the contrary, many women do protest their sons being called to war and publicly mourn their deaths in ways that defy the state.

Mourning

While some wives, lovers, sisters, and mothers mourn the war dead in private, others mourn publicly as a form of resistance. Some women's groups, such as Women in Black, rather than mourning the loss of particular family members, symbolically mourn the continuing deaths caused by the Israeli occupation of Palestine. Sara Ruddick writes in this volume that the figure of the *mater dolorosa*, the suffering mother, is the predominant image of women in war. Indeed, many mothers' groups have been formed that express the women's suffering, not only in private, but as a form of protest against the war.

Mothers' groups may also organize to glorify their lost sons, providing support for revolutionary struggles against interventionist powers. Such was the case of the Mothers of the Heroes and Martyrs in Nicaragua, who not only honored their dead sons but also called for the Contras to stop their war (Bayard de Volo, this volume).

Resisting

Some women's groups actively resisting war have also drawn on gender roles and employed stereotypic symbols in their activism. For example, at the Greenham Common women's peace camp in England, women hung diapers on the wire fence around the nuclear installation and wore pictures of their children around their necks. The members of Women Strike for Peace in the United States declared a "strike" on their domestic work, refusing to perform household work as a form of protest against nuclear war preparations. When they appeared in public spaces such as courthouses and parliaments, these women dressed up in traditionally feminine clothing to unsettle the men and appeal to them as might their sisters, wives, and mothers (Hyman Alonso 1993). The Materinskoe Serdise, Soviet mothers who drew attention to their killed sons in Afghanistan, organized demonstrations and hunger strikes and broke into official meetings (Enloe 1993). The women of Another Mother for Peace in the United States sent a Mothers' Day card to members of the United States Congress during the Vietnam War. It said:

> For my Mothers' Day gift this year
> I don't want candy or flowers.
> I want an end to killing.
> We who have given life
> Must be dedicated to preserving it.
> Please, talk peace!
> (Hyman Alonso 1993:218)

This group created a creed of "Pax Materna," or mother's peace and a logo that was translated into twenty languages and distributed worldwide. These groups demonstrated that feminine symbols, often associated with passivity, can be transformed into effective forms of political protest.

Women's association with peace is an ancient historical theme (Reardon 1993). Women have developed national organizations as well as transnational groups such as Women's International League for Peace and Freedom (WILPF), World Women Parliamentarians for Peace, and the International Feminist Network (IFN) (Boulding 1995). Women's involvement in the peace movement worldwide through both gender-specific and gender-inclusive peace organizations suggests that, although we may reject arguments that women are inherently peaceful, we must question why so many women are drawn to peace work.

Contemporary Debates

Scholarship on women and war has generated a wealth of knowledge and challenged traditional approaches to studying war that typically ignore the role of gender and the impact of war on women. Within the subfield of women and war, a number of debates are underway.

Essentialism versus Difference

The debate over whether or not women have a feminine nature that is distinct from men's has raged both within conservative political circles and among feminists (Elshtain 1987). Are women and men fundamentally different because of biology? While conservatives have answered "yes," their answer leads to the policy conclusion that men should fight wars and women should support them in distinctly feminine, maternal ways. Ironically, some feminists have also answered "yes," but conclude that women, as natural peacemakers, should resist wars, and that women should be accorded more power over world affairs so as to make the world less violent.

This debate has become more nuanced and complicated. Cross-cultural analyses have yielded evidence that neither men nor women have an "essential" nature: rather, gender is a fluid social category that people express differently in varied cultural contexts and diverse roles. Neither men nor women have proven to be inherently violent or peaceful; instead, humans have the capacity to be both. The fact that states produce so much propaganda to instruct men and women how to behave properly suggests that masculinity and femininity are learned rather than inherent traits. A group of internationally renowned scientists concluded in the Seville Statement on Violence that humans are not inherently violent, and therefore social and political factors are more likely to contribute to war and its gendered nature (Adams 1992; Hunter 1991).

The Politics of Motherhood

A second debate within the field concerns the relationship between motherhood and war. As discussed earlier, mothers can respond in quite different ways to war, again depending on the social and political context. Yet patterns emerge over time, with significant numbers of mothers' groups organizing to protest wars in different parts of the world. At the same time, many mothers support decisions to go to war and willingly send their sons to fight.

Women in the Military

A third major debate, especially among feminists, centers on women's participation in the military. It includes a number of questions. Should women join the military? While some argue that women should be free to join whatever organizations they choose, others protest that the military is a fundamentally sexist institution, and women should not participate in it. Some argue that women in greater numbers will change the military for the better, while others claim that it is more likely the military will change women.

Should women serve in combat roles? Equal-rights/liberal feminists argue for women's access to the same military jobs as men, claiming that women will also gain greater political power as a consequence. Conservatives and cultural feminists reject the notion of women in combat.

Women and Collective Organizing

A final debate that has emerged from women's multiple responses to war concerns whether women constitute a group for organizing, in any unified fashion, around issues of war and peace. Do women across cultures and social groups share the same concerns? Do women have a collective identity that can be mobilized? Elise Boulding points out that women have over time organized transnationally to oppose war, sexism, and inequality. She believes that women's collective sensibility stems not from some biological commonality, but rather from their unique social roles and knowledge. Women, she argues, can make a distinct contribution to peacemaking (Boulding 1995).

Research Questions

Some of the most fruitful areas for research draw on the previous debates. Some of these areas are listed below.

Factors That Determine Women's Responses to War

Scholarship that examines women's responses to war in different historical, cultural, and geopolitical contexts will help us to understand why and under what conditions women support war or peace; why some women respond to war by becoming prostitutes while others are munitions workers, soldiers, or protesters. As a part of this analysis, we need to better understand the ways in which women's class status, race, ethnicity, sexuality, and nationality affect their experiences.

Militarism in Peacetime

Much of the research on women and war suggests that war magnifies already existing gender inequality and women's subordination. We need more research that examines the ways that violence against women and women's lower social status in peacetime are connected to those at wartime. Sexual violence against women, for example, is routine in most contemporary societies, and yet is magnified in wartime. We need to understand how women's lives are militarized in times of "peace" in order to understand how their lives are transformed by war.

The State's Role in Mobilizing Women

Further research should examine the different strategies that states utilize to mobilize women to support war. Which states, for example, attempt to recruit women into military service, and which attempt to mobilize mothers to support war? How do cross-cultural differences, historical circumstances, and dynamics of the war in question shape states' behavior? Which strategies are most effective for mobilizing which women? What resources do states invest in these efforts, and who makes decisions about mobilization campaigns? How do women's reactions figure into declarations of war and defense department press releases?

Women Making Security Policy

Another question that merits further research elaborates on the debate concerning women and men's standpoints toward war, whether they be based in essential nature or acquired attitudes. Would women, if represented in greater numbers in policymaking positions, change security policy? Some contend that if women were in key political and military positions, such as Secretary of Defense or a position on the Joint Chiefs of Staff, nations would be less likely to go to war, or would at least exercise greater attempts at diplomacy and conflict resolution. However, we have numerous examples of women political leaders who pursued militaristic policies and led their nations to war (Fraser 1988). Another argument suggests that simply having a woman in a key position is not the issue; rather a "critical mass" of women would make a difference in decision making (Dahlerup 1991, 1994). Since so few women make security policy around the world, this question remains unanswered.

Gendered Social Relations as a Cause of War

Perhaps the most significant issue raised by the scholarship on women and war and by the women who have experienced war concerns the link between militarism and patriarchy. This relationship is dialectical: militarism relies on patriarchal patterns, and patriarchy relies on militarization. First let us consider how militarism relies on patriarchy. Militaries rely on male privilege and female subordination in order to function. That privilege takes both structural and cultural forms. Structurally, because women have less political, social, and economic power in society, they also have less power to make security decisions and very little power in military institutions. Poor women are compelled by their economic need to occupy low-ranking positions in the defense industry or the military. Other poor women are coerced into serving as prostitutes around military bases.

Cynthia Enloe (1989, 1993) has shown that the structural conditions are complemented by cultural ones: militaries need men and women to behave in gender-stereotyped ways. Women should behave in maternal fashion, they should need men to protect them, and their wartime experience should be sexualized. Men should feel that in order to prove their masculinity they should fight and generally support their nation going to war. Men should take on exceptionally masculine behaviors and attitudes through their military training.

The complementary argument suggests that in order for societies to be patriarchal or male dominated, military values must predominate—that masculine values must be privileged over feminine values, and masculine values become equated with military ones. Those values will be evident in various cultural forms, including gendered, militarized rhetoric, in popular culture, and in religious symbols (Cohn 1990; Miedzian 1991; Turpin and Patterson 1996). Gendered social relations encourage militarism, and militarism in turn relies on gendered social relations. As Betty Reardon (1985) has argued, without sexism the "war system" cannot function, and sexism is based on militarized notions of masculinity. For persons concerned about war and about sexism, this suggests that these interlocking problems must be addressed simultaneously.

REFERENCES

Adams, David, et al. 1992. "The Seville Statement on Violence." *Peace Review* 4:3, 20–22.

Beilstein, Janet. 1995. "The Role of Women in United Nations Peace-Keeping." *Women 2000*, no. 1 (December), 1–10. United Nations Division for the Advancement of Women, New York.

Boulding, Elise. 1995. "Feminist Inventions in the Art of Peacemaking: A Century Overview." *Peace and Change* 20:4, 408–439.

Brownmiller, Susan. 1994. "Making Female Bodies in the Battlefield." In Alexandra Stiglmayer (ed.), *Mass Rape*. Lincoln: University of Nebraska Press.

Cohn, Carol. 1990. "Clean Bombs and Clean Language." Pp. 33–56 in Jean Bethke Elshtain and Sheila Tobias (eds.), *Women, Militarism, and War: Essays in History, Politics, and Social Theory*. Savage, MD: Rowman and Littlefield.

Dahlerup, Drude. 1991. "From a Small to a Large Minority: A Theory of Critical Mass Applied to the Case of Women in Scandinavian Politics." In Hem Lata Swarup and Sarojini Bisaria (eds.), *Women, Politics and Religion*. Etawah, India: AC Brothers.

———. 1994. "Learning to Live with the State: State, Market and Civil Society, Women's Need for State Intervention in East and West." *Women's Studies International Forum* 17: 2–3, 117–128.

Elshtain, Jean Bethke. 1987. *Women and War*. New York: Basic Books.

Enloe, Cynthia. 1989. *Bananas, Beaches and Bases*. London: Pandora.

————. 1993. *The Morning After: Sexual Politics at the End of the Cold War.* Berkeley: University of California Press.

————. 1996. "Spoils of War." *Ms. Magazine,* March/April, p. 15.

Fetherston, A. B. 1995. "U.N. Peacekeepers and Cultures of Violence." *Cultural Survival Quarterly* 19:1, 19–23.

Forbes Martin, Susan. 1992. *Refugee Women.* London: Zed Books.

Fraser, Antonia. 1988. *The Warrior Queens.* London: Mandarin.

Hauchler, Ingomar, and Paul M. Kennedy. 1994. *Global Trends.* New York: Continuum Publishers.

Holm, Jeanne. 1992. *Women in the Military: An Unfinished Revolution, rev. ed.* Novato, CA: Presidio.

Hunter, Anne E. (ed.), 1991. *Genes and Gender VI. On Peace, War and Gender: A Challenge to Genetic Explanations.* New York: Feminist Press.

Hyman Alonso, Harriet. 1993. *Peace as a Women's Issue.* Syracuse, NY: Syracuse University Press.

Lorentzen, Lois Ann, and Jennifer Turpin. 1996. "Introduction: The Gendered New World Order." In Jennifer Turpin and Lois Ann Lorentzen (eds.), *The Gendered New World Order.* New York: Routledge.

MacKinnon, Catharine. 1994. "Rape, Genocide, and Women's Human Rights." In Alexandra Stiglmayer (ed.), *Mass Rape.* Lincoln: University of Nebraska Press.

Miedzian, Miriam. 1991. *Boys Will Be Boys.* New York: Doubleday.

Nikolić-Ristanović, Vesna. 1996. "War and Violence against Women." In Jennifer Turpin and Lois Ann Lorentzen (eds.), *The Gendered New World Order.* New York: Routledge.

Oniang'o, Ruth K. 1996. "African Women's Strategies to Advance Household Food Security." In Jennifer Turpin and Lois Ann Lorentzen (eds.), *The Gendered New World Order.* New York: Routledge.

Peace Pledge Union. 1997. *Women and Peace Resource Guide.* London: Peace Pledge Union.

Peterson, V. Spike, and Anne Sisson Runyan. 1993. *Global Gender Issues.* Boulder: Westview Press.

Reardon, Betty. 1993. *Women and Peace.* Albany: SUNY Press.

————. 1985. *Sexism and the War System.* New York: Teachers College Press.

Riley, Robin. 1997. "Practical Warriors: Gender and Militarism." Paper presented at the American Sociological Association Meetings, August 7-13, Toronto, Canada.

Ruddick, Sara. 1990. *Maternal Thinking: Towards a Politics of Peace.* Boston: Beacon Press.

Scheper-Hughes, Nancy. 1992. *Death without Weeping: The Violence of Everyday Life in Brazil.* Berkeley: University of California Press.

Segal, Mady Wechsler. 1995. "Women's Military Roles Cross-Nationally: Past, Present, and Future." *Gender and Society* 9:6, 757–775.

Sivard, Ruth Leger. 1996. *World Military and Social Expenditures.* Washington, DC: World Priorities Institute.

Stiehm, Judith Hicks. 1989. *Arms and the Enlisted Woman.* Philadelphia: Temple University Press.

Stiglmayer, Alexandra (ed.). 1994. *Mass Rape: The War against Women in Bosnia-Herzegovina.* Lincoln: University of Nebraska Press.

Tenhula, John. 1991. *Voices from Southeast Asia.* New York: Holmes and Meier.

Turpin, Jennifer, and Lois Ann Lorentzen (eds.). 1996. *The Gendered New World Order: Militarism, Development and the Environment.* New York: Routledge.

Turpin, Jennifer and Patience E. Patterson. 1996. "Sacrilizing Total War." *Peace Review* 8: 2, 195–200.

Vickers, Jeanne. 1991. Women and the World Economic Crisis. London: Zed Books.

———. 1993. *Women and War*. London: Zed Books.

Woollacott, Angela. 1994. *On Her Their Lives Depend: Munitions Workers in the Great War*. Berkeley: University of California Press.

Chapter Two

The Truth about Women and Peace

Jodi York

Much has been made in Western culture of the dichotomy between "women's peace" and "men's war." We can see the importance of this dichotomy in politics, media, education, and socialization, where women are expected to be inherently creative, nurturing, and peaceful, while men are bold, courageous warriors. For more than a hundred years, these differences have been the foundation for banal arguments that peace is a "women's issue."

Historically, conceptions of "womanhood" generally have been used to rally women into peace movements via two hackneyed arguments. The first claims war is antithetical to women's natural/biological role of bearing and nurturing children; therefore women must band together as mothers to demand its end. The second argument claims that devalued "feminine" traits of cooperation, caring, and nurturing are superior to masculine values of individuality, dominance, and violence—and that we can thus achieve peace by revaluing these "feminine" traits. From each of these positions, activist groups have argued that women have a special interest in peace, sometimes going so far as to exclude men entirely.

More recently, a holistic argument has also emerged, articulated by ecofeminists (among others). This theory holds that all oppression (from war to domestic violence to environmental exploitation) is interrelated, and all must be stopped for social justice to be achieved. In this view, rather than being part of their "duty," or being an outcropping of their traditional roles, the striving for peace constitutes radical behavior for women—a way of taking control of their lives.

The most "traditional" logic behind women's peace groups relies on the conservative, uncontroversial—even Victorian—ideal of motherhood, where women function as caring, nurturing, and protective moral guides for their children. This position does not encourage women to question their primary identities as helpmates and mothers. Instead, the argument continues, women are inherently concerned about peace because of their special connection to life preservation and moral guardianship. As activist and pediatrician Helen Caldicott has suggested:

> As mothers we must make sure the world is safe for our babies. . . . Look at one child, one baby . . . I have three children, and I'm a doctor who treats children. I live with grieving parents. I understand the value of every human life. . . . I appeal especially to

the women to do this [peace] work because we understand the genesis of life. Our bodies are built to nurture life. (Harris and King, 1989: 81)

This "motherist" posture demands an end not only to war itself, but to the by-products of militarism: famine, refugee camps, nuclear fallout, and early death in the military—because children deserve to live and be loved. This logic extends to all people, who were once children. Suffragist Anna Shaw once argued that "looking into the face of . . . one dead man we see two dead, the man and the life of the woman who gave him birth; the life she wrought into his life" (Harris and King, 1989: 84).

There is sober basis for this rhetoric. Traditional "women's work"—nursing, feeding, sheltering, teaching the young, tending the elderly—is threatened by violence. Mothering (and, consequently, womanhood) focuses on life, war making emphasizes death. Author Sara Ruddick explains this "dichotomy": "A mother preserves the bodies, nurtures the psychic growth and disciplines the conscience of the children; although the military trains the soldiers to survive the situations it puts them through, it also deliberately endangers their bodies, minds and consciences in the name of victory and abstract causes" (Harris and King, 1989: 81).

Women Strike for Peace (WSP), a United States grass-roots, middle-class women's peace movement of the 1960s, relied on this "motherist" image. Comprised largely of homemakers, WSP used the informal organizational networks developed in their daily practice of managing households, running church luncheons, and organizing bake sales or car pools. Their first major action, called in response to women's fears about nuclear war and fallout from atmospheric testing, was a one-day peace strike on November 1, 1961. On this day, in the largest female peace action of the twentieth century, an estimated fifty thousand women in more than sixty cities walked out of their kitchens and off their jobs.

The symbols WSP used consciously relied on their identity as "outraged housewives and mothers": at one White House demonstration, they unrolled a block-long dishtowel signed by thousands of American women. When called before the House Un-American Activities Committee, demonstrators were urged to dress neatly, and thus arrived in white gloves and hats, looking more like the committee members' wives and sisters than potential communists. Historian Amy Swerdlow describes how they undermined the committee's coercive control, transforming the usually grim atmosphere by bringing babies and giving flowers to each witness. Answering the committee irreverently—sometimes lecturing its members as though they were schoolboys—they stressed "the rights of ordinary mothers to protect children from nuclear death over the rights of governments to kill them" (Harris and King, 1989: 234).

For many women, the motherist position poses problems because it accepts women's subordinate role in our society. Some argue that doing "women's work," rather than making life better or increasing the likelihood of peace, merely collaborates with patriarchy by ameliorating its worst aspects, making patriarchal and militaristic oppression more bearable.

A critique of the motherist position, even though it was the primary argument used by women's peace groups in industrialized countries for most of this century, generally leads to a cultural feminist argument as an alternative. The basic reasoning for cultural feminists goes like this: women's psychosocial development prepares them to be connected caretakers. Men's psychosocial development prepares them to be individuated competitors. The prevalence of this masculine mentality leads to war. Therefore, war can be averted by promoting the female mentality. The basic premise is that if men were more like women, if our culture didn't alienate them from all that is female, we wouldn't have wars.

This position has been widely embraced by more radical feminist peace activists. But they still differ among themselves in explaining how this situation has arisen: In the extreme view, the difference is biological, while in the more moderate (and common) view, gender differences have instead been a result of culture and socialization. Either way, according to this argument women (i.e., mothers), because they are generally responsible for the rearing of young children, can choose not to promote patriarchal values. By rewarding cooperation instead of competition, by discouraging violent play and entertainment in both sexes, and by teaching both boys and girls to honor caring, women can shift the paradigm.

This philosophy has motivated many women's peace encampments. In the early 1980s, after centuries of women watching men leave home for war, some feminists decided women needed to leave home for peace. They met in places like Greenham Common in Britain to protest the militarization of their lands and culture that put them and their families at risk of nuclear destruction every day in a conflict in which Britain wasn't even directly participating. The goal was to create an alternative, female peace culture for all to witness. Many women's peace camps, such as Seneca Falls in the United States, were organized according to a more "female" model, emphasizing consensus decision making, shared tasks, and a rejection of hierarchy.

However, the cultural feminist position has been criticized as well. Critics argue that it fails to adequately challenge the patriarchal dualism that constitutes the "self" by devaluing the "other," and that it ignores the roles women play in the service of war. Laura Duhan Kaplan goes so far as to argue that focusing on women as caretakers (even with value added) employs an archetype that actually supports patriarchal militarism (Kaplan, 1994).

By emphasizing differences between women and men, cultural feminists perpetuate the same dichotomy that underlies patriarchy itself: it polarizes differences between genders and minimizes shared characteristics. It assumes an "essential" nature of men and women: the problem thus amounts merely to masculinity being enthroned by our culture while femininity is degraded. But by emphasizing women's role as caretakers in society, Kaplan argues that cultural feminist activists "do not challenge conceptions of femininity which have served to silence women; [they] accept hierarchical thinking about gender but invert the hierarchy, placing femininity on top" (Kaplan, 1994: 127).

Further, by employing dichotomous gender definitions, this position accepts the devaluation of the "other" that has so plagued women under patriarchy. This troubles Kaplan, who argues that "a feminist peace theory begins by questioning the categories of masculinity and femininity, rather than by formulating solutions within this dichotomous world view" (Kaplan, 1994: 127).

The critique of cultural feminism broadens when we examine the roles women play in supporting the war system. Women's support is as necessary to war as that of men; women serve as nurses, prostitutes, primary school teachers who glorify war, and patriotic mothers who raise their sons to be soldiers. As Kaplan argues, "Women are constituted as weepers, occasions for war, and keepers of the flame of non-warlike values who cannot effectively fight the mortal wounding of sons, brothers, husbands, fathers" (Kaplan, 1994: 130). The ideal of woman-as-caretaker has been utilized to silence or derail women's resistance to war. Kaplan claims it helps "co-opt women's resistance to war by convincing women that their immediate responsibility to ameliorate the effects of war takes precedence over organized public action against war" (Kaplan, 1994: 131).

Increasingly, women's roles go beyond mere support for war: women soldiers have been fighting in national liberation struggles for years, and were used in [what were effectively] combat roles in the Gulf War, and thus have become perpetrators of direct violence. Often, it is claimed that "if women were in charge, things would be different" But Margaret Thatcher, Jeane Kirkpatrick, or Indira Gandhi could easily "out-hawk" the average male.

The socialization argument cannot account for all women who engage in violence. Cynthia Enloe calls our attention to this "affront" to the ideas of cultural feminism: how do we account for the Nicaraguan female guerrilla fighting alongside her brother with a baby in one hand and an Uzi in the other? The guerrilla does not feel she is being unfeminine. In fact, the argument in many ways merely extends the motherist perspective: she is doing what she needs to do to protect her children's future. How can she use the same argument to go to war that others use to strike for peace? If "female" nature is not monolithic, where does this leave cultural feminism?

In response to the critique of cultural feminism, ecofeminism provides an alternative. This perspective argues that all oppression exists on a continuum; the differences among exploiting the earth, domestic violence, and all-out warfare are simply a matter of degree. According to this view, women are associated with the natural world, culturally, linguistically, and symbolically: we cannot understand one without the other.

Ecofeminists take the meaning of phrases like "Mother Earth," "raping the land," and "virgin soil" very seriously. They argue that exploitation characterizes the relationship between men and either women or the Earth—the latter are there to be used and conquered. Thus, those who perpetuate militarism cannot take women's peace protests seriously because they cannot take women seriously. From this perspective, if women want to improve their lives, they must work for both peace and the environment.

Ecofeminists argue that women's oppression constitutes the "original" oppression, the model for all other forms of oppression. Since in this view all oppression is essentially the same, the implication is that men and whole ethnic groups or nations are also oppressed to the extent that they can be seen as "feminine" or "unmanly." As such, all forms of "power-over" in relationships among people and nations reflect the oppression of women and the Earth. Thus peace, while particularly important to women, is crucial for everyone in unequal relationships (and thus for all but a few elites).

While the motherist and cultural feminist views have merit, ecofeminism provides the most compelling argument since it provides undeniable reasons for women to be concerned about peace. These reasons have nothing to do with who she feels like she is, what her gender means to her, or how she feels about patriarchy. It is an argument of simple arithmetic: women pay for war. Whether you look at economics, families, refugees, or war casualties, the costs of war are borne disproportionately by women and their children.

Jeanne Vickers illustrates the ugly picture, which could be set anywhere in the world:

> Left to sustain the family and endure the loneliness and vulnerability of separation, women suffer great hardships in wartime. They, and those they care for, may be killed or injured in ethnic fighting or civil disturbances. . . . Their houses may be damaged, or they may flee from home in fear of their lives. Dwindling food supplies and hungry children exacerbate tensions. And so, to the loss of husbands, fathers, sons and brothers who are killed in battle, is added the longer-term suffering of further deprivation. Often defenseless against invasion, women can find that armed conflict means rape and other forms of abuse by occupying troops, as well as loss of the means of livelihood. Rural women must carry additional responsibilities while their menfolk are absent, left to tend both to their farms and domestic needs, and many have been the cases in which women farmers have lost their crops first to occupying troops and then to their own. (Vickers, 1993: 18)

The cost to women starts long before war breaks out. Poor women worldwide pay it daily when governments divert funds from social services that benefit the poor to defense spending. Women, who comprise the majority of the poor, who constitute more than half the world's population and who do two-thirds of the labor, make only one-tenth of the money and own only one one-hundredth of the property. Since the poor are predominantly women and children, it is from their mouths that social spending is diverted to feed war-making capabilities.

If war actually breaks out, the costs rise further. War was once fought between armed opponents, but increasingly civilians account for the casualties. Civilians, mostly women, children and the elderly, represent 90 percent of the deaths in recent fighting in Lebanon. In guerrilla conflict the toll hovers around 80 percent civilian. Intentional targeting of civilian and humanitarian outposts, once considered taboo, is now not uncommon.

When women lose their husbands to war, they typically lose the family breadwinner. In societies where women's status and welfare depend on their relationship to men, widows are often left without the means to provide for themselves and their children, a situation compounded by routine scarcity. With the loss of income and protection, their risk increases for a variety of abuses, especially rape.

Rape is a common tool during war. It is used to extract information and to punish women who are of a certain ethnicity or religion, or even for just living in an area known to be sympathetic to insurgents. The examples are nearly limitless, and military forces tacitly condone it—to such an extent that the rhetoric of rape and brutal murder of innocent women even shows up in military marching songs.

Of Korean women who had been pressed into service as "comfort girls" by the Japanese army during World War II, Jeanne Vickers tells of one who "was sent to a Japanese naval base at the age of 16 and forced to undergo intercourse 10 to 15 times a day, every day. She was regularly beaten and once stabbed. Eventually she returned to Korea but she was too ashamed to marry or even go back to her family" (Vickers, 1993: 21). Similar stories have emerged from the former Yugoslavia, where Muslim women have been systematically raped and intentionally impregnated as a form of "ethnic cleansing."

Refugees constitute the most numerous victims of war. According to the UNHCR [United Nations High Commission on Refugees], there are over 20 million refugees in the world today, and a similar number are displaced within the borders of their own countries. Women and young girls now constitute at least 80 percent of this figure. Reaching a refugee camp usually requires a woman to sacrifice everything she owns to pay for bribes and avoid repeated rapes, only to arrive in a situation where her physical safety is just as endangered. Vickers reports: "Abuse and abduction of refugee women by, for example, camp guards continue to be of great concern to UNHCR field officers, who report that it is also distressingly common for female refugees to fall victim to extortion and brutality both within and outside such camps and settlements" (Vickers, 1993: 29).

In the refugee camps, women and their children also suffer from many preventable diseases, compounded by a lack of nutrition, sanitation, proper shelter, and safe water. The High Commission acknowledges that "relief workers have become familiar with the sight of well-fed men alongside under-fed and sickly women and children" (Vickers, 1993: 30). For the majority of women, who occupy the camps with only their children, refugeeism is not a brief but rather a nightmarish experience that they cannot easily put behind them. Once new and independent social patterns have been established to cope with life in the camps, readjustment to normal family life tends to be very difficult—if they are ever reunited with their families.

The ecofeminist argument, however, goes beyond mere pragmatics. If we consider these statistics from an ecofeminist perspective, then all oppression is essentially the same. All wars are fought against the weak, the different and the "other"—all of which are symbolically women. War and militarism must be stopped if women, and those associated with them—the weak, the very young and very old, the poor, those of "wrong" color—are to change their situation. War, with its necessary death, misogyny, homophobia, and economic inequities, provides a primary impediment to women's equality anywhere in the world. If women cannot have equality, no one can.

Although it sounds like a cliché, peace remains a "women's issue," not for reasons of motherhood or biological difference, but for reasons of justice. It's not exclusively their domain, but since they pay the primary price when peace is absent, women have a particular interest in pursuing peace. Peace has been viewed as a women's issue for nearly as long as there has been war. But the reasons have shifted through time, as has the danger and the ways in which wars are fought. Perhaps now more than ever, peace is something women need to pursue: it stands between them and their goals, even when those objectives are as disparate as getting adequate nutrition on the one hand, and breaking through glass ceilings on the other.

REFERENCES

Brock-Utne, Birgit. 1985. *Educating for Peace: A Feminist Perspective.* New York: Pergamon.

Elshtain, Jean Bethke, and Sheila Tobias (eds.). 1990. *Women, Militarism and War.* Savage, MD: Rowman and Littlefield.

Enloe, Cynthia. 1993. *The Morning After: Sexual Politics at the End of the Cold War.* Berkeley: University of California Press.

Harris, Adrienne, and Ynestra King (eds.). 1989. *Rocking the Ship of State: Toward a Feminist Peace Politics.* Boulder, CO: Westview Press.

Kaplan, Laura Duhan. 1994. "Woman as Caretaker: An Archetype That Supports Patriarchal Militarism." *Hypatia* (Spring): 123–134.

Vickers, Jeanne. 1993. *Women and War.* London: Zed Books.

Warren, Karen, and Duane Cady. 1994. "Feminism and Peace: Seeing Connections." *Hypatia* (Spring): 4–21.

Chapter Three

After Feminist Analyses of Bosnian Violence

Darius M. Rejali

As events in Bosnia unfolded, American feminists found themselves wondering about the relevance of their theories of rape beyond North Atlantic shores. Their analyses provide excellent ways of thinking about gender and rape in war, yet they are limited by an impoverished concept of ethnicity. To think comparatively about rape in war, we must understand gender's relationship to ethnicity in more complicated ways. Bosnia is the place to see this most clearly.

Analysts have distinguished three kinds of rape in Bosnia: rapes that occurred when Serbs first occupied a village; rapes committed by prison guards in detention camps; and rape camps or houses temporarily commandeered by Serbs to keep women expressly for that purpose. Reports have also emphasized that rapes often took place publicly or with other witnesses; that rapes included acts designed to degrade the victim; and that often the victims knew the aggressors.

In assessing this information, American feminists agreed that wartime rape could not be reduced to the psychological attributes of the individual aggressors or their mere aggregate in war. Rape must be understood in relation to social structures and practices. Mass rape also cannot be understood by emphasizing its unique or exceptional wartime character; rather it can only be comprehended in terms of everyday forms of violence that are considered legitimate. Finally, a rape account must identify the interrelationship between ethnicity and gender.

Rape in a national context often touches on, if not centers on, issues of race and ethnicity. The American context, for example, emphasizes the stereotype of the black rapist or the idea that black women are less worthy rape victims. In a war context, racial and ethnic distinctions have particular salience because they are violently renegotiated, complicating the relationship between ethnicity and gender. So rape in Bosnia was systematic, but how was it systematic: that is, in relation to what policies or sociocultural forms? Can one specify the processes that make a rapist? How did the seemingly pathological violence reflect everyday life in the former Yugoslavia? Here, key feminists have given different answers.

Catharine MacKinnon has analyzed the Bosnian rapes by focusing on pornography's role in the former Yugoslavia. She notes that pornographic products were more common in Yugoslavia than in any other socialist country. "When pornography is this normal a whole population of men is primed to dehumanize women and to enjoy inflicting assault sexually. . . . Pornography is the perfect preparation—motivator and instruction manual in one—for the sexual atrocities ordered in this genocide" (MacKinnon, 1993: 28). MacKinnon notes that rapes in detention camps always involved performing for a male audience, just as in pornographic shows. Some rapes were not only publicly performed but also filmed with video technology. These films were sold as pornography: they were indistinguishable from the real thing. Women were ordered to copy poses from pornographic magazines stuck on the walls during the rapes, thus reproducing pornography as reality. Finally, these pornographic films were turned out for mass consumption much like news and entertainment, except that here they were used to whip up a popular frenzy for the Serbian war effort.

Analyzing the films, MacKinnon notes that the Serbs who directed the films used sophisticated staging, providing props and dubbing dialogue to implicate Croatian soldiers. This suggests the government's involvement. "The world has never seen sex used this consciously, this cynically, this elaborately, this openly, this systematically with this degree of technology and psychological sophistication, as a means of destroying a whole people" (MacKinnon, 1993: 27). Rape pornography encourages more men to enlist who in turn rape and produce more pornography that generates still more enlistees.

Susan Brownmiller has analyzed rape in Bosnia quite differently. Rape in Bosnia, she asserts, has been produced not merely by a crisis in ethnic identity but rather by a crisis in male ethnic identity (Brownmiller, 1993). In "protecting their women" from their enemies, Balkan men have found an ethnic cause to fight and die for. Whereas MacKinnon locates rape in male/female dynamics, Brownmiller locates it in the conflict between males. "Sexual trespass on the enemy's women is one of the satisfactions of conquest, like a boot in the face, for once he is handed a rifle and told to kill, the soldier becomes an adrenaline-rushed young man with permission to kick in the door to grab, to steal, to give vent to his submerged rage against all women who belong to other men" (Brownmiller, 1993: 37). Here, women's bodies constitute the battlefield where men communicate their rage to other men.

Brownmiller knows the scale of the Bosnian rapes is not historically unprecedented. Whereas MacKinnon sees a technological sophistication unique in modern history, Brownmiller sees it as history repeating itself. She recognizes that rape dehumanizes women but acknowledges that it is not the only force in wartime that promotes dehumanization. "Rape of a doubly dehumanized object—as woman, as enemy, carries its own terrible logic. In one act of aggressiveness, the collective spirit of women and the nation is broken, leaving a reminder long after the troops depart" (Brownmiller, 1993:37). Pornography is not the only social form that dehumanizes women: war itself introduces a process that dehumanizes the enemy. Therefore, for Brownmiller, rape is predictable in a war context.

These analyses have an odd symmetry. MacKinnon claims that the social dynamic between men and women causes rape in a war context. Yet her focus on the eroticized body leaves almost no space for discussing ethnicized bodies and how they are constituted. That ethnic bodies exist primordially is assumed. Brownmiller, on the other hand, emphasizes the ethnic dynamic between men and men, where women are marginalized and torture's eroticization is ignored. Such a singleminded focus can be blinding. Brownmiller may be right about the intra-male dynamics of rape, but heterosexual rape is often only a substitute for homosexual rape. Yet Brownmiller provides no such evidence to vindicate her thesis. MacKinnon's focus on male-female dynamics, on the other hand, rules this inquiry out by fiat.

To transcend these problems, we should consider American feminist analyses of rape in Latin America. Throughout the 1980s, wartime rape by government soldiers was common throughout Central and Latin America, most notably in Peru and El Salvador. For Cynthia Enloe and Julie Phillips, who have examined this situation, the feminist debate on Bosnia seemed disproportionate to the issue's gravity. "As the highly visible rapes in Bosnia reshape feminist thinking on women and war," Phillips remarked bitterly, "the conflict in Peru quietly goes into its 13th year" (Phillips, 1993: 2). And Enloe emphasizes the limited knowledge we have about this phenomenon. "We still know surprisingly little about why the government's male soldiers in Guatemala or the Contra's male insurgents in Nicaragua engaged in sexual assault on women so insistently" (Enloe, 1993: 120–21). Were these soldiers in or out of control? Was this a conscious government strategy to intimidate or simply one more product of a mostly militarized society? What would count as evidence for one or the other?

Unlike many other kinds of violence, rape carries greater symbolic significance and must be analyzed contextually. Enloe criticizes those who list rape as one of "an assortment of repressive acts, as if rape were not qualitatively different in both its motivations and repercussions" (Enloe, 1993: 121). Rape's consequences may be either shame, as in Bosnia (Drakulic, 1993), or heroic martyrdom (Phillips, 1993). Similarly, rapists may be seeking to intimidate the woman being raped, the men whose property she represents, or even other rapists. For example, Enloe maintains that in Central America, rape socialized the new military recruit and separated him permanently from his civilian compatriots; many soldiers were forced recruits who had to be isolated, through rape, from their communities before they could undertake repressive operations (Enloe, 1993: 121).

Analyzing the Peruvian rapes in the 1980s, Phillips claims that rape does not merely have one function but rather is multifunctional, "a uniquely versatile type of violence" (Phillips, 1993: 28). Rape intimidates independent community organizers. "If traditional 'women's work'—tending families, raising children, holds communities together, assaults on women do much to tear the social fabric apart. When you are out to subdue a population, women are the population" (Phillips, 1993: 28). Rape may be used as a terror tactic to force confessions or destabilize whole areas. In the case of female guerrillas, rape provides a particularly vicious means of reinforcing the gendered division of labor. Rape also imitates and reinforces ethnic and racial divisions: in Peru, *mestizo* guerrillas are raped by *mestizo* and white soldiers, whereas Indian guerrillas are raped by dark-skinned as well as *mestizo* soldiers.

Similarly, Enloe emphasizes the way rape reinforces a sense of community. "Men in war almost always relate to each other in terms of rank and in a lot of circumstances, rape serves to rebond men across personal differences and hierarchies" (Phillips, 1993: 28). This becomes even more likely, as in the case of U.S. soldiers in Vietnam, where divisions in rank mirrored racial differences between blacks and whites. While Enloe agrees with Brownmiller that "we need to look at what dynamics between men lead to rape and what dynamics between men influence how men think about rape," she includes a broader range of possible male relationships than the simple categories of enemies and friends.

We can analyze rape by its effects on military rankings, state and ethnic formations, forms of political recruitment, family reorganization, gender divisions, economic and rural/urban differentiation, and forms of political recruitment and religious purity/pollution. Its effects may not explain why mass rape occurred, but they may clarify why it systematically continues. It is important, therefore, to work outward from rape rather than inward toward rape from a particular social system. We should examine rapes by their specific constellation of practices and discourses.

In the debate on Bosnia, American feminists have a rich understanding of gender formation, but their analysis of ethnicity is remarkably impoverished. American feminists, like the popular press, view ethnic identity as a property of individuals, assuming it is somehow inherited or readily visible. But this notion of ethnicity cannot be sustained in light of contemporary ethnic conflicts. In the Balkans, for example, while no immediate racial, physical, or even linguistic traits facilitate immediate identification, group solidarity and ethnic conflict is nevertheless quite pronounced.

Donald Horowitz has persuasively argued that ethnicity is not a property but rather a relationship between groups in specified contexts (Horowitz, 1985: 1–92). He distinguishes two ethnic systems: "ranked" and "unranked." In ranked systems, groups stand in clear superordination or subordination to one another, often stemming from particular occupational positions. In unranked systems, each group spans the whole available range of occupations and statuses. Horowitz argues that ranked systems are more stable but can break down from changes in technology that deskill the superordinate group or from upward mobility by the subordinate group. When ranked systems collapse, the higher-ranked group desperately struggles to maintain its position, and thus the violence that results may be much more extreme than in unranked systems.

In contrast, in unranked societies such as the former Yugoslavia, each group is potentially a whole society. The groups relate to one another as if they were in a small international system. Conflict in an unranked system is endemic, as in the international community, but can escalate markedly if one group progresses much more (or less) rapidly than others, thereby threatening to monopolize key positions in the economy.

Horowitz's analysis fits well with some feminist analyses of rape. Feminists argue that rape often involves the intersection of race and gender. But this neglects the particular saliency racial or ethnic categories assume in relation to wartime rape. In a stable state, rapes move through ethnic categories that are relatively secure. In war situations, however, racial and ethnic conventions are themselves at stake.

Their renegotiation is the context of rape, not merely something through which rape moves. Here, rape constitutes an ethnomarker. This illustrates a difference in degree, instead of kind, but an important one nevertheless.

If ethnic groups identify themselves mainly in relation to one another, if ethnic war renegotiates these relations, and if rape marks the new boundaries of those relations, then we can expect rape to vary with the kind of ethnic system we are dealing with. In conflicts involving ranked ethnic systems, rape marks how groups are subordinated and superordinated.

Take the example of Peru. According to Phillips, rape minimizes hierarchical relations within a ranked, ethnically divided Peruvian military while reinscribing, through rape, those same hierarchical relations onto the female enemy. In contrast, when conflict breaks out in unranked systems, rape cannot reinscribe hierarchical relations between males of different ethnicities because no clear pattern of dominance exists to begin with. Instead, a competition exists for an economic niche and a demographic majority in an ethnically divided country. As Horowitz indicates, in unranked systems the national census and women's birthrate are highly contested among men in politics (Horowitz, 1985: 194–96). When an unranked system collapses, as in Bosnia, women's bodies become a battlefield where men communicate their rage to other men—because women's bodies had been the implicit political battlefield all along.

We can better use theories of rape if we consider the effects of rape in relation to the kind of ethnic conflicts that exist. Brownmiller's analysis helps us understand how rape shapes an unranked ethnic conflict, but falters when it encounters the complexity of a situation like that in Peru. Phillips's analysis of Peru would probably help us understand little about how rape shapes an unranked ethnic conflict since the male solidarity-through-rape analysis presupposes ranked ethnic divisions.

Rape is an ethnomarker in a massive social conflict, but as an ethnomarker its effects differ depending on the society's ethnic makeup. This does not mean that rape is an ethnomarker solely in war situations, but rather that gender and ethnicity gain greater saliency in these situations. Rape in a war context is the means by which differentials of power and identity are defined.

So how did rape serve as an ethnomarker in Bosnia? The Croatian sociologist Silva Meznaric studied the discourse of rape in the Serbian-Albanian conflict in Kosovo in 1990 to illustrate how gender is used and abused in ethnic conflict. Like Bosnia, Kosovo was an unranked ethnic society, with each group spread across many occupations. The groups were bound by actors who crossed the boundaries either because of their stable social roles (Serbian and Albanian women) or because of informal networks within the local community (Albanian men and Serbian women). Phillips has argued that in Peru women became targets in the guerrilla war because "traditional women's work" was precisely what kept communities together and stable.

Meznaric's account, in contrast, shows how females working in the public sector acted as crucial bridges in divided communities. The daily interactions of Serbian women and Albanian males, and the life-work that went on in these interactions, bound Kosovans together. Meznaric further argues that population growth, modernization, and migration in the 1980s upset the relationship between Serbs and Albanians: Serbs moved out but Albanians remained. While both groups spent enormous amounts of energy and money to emphasize tradition and continuity, problems emerged. As Meznaric puts it:

> Identification of ethnic markers frequently entails recognition of ethnic identifiers such as language, dress, lifestyle and housing—these are customary for every ethnic group. What happens when these identifiers are similar and cannot easily distinguish the groups? In the case of Serbs and Albanians, not only did they demarcate themselves in terms of language, dress, and housing, but they also insisted on separation of schools, instruction, literature, history and so on. Even so, overt signals and signs for defining boundaries were not enough. . . . Classic markers of ethnic difference (language, religion, housing, territory) were insufficient because they could be erased or blurred by the modernization of life. (Meznaric, 1994: 82)

In this context, rape became an ethnomarker by defining moral excellence and "by constructing ethnic difference on the basis of one group's cultural proclivity to violence and rape, the boundary between the two groups became fixed" (Meznaric, 1994: 82; see also Horowitz, 1985: 201–2). Meznaric also notes the media campaign on rape (that presented Albanian men as rapists) that sharpened the ethnic border between Serbs and Albanians. Also, Serbian criminal law was amended to include the category of ethnic rape, that is, "if a perpetrator and victim are of different ethnic origin, the criminal law recognizes this fact as aggravating" the crime (Meznaric, 1994: 94). As a result, public interaction between working women—who were mostly Serbian—and Albanian men was rendered unpredictable and dangerous. Thus, the informal channels connecting Albanians and Serbs in Kosovo were interrupted and "Kosovo ceased to exist as a multiethnic region. Kosovo became a deeply divided society." There was, in other words, "a total breakdown in communication between ethnic groups" (Meznaric, 1994: 88).

Meznaric's implicit argument about Bosnia suggests that the lines between ethnic groups were blurred; ethnic identification was not easy. Unlike in Kosovo, the war in Bosnia was not preceded by a gradual process through which unranked peoples who once knew each other learned to fear one another through rape-talk. In this context, rape served as an ethnomarker particularly in areas where the interaction between groups was most dense. Meznaric argues that if one plots the location of camps and information about rapes against a map of the population distribution, "one can notice that massive rapes occur in areas where Serbs are a minority and Muslims are in relative or absolute majority . . . or else in areas where Serbs are in the majority position but where there are significant Muslim and/or Croat minorities" (Meznaric, 1994:93).

Just as in Central America, rape socialized the new military recruit and separated him from his civilian compatriots. This is why rapes occurred in front of fellow soldiers and victims who knew the perpetrators. Rape isolated the recruit from his community and prepared him for further military operations. Just as in Kosovo, rape was also used to underline the moral superiority of the Serbians, using—for example—the videotaped rapes that were later used to implicate Croatian forces.

This account generates hypotheses about rape in war that differ from accounts provided by American feminists. If Meznaric is right, we should witness a decline in Bosnian war rapes over time as the work of isolating ethnic groups is accomplished.

Fred Halliday writes that "a history of world war as a gendered conflict, ranging from the Japanese 'rape' (in both senses) of Nanking in 1937 through the legitimation of rape by the Red Army as it advanced westwards, remains to be written" (Halliday, 1994: 327). Such a history, like the unwritten history of rape and decolonization, would inevitably relate gendered conflict to ethnic conflict in specified contexts. The account I've sketched here poses a more specific and contextualized analysis than the accounts provided by Brownmiller, MacKinnon, Enloe, and Phillips. It incorporates their theories of rape but situates them according to variations in ethnic relations rather than merely gender relations.

REFERENCES

Blatt, Deborah. 1992. "Recognizing Rape as a Method of Torture." *Review of Law and Social Change* 19:4, 821–865.

Brownmiller, Susan. 1993. "Making Female Bodies the Battlefield." *Newsweek*, 4 January, p. 37.

Drakulic, Slavenka. 1993. "Women Hide Behind a Wall of Silence." *The Nation*, 1 March, pp. 268–272.

Enloe, Cynthia. 1993. *The Morning After: Sexual Politics at the End of the Cold War.* Berkeley: University of California Press.

Halliday, Fred. 1994. *Rethinking International Relations.* Vancouver: University of British Columbia Press.

Horowitz, Donald. 1985. *Ethnic Groups in Conflict.* Berkeley: University of California Press.

MacKinnon, Catharine. 1993. "Turning Rape into Pornography: Postmodern Genocide." *MS.*, July/August, pp. 24–30.

Meznaric, Silva. 1994. "Gender as an Ethno-Marker: Rape, War, and Identity Politics in the Former Yugoslavia." In Valentine M. Moghadam (ed.), *Identity, Politics and Women: Cultural Reassertions and Feminisms in International Perspective.* Boulder, CO: Westview Press.

Phillips, Julie. 1993. "Crossfire's Targets: Women in Peru Fight Violence from Both Sides." *Village Voice*, 13 July, pp. 28–29.

Stiglmayer, Alexandra (ed.). 1994. *Mass Rape: The War against Women in Bosnia–Herzogovina.* Lincoln: University of Nebraska Press.

Chapter Four

Should Women Be Soldiers or Pacifists?

April Carter

Even with the upsurge of feminist scholarship in the last twenty-five years, relatively little attention has been given to war's impact on women. Some feminist historians and sociologists have nevertheless contributed important research. Cynthia Enloe, in particular, explores the roles the military assigns to women in her books, beginning with *Does Khaki Become You?* in 1983. Others such as Sara Ruddick and Jean Bethke Elshtain have examined the actual theme of women and war.

Nevertheless, debates on the theme have largely stalled around the starkly opposed views among Western feminist activists about women's future roles within wars. Liberal feminists promote women's equal right to become front line soldiers, while many women who flocked to peace movements in the 1980s view war as a masculine enterprise and urge women to reject war and work for peace. So which side is right? Should women press for full equality in the armed services or should they campaign against militarism? Unfortunately, feminist theory thus far cannot, for several reasons, satisfactorily answer these questions. Rather, women must make political judgments within the context of fundamental debates about war and peace, and not merely within the context of feminist goals.

The dominant image of women in war shows women suffering: weeping for husbands or sons in battle and, if defeated, becoming the sexual booty of their conquerors. Obversely, much military rhetoric emphasizes the need to protect the home and the purity of womenfolk. In return for that protection, women have been expected to support their men—cheering their warriors, offering sympathy and companionship, and nursing the wounded. Another group of women is assigned to meet soldiers' immediate sexual needs, as camp followers and prostitutes.

Newspaper accounts over the last few years suggest that such traditional roles still survive. We are reminded that the Japanese Army used captured females as "comfort women" for their troops in World War II. We see that rape is still closely associated with war; as in Bosnia, it may be organized systematically to impress upon the captured the totality of their submission. Still, women's primary roles in war are as wives, girlfriends, and mothers, waiting for their soldiers to return and caring for the wounded.

But there's also a close association between women gaining greater social status and their playing a more active part in war. Women's emancipation during this century and the demands on manpower in the two world wars have led many women to contribute directly to war efforts—such as serving in munitions factories and directly serving in the armed forces. During the Second World War, women were barred from actual fighting—except in the Soviet Union and in partisan warfare in Eastern Europe. But since the 1980s the armed services have, in response to the second wave of the women's liberation movement, integrated women into their ranks and given them front-line roles. In the Gulf War, over thirty-three thousand American women, along with one thousand British women, were sent into duty. Today, even more opportunities exist for women in combat, as a result of the United States Defense Department's January 1994 revision of rules on risk in ground combat. Many Western countries now only explicitly exclude women, if at all, from infantry assignments. Although the number of women in front-line military roles—as opposed to support services—is still small, ordinary Western women, including mothers of small children, are going to war.

Since war generally dramatizes women's powerlessness and suffering and the way they are forced into roles required by soldiers in a male-dominated society, liberating women might naturally require their symbolic equality on the battlefield. Emancipatory socialist and nationalist movements have given women symbolic status as fighters in varying cultural contexts, such as the Chinese Communists in the 1930s and 1940s, the Jewish independence campaign in the 1940s, and the African National Congress in its armed struggle in South Africa in the 1970s and 1980s. But once in power, emancipatory movements tend to move women back into more traditional activities, perhaps as a reflection of the waning of emancipatory aspirations.

Some Western feminists, such as Judith Hicks Stiehm, argue that women must join the protectors and abandon their age-old status as the weak and protected. In the United States in particular, liberal equal-rights feminism advocates women's incorporation into the armed forces on the same terms as men, so that women will have an equal opportunity to perform challenging jobs and gain promotions. Some liberal feminists believe claims to full equality of rights require women to accept the same duties of citizenship as men. This linkage was made, for example, by a legal brief filed by the National Organization for Women in 1981, which challenged the constitutionality of an all-male draft and called for women to register for the draft the same as men.

The strategy of creating societies that give women genuine equality by giving them the right (and the duty) to fight has provoked objections from a purely feminist standpoint. The armed services are exceptionally macho institutions—soldiers are regularly inducted into manly valor by being encouraged to despise effeminacy, as the language of the barrack square vividly illustrates. And rape and sexual harrassment provide special problems for women in the armed services. Women in war zones are vulnerable not only to rape by the enemy, but by soldiers on their own side. Horrific examples of this from the Vietnam War have been documented by the Australian author Siobhan McHugh in *Minefields and Miniskirts*.

The entry of women will not easily transform the military services. The 1992 Tailhook scandal, for example, illustrates the continuing sexism in the United States armed forces. (Even longer-standing problems of prejudice still linger: consider the March 1996 report on the extreme racism still suffered by black recruits to the British army.) In the foreseeable future, women will likely have no more than token representation in front-line combat. Either way, the most fundamental objection to women seeking equality via combat is that the values and institutions of militarism clash with those of a "woman-friendly" society. To take an extreme example, it is no accident that fascism—the political ideology that exalts warrior values—relegates women to their homes and their warrior's beds.

Since women in war traditionally serve as victims and appendages to men, and since there is reason to question the pursuit of equality within male-determined military institutions (even if it might promote challenging possibilities for individual women), it is tempting to have women instead actively oppose war and militarism. Some feminists believe that women "naturally" oppose war and militarism because they're committed to creating and nurturing life. This had produced the hope, especially among women's suffrage movements, that women—once in political power—would create a world without war. During the First World War, feminists pursued international action to end the war, and feminist pacifists in the interwar years counted on women to resist men's nationalism and militarism.

More recently, militant feminism combined with radical antiwar beliefs in women's peace camps in the peace movement of the 1980s—the most famous of which was the Greenham Common camp at the cruise missile base in England. Feminists were also among those in the former Yugoslavia who resisted extremist nationalism and military violence. Belgrade feminists, for example, created Women in Black in 1991, which opposed the war in Croatia, and then in Bosnia.

The image of women as active peacemakers suggests that women can transcend their destiny as helpless victims of men's wars, without accepting the values of a male-dominated society. So feminist pacifism also appears most compatible with feminist hopes of transforming society. But there have been major challenges to the argument that women are necessarily more peace-loving than men. Especially challenged has been the claim that women are motivated to act as mothers, as suggested in *Women and Russia* by Tatyana Mamonova. This pioneer Soviet argued in the early 1980s: "Our sense of responsibility for our children compels us to take to the streets with our demands for peace." This reflects similar beliefs among many women activists in the Western peace movement, such as those attracted to Women for a Non-Nuclear Future.

There are several objections to the notion that women's maternal instincts make them naturally pacifist. First, the implication would be that men are therefore aggressive by "nature" and drawn irresistibly to deadly technology. This inappropriately pits men against women in the quest for peace. Second, this biological determinism ignores the crucial role of culture in shaping personality. Even Sara Ruddick's more sophisticated consideration of women's cross-cultural experiences of "maternal thinking" falls short. Being a mother does not necessarily lead to a hatred of war and an empathy with mothers on the enemy side. A mother has a gut concern for the safety of her own children; only if mother love becomes more generalized does it sustain a peace politics. Moreover, for the past two hundred years feminists have struggled to extend our notion of women's roles and experiences beyond only motherhood. Thus to define women's approach to war primarily in terms of that role provides a questionable feminist position.

Recent feminist developments, including political opposition to the dominance of feminist organizations by white middle-class women and challenges by postmodernists to all universalizing claims, cast doubt on the possibility of speaking about "women" as a category at all. Feminism in the 1990s strives to respect the cultural and other differences among women, both within and between countries, and thus many feminists hesitate to make general claims about women and war based on maternal thinking. Radical feminist theorists such as Catharine MacKinnon, and some feminist international lawyers, address rape in war as a universal issue specific to women. But a focus on rape only addresses women's suffering, not their positive potential.

A qualified feminist case can also be made that women, although they have often been co-opted into promoting bellicose policies, do on balance have a substantial interest in resisting war, given their roles in society. Many women are mothers hoping for a secure world for their children. Many are wives or lovers of men who may be killed or wounded in war, or who may be more subtly damaged and made more prone to use violence in their private lives. Moreover, the association between war and rape, and the tendency for women to be pushed into the background in many wars, suggests that women will usually—though not always—gain greater freedom and equality in peace.

Feminist theory alone cannot, however, provide a convincing case for feminist pacifism. This stems from more than merely the political divisions between equal-rights feminists and feminist pacifists, and the theoretical disputes between radical feminists (who make universal claims about women) and postmodern feminists (who stress differences and the impossiblity of generalizing about women). The limitations result also from the failure to confront fundamental questions about war and pacifism. If, for example, war is inevitable—as realist theories of international relations suggest—or if there are some genuinely just wars, then women's responsibility as citizens may sometimes require them to fight, regardless of whether fighting clashes with women's biological or culturally created "nature." Jean Bethke Elshtain, for example, seems to have moved toward this view: while her early work on women and war sought to develop "maternal thinking" as a basis for feminist pacifism, she began arguing in 1987 that women should as citizens play a role in just wars.

The recent development of a specifically feminist approach to international relations promises to bridge the gap between feminism and theorizing about war. But it still must overcome the continuing disputes between different schools of thought within 1990s feminist theory, including whether we can generalize about the category of "women." Although feminist scholarship provides us with fascinating insights into the relationship between war and masculinity and into the roles women play in supporting militarism, women who want to know whether they should be soldiers or pacifists still need to go beyond feminism: they must consider the arguments for and against pacifism, and for and against the notion of just wars.

REFERENCES

Alcoff, Linda. 1994. "Cultural Feminism versus Post-Structuralism: The Identity Crisis in Feminist Theory." In S. M. Okin and J. Mansbridge (eds.), *Feminism*. Vol. 2. Aldershot, U.K.: Edward Elgar.

Elshtain, Jean Bethke. 1987. *Women and War*. New York: Basic Books.

Enloe, Cynthia. 1983. *Does Khaki Become You? The Militarization of Women's Lives*. London: Pluto Press.

———. 1989. *Bananas, Beaches and Bases: Making Feminist Sense of International Politics*. Berkeley: University of California Press.

———. 1990. *The Morning After: Sexual Politics at the End of the Cold War*. Berkeley: University of California Press.

Mamonova, Tatyana. 1984. *Women and Russia: Feminist Writings from the Soviet Union*. Boston: Beacon Press.

McHugh, Siobhan. 1993. *Minefields and Miniskirts: Australian Women and the Vietnam War*. Sydney: Doubleday.

Muir, Kate. 1993. *Arms and the Woman*. London: Hodder and Stoughton, Coronet.

Ruddick, Sara. 1990. *Maternal Thinking: Towards a Politics of Peace*. London: Women's Press.

Part II

Nationalism, Victimization, and War Culture

Chapter Five

Gendered Nationalism
Reproducing "Us" versus "Them"

V. Spike Peterson

[I]n international theory—neorealism in particular—
nations and nationalisms register as a key area of empirical neglect and theoretical infertility. . . . Despite the
manifest salience of the "national factor" in some extraordinary recent transformations of our global political landscape, we have yet to see a serious disciplinary
effort to reconsider nationalism in light of contemporary transformations.

—(Lapid 1991:1–2)

This essay explores the politics of identity and the problematics of nationalism
through a gender-sensitive lens. It argues that gender is a structural feature of the
terrain we call world politics, shaping what we study and how we study it. Mapping
practices conventionally employed in international relations fail to "see" and
therefore do not analyze this pervasive ordering principle. As a consequence, our
conventional maps are not simply limited but actually misleading.

Gender refers not to anatomical or biological distinctions but to the social construction, which is always culturally specific, of masculine and feminine as hierarchical and oppositional categories. Symbols, theories, practices, institutions, and, of
course, individuals are gendered, meaning that their characteristics can be associated
with, or construed as manifestations of, masculinity or femininity. A gender-
sensitive lens enables us to see how gender hierarchy shapes our ways of thinking,
knowing, and doing and therefore has patterned consequences that are relevant to
the study and conduct of foreign policy.[1]

Nationalism and International Relations

We recognize nationalism as problematic from the vantage point of conflict between
groups: sameness within is purchased at the price of institutionalizing difference—

and too often, conflict—between groups. But nationalism is also problematic from the vantage point of those within the nation who share least in elite privilege and political representation. Gregory Gleason (1991:223–228) identifies three "faces" of nationalism: liberation (the self-determination associated positively with nationalism), exclusivity (the promotion of group uniformity and "difference" from "others"), and domination (the negative effects of suppressing difference within the group and/or domination of "outsiders" in the name of the group). How particular individuals and subgroups are situated in relation to the homogenizing project will depend on a variety of historical factors: there is no essential or predetermined "givens" in how race, class, ethnicity, gender, etc. are linked to nationalist projects.[2] It is possible, however, to identify historical patterns in regard to the gendered dynamics—and problematics—of group identity formation and reproduction. This chapter explores such dynamics with a particular focus on nationalism.

In spite of its contemporary significance, nationalism remains poorly understood and insufficiently studied. Jill Vickers argues that "this difficulty of understanding nationalism as a form of self-identification and of group organization reflects the profound difficulty that male-stream thought, in general, has had in understanding the public manifestations of the process of identity construction" (1990:480). The dilemma is this: once we move beyond the biological parameters of females bearing and breast-feeding infants, how are groups—and the social relations they entail—formed and reproduced?

Vickers argues that patriarchal social relations can be interpreted as one way of "constructing enduring forms of social organization, group cohesion and identity" (1990:483).[3] Insofar as men seek group affiliation and continuity, they attempt to control women's sexual reproduction and to institutionalize social relations that engender loyalties to a male-defined group extending beyond the mother-infant bond. Lacking an immediate biological connection, men appropriate an abstract concept of the blood tie and employ it to promote bonding among males and group identity based on male-defined needs.

Implementation of this strategy involves a "battle of the cradle" over women's sexual reproduction and a "battle of the nursery" over identities and loyalties (Vickers 1990:485). To the extent that women are excluded from the definition of group interests and compelled to comply with male-defined needs, their freedom and autonomy are limited. So excluded, women are at the same time denied the status of "personhood" attached to group decision makers (in the modern state, this is institutionalized through the public-private dichotomy). In sum, the coherence and continuity of the group—and the gender hierarchy it imposes—is "maintained and secured only by limiting the autonomy, freedom of choice and social adulthood of the group's physical and social reproducers" (Vickers 1990:482).

What this analysis points out is that reproduction is the most political—power-laden and potent—of activities. Conventionally ignored as a dimension of the ostensibly apolitical private sphere, the power relations of reproduction fundamentally condition who "we" are and how groups/nations align themselves in cooperative, competing, and complementary ways. On this view, gender relations are a crucial, not peripheral, dimension of the dynamics of group identities and intergroup conflicts.

Gendered Nationalism

To illustrate the politics of reproduction, I draw upon (but alter) a framework for analyzing gendered nationalism introduced by Yuval-Davis and Anthias (1989). The following discussion identifies and briefly discusses five gender-differentiated dimensions or ways in which women have typically been situated in relation to nationalist processes.

Women as Biological Reproducers of Group Members

The battle of the cradle is about regulating under what conditions, when, how many, and whose children women will bear. The forms it takes are historically specific, shaped by socio-religious norms, technological developments, economic pressures, and political priorities. Pronatalist policies may include restriction of contraceptive knowledge and techniques, denial of access to abortions, and provision of material rewards for bearing children. From Sparta, where a mother "reared her sons to be sacrificed on the alter of civic necessity" (Elshtain 1992:142) to South Africa, where white women were exhorted to bear "babies for Botha" (McClintock 1991:110–11), women have been admonished to fulfill their "duty" by bearing sons to fight for and daughters to care for the Motherland.

Population control works both ways. To limit the size of "undesirable" groups, immigration controls, expulsion, sterilization, and even extermination have been—and are being—practiced. Women's bodies are often used as a battleground of men's wars. In Bosnia, systematic rape and sexual enslavement not only violate countless Muslim women but sabotage the underpinnings and therefore the continuity of community.

Women as Social Reproducers of Group Members and Cultural Forms

The battle of the nursery is about ensuring that children born are bred in culturally appropriate ways. This may involve the regulation—through religious dogma, legislation, social norms, and coercion—of sexual liaisons so that religious, ethnic, class, and citizenship boundaries are maintained. By enforcing legislation regarding marriage, child custody, and property and citizenship inheritance, the state controls the reproduction of membership/citizenship claims. As states assume ever greater responsibility for provision of basic needs, claims to citizenship assume ever greater significance, determining not only one's obligations but also one's rights—to work, to a stable residency, to legal protections, and to educational and welfare benefits.

The battle of the nursery also involves the ideological reproduction of group members. Under patriarchal relations, women are the primary socializers of children, both within the family and in early education. They are largely responsible for inculcating beliefs, behaviors, and loyalties that are culturally appropriate and ensure intergenerational continuity. This cultural transmission includes learning the "mother tongue," as well as the group's symbols, rituals, divisions of labor, and worldviews.

Women as Signifiers of Group Differences

As biological and social reproducers, it is women's capacities and activities that are "privatized" in the name of male-defined groups. But women also serve as symbolic markers of the nation and of the group's cultural identity. Shared images, symbols, rituals, myths, and language play essential roles in the reproduction of social groups that are based on abstract bonds among men who are distanced from reproductive activities. In this context, the symbolic realm is elevated to strategic importance: symbols become what's worth fighting—even dying—for, and cultural metaphors become weapons in the war. The metaphors of nation-as-woman and woman-as-nation suggest how women—as bodies and cultural repositories—become the battleground of group struggles.

The personification of nature-as-female transmutes easily to nation-as-woman, where the Motherland is a woman's body and as such is ever in danger of violation—by "foreign" males. To defend her frontiers and her honor requires relentless vigilance and the sacrifice of countless citizen-warriors (Elshtain 1992). Nation-as-woman expresses a spatial, embodied femaleness: the land's fecundity, upon which the people depend, must be protected by defending the body/nation's boundaries against invasion and violation. But nation-as-woman is also a temporal metaphor: the rape of the body/nation not only violates frontiers but disrupts—by planting alien seed or destroying reproductive viability—the maintenance of the community through time. Also implicit in the patriarchal metaphor is a tacit agreement that men who cannot defend their woman/nation against rape have lost their "claim" to that body, that land.

Clearly, the nation/woman is being denied agency. Rather, "she" is man's possession, and like other enabling vessels (boats, planes) is valued as a means for achieving male-defined ends: the sovereign/man drives the ship of state. Thus, the motherland is female but the state and its citizen-warriors are male. The homogenizing identity of the group/state is one of fraternal bonding in the literal sense of "liberty, fraternity, equality." Excluded intentionally from the public domain, women are not agents in their own right but instruments for the realization of male-defined agendas.

Woman-as-nation signifies the boundaries of group identity, marking its difference from alien "others." Assigned responsibility for reproducing the group through time, women are singled out as "custodians of cultural particularisms" and "the symbolic repository of group identity" (Kandiyoti 1991:434). Because symbols of cultural authenticity are jealously guarded, actual women face a variety of pressures to conform to idealized models of behavior. In Jan Jindy Pettman's words,

Women's use in symbolically marking the boundary of the group makes them particularly susceptible to control in strategies to maintain and defend the boundaries. Here women's movements and bodies are policed, in terms of their sexuality, fertility, and relations with "others," especially with other men. This suggests why (some) men attach such political significance to women's "outer attire and sexual purity," seeing women as their possessions, as those responsible for the transmission of culture and through it political identity; and also as those most vulnerable to abuse, violation or seduction by "other" men. (Pettman 1992:5–6)

Women as Participants in Political Identity Struggles

In reality, women are not only symbols, and their activities extend well beyond the private sphere. In contrast to the stereotype of women as passive and peace-loving, women have throughout history supported and participated in conflicts involving their communities. They have provided essential support in their servicing roles (feeding, clothing, and nursing combatants), worked in underground movements, passed information and weapons, organized their communities for military action, taken up arms themselves, and occasionally led troops into battle (Peterson and Runyan 1993, chap. 4). Yet the significance of their contributions remains "hidden" and therefore unanalyzed in conventional accounts.

Women have historically been denied public sphere activities: they rarely appear in combatant or leadership roles and in the arena of high politics. Because conventional accounts of war focus on these activities, it is not surprising that women appear only as "an off-stage chorus to a basically male drama" (Enloe 1987:529). Contemporary analysts continue to understand war as a "basically male drama" but they recognize that battlefield action is only the tip of the iceberg. Leadership personalities, production capabilities, popular sentiments, communication technologies, historical animosities, political alignments, media politics and normative principles are some of the multiple variables upon which battlefield outcomes depend. There is no fixed pattern in how gender shapes the most pertinent variables and their interaction in a specific case. But our knowledge of the iceberg is inaccurate and therefore inadequate unless we "see" how gender is at work and undertake systematic study of its effects.

Women as Societal Members Generally

This category extends our mapping of gender beyond the immediate context of nationalist struggles. It reminds us that women are not homogeneous or typically united. Social hierarchies—racism, classism, ageism, heterosexism, ablism, etc.—structuring any particular society are interactive: racism is not independent of but mutually shapes expressions of sexism (Mohanty, Russo, and Torres 1991). As a consequence, allegiance to particular causes may complement, coexist with, or contradict allegiance to other group objectives. How and to what extent feminist and nationalist projects converge depends on contextual specifics. Kumara Jayawardena found that at the end of the nineteenth and the beginning of the twentieth centuries, feminism was compatible with the modernizing dynamic of anti-imperialist national liberation movements in Asia and a number of other colonized countries (Jayawardena 1986). In contrast, Val Moghadam examines contemporary movements and finds that "feminists and nationalists view each other with suspicion, if not hostility, and nationalism is no longer assumed to be a progressive force for change" (Moghadam, forthcoming). She argues that nationalism has been recast from a secular, modernizing project to one that emphasizes "the nation as an extended family writ large" or "a religious entity"; "women become the revered objects of the collective act of redemption, and the role models for the new nationalist, patriarchal family" (Moghadam, forthcoming). In this context, women face a variety of pressures to support nationalist objectives even, or especially, when these conflict with feminist objectives.

In general, women are situated differently than men (and differently among themselves) in regard to divisions of power, violence, labor, and resources. In the context of nationalism, these various locations shape the allegiance that various women, or women in concert, will have toward group identity and objectives. How the trade-offs are played out may have international consequences. For example, Denmark's initial rejection of the Maastricht Treaty—a "no" vote that threatened to undermine community solidarity—was significantly shaped by gender issues. Danish feminists campaigned against the treaty because work and welfare provisions in the community structure are less progressive than those obtained already in Denmark (True 1993:84). Different trade-offs pertained in the United Kingdom. There, lack of equal opportunity legislation meant that British women had a political interest in seeing their country's adoption of more progressive community policies, even though this represented a loss of traditional sovereignty (Walby 1992:95).

These examples remind us that there is no "given" or automatic relationship between women's interests and national interests. But they also demonstrate that gender is a pervasive feature of the territory—group conflicts and world politics—we are attempting to map.

Conclusion

The whole study of states is today being reconfigured. . . . [N]ew attention is being given to the salience of the forces of nationalism in all their modern manifestations, at the same time that more fundamental questions are being asked about the international order. (Graubard 1993:vii)

Conventional simplifications—exemplified in traditional dichotomies of public-private, domestic-international, production-reproduction—provide not only limited but actually misleading "maps" of today's systems of power. Gender is a structural feature of social reality and as such must be "put on the map," systematically studied, and its symbolic and material effects incorporated in our production of historical, contextual accounts that enable effective social transformation.

One important consequence of conventional dichotomies is our neglect of activities associated with the private sphere. The latter include individual and group identity formation, cultural socialization, and social reproduction: the maintenance of social relationships and meeting of basic needs upon which the continuity of our world(s) ultimately depends. When we neglect reproductive processes we easily lapse into reifying our constructs rather than understanding them in historical context. When we ignore these activities we fail to contextualize sources of group compliance, cooperation, and conflict.

As the identity people are willing to kill and to die for, nationalism demands our best mapping techniques. A gender-sensitive analysis improves our map of nationalism. It illuminates the processes of identity formation, cultural reproduction, and political allegiance that are key to understanding collective identities and their political effects. It also informs our understanding of domination dynamics. In patriarchal societies (currently the norm worldwide), group coherence and continuity are achieved through denial of equality within the group. The battle of the cradle and nursery are at the expense of women's autonomy internally and mutually respectful relations externally. As the inequality that is most naturalized, and therefore used to justify multiple hierarchies, gender hierarchy is central to the construction and reproduction of asymmetrical social relations. The exclusivity and domination "faces" of nationalism typify such asymmetrical relations.

In short, the gender hierarchy of masculine over feminine and the nationalist domination of insiders over outsiders are doubly linked. As described earlier, nationalism is gendered in terms of how the construction of group identity (allegiance to "us" versus "them") depends upon divisions of masculinity and femininity. In this sense, the process itself presupposes gendered social relations. Nationalism is also gendered in terms of how the naturalization of domination ("us" at the expense of "them") depends upon the prior naturalization of men/masculinity over women/femininity. In this sense, taking domination as natural obscures its historical context and disables our knowledge of and attempts to transform hierarchical relations. The point of gender-sensitive analyses is not that gender is always the primary or most salient dimension of a particular context. But it is consistently at work, making a difference and, in the context of nationalism and intergroup conflicts, may be the difference we most need to see—and move beyond.

NOTES

1. Gender hierarchy and patriarchy both refer to systems of power that privilege men and that which is associated with masculinity over women and that which is associated with femininity. Androcentrism refers to male-centered orientations that privilege men's ways of being and knowing as the norm or standard for all people, thus eclipsing alternative perspectives. Masculinism, like sexism, is an orientation that justifies and "naturalizes" gender hierarchy by not questioning the elevation of ways of being and knowing associated with masculinity over those associated with femininity. Feminism is an orientation that views gender as a fundamental ordering principle in today's world, values women's diverse ways of being and knowing, and promotes the transformation of gender and related hierarchies.

Gender-sensitive research both "deconstructs" androcentric (male-as-norm) accounts—by locating "invisible" women and incorporating women's experiences and perspectives in the study of humankind—and "reconstructs" them—by rethinking fundamental relationships of knowledge, power, and community and developing feminist epistemologies. See, for example, Butler and Scott 1992; Hekman 1990; Mohanty, Russo and Torres 1991; Nicholson 1990. On the basis of this research, many contemporary feminist scholars argue that "all of social life is gendered" (Nelson 1989:4) and allegedly "gender-neutral" accounts distort our understanding by obscuring the significance of gender.

2. For an overview of the literature on state making, political identity, feminism, and nationalism, see Peterson 1993. To the extent that states have historically institutionalized class, gender and race/ethnic hierarchies, state-led or state-seeking nationalisms are problematic from the perspective of struggling against these hierarchies.

3. With Vickers, I emphasize that the development of gender hierarchy was neither "necessary" nor "inevitable" but represents one among numerous possibilities. Like states, racism, and nationalism, gender hierarchy is a complex, contingent, historical development. Approaches that reduce these developments to "nature" inevitably sustain—by their naturalizing, depoliticizing effects—the phenomena they purport to explain and in effect promote the hierarchical relations characteristic of states, racism, nationalism, and sexism.

REFERENCES

Butler, Judith, and Joan W. Scott, eds. 1992. *Feminists Theorize the Political.* New York and London: Routledge.

Elshtain, Jean Bethke. 1992. "Sovereignty, Identity, Sacrifice." In V. Spike Peterson (ed.), *Gendered States.* Boulder, CO: Lynne Rienner Press.

Enloe, Cynthia. 1987. "Feminists Thinking about War, Militarism, and Peace." In Beth B. Hess and Myra Marx Ferree (eds.), *Analyzing Gender.* Newbury Park, CA: Sage.

Gleason, Gregory. 1991. "Nationalism in Our Time." *Current World Leaders* 34(2) April: 213–234.

Graubard, Stephen R. 1993. "Preface. Special Issue: Reconstructing Nations and States." *Daedalus* 122 (3) Summer:v–viii.

Hekman, Susan J. 1990. *Gender and Knowledge: Elements of a Postmodern Feminism.* Cambridge, U.K.: Polity Press.

Jayawardena, Kumari. 1986. *Feminism and Nationalism in the Third World.* London: ZED Books.

Kandiyoti, Deniz. 1991. "Identity and Its Discontents: Women and the Nation." *Millennium* 20 (3):429–443.

Lapid, Yosef. 1991. "Theorizing the 'National' in International Relations Theory: Reflections on Nationalism and Neorealism." Paper presented at the 32nd Annual Meeting of the International Studies Association, Vancouver, BC, March.

McClintock, Anne. 1991. " 'No Longer in a Future Heaven': Women and Nationalism in South Africa." *Transition* 51:104–123.

Moghadam, Valentine M., ed. Forthcoming. *Gender and National Identity: Woman in Muslim Society.* London: ZED Books.

Mohanty, Chandra, and Satya P. Mohanty. 1990. "Contradictions of Colonialism." *Women's Review of Books* 7 (6) March:19–21.

Mohanty, Chandra Talpade, Anne Russo, and Lourdes Torres, eds. 1991. *Third World Women and the Politics of Feminism.* Bloomington: Indiana University Press.

Nelson, Barbara J. 1989. "Women and Knowledge in Political Science." *Women and Politics* 9 (2):1–25.

Nicholson, Linda, ed. 1990. *Feminism/Postmodernism.* New York: Routledge.

Peterson, V. Spike. 1993. *The Politics of Identity in International Relations.* Fletcher Forum of World Affairs 17 (2) Summer:1–12.

Peterson, V. Spike, and Anne Sisson Runyan. 1993. *Global Gender Issues.* Boulder, CO: Westview Press.

Pettman, Jan Jindy. 1992. "Women, Nationalism and the State: Towards an International Feminist Perspective." Occasional Paper 4 in Gender and Development Studies, Asian Institute of Technology, Bangkok.

True, Jacqui. 1993. "National Selves and Feminine Others." *Fletcher Forum of World Affairs* 17 (2) Summer:75–89.

Vickers, Jill McCalla. 1990. "At His Mother's Knee: Sex/Gender and the Construction of National Identities." In Greta Hoffman Nemiroff (ed.), *Women and Men: Interdisciplinary Readings on Gender.* Toronto: Fitzhenry and Whiteside.

Walby, Sylvia. 1992. "Women and Nation." *International Journal of Comparative Sociology* 32 (1–2) Jan.–April.

Yuval-Davis, Nira, and Floya Anthias, eds. 1989. *Woman-Nation-State.* London: Macmillan Press.

Chapter Six

All the Men Are in the Militias,
All the Women Are Victims
The Politics of Masculinity and Femininity in Nationalist Wars

Cynthia Enloe

Borislav Herak was an ordinary man.[1] He had not yet married and so lived with his parents in Sarajevo. Although ethnically a Serb, he, like so many Sarajevans, lived within an ethnically mixed family. His sister had married a Sarajevan Muslim Bosnian man. Borislav himself didn't have much luck with girlfriends, and maybe that is why he read pornographic magazines up in his room. This disturbed his father, a welder. Nor could his son's work life have been called a success. He had done poorly in school and had an undistinguished career as a conscript in the Yugoslav navy. In the early 1990s he was employed pushing a cart in one of the city's textile factories. Yet Borislav didn't seem to be a violent man. In his twenty-one years there were no records of his having vented his personal frustrations with assaults on women. And politics did not appear to provide an alternative outlet. He scarcely knew anything about either Yugoslav or Serbian history. Perhaps the political debates that had grown steadily more intense since the outbreak of controversy over control of Kosovo just seemed to this twenty-one-year-old less immediately relevant than the centerfolds of the magazines he stored in his bedroom.

All this changed in 1992. War came to Sarajevo. Like many of the besieged city's residents, Borislav fled to its surrounding mountains. He was taken into one of the scores of semi-autonomous militias formed with the intent of pursuing ethnic Serbian territorial control. One, however, could scarcely describe Borislav Herak as having "joined" or been enlisted into this militia. The process was a far cry from the formal routines by which young men were conscripted into the now-disintegrating Yugoslav state army. From his own rather vague account, he seemed, rather, to have fallen into the company of these Serbian militiamen. They offered shelter and protection in the midst of an increasingly chaotic social environment. Gradually, his new comrades would also provide this unfocused and listless young man a purpose larger than himself.

We know these details about Borislav Herak because he had nothing to do in prison but talk. Speaking to French and American journalists broke the boredom during the days he waited for his trial. By late 1992, he had been captured by the Bosnian forces he had come to see as his militia comrades' and his own enemy. He was to be tried on charges not only of murder, but of rape. Mass rape. He was prepared to confess. Borislav Herak, a man who merely a year ago had been one of history's nonentities, now had his photograph on the front pages of major newspapers. He would forever after be among the most widely recognized human faces behind that abstracted horror that had come to be called "the Bosnian rapes."[2]

It is clear that a student of ethnicity and nationalism has much to explain before the story of Borislav Herak makes sense. Why did he come to sexually assault Bosnian Muslim women when a person of the same religion and ethnicity was the object of familial affections? How had such an apparently unpoliticized individual come to take risks in the name of Serbian nationalism? But these questions expose only the tip of the analytical iceberg.

Buried in the story of this once unexceptional person are important puzzles—and potential revelations—about how ethnicity gets converted into nationalist consciousness, how consciousness becomes organized, and how organized nationalism becomes militarized. None of these transformations is automatic. Nor is their sequence from one to the next. Each calls for explanation. But exploring these questions, melting down the analytical iceberg, requires taking a close look at gender.

For Borislav Herak was more than simply (or not so simply) a Serbian working-class Sarajevan who grew to young adulthood under the post-World War II Yugoslav multi-ethnic Communist state. He was a man. More to the point, he was a man raised in the 1960s, '70s, and '80s to think of himself as masculine. Or perhaps it is more useful to say that Borislav was a man raised to think of himself as *needing* to be masculine. If we leave this process out of his story, if we treat this process as unproblematic, then we leave out an exploration of the gendered politics of nationalism. With such a gaping omission, we will have a hard time arriving at a satisfactory explanation of why a factory worker became a militarized rapist.

There has been a burgeoning literature in recent years on the gendering of nationalist identities and—quite distinct—the gendering of nationalist ideologies and organizations. Most of this revealing research has been done by feminist scholars. They have found the existing literature on ethnicity and nationalism incapable of fully describing, much less explaining, how it is that women have experienced either ethnic communalism or nationalist politics so differently than men, different even from those men who have shared common ethnic, generational, and class conditions with them.[3] These feminist researchers have, quite wisely, focused their primary attention on women's experiences of ethnicity and of nationalism precisely because so much of the previous attention—particularly that concerning nationalism—privileged men's experiences.

Written between the lines of many of the most influential investigations of politicized ethnicity or of nationalist movements were several assumptions. First was the frequent assumption that men's experiences of both politicized ethnicity and nationalism deserved to be featured because it had been men (in Ireland or Algeria or

Kenya or Quebec) whose ideas and actions had been the crucial shapers of those processes, leaving women to be spectators on the side of the collective road. Second, there was the common unspoken belief that men and women in any given community had roughly the same experiences and, since the experiences of men were the easiest to research—they left the most evidence in their wake—the investigator need not look further. Third, while few imagined that women and men actually cooked, negotiated, shot, or gave birth equally, it seemed convenient for some observers to assume that uneven task distribution had little impact on individuals' senses of belonging or on the strategies selected for collective mobilization.

New feminist research starts from the conviction that assumptions this sweeping are worthy of explicit testing. The result has been evidence that all three assumptions not only are seriously flawed, but that they yield an imperfect understanding of how both ethnic and nationalist processes actually operate.[4]

The research that takes women's experiences of nationalism seriously reveals that many more decisions are made that determine the course of any ethnic transformation or nationalist mobilization than most of us could ever imagine. Decisions about what to cook, decisions about who would drop out of school, decisions about what to wear, decisions about whether to use contraceptives, decisions about who should go to meetings at night—decisions that frequently have been treated as merely "personal" or "trivial"—suddenly were shown to be significant. They also were found to be contested.

Decisions involve power. Many observers of nationalism, by ignoring women's experiences and by trivializing relationships between women and men, have underestimated the number of decisions it has taken to construct nationalism. Those who have underestimated the number of decisions it actually required to develop ethnic consciousness, to politicize it, to transform it into nationalism, and—on occasion—to turn it into a violent force, in turn, have vastly underestimated the flows of power.

Furthermore, paying attention to women's experiences of nationalism not only made women visible, it also made it possible for researchers to see men. Where once there were militiamen, workers, and political elites, now there were women workers, men workers, women refugees, men refugees, militiamen. That is, as soon as we start making the experiences of Bosnians problematically gendered, we no longer can subsume all women under the sprawling canopy of "victims" nor all men under the category of "militia fighters." In fact, we may hesitate before we even use the easy term "militiamen" unthinkingly. Instead we try to determine if there were some men in Bosnia or the other regions of the former Yugoslavia who perhaps were more likely to have been marginalized, silenced, or injured—to have been victimized—than at least some women. We have to ask which women exactly have been the most likely targets of assault, which women by contrast have been best situated to speak out publicly for themselves, which women have developed antiviolent interpretations of nationalism, which women have theorized in ways that led them to reject nationalist political identities altogether. To engage in this analytical activity is not designed to push women's vulnerability back into the shadows; rather, it is to roll back the canopy that discourages observers from taking a close look at women's varied experiences of nationalist conflict and thereby to specify the conditions and decisions that have turned some women into victims. Accepting a priori the assumption that women are best thought of as victims in any nationalist mobilization that has turned violent dulls the analytical curiosity. Ultimately, this dulled curiosity produces explanations that are naive in their descriptions of power and camouflage men as ungendered actors.

Thus it would be a mistake to file Borislav Herak's experiences solely under "militia fighter," or "factory worker," or "Sarajevan Serb." He is also a man. We don't know at the start if his maleness is significant in making sense of how and why ethnicity becomes nationalist and how nationalist consciousness feeds violent conflict. Did all Sarajevan men join militias? Was there something in the 1990s' gendered urban labor force that pushed more male factory workers than female factory workers to resort to arms? Having put on our gender goggles, we are compelled to inquire whether Borislav's being male has mattered and, if so, why. The answers may reveal something about the gendered ethnic and nationalist processes shaping the recent actions of Borislav Herak. Pursuing gendered lines of inquiry also may expose more about the path of intercommunal violence in the 1990s, which could help us to make fuller sense of how and why nationalisms develop so differently in Flanders, Burundi, Scotland, Armenia, Quebec, and Slovenia.

Borislav Herak, from the little we know, did not seem motivated by nationalist conviction to join the Serbian militia in the hills above Sarajevo. From his recounting, it would appear that the sequence was the reverse: he began to see his Serb identity as justifying military action only after he joined the militia. Although there are reports of some Serbian and Croatian women having joined militia forces, the particular militia Borislav joined in 1991 was an all-male company composed of men who self-consciously thought of themselves as Serbs (Women in Black, 1993).[5] The micro-culture these men were developing was simultaneously masculinized, militarized, and ethnically politicized. From the older men in the militia, Borislav first learned that Muslims, ancestors of his urban neighbors and his extended family, had oppressed his own ancestors. According to his new militia tutors, it was Muslims, from the Ottoman imperialists in the past to Islamic believers in the present, who were largely to blame for his own personal lack of success. Borislav Herak, he now learned, was a man oppressed. A *man* oppressed. Maybe that was why he was pushing a textile cart to earn a living. Maybe that was why girls didn't find him attractive. Maybe that was why he had to find solace in pornographic centerfolds.

While the young man's entrance into the evolving world of Serbian militias apparently was not politically premeditated or deliberate, there still are decisions here to explore. First, some Serbian men made the decision to form armed all-male militarized groups rather than to trust their destiny to civilian parties or to the state's own shrunken but still potent and largely Serb military. What calculations prompted their decision? Perhaps a number of these male militia founders already had done their tours as military conscripts in the Yugoslav army and had learned there that the manly thing to do when faced with perceived threat was to take up arms in company with other men. Perhaps as conscripts in the Yugoslav army they had mixed with Slovene, Muslim, and Croatian conscripts, but had been socialized by their Serb officers to think of military activity as the special calling of men who identify themselves as Serbs. We don't have the answers yet, but we need them if we are going to make adequate sense of the Yugoslav conflict and if we are going to venture to use that conflict in any comparative analysis of post-Cold War nationalism. Have the British, Russian, Canadian, and Indian armies, for example, had the same impacts on the masculinization of ethnic identities of their respective male enlistees?

There is evidence that the warrior is a central element in the twentieth-century cultural construction of the Serbian ideal of masculinity. Researchers are also demonstrating that the ideals of Serbian femininity have been constructed in ways deliberately intended to bolster the militarization of masculinity. Constructing ideals of masculine behavior in any culture cannot be accomplished without constructing ideals of femininity that are supportive and complementary. Thus, many feminist analysts search for the decisions and actors that have the greatest stake in controlling notions of feminine respectability, feminine patriotism, and feminine attractiveness. For it is these ideas that need to be shaped and monitored if standards of manliness are to remain persuasive and legitimate. For instance, cultural constructions of masculinity in many societies have been dependent not simply on celebrating men as soldiers, but on simultaneously elevating women as mothers-of-soldiering-sons, valuing women chiefly for their maternal sacrifices for the nations. Consequently, pro-natalist policies by government officials espouse a militarized nationalism. This means that to make full sense of what has been happening to Borislav, we need to be curious about his mother and his sister as well. Journalists who tried to understand the Serb militiaman spoke only to his father. That is a start, but it is not enough.

Paying attention to cultural ideals of femininity and masculinity and the processes by which they are propagated and made mutually reinforcing, however, should not be the end of the investigation of the gendering of nationalism. Cultural ideals under certain circumstances can be challenged, they can become confused, contradictory; even widely accepted ideas about what it means to be manly or to be a good woman can become the objects of social controversy rather than veneration. Thus, for example, the notion of communally legitimated maternalized femininity has been contradicted by the occasional promotion of women as fighters for the Serbian nation, though the contradiction has been partially contained by assigning far more importance to the patriotic mother than to the patriotic woman soldier. Such norms, even when bolstered by potent historical myths, as in Serbian communal lore, do not, however, automatically lead all men to take up arms all the time. Borislav's father didn't. Nor, apparently did his brother. Thus the existence of such norms and legends are not sufficient explanations for the rapid multiplication of mostly-male militias in the early 1990s.

When war with Croatia broke out in 1990, many young Serbian men, often with the explicit assistance of their mothers—women whom Serbian nationalist propagandists were urging to meet the standards of the Serbian "patriot mother"—in fact fled the country to escape the increasingly dangerous and politically controversial military service (Kaser, 1993; Papic, 1993).[6] We do not yet have a gender-curious analysis of the pre-1990 Yugoslav military, so we do not yet even know how successful or unsuccessful cultural elites and public authorities were in masculinizing soldiering and militarizing manliness. We do know, however, that in the decades prior to the current conflict some Yugoslav women activists had complained that by so thoroughly masculinizing the idea of national service, the central federal government was diminishing women's contribution in the creation of the post-World War II nation. By raising this as a public issue, these women were not only attempting to pry military service apart from masculinity; they also were attempting to problematize the gendered historical memory of nation-building (Women in Black, 1993).[7]

Militarization of ethnic nationalism often depends on persuading individual men that their own manhood will be fully validated only if they perform as soldiers, either in the state's military or in insurgent autonomous or quasi-autonomous forces. But although the most persuasive socialization strategies succeed because they manage to portray soldiering as a "naturally" manly activity, in reality socialization requires explicit and artificial construction, sometimes backed by coercion. Large advertising budgets allocated to defense ministries in countries that rely on volunteer militaries, and harsh penalties assigned by the state to draft-dodgers in countries dependent on conscription, both signal a degree of deliberateness in sustaining militarized notions of masculinity. One of the most interesting studies on the artificiality of the connection between manhood and soldiering comes from South Africa. Zulu men are deliberately encouraged by leaders of the Inkatha movement to imagine their ethnicized manhood as rooted in the performance of warrior roles. Not all Zulu men have been persuaded. Furthermore, as in contemporary Serbia, the contradictions within the nationalist rhetoric over whether the ideal woman should be herself a fighter for the nation or merely a maternal supporter of the nation's male fighters have served to undermine the militarizing process (Hassim, 1993).[8]

Thus the process by which the Serbian men in Borislav's militia initially decided to form an armed group and the process by which they recruited other men are not at all obvious. Each of these social processes calls for detailed descriptions and subtle analyses. If Borislav Herak's story is at all representative, it may well be that many Serbian men were very incompletely militarized in their manhood by their experiences as lowly conscripts in the Yugoslav state military, so they fell into militias in the early 1990s rather than self-consciously seeking them out, and that they were militarized in their own ethnicized masculinity only after they experienced physical and emotional dependence on these deeply masculinized groups.

There are yet other decisions that need investigation. What were the decisions—and by whom were they made—that led Borislav Herak to rape sixteen Muslim Bosnian women, some murdered afterwards? An ethnicized, masculinized man, even one enrolled in a group that wields violent weaponry, does not *inevitably* commit atrocities.

A blueprint for conducting this investigation may be found in another study of men who committed war atrocities. Historian Christopher Browning's curiosity was provoked by a group of working-class men from the city of Hamburg, who in the early 1940s had been conscripted into a special police unit by the Nazi government that took part in several mass murders of Polish Jewish civilians in the later years of World War II (Browning, 1992). How should one think about these men? Is it enough to assume that they were anti-Semitic in their German identities before joining the Reserve Police Battalion 101? Maybe some of these men sought service in a police unit because they hoped it would save them from performing more militarized duties that would involve killing other people. Were their own notions of themselves as manly—as longshoremen, or as fathers, or as heterosexuals— deliberately manipulated by their police superiors in an effort to insure that they would kill Jewish civilians? Was that manipulation totally successful? All of these questions are relevant to our making sense of Borislav Herak's behavior in 1991– 92 Bosnia.

Each question suggests that the location of a man—or woman—in an organized group such as an autonomous militia or a state police force has to be understood if the processes of militarized nationalism are to be accurately portrayed.

Christopher Browning used archival documents, postwar trial testimonies, and more recent interviews with the men of Reserve Police Battalion 101 and their bureaucratic superiors to answer the question: What would make ordinary German men shoot defenseless Jewish children, women, and men between June 1942 and early 1943? Browning's intent was not to relieve these middle-aged policemen of responsibility. Rather, he was curious to know what exactly it took to turn these men into mass killers.

According to Browning's account, these shootings were not preceded by rapes. Why not? Were the men's sexual frustrations less intense before joining the armed unit? Was their anti-Semitism less dependent on misogyny? Did their officers construct their male subordinates' ethnic militarism with less reliance on sexuality? Browning didn't inquire. Perhaps if he or another historian looked at these policemen's killing activities in light of the puzzle surrounding Borislav Herak, these questions would be pursued.

What Browning did discover was that most of the German men in Battalion 101 had not been actively involved in politics before the war, although some had joined Nazi youth groups. He also found that, while several of their commanders were committed Nazi careerists and self-conscious anti-Semites, and while anti-Semitic messages were part of the battalion's training manuals, an anti-Semitic form of German nationalism was not deeply imbedded in the personal identities of most of the men who eventually followed orders to shoot unarmed Polish Jews. What Browning uncovered instead were conflicting messages coming to these men from their officers—their immediate superior tried to give his men a non-killing option. On the other hand, these men were socialized to kill by a steady stream of assignments devised in Berlin over several months, assignments that gradually escalated in their levels of dehumanizing harshness.

These male police troops' male superiors, however, did not assume that either their troops' preconscription notions of their masculinity or their personal commitments to German nationalism would in themselves be sufficient to guarantee that they would follow orders to shoot on command. Documents reveal that steps were taken by male superiors to lower the "psychological stress" they believed would be experienced by the men on killing assignments (Browning, 1992: 49). An effective commander does not leave morale to chance. Yet morale is thoroughly gendered in the minds of most military commanders. Dignity as fathers, reassurance as boyfriends, pride as sons, comradeship as fictive brothers-in-arms, satisfaction as masculinized heterosexuals—each has been weighed and employed by commanders in male military forces as different from each other as the American army in 1960s Vietnam and the German police in 1940s Poland.

From his interviews, Browning learned that the men who chose their commander's nonshooting option especially worried that they risked being ostracized by fellow policemen: "The nonshooter was potentially indicating that he was 'too good' to do such things." Rather than risk losing his comrades' valued masculine friendship, nonshooters appealed to their fellow policemen to excuse their failures of masculine toughness: "They pleaded not that they were 'too good' but rather that they were 'too weak' to kill" (Browning, 1992: 185). But Browning is not a feminist investigator. Thus it is only toward the conclusion of his otherwise richly detailed account that he confronts directly the role played by the social construction of masculinity. Considering the pressures to shoot on command that came from within the group rather than simply from above or outside, Browning observes, "Insidiously, therefore, most of those who did not shoot only reaffirmed the 'macho' values of the majority—according to which it was a positive quality to be 'tough' enough to kill unarmed, noncombatant men, women and children—and tried not to rupture the bonds of comradeship that constituted their social world" (Browning, 1992: 185).

Browning's study of these particular Nazi male police conscripts suggests that ungendered nationalist propaganda alone is not sufficient to transform a male recruit into a committer of atrocities. Nor did he find that mere maleness or even simply a culture of masculinity was adequate. Instead, it took a complex set of bureaucratic relationships among officers at different ranks who not always held harmonious ideas about what policing or soldiering might rightly justify. It also took the sometimes confusing relationships between male officers and male troops. And it required the evolution of a particular brand of masculinized comradeship between peers. Each was infused with deliberateness.

Another study of military men that might shed light on the making of Borislav Herak is the United States Defense Department's 1993 "Tailhook Report." [9] While it does not portray violence at the extreme levels found in Poland or Bosnia, this report's authors also seek to explain what caused an all-male military unit to engage in assaults and the harassment of women. Like Browning, the American Defense Department investigators looking into the Tailhook convention of 1991 concluded that a potent mixture of bureaucratic decisions and masculinized social pressure to turn men in military units into assailants were at fault. The American aircraft pilots, according to this highly critical report, only adopted misogynist practices at their annual Las Vegas meeting when their hospitality suites were no longer sponsored by weapons manufacturers but instead were sponsored by different pilots' units, which had been encouraged by their commanders to look at one another as fierce competitors. Competition in fighter-raid targeting hits off aircraft carriers translated, it seems, into competition in stripping women of their clothes in hotel corridors. These pilots' naval superiors explained that they had come to believe that aircraft pilots—"tailhookers"—were a particular breed of men, that they were especially brash, immature males who needed to have the opportunity to drink in excess and chase after women if they were going to perform successfully as fighter pilots. The Pentagon investigators, unfortunately, did not devote any attention to nationalism. But they did note in passing that the 1991 convention—the gathering that first attracted public criticism when one naval woman officer went to the press after her own superior officer brushed aside her charges of abuse—was held in the heady atmosphere of victory of United States military forces against Iraq in the Gulf War, an atmosphere that may have intensified the male pilots' peculiar form of masculine behavior.

The following excerpt is from an interview by *Dallas Morning News* reporter George Rodriguez.[10]

> *Borislav:* We had an order to go to restaurant Sonja in Vogosca. We were told that we were going to rape girls there.[11]
> *Journalist:* Who told you this?
> *B:* My captain. The commander of our unit. So as to increase the morale of our fighters. . . .
> *J:* You had never raped a woman before this?
> *B:* No, I had not.
> *J:* And if the women had been Serbian, would you have thought it OK to rape them?
> *B:* The order was to rape them. . . .
> *J:* What would have happened to you if you had not?
> *B:* They would have sent me to the worst front line in Trebinje, in Herzegovina, or sent me to jail.
> *J:* They would not have killed you?
> *B:* I cannot say that. But I know they would have taken away the house that they had given me. . . .
> *J:* They picked out one girl for the four of you?
> *B:* Yes.
> *J:* You were all in the room when she was raped?
> *B:* Yes.
> *J:* Didn't this seem strange to you?
> *B:* Just a little bit.
> *J:* Why did you do it?
> *B:* Because I had those guys with me. I had to listen to the order, or I would have consequences if I did not. . . . We told her to take off her clothes. . . . She didn't want to. And that guy Damjanovic Mish started to beat her. . . .
> *J:* Did he beat her with his rifle butt or his hands?
> *B:* With his hands. And then she took her clothes off and we raped her. And she put her clothes back on, and we took her away.

J: Did you feel good about this, or guilty?

B: I felt guilty. But I didn't want to say anything or to show it to the others. . . .

J: I do not want to sound anti-Serb, because I am not. But how could you stand to fight for such people?

B: I could not return to Sarajevo to join the Bosnian army. . . .

J: What happened on the drive back after you had killed this woman? Was anything said? Did anyone laugh, or say they felt bad?

B: We never talked about that.

J: Was this good for your morale?

B: Not at all. And before that and after that I had to go to the front lines, so it was the same for me. . . .

J: Was there anything good about fighting with the Serbs? A feeling of togetherness or being part of a team? A feeling of being important?

B: The only good time was when we found schnapps, and we could drink together. Or when we had barbecues. Then we could be together and drink and eat.

J: But I think that in the same way your bosses gave you the drink and food, they gave you the women. As a way to show you were important. Is that right?

B: Yes. For me and for all the soldiers. They wanted to keep us together.

Reports of the number of women raped by male combatants during the 1991–93 war in the former Yugoslavia vary between 3,000 and 30,000. Muslim women residing in Bosnia appear to comprise the majority of women raped by male soldiers, but human rights monitors have documented rapes of ethnic Croat and Serb women as well. Rapist men include both soldiers in the Yugoslav army and in the militias, and Serbs as well as Croats and Muslims. Yet the incidence of rape by Serbian men serving in autonomous militias fighting in Bosnia appears to be the highest.[12]

Even a skeletal outline of one male militia fighter's thinking about his participation in wartime rape leaves more puzzles than certainties. Borislav Herak, the twenty-one-year-old former navy conscript, a lonely textile worker from an ethnically mixed family, fought with fellow Serbs. But he seemed to weigh the possibilities of returning to Sarajevo to join their Bosnian adversaries. He did not object to raping Muslim women when commanded to do so, but he appears to have felt that male bonding was most authentic over barbecues and schnapps. He was accepted as a Serb man among Serb men, but what he cared most about was avoiding the front and holding on to the once Muslim-owned house given to him. He acted violently on numerous occasions but expressed no warrior's joy in his actions.

The gendered politics of militarized ethnic rape in Bosnia will not end when the leaders of each faction finally call a halt to the war. There will be thousands of men who will be left to make sense of their militarized or nonmilitarized actions, including figuring out—with help from cultural elites in their own communities—whether they should have been able to protect "their" women from male opponents' assaults and, if they could not, what this means for their own ideas about manliness and the future relations of men toward women in their ethnic groups. These women will not be mere victims, real or symbolic. There will be thousands of women who will attempt to reimagine what it means to be feminine in a postwar society, who will actively respond to pressures to restore the community's purity or replenish their community's pool of male fighters, who will devise ways to come to terms with having been raped or with having lived in fear of being raped.

Out of these efforts at social construction—imagining, policymaking, persuasion, and response—will come postwar societies. Borislav Herak, now convicted of murder and rape, may not be alive to take part in this process. But there will be other ordinary men and ordinary women. And their notions about masculinity and femininity will call for just as much serious attention as did that of the youth who pushed a cart by day and read pornographic magazines by night when life was peaceful in Sarajevo.

NOTES

1. The following material on Borislav Herak is derived from two journalists' interviews with Herak after he was captured and imprisoned by the Bosnian authorities. While awaiting trial on charges of murder and rape he was permitted to talk to a variety of foreign journalists; see John Burns, "A Serbian Fighter's Trail of Brutality," *New York Times*, November 27, 1992; also George Rodriguez, transcript of interview with Borislav Herak conducted for the *Dallas Morning News* at the Viktor Buban military prison, Sarajevo, in January 1993, reprinted in Alexandra Stiglmayer (ed.), *Mass Rape: The War against Women in Bosnia-Herzegovina* (Lincoln: University of Nebraska Press, 1994).

2. John Burns, "Bosnia War Crime Trial Hears Serb's Confession," *New York Times*, March 14, 1993. For detailed reporting on the rapes of women that occurred during 1991–92 in Bosnia, see Stiglmayer, *Mass Rape*; "Serbia's War Against Bosnia and Croatia," *Off Our Backs*, special supplement, May 1993; Ivana Balen, "Responding to War-time Rapes, *Helsinki Citizens Assembly Newsletter*, no. 6 (Winter 1993): 12–13; Cornelia Sorabji, "War Crimes: Crimes against Gender or Nation?" *War Report* (Feb.–Mar. 1993): 16–17; the United Nations War Crimes Commission report as described in Paul Lewis, "Rape Was a Weapon of Serb, U.N. Says," *New York Times*, October 20, 1993; "Correction: Report on Rape in Bosnia," *New York Times*, October 23, 1993.

3. For those wishing to become acquainted with this literature, here are some starting places: Nira Yuval-Davis and Floya Anthias (eds.), *Woman-Nation-State* (London: Macmillan, 1989); Floya Anthias and Nira Yuval-Davis, with Harriet Cain (eds.), *Racialized Boundaries: Race, Nation, Gender, Colour and Class and the Anti-Racist Struggle* (London: Routledge, 1993); Roberta Hamilton and Michele Barrett (eds.), *The Politics of Diversity: Feminism, Marxism and Nationalism* (London: Verso, 1987); Constance Sutton (ed.), *Feminism, Nationalism and Militarism* (Fairax, VA: American Association of Anthropology, 1993); *Feminist Review*, special issues on "Nationalisms and National Identities" Summer 1993, and "Thinking through Ethnicities," Autumn 1993; Nanette Funk and Magda Mueller (eds.), *Gender Politics and Post-Communism* (New York and London: Routledge, 1993); Jan Pettman, *Living in the Margins: Racism, Sexism and Feminism in Australia* (Sydney: Allen and Unwin, 1992); Angela V. John, *Our Mother's Land: Chapters in Welsh Women's History, 1830–1939* (Cardiff: University of Wales Press, 1991); Hue-Tam Ho Tai, *Radicalism and the Origins of the Vietnamese Revolution* (Cambridge, MA: Harvard University Press, 1992); Andrew Parker et al. (eds.), *Nationalisms and Sexuality* (New York and London: Routledge, 1992); *Gender and History*, special issue, "Gender, Nationalism and History," Summer 1993.

4. My own recent efforts to use feminist analysis to think freshly about nationalism can be found in: *The Morning After: Sexual Politics at the End of the Cold War* (London and Berkeley: University of California Press, 1993); and *Bananas, Beaches and Bases: Making Feminist Sense of International Politics* (Berkeley: University of California Press, and London: Pandora Press, 1990).

5. Women's presence in some militias on all sides was confirmed by Yugoslav scholars participating in the Conference on Gender, Nationalism and Democratization: Policy Initiatives for Central and Eastern Europe, sponsored by the Network of East-West Women, Washington, DC, October 26, 1993.

6. Karl Kaser is a professor of history at the Austrian University of Graz, specializing in Serbian folklore and symbolism; Zarana Papic is professor of anthropology at the University of Belgrade, who also investigates the gendered ideals of Serbian masculinity and femininity. In the discussion that followed these papers, Professor Papic was joined by Professor Perunovic, a Serbian scholar who is now a Professor of Anthropology at the City University of New York, in describing the inconsistencies between the militarization of the Serbian ideal of manhood and the actual behaviors of many Serbian young men in the years 1990–93.

7. My own gender-ignorant examination of the ethnic politics shaping the Yugoslav military is *Ethnic Soldiers: State Security in Divided Societies* (London: Penguin, 1980). My brief attempt to understand the Yugoslav women's postwar meaning of having served in what they saw as a war of liberation is contained in *Does Khaki Become You? The Militarization of Women's Lives* (London and San Francisco: Pandora/HarperCollins, 1988).

8. For an exploration of white and black South African men's and women's attitudes toward soldiering during the 1980s, a period of intense militarization, see Jacklyn Cock, *Women and War in South Africa* (London: Open Letters Press, 1992).

9. A more extensive discussion of the "Tailhook affair" is included in Enloe, *The Morning After*.

10. Reprinted in Stiglmayer, *Mass Rape*.

11. A report of the United Nations' war crimes commission is summarized in Paul Lewis, "Rape Was Weapon of Serbs, UN Says," *New York Times,* October 20, 1993. A clarifying afternote was added by the *New York Times* three days later: "Correction: Report on Rapes in Bosnia."

12. A Danish psychologist's study of how Middle East and Latin American refugee women reacted to the traumas—including rape—of civil conflict is Inger Agger, *The Blue Room: Trauma and Testimony among Refugee Women* (London: Zed Books, forthcoming).

REFERENCES

Browning, Christopher. 1992. *Ordinary Men: Reserve Police Battalion 101 and the Final Solution in Poland.* New York: HarperCollins.

Hassim, Shireen. 1993. "Family, Motherhood and Zulu Nationalism: the Politics of the Inkatha Women's Brigade," *Feminist Review* (Spring): 5-12.

Helsinki Citizens' Assembly Women's Commission. 1992. *Reproductive Rights in East and Central Europe.* Prague: Citizens' Assembly Publication Series.

Kaser, Karl. 1993. "Ex-Yugoslavia, a Case Study." Paper presented at the Conference on Gender, Nationalism and Democratization: Policy Initiatives for Central and Eastern Europe, sponsored by the Network of East-West Women, Washington DC, October 26.

Papic, Zarana. 1993. "Ex-Yugoslavia, a Case Study." Paper presented at the Conference on Gender, Nationalism and Democratization: Policy Initiatives for Central and Eastern Europe, sponsored by the Network of East-West Women, Washington, DC, October 26.

United States Department of Defense. 1993. *Tailhook Report.* New York: St. Martin's Press.

Women in Black. 1993. Compilation of Information on Crimes of War Against Women in Ex-Yugoslavia—Actions and Initiatives in Their Defence. Belgrade: Women in Black.

Chapter Seven

Surfacing Gender
Reconceptualizing Crimes against Women in Time of War

Rhonda Copelon

Historically, the rape of women in war has drawn occasional and short-lived international attention. Most of the time rape has been invisible or comes to light as part of the competing diplomacies of war, illustrating the viciousness of the conqueror or the innocence of the conquered. When war is done, it is comfortably cabined as a mere, inevitable "by-product of war," a matter of indiscipline, of soldiers revved up by war, needy, and briefly, "out of control."

Military histories rarely refer to rape, and military tribunals rarely either charge or sanction it. This is true even where rape and forced prostitution are mass or systematic, as with the rape of women in both theaters of the Second World War; it is even true where the open, mass, and systematic rape has been thought to shock the conscience of the world, such as in the "rape of Nanking"[1] or the rape of an estimated 200,000 Bengali women during theaters of independence from Pakistan (Brownmiller, 1975).[2] Though discussed in the judgment of the International Military Tribunal in Tokyo, rape was not separately charged against the Japanese commander as a crime. In Bangladesh, amnesty was quietly traded for independence.

The question today is whether the terrible rape of women in the war in the former Yugoslavia will likewise disappear into history, or at best will survive as an exceptional case. The apparent uniqueness of the rape of women in Bosnia-Herzegovina, directed overwhelmingly against Bosnian-Muslim women, is a product of the invisibility of the rape of women through history as well as in the present. Geopolitical factors—that this is occurring in Europe, is perpetrated by white men against white, albeit largely Muslim women, and contains the seeds of a new world war—cannot be ignored in explaining the visibility of these rapes. By contrast, the rape of 50 percent of the women of the indigenous Yuracruz people in Ecuador by

The issues discussed in this chapter are further elaborated in Rhonda Copelon, 1994. "Surfacing Gender: Re-Engraving Crimes against Women in Humanitarian Law," 5 *Hastings Women's Law Journal* 243 (2) (Summer 1994).

mercenaries of an agribusiness company seeking to "cleanse" the land is invisible, just as the routine rape of women in the civil wars in Peru, Liberia, and Burma, for example, has gone largely unreported.[3]

Moreover, just as historically the condemnation of rape in war has rarely been about the abuse of women as a crime of gender, so the mass rape in Bosnia has captured world attention and remains there largely because of its association with "ethnic cleansing," or genocide. In one week a midday women's talk show opened with the script, "In Bosnia, they are raping the enemy's women," and a leading Croatian-American scholar blithely distinguished "genocidal" rape from "normal" rape. Our ad hoc Women's Coalition against Crimes against Women in the Former Yugoslavia spoke of rape as a weapon of war whether used to dilute ethnic identity, destabilize the civilian population, or reward soldiers. But the public was nodding yes, when rape is a vehicle of genocide.

The elision of genocide and rape in the focus on "genocidal rape" as a means of emphasizing the heinousness of the rape of Muslim women in Bosnia is thus dangerous. Rape and genocide are separate atrocities. Genocide—the effort to destroy a people—based on its identity as a people evokes the deepest horror and warrants the severest condemnation. Rape is sexualized violence that seeks to humiliate, terrorize, and destroy a woman based on her identity as a woman. Both are based on total contempt for and dehumanization of the victim, and both give rise to unspeakable brutalities. Their intersection in the Serbian and, to a lesser extent, the Croatian aggressions in Bosnia defines an ineffable living hell for women. From the standpoint of these women, they are inseparable.

But to emphasize as unparalleled the horror of genocidal rape is factually dubious and risks rendering rape invisible once again. Even in war, rape is not fully recognized as an atrocity. When the ethnic war ceases or is forced back into the bottle, will the crimes against women, the voices of women, and their struggles to survive be vindicated? Or will condemnation be limited to this seemingly exceptional case? Will the women who are brutally raped for domination, terror, booty, or revenge—in Bosnia and elsewhere—be heard?

Whether the rape, forced prostitution, and forced impregnation of women will be effectively prosecuted before the recently created United Nations ad hoc International Tribunal,[4] whether the survivors will obtain redress, or whether impunity will again be the agreed-upon or de facto cost of "peace" is up for grabs. The pressure of survivors and their advocates, together with the global women's human rights movement, will make the difference. The situation presents a historic opportunity as well as an imperative to insist on justice for the women of Bosnia as well as to press for a feminist reconceptualization of the role and legal understanding of rape in war.

To do this, we must surface gender in the midst of genocide at the same time as we avoid dualistic thinking. We must critically examine the claim that rape as a tool of "ethnic cleansing" is unique, worse than or not comparable to other forms of rape in war or in peace, at the same time as we recognize that rape together with genocide inflicts multiple, intersectional harms.[5] This combination of the particular and the general is critical if the horrors experienced by women in Bosnia are to be appreciated and if that experience is to have meaning for women brutalized in less-known theaters of war or in the byways of daily life.

This chapter examines the evolving legal status of rape in war with attention given to both the particular and the general, as well as to the tension between them. The opening section focuses on the two central questions of conceptualization. The first is whether these gender crimes are fully recognized as war crimes under the Geneva Conventions, the cornerstone of what is called "humanitarian" law—that is, the prohibitions that have made war itself permissible. The second is whether international law does or should distinguish between "genocidal rape" and mass rape for other purposes. In this regard it examines the limitations and the potential in the concept of "crimes against humanity," as well as the relation between gender and nationality/ethnicity in the crimes committed against women in Bosnia. The second section looks at the viability of the ad hoc International Tribunal as well as the gender issues presented.

Reconceptualizing Rape, Forced Prostitution, and Forced Pregnancy in War

Is Rape a War Crime?

Although news of the mass rapes of women in Bosnia had an electrifying effect and became a significant factor in the demand for the creation of an international war crimes tribunal, the leading question for a time was whether rape and other forms of sexual abuse are "war crimes" within the meaning of the Geneva Conventions and the internationally agreed-upon norms that bind all nations whether or not they have signed the conventions. The answer is not unequivocal.

The question is not whether rape is technically a crime or prohibited in war. Rape has long been viewed as a criminal offense under national and international rules of war (Khushalini 1982). The 1949 Geneva Conventions as well as the 1977 protocols regarding the protection of civilians in war explicitly prohibit rape, enforced prostitution, and any form of indecent assault and call for special protection of women, including separate quarters with supervision and searches by women only.[6] Yet it is significant that where rape and other forms of sexual assault are explicitly mentioned, they are categorized as an outrage upon personal dignity, or as crimes against honor.[7] Crimes of violence, including murder, mutilation, cruel treatment, and torture, are treated separately.

The concept of rape as a crime against dignity and honor as opposed to a crime of violence is a core problem. Formal sanctions against rape range from minimal to extreme. Where rape has been treated as a grave crime, it is because it violates the honor of the man and his exclusive right to sexual possession of his woman as property. Thus, in the United States the death penalty against rape was prevalent in Southern states as a result of a combination of racism and sexism.[8] Similarly, the media often refer to the mass rape in Bosnia as the rape of "the enemy's women"—the enemy in this formulation being the male combatant and the seemingly all-male nation, religious, or ethnic group.

Under the Geneva Conventions, the concept of honor is somewhat more enlightened: rape is a crime against the honor and dignity of women (Khushalani 1982). But this too is problematic. Where rape is treated as a crime against honor, the honor of women is called into question and virginity or chastity is often a precondition.[9] Honor implies the loss of station or respect; it reinforces the social view, internalized by women, that the raped woman is dishonorable. And while the concept of dignity potentially embraces more profound concerns, standing alone it obfuscates the fact that rape is fundamentally violence against women—violence against a woman's body, autonomy, integrity, selfhood, security, and self-esteem as well as her standing in the community. This failure to recognize rape as violence is critical to the traditionally lesser or ambiguous status of rape in humanitarian law.

The issue then is not whether rape is a war crime, but whether it is a crime of the gravest dimension. Under the Geneva Conventions, the term is "grave breach." The significance of a war crime being a "grave breach" is threefold. On the level of discourse, it calls attention to the egregiousness of the assault. On the practical level, it is not necessary that rape be mass or systematic: one act of rape is punishable. Finally, only crimes that are grave breaches give rise to universal jurisdiction under the Geneva Conventions. Universal jurisdiction means that every nation has an obligation to bring the perpetrators to justice through investigating, arresting, and prosecuting offenders in its own courts or extraditing them to more appropriate forums. The existence of universal jurisdiction also provides a legal rationale for trying such crimes before an international tribunal and for the obligation of states to cooperate. If rape were not a "grave breach" of the Geneva Conventions, some international jurists would argue that it can be redressed only by the state to which the wrongdoer belonged or in which the wrong occurred, and not by an international tribunal.[10]

The relevant portions of the Geneva Conventions do not specifically mention rape in the list of crimes considered "grave breaches." Included are "willful killing, torture, or inhumane treatment" and "willfully causing great suffering or serious injury to body or health."[11] Clearly these categories are broad and generic enough to encompass rape and sexual abuse (Khushalani 1982). But in addition to qualifying as "willfully causing great suffering or serious injury to body or health" or as "inhumane treatment," it is important that rape be recognized as a form of torture.

When the Geneva Conventions were drafted, the view that torture was a method of extracting information was dominant. Today, however, this distinction has been largely abandoned, although it endures in popular thinking. The historian Edward Peters writes: "It is not primarily the victim's information, but the victim, that torture needs to win—or reduce to powerlessness" (Peters 1985: 164). Recent treaties define torture as the willfull infliction of severe physical or mental pain or suffering not only to elicit information, but also to punish, intimidate, or discriminate, to obliterate the victim's personality or diminish her personal capacities (*U.N. Convention against Torture* 1988). Thus torture is now commensurate with willfully causing great suffering or injury. Moreover, it is not simply or necessarily the infliction of terrible physical pain; it is also the use of pain, sensory deprivation, isolation, and humiliation as a pathway to the mind. Indeed, in the contemporary understanding of torture, degradation is both vehicle and goal (Amnesty International 1974).

Although largely ignored until recently by human rights advocates, the testimonies and studies of women tortured by dictatorial regimes and military occupations make it clear that rape is one of the most common, terrible, and effective forms of torture used against women.[12] Rape attacks the integrity of the woman as a person as well as her identity as a woman. It renders her, in the words of Lepa Mladjenovic, a psychotherapist and Serbian feminist antiwar activist, "homeless in her own body."[13] It strikes at a woman's power; it seeks to degrade and destroy her; its goal is domination and dehumanization.

Likewise, the testimonies of raped women, whether they were attacked once or forced into prostitution, make it clear that rape is both a profound physical attack and a particularly egregious form of psychological torture. They document the intersection of contempt for and conquest of women based on their sex as well as on their national, religious, or cultural identity. They demonstrate the significance of the threat, fear, or reality of pregnancy as well as of the fact that in Bosnia the rapists are in many cases former colleagues, neighbors, or even friends.

Indeed, torturers know well the power of the intimate in the process of breaking down their victim.[14] Because rape is a transposition of the intimate into violence, rape by acquaintances, by those one has trusted, is particularly world shattering and thus a particularly effective tool of ethnic cleansing. It is no wonder that local Bosnian Serbs are being incited and, in some cases, recruited to rape. Their stories, notwithstanding their self-justificatory quality, reflect the common methods of training torturers—exposure to and engagement in increasingly unthinkable violence and humiliations.[15]

Despite the fact that rape in Bosnia has drawn substantial international condemnation, the United Nations' position on the status of rape as a grave breach of humanitarian law is not clear. The U.N. Human Rights Commission condemned "the abhorrent practice of rape and abuse of women and children in the former Yugoslavia which, *in the circumstances*, constitutes a war crime," and urged all nations to "exert every effort to bring to justice . . . all those individuals directly or indirectly involved" (U.N. Commission on Human Rights 1993: 122). While this implies that rape is a "grave breach," the limitation to the particular "circumstances" could be read as a limitation to the context of ethnic cleansing. The declaration of the 1993 World Conference of Human Rights in Vienna, though strongly worded, is limited to "systematic" rape and abuse.[16]

Most significantly, the report subsequently adopted by the Security Council that constitutes the statute establishing the jurisdiction of the international tribunal largely tracks the Geneva Conventions' definition of grave breach and does not explicitly list rape as a grave breach or describe it as implicit in the recognized categories.[17] But if, as a consequence of women's pressure, it is prosecuted as such and the various bodies of the United Nations begin to refer to rape as a grave breach, then this practice will effectively amend or expand the meaning of grave breach in the conventions and protocols. This emphasizes the importance, from a practical as well as a moral perspective, of insisting that all rape be subject to punishment, not only mass or genocidal rape. It should be noted that under the Geneva Conventions, responsibility is imputed to commanders where they knew, or should have known, of the likelihood of rape and failed to take all measures within their power to prevent or suppress it.[18]

It is also important to point out the importance of the Vienna Declaration's explicit inclusion of forced pregnancy in its condemnation of the mass atrocities in the former Yugoslavia. This is clearly a product of the intensive women's mobilization that preceded the World Conference on Human Rights. Forced pregnancy must be seen as a separate offense: the expressed intention to make women pregnant is an additional form of psychological torture; the goal of impregnation leads to imprisoning women and raping them until they are pregnant; the fact of pregnancy, whether aborted or not, continues the initial torture in a most intimate and invasive form; and bearing the child of rape, whether placed for adoption or not, has a potentially lifelong impact on the woman and her place in the community (Goldstein 1993).

Genocidal Rape versus "Normal" Rape: When Is Mass Rape a Crime against Humanity?

"Crimes against humanity" were first formally recognized in the Charter and Judgment of the Nuremberg Tribunal; they do not depend on adherence to a treaty, and they too give rise to universal jurisdiction. Since crimes against humanity can be committed in any war, it is irrelevant whether the war in the former Yugoslavia is international or internal.

Rape has been separately listed, and forced prostitution acknowledged, as a "crime against humanity" in the report establishing the statute of the International Tribunal.[19] This is not without precedent. After the Second World War, Local Council Law No. 10, which provided the foundation for the trials of lesser Nazis by the Allied forces, also listed rape as a crime against humanity, although no one was prosecuted (Khushalani 1982). Nonetheless, the Security Council's reaffirmation that rape is a "crime against humanity," and therefore among the most egregious breaches of civilization, is profoundly important. But the meaning of this designation and its import for other contexts in which women are subjected to mass rape apart from ethnic cleansing are not clear. The danger, as always, is that extreme examples produce narrow principles.

The commentary on this aspect of the jurisdiction of the current tribunal signals this danger. It explains crimes against humanity as "inhumane acts of a very serious nature, such as willful killing, *torture or rape*, committed *as part of* a widespread or systematic attack against any civilian population on national, political, ethnic, racial, or religious grounds."[20] Several aspects of this definition deserve comment.

First, on the positive side, the statute correctly encompasses violations that are widespread but not necessarily systematic. The law wisely does not require massive numbers but specifies patterns of abuse. Particularly with rape, numbers are unprovable: a small percentage of women will ultimately come forward, and the significance of rape threatens to become drowned in statistical claims. Moreover, the statute does not require that rape be ordered or centrally organized. Commanders can be held responsible where widespread violence is known.[21] In Bosnia, rape is clearly a conscious tool of war and ethnic cleansing. It is politically and ethically important for the tribunal to investigate and prove the chain of command, but it is likewise important that leaders can be held legally responsible without proof that rape was systematic or committed under orders.

Second, the commentary on the statute does rank rape with torture, at least where it is widespread or systematic. But it undercuts this by appearing to conflate what were originally understood as two separate and independent criteria of crimes against humanity: gross acts of violence and persecution-based offenses. Under the original concept, rape should qualify as a gross act of violence and accordingly, if widespread or systematic, would independently qualify as a crime against humanity. By merging the criterion of gross violence with persecution-based offenses, the commentary could limit prosecution to rape that is undertaken as a method of persecution on the specified grounds. Since the statute of the tribunal lists rape and persecution separately, it is not clear, until put in practice, whether the broader understanding will prevail.

The narrow view is quite prevalent, however. The international and popular condemnation of the rapes in Bosnia tends to be either explicitly or implicitly based on the fact that rape is being used as a tactic of ethnic cleansing. Genocidal rape is widely seen not as a modality of rape but as unique. The distinction commonly drawn between genocidal rape and "normal" rape in war or in peace is proffered not as a typology, but rather as a hierarchy. But to exaggerate the distinctiveness of genocidal rape obscures the atrocity of common rape.

Genocidal rape often involves gang rapes, is outrageously brutal, and is done in public or in front of children or partners. It involves imprisoning women in rape "camps" or raping them repetitively. These are also characteristics of the most common rape in war—rape for booty or to boost the morale of soldiers; and they are common characteristics of the use of rape as a form of torture and terror by dictatorial regimes.[22]

The notion that genocidal rape is uniquely a weapon of war is also problematic. The rape of women is a weapon of war where it is used to spread political terror, as in the civil war in Peru. It is a weapon of war where, as in Bosnia and elsewhere, it is used against women to destabilize the society and force families to flee, because in time of war women are the mainstay of the civilian population, even more than in peacetime.[23]

The rape of women, where permitted or systematized as "booty" of war, is likewise an engine of war: it maintains the morale of soldiers, feeds their hatred and sense of superiority, and keeps them fighting. The Japanese military industrialized the sexual slavery of women in the Second World War: 200,000 to 400,000 mostly Korean, but also Philippine, Chinese, and Dutch women from Indonesia, were deceived or disappeared into "comfort stations," raped repeatedly, and moved from battlefield to battlefield to motivate as well as reward the Japanese soldiers. Genocide was not a goal, but it is believed that 70 to 90 percent of these women died in captivity, and among the known survivors, none were subsequently able to bear children.[24] For similar reasons, the U.S. military in Vietnam raped Vietnamese women and established brothels, relying on dire economic necessity rather than kidnapping to fill them (Brownmiller 1975). Indeed, the testimonies of the Bosnian Serbian rapists reveal an admixture of all these goals.

At the same time, genocidal or ethnic-cleansing rape as practiced in Bosnia does have some aspects that are particularly tailored to its goals of driving women from their homes or destroying their possibility of reproducing within and "for" their community. As the preceding testimonies suggest, that women are raped by men familiar to them exacerbates their trauma and the impulse to flee the community because trust and safety are no longer possible. This is particular to the Bosnian situation, where war and propaganda have made enemies out of neighbors.

The second and more generally distinctive feature of genocidal rape is the focus on women as reproductive vessels. The explicit and common threat to make Muslim women bear "Serbian babies" (as if the child were the product of sperm only) justifies repetitive rape and aggravates her terror and potential unacceptability to her community. Bengali women were raped to lighten their race and produce a class of outcast mothers and children. Enslaved African women in the southern United States were raped as property to produce babies bartered, sold, and used as property (Davis 1983). While intentional impregnation is properly treated as a separate offense, it should also be noted that pregnancy is a common consequence of rape. In situations where women are raped repeatedly, most fertile women will become pregnant at some point. When the U.S. Navy took over Saipan, for example, one observer reports that virtually all the women who had been enslaved as comfort women for the Japanese army were pregnant.[25]

These distinctive characteristics do not place genocidal rape in a class by itself; nor do they reflect the full range of atrocities, losses, and suffering that the combination of rape and ethnic cleansing inflicts. The women victims and survivors in Bosnia are being subjected to crimes against humanity based on ethnicity and religion, and based on gender. It is critical to recognize both and to acknowledge that the intersection of ethnic and gender violence has its own particular characteristics.

This brings me to the third concern: the complete failure of the United Nations and the international community in general to recognize that persecution based on gender must be recognized as its own category of crimes against humanity. The crystallization of the concept of crimes against humanity in the wake of the Holocaust has meant that "it" is popularly associated with religious and ethnic genocide. But the concept is a broader one, and the categories of persecution are explicitly open-ended, capable of expanding to embrace new understandings of persecution.

With respect to women, the need is to acknowledge that gender has historically not been viewed as a relevant category of victimization. The frequency of mass rape and the absence of sanction are sufficient evidence. In the Holocaust, the gender persecutions—the rape and forced prostitution of women as well as the extermination of gay people—were obscured.[26] The absence of gender as a basis for persecution is not peculiar to the concept of crimes against humanity. A parallel problem exists in the international standards for political asylum, which require a well-founded fear of persecution but do not explicitly recognize gender as a source of persecution.[27] The expansion of the concept of crimes against humanity to include gender is thus part of the broader movement to end the historical invisibility of gender violence as a humanitarian and human rights violation.

Moreover, the particular goals and defining aspects of genocidal rape do not detract from but rather elucidate the nature of rape as a crime of gender as well as ethnicity. Women are targets not simply because they "belong to" the enemy but precisely because they keep the civilian population functioning and are essential to its continuity. They are targets because they too *are* the enemy, because of their power as well as vulnerability as women, including their sexual and reproductive power. They are targets because of *hatred* of their power as women; because of endemic objectification of women; because rape embodies male domination and female subordination.

The crime of forced impregnation—central as it is to genocidal rape—also elucidates the gender component. Since under patriarchy, women are little more than vessels for childbearing, involuntary pregnancy is commonly viewed as natural—divinely ordained, perhaps—or simply an unquestioned fact of life. As a result, the risk of pregnancy in all rape is treated not as an offense, but as a sequela. Forced pregnancy has drawn condemnation only when it reflects an intent to harm the victimized race. In Bosnia, the taunt that Muslim women will bear Serbian babies is not simply an ethnic harm, particularly in light of the prevalence of ethnically mixed families. When examined through a feminist lens, forced pregnancy appears as an assault on the reproductive self-determination of women; it expresses the desire to mark the rape and rapist upon the woman's body and upon the woman's life.

Finally, that the rape of women is also designed to humiliate the men or destroy "the enemy" itself reflects the fundamental objectification of women. Women are the target of abuse at the same time as their subjectivity is completely denied. The persistent failure to acknowledge the gender dimension of rape and sexual persecution is thus a most effective means of perpetuating it.

In sum, the international attention focused on Bosnia challenges the world to squarely recognize sexual violence against women in war as torture. Moreover, it is not enough for rape to be viewed as a crime against humanity when it is the vehicle of some other form of persecution; it must also be recognized as a crime against humanity because it is invariably a persecution based on gender. This is essential if the women of Bosnia are to be understood as full subjects as well as objects in this terrible victimization and if the international attention focused on Bosnia is to have meaning for women subjected to rape in other parts of the world.

Seeking Gender Justice

The history of atrocities and oppression and of festering hatreds among the peoples of the former Yugoslavia underscores the necessity of the demand, articulated by feminist critics of the war, for "justice, not revenge.[28] It is troubling as well as significant that the United Nations has taken steps to establish an International Tribunal to try the perpetrators of war crimes and crimes against humanity in the former Yugoslavia. On the negative side, the choice of an ad hoc tribunal rather than a permanent international criminal court reveals the shallowness of the international commitment to justice and opens the process to excessive politicization. At the same time, the creation of this tribunal lessens the possibility that legal amnesty will be the price of peace. But it is no guarantee against de facto impunity; nor does it guarantee that the suffering of the women will be vindicated. This section outlines some of the problems with the tribunal as it is at present envisaged and suggests some alternative routes.

The International Tribunal

The potential efficacy of the new International Tribunal is riddled with doubt. Unless there is a radical change in the military context, this tribunal, unlike those at Nuremberg and Tokyo, will not sit in judgment of conquered aggressors, but will be called upon primarily to judge the victors—the Bosnian Serbs and the Serbian leaders. Since the tribunal cannot compel the presence of the indicted criminals, it must count on their being arrested if they move beyond their own countries or those that protect them. Thus the rejection of the option of trials in absentia is likely to reduce the tribunal to publishing detailed, formal indictments—an international "wanted list"—as a historical record and a constraint on the movement of the accused.

Beyond its formal powers, the United Nations has utterly failed to provide the tribunal with the resources necessary to do the extensive and careful fact finding required. The U.N. Commission of Experts that laid the foundation for the tribunal operated on a shoestring at a time when the survivors of atrocities were most accessible. To prosecute the leaders, the issues of command responsibility and Serbian complicity require an investigation, and yet the United Nations relies on the investigations of a grossly underfinanced Special Rapporteur and independent human rights missions. Moreover, the tribunal, modeled after Nuremberg, is likely to consider only thirty cases. There is no mechanism for trying the thousands of direct perpetrators and low-level commanders. The United Nations seems to have forgotten that most of the Nazis were tried under the Local Council Law, which established the lesser war crimes tribunals. Moreover, the statute creating the tribunal makes no provision for compensation or rehabilitation of the survivors.

Beyond these general defects are the gender defects. In addition to the ambiguous status of gender crimes in the statute that defines the substantive power of the tribunal, there are substantial process concerns as well. Will women come forward?

And how will they be treated if they do? It is a given that women are terrified and, at best, reluctant to come forward to charge rape. Admitting rape in a sexist society is a public dishonoring and has consequences for the ability to continue or build relationships with one's community and with male partners. Most women are silent about it.[29] To charge rape is to risk retaliation and death, a risk heightened by war and by knowing and being known to the rapist. To charge rape usually is to risk being raped again—figuratively, at least—by the law enforcers. The callous, humiliating, and debilitating treatment of women refugees by some members of the press and some human rights missions in this war only confirms the expectation of abuse by official investigatory bodies.

The designers of the tribunal have done nothing to mitigate these fears. Ensuring sensitive and empowering gender justice ought to have been a central concern in the creation of the tribunal.[30] This would include, at a minimum, gender sensitivity training of all personnel as well as the establishment of a special sex crimes unit staffed primarily by women experienced in eliciting evidence in an empowering as opposed to a traumatizing way. In respect to indictments and trials, survivors should not be publicly identified without their consent; certain proceedings should be held in camera with safeguards to prevent abuse; victims should be able to testify without face-to-face confrontation with the perpetrators while preserving the accused's rights through video and one-way observation; rules of evidence should forbid reference to a woman's prior sexual conduct, restrict the consent defense, and control cross-examination to prevent abuse as well as distortion; expert testimony on trauma should be permitted but not required; and victims should be entitled to the assistance of their own counsel and counselors. But these concerns have been effectively ignored. The statute creating the tribunal recognizes the need to protect victims and witnesses from retaliation and to design rules of procedure and evidence that take into account the protection of victims in cases of rape and sexual assault. But beyond calling for protection of the victim's identity, the statute leaves to the tribunal the responsibility to develop the rules.

As part of a broader demand for participation at all diplomatic and international levels, and in light of the particular salience of gender to the tribunal process, women have also called for gender parity in staffing the tribunal at every level. It is likely, however, that women's participation will be token.[31] This alone attests to the lack of concern for encouraging the participation of women survivors. Moreover, that it will devolve upon the tribunal to design the rules under which rape and sexual abuse will be prosecuted highlights the disregard of this effort for the rights of women. Without continuing pressure, it is likely that the integrity of this tribunal as well as its receptivity to women will be sacrificed.

Alternative Routes

At the same time, it is essential that women create their own strategies for vindication and redress. Women have, of course, the possibility of establishing independent tribunals to symbolically try the perpetrators in Bosnia and other contexts. Beyond that, international law provides some other tools.

The concept of universal jurisdiction, which applies to grave breaches, torture, genocide, and crimes against humanity, confers upon the separate nations both the power and obligation to try violators when they enter their territory. The nations of the world, and particularly of Europe, where the perpetrators are most likely to travel, might have a significant effect if they simply announced that they would vigorously search out, investigate, arrest, and prosecute or extradite those who crossed their borders. The tribunal cannot function without this, and given its meager resources, national courts are an essential alternative. The absence of such declarations to date underscores the questions raised about the political will to try the offenders.

There is also the possibility of a more women-controlled legal remedy—the filing of private civil lawsuits for compensatory and punitive damages against the perpetrators when they enter their countries. In the United States a line of cases, instigated largely by victims of torture by military or dictatorial governments, has established the right of aliens to sue for human rights violations occurring anywhere in the world so long as the alleged perpetrator can be physically sued in the United States. The possibility of such suits in other countries that either follow the principles of Anglo-American jurisprudence or incorporate international law in their domestic law is being explored.[32]

Two such lawsuits have been filed against the Bosnian-Serbian leader Radovan Karadzic on behalf of Bosnian Muslim and Croatian women, women's organizations, and unnamed victims of atrocities committed under his command.[33] Karadzic was sued during successive stays in New York City in connection with U.N.-sponsored peace negotiations. If the court rejects his initial contention that he is entitled to immunity from suit because he was here on U.N. business, the case is likely to reach the issue of his responsibility for gross violations of human rights and humanitarian law. At this stage it is common for human rights violators to refuse to appear before the court, which then results, after a factual hearing, in a judgment for the plaintiffs by default.

These lawsuits cannot stop all atrocities or guarantee concrete relief, but they have a profound symbolic value. They provide an official forum for examining atrocities and the responsibilities of individuals for them, and they usually result in a judgment of wrongdoing and an award of substantial money damages, usually millions of dollars. Only in rare cases where the wrongdoer has substantial assets that can be discovered will the survivors actually recover the money. But these cases are not brought primarily for money. They are pursued as a wedge against impunity and an opportunity for survivors to tell the story and obtain vindication. They also make the perpetrators a little less secure: they cannot travel without risking the revelation of their crimes and the compromise of their political standing, personal reputations, families, property, or wealth.

Such lawsuits require international coordination, for which the growth of the global women's movement provides the foundation. The leaders responsible should be arrested, not feted, in the countries to which they travel, and the actual rapists should not enjoy vacations or carry out international business without sanction. The cost of their atrocities, if it is not prison, should at the least be confinement to their own countries. Women can build the capacity to do this. We can publicize the violators' identities, track their peregrinations, and mobilize the legal and political resources to pressure countries to arrest and prosecute them and find lawyers to bring private suits. We can do it for the raped women in the former Yugoslavia, and we can do it wherever women's human rights are violated.

Conclusion

Given the formidable pressure being brought to bear by women survivors and the women's movement globally, it may well be that some few men will be indicted and even tried before the International Tribunal or national courts, at least if impunity is not again the price of peace. This would be precedent setting in international law and offer symbolic vindication to the untold numbers of women this war has rendered homeless in so many senses. Unless the gender dimension of rape in war is recognized, however, it will mean little for women where rape is not also a tool of genocide.

Emphasis on the gender dimension of rape in war is critical not only to surfacing women as full subjects of sexual violence in war, but also to recognizing the atrocity of rape in the time called peace. When women charge rape in war they are more likely to be believed, because their status as enemy, or at least "the enemy's" women, is recognized and because rape in war is seen as a product of exceptional circumstances. When women charge rape in everyday life, however, they are disbelieved largely because the ubiquitous war against women is denied.

From a feminist human rights perspective, gender violence has escaped sanction because it has not been viewed as violence and because the public/private dichotomy has shielded such violence in its most common and private forms.[34] The recognition of rape as a war crime is thus a critical step toward understanding rape as violence. The next is to recognize that rape that acquires the imprimatur of the state is not necessarily more brutal, relentless, or dehumanizing than the private rapes of everyday life.

This is not to say that rape is identical in the two contexts. There are differences here, just as there are differences between rape for the purpose of genocide and rape for the purpose of booty. War tends to intensify the brutality, repetitiveness, public spectacle, and likelihood of rape. War diminishes sensitivity to human suffering and intensifies men's sense of entitlement, superiority, avidity, and social license to rape. But the line is not so sharp. Gang rape in civilian life shares the repetitive, gleeful, and public character of rape in war. Marital rape, the most private of all, shares some of the particular characteristics of genocidal rape in Bosnia: it is repetitive, brutal, and exacerbated by betrayal; it assaults a woman's reproductive autonomy, may force her to flee her home and community, and is widely treated as legitimate in law and custom. Violation by a state official or enemy soldier is not necessarily more devastating than violation by an intimate.[35]

Every rape is a grave violation of physical and mental integrity. Every rape has the potential to profoundly debilitate, to render the woman homeless in her own body and destroy her sense of security in the world. Every rape is an expression of male domination and misogyny, a vehicle of terrorizing and subordinating women. Like torture, rape takes many forms, occurs in many contexts, and has different repercussions for different victims. Every rape is multidimensional, but not incomparable.

The rape of women in the former Yugoslavia challenges the world to refuse impunity to atrocity as well as to resist the powerful forces that would make the mass rape of Muslim women in Bosnia exceptional and thereby restrict its meaning for women raped in different contexts. It thus demands recognition of situational differences without losing sight of the commonalities. To fail to make distinctions flattens reality; and to rank the egregious demeans it.[36]

NOTES

1. The "rape of Nanking" refers to the brutal taking of Nanking by Japanese soldiers, which involved mass and open killing, looting, and rape that went on for several months. It is estimated that twenty thousand women were raped in the first month. See Leon Friedman, *The Law of War: A Documentary/History*, vol. 2 (New York: Random House, 1972), p. 46.

2. Susan Brownmiller, *Against Our Will* (New York: Simon and Schuster, 1975), pp. 78–86. Among the motives for these rapes was a genocidal one—to destroy the racial distinctiveness of the Bengali people.

3. Presentation of Guadelupe Leon, Panel on Military Violence and Sexual Slavery, 1993 U.N. Conference on Human Rights, NGO Parallel Activities, June 1993; America's Watch and Women's Rights Project, *Untold Terror: Violence against Women in Peru's Armed Conflict* (New York: Human Rights Watch, 1992); Asia Watch and Women's Rights Project, *Burma: Rape, Forced Labor, and Religious Persecution in the Northern Arakan* (New York: Asia Watch, 1992); Shana Swiss, *Liberia: Women and Children Gravely Mistreated* (Boston, 1991). For other examples, see Shana Swiss and Joan E. Giller, "Rape as a Crime of War," *JAMA* 270 (August 4, 1993): 612.

4. The full title is International Tribunal for the Prosecution of Persons Responsible for Serious Violations of International Humanitarian Law Committed in the Territory of the Former Yugoslavia since 1991. See Report of the Secretary General Pursuant to Paragraph 2 of the Security Council Resolution 808 (1993), S/25704 (May 3, 1993), para. 25, p. 8.

5. On the concept of the significance of the intersection of categories of oppression, see Kimberle Crenshaw, "Demarginalizing the Intersection of Race and Sex: A Black Feminist Critique of Anti-Discrimination Doctrine, Feminist Theory, and Antiracist Politics," *University of Chicago Legal Forum*, 1989, pp. 139–67.

6. *Geneva Conventions Relative to the Protection of Civilian Persons in Time of War*, common art. 3, I(a) and (c); arts. 27 and 76, 97 (hereafter, *Geneva Convention IV*); *Protocol Additional to the Geneva Conventions of 12 August 1949, and Relating to the Protection of Victims of Non-International Armed Conflicts (Protocol II)*, art. 76, and *Protocol Additional to the Geneva Conventions of 12 August 1949, and Relating to the Protection of Victims of Non-International Armed Conflicts (Protocol II)*, art. 4, reprinted in Center for Human Rights, *Human Rights: A Compilation of International Instruments*, vol. 1, part 2 (1993), pp. 799–939.

7. See, e.g., ibid., *Geneva Convention IV*, art. 27, para. 2; *Protocol II*, art. 4.

8. This was recognized by the United States Supreme Court in striking the death penalty in *Coker* v. *Georgia*, 433 United States 584 (1977).

9. See, e.g., America's Watch and Women's Rights Project, *Untold Terror*.

10. It should be noted here that the concept of "grave breach" applies only to international conflict and not to civil war. Although there is debate about whether the conflict in the territory of the former Yugoslavia is international or internal, the United Nations has taken the position that the warring parties have agreed to abide by the rules governing international conflicts. *Report of the Secretary-General*, para. 25, p. 8.

11. *Geneva Convention IV*, art. 147; *Protocol I*, arts. 11 and 85 (3).

12. See, e.g., Ximena Bunster-Burotto, "Surviving beyond Fear: Women and Torture in Latin America," in *Women and Change in Latin America*, ed. June Nash and Helen Safa (South Hadley, MA: Bergin and Garvey, 1986), pp. 297–325; F. Allodi and S. Stiasny, "Women as Torture Victims," *Canadian Journal of Psychiatry* 35 (March 1990): 144–48; Inge Lunde and Jorge Ortmann, "Prevalence and Sequelae of Sexual Torture," *Lancet* 336 (August 1990): 289–91. While not the subject here, the rape of men is also a devastating crime of gender, designed as it is to humiliate through feminization.

13. Testimony before the Global Tribunal on Violations of Women's Human Rights, part of the NGO, Parallel Activities, 1993 World Conference on Human Rights, Vienna, June 15, 1993.

14. See Amnesty International, *Report on Torture*; Elaine Scarry, *The Body in Pain: The Making and Unmaking of the World* (New York: Oxford University Press, 1985), p. 41; Judith Lewis Herman, *Trauma and Recovery* (New York: Basic Books, 1992).

15. See, e.g., Stanley Milgram, "Some Conditions of Obedience and Disobedience to Authority," *Human Relations* 38 (1965): 57–74. On the training of torturers, see Amnesty International, *Torture in Greece: The First Torturers' Trial* (London: Amnesty International, 1977); Mika Haritos-Fatouros, "The Official Torturer: A Learning Model for Obedience to the Authority of Violence," *Journal of Applied Social Psychology* 18 (1988): 1107–20.

16. The conference agreed: "Violations of the human rights of women in situations of armed conflict are violations of the fundamental principles of international human rights and humanitarian law. All violations of this kind, including in particular murder, systematic rape, sexual slavery, and forced pregnancy, require a particularly effective response." *Report of the Drafting Committee, Addendum, Final Outcome of the World Conference on Human Rights*, A/conf. 157/PC/add. I (June 24, 1993) (hereafter "Vienna Declaration").

17. Article 2 identifies as grave breaches "(a) willful killing; (b) torture or inhuman treatment, including biological experiments; (c) willfully causing great suffering or serious bodily injury to body or health." *Report of the Secretary-General*, art. 2, paras. 37–40, pp. 10–11,

18. *Protocol I*, art. 86.

19. *Report of the Secretary-General*, art. 5, paras. 47–49, p. 13.

20. *Report of the Secretary-General*, art. 5, para. 48, p. 13.

21. Ibid., art. 7, *Draft Code of Offenses against Peace and Security of Mankind*, U.N. GAOR, 6th sess. (1951), suppl. 9, doc. A/1858, art. 2(II).

22. See, e.g., Brownmiller, *Against Our Will*; Bunster-Burrotto, "Surviving beyond Fear"; Amnesty International, *Women on the Frontline* (New York, 1991).

23. America's Watch and Women's Rights Project, *Untold Terror*; Swiss and Giller, "Rape as a Crime of War."

24. Testimony of Bok Dong Kim before the Global Tribunal on Violations of Women's Human Rights, NGO Parallel Activities, 1993 World Conference on Human Rights, Vienna,

June 15, 1993. See also *Hearings before the United Nations Secretary-General* (February 25, 1993) (testimony of Hyo-chai Lee, MA, Soon-Kum Park, and Chung-Ok Yum, MFA, Korean Council for the Women Drafted for Military Sexual Service in Japan); Lourdes Sajor, "Women in Armed Conflict Situations," MAV/1993/WP.I (September 21, 1993), prepared for Expert Group Meeting on Measures to Eradicate Violence against Women, U.N. Division for the Advancement of Women.

25. Conversation with D.B.

26. See Brownmiller, *Against Our Will*, pp. 48–78, for the unrecognized sexual violence against women on the part of Allied as well as Axis forces. See also Erwin J. Haeberle, "Swastika, Pink Triangle, and Yellow Star: The Destruction of Sexology and the Persecution of Homosexuals in Nazi Germany," in Martin Duberman, Martha Vicinus, and George Channcez, Jr. (eds.), *Hidden from History: Reclaiming the Gay and Lesbian Past* (New York: New American Library, 1989), pp. 365–79 (noting the gender aspect of the Nazi attacks on homosexuals reflected in the use of the pink triangle and charges of emasculation).

27. The Convention Relating to the Status of Refugees recognizes persecution based on race, religion, nationality membership in a particular social group, or political opinion. The "social group" cartoon is currently being expanded to encompass gender claims, but this is not enough. See Pamela Goldberg and Nancy Kelly, "International Human Rights and Violence against Women," *Harvard Human Rights Journal* 6 (Spring 1993).

28. Testimony of Slavika Kusic, Center for Women War Victims in Zagreb, before the Global Tribunal (see note 13).

29. At the Global Tribunal in Vienna, Fadila Memisevic of the Center for the Registration of War Crimes and Genocide in Zenica spoke of a woman in the refugee camp who was hated by the other women because she spoke out about the practice of rape and therefore cast the stigma on her sisters, who did not want to talk about it. For a discussion of the tensions between human rights documentation and the needs of survivors, see Swiss and Giller, "Rape as a Crime of War."

30. See International Women's Human Rights Law Clinic, Gender Justice and the Constitution of the War Crimes Tribunal Pursuant to Security Council Resolution 808, photocopy, 1993, on file with author.

31. For example, a list of twenty-three names proposed to the General Assembly for the eleven judgeships contained only two women. Both were elected, but not easily. None of the nominees for chief prosecutor were women, and expertise in the issue of violence against women was not a criterion of selection.

32. The original case, *Filartiga* v. *Pena-Irala*, 630 F. 2d 876 (second circuit, 1980), resulted in a $10.4 million award against a Paraguayan torturer who was sued by the affected family after he was arrested by the Immigration and Naturalization Service, as a result of pressure from the Paraguayan community, because he was discovered residing illegally in the United States. Information on subsequent suits and on bringing such cases is available from Beth Stevens, Michael Ratner, or Peter Weiss at the Center for Constitutional Rights, 666 Broadway, New York, NY 10012; FAX (212) 614-6499.

33. *Jane Doe* v. *Radovan Karadzic*, Civil Action no. 93 Civ. 0878 (PKL)(United States Southern District of New York, filed 1993); *S. Kadic* v. *Radovan Karadzic*, Civil Action no. 93 Civ. 1163 (PKL) (United States Southern District of New York, filed 1993).

34. See, e.g., Charlotte Bunch, "Women's Rights as Human Rights: Toward a Revision of Human Rights," *Human Rights Quarterly* 12 (1990): 486; Rhonda Copelon, "Intimate Terror: Understanding Domestic Violence as Torture"; and Celina Romany, "State Responsibility Goes 'Private': A Feminist Critique of the Public/Private Distinction in International

Human Rights Law," in Rebecca Cook (ed.), *International Women's Human Rights* (Philadelphia: University of Pennsylvania Press, 1994).

35. Herman, *Trauma and Recovery*.

36. As the tribunal proceeds, you can write to United Nations Secretary-General Boutros Boutros-Ghali, to your country's ambassador to the United Nations, and to the judges and chief prosecutor of the tribunal, which will be situated in The Hague. The two women judges are Gabrielle Kirk-MacDonald (United States) and Elizabeth Odio-Benito (Costa Rica).

REFERENCES

Amnesty International. 1974. *Report on Torture*. New York.

Brownmiller, Susan. 1975. *Against Our Will: Men, Women, and Rape*. New York: Simon and Schuster.

Burgers, J. Herman, and Hans Danelius. 1988. *The United Nations Convention against Torture: A Handbook on the Convention against Torture and Other Cruel, Inhuman or Degrading Treatment or Punishment*. Dordrecht and Boston: M. Nijhoff Publishers.

Davis, Angela Y. 1983. *Women, Race and Class*. New York: Vintage.

Goldstein, Anne Tierney. 1993. *Recognizing Forced Impregnation As a War Crime under International Law*. New York: Center for Reproductive Law and Policy.

Khushalani, Yougindra. 1982. *Dignity and Honour of Women As Basic and Fundamental Human Rights*. The Hague and Boston: M. Nijhoff Publishers.

Peters, Edward. 1985. *Torture*. New York: Basil Blackwell.

U.N. Commission on Human Rights. 1993. *Rape and Abuse of Women in the Territory of the Former Yugoslavia*. Report on the 49th sess., February 1–March 12, Economic and Social Council, suppl. no. 3, E/CN4/1993/122 (emphasis supplied).

U.N. Convention against Torture, art. I; *Inter-American Convention against Torture*, art. 2. Reprinted in J. Herman Burgers and Hans Danelius, *The United Nations Convention against Torture: A Handbook on the Convention against Torture and Other Cruel, Inhuman and Degrading Treatment or Punishment* (Dordrecht and Boston, M. Nijhoff Publishers, 1988), appendix.

Chapter Eight

Girls Behind the (Front) Lines

Carolyn Nordstrom

Q: What did you do?
A: I held my M-16 on them.
Q: Why?
A: Because they might attack.
Q: They were children and babies?
A: Yes.
Q: And they might attack? Children and babies?
A: They might've had a fully loaded grenade on them. The mothers might have thrown them at us.
Q: Babies?
A: Yes.
Q: Were the babies in their mother's arms?
A: I guess so.
Q: And the babies moved to attack?
A: I expected at any moment they were about to make a counter-balance.

> —Paul Meadlo, court-martial testimony
> in Hammer 1971: 161–62

Behind the rhetoric of soldiers fighting soldiers that fuels military propaganda and popular accounts of war around the world, children are maimed, tortured, starved, forced to fight, and killed in numbers that rival adult civilian casualties, and they outnumber those of soldiers who die. These youthful casualties—some one and a half million in recognized armed conflicts in the last decade alone—are largely invisible: most of the military texts, the political science analyses, and the media accounts of war ignore the tactical targeting of children.

In over a decade of studying war, I have seen children as victims of war, lying maimed in hospitals or dead in bombed-out villages, and living or dying of starvation in refugee camps and on the streets after their families and homes have been attacked. I have seen children sold into forced labor and sexual servitude by international networks of profiteers who exploit the tragedies of war and the powerlessness of children. This constitutes a multibillion dollar transnational "industry."

Despite seeing all of this, I have witnessed only a very small percentage of *all* the children who are directly affected by war. In trying to find out what happens to other children in war, I discovered that the (very) little data that exist concern mainly boys. This prompts me to ask: Where are the girls?

The more I ask this question, the less I find an answer. Cynthia Enloe demanded a new sensibility in political studies when she insisted we ask: "Where are the women in politics, in conflict, and in political solutions?" (Enloe, 1989, 1993). To answer Enloe's question, I found women, I could follow their stories. Not all women and their stories, by any means. But I could see women during the time I was in war zones: they told stories and traded and set up healing programs. But *girls* were largely, dangerously, invisible. Outside of families, they disappeared from sight; they had no agency to direct their lives, to talk and trade and set up healing programs, they never spoke on the radio, their words were not recorded in newsprint, political scientists did not quote them, non-governmental organizations (NGOs) did not interview them.

When one tries to track the plight of girls in war zones, one finds that the images of children in war are obviously circumscribed. While bombing victims are plentiful in military and media presentations, discussions of the torture of children by state security forces are rare. While starvation among refugee children is frequently analyzed and photographed, the rape of these children is far less evident. While forcefully conscripting children into militaries has been studied in both academia and popular documentaries, the contemporary slaving of war orphans has been far more hidden, especially when the buyers are Westerners. Likewise, military texts seldom publicly document the strategic targeting of children, even though frontline realities show how frequent these strategies are pursued.

In the war zones I have visited, girls are actors in the drama and tragedy of war along with adults. They are targeted for attack, they devise escapes, they endure torture, they carry food to the needy, they forge a politics of belief and action. In general accounts of war—not the few excellent ethnographies focusing specifically on children—I look for children actors, and usually find none. Girls, children, are acted upon; they are listed as casualties—they do not act. They are not presented as having identities, politics, morals, and agendas for war or peace.[1]

What we hear and do not hear about the world we occupy is no accident. If reality is socially constructed, if we are the architects of our world and the cultures that give it meaning and vibrancy, knowledge is a profound resource. Shaping knowledge, and a lack of knowledge, constitutes a basic element of power. Silences—spheres where knowledge has been kept from public awareness—are undeniably political. So, what lies behind the silence about children in war, and why does it happen?

Following Girls' Stories during the War in Mozambique

My two years of trying to locate girls in the war zones of Mozambique have raised many questions about the very premises of war. In this section, I explore three locations where war impinges directly on the health and well-being of girls—the frontlines of war, the borders of war zones proper, and the peace process.

In 1991 I visited a town in north-central Mozambique during the war, which claimed some one million lives in a decade. I flew on one of the few emergency relief cargo planes that were trying to supply an entire country's needs. As I listened to local citizens' experiences of war and military occupation, one concern predominated: people stressed to me that every woman and girl in the town had been sexually assaulted during Renamo control. The townspeople told me that virtually all the women and young females had sexually transmitted diseases. For those infected with HIV, the war would claim casualties long after the peace accord had been signed. Such conditions—common both throughout Mozambique and in other wars around the world—have neither been labeled "rape camps" nor generated international awareness and outrage.

Few non-locals or foreigners visited this town. Shortly after my visit, the emergency supply planes were diverted elsewhere. With no telephones or communications equipment, the town fell to a silence in the landscape of war. The people's lives became invisible once again to the outside world.

Where war is the worst, where suffering is at its greatest, the least is known. It is simply too difficult to travel to the hotspots erupting in the world, too difficult to get people's stories on the frontlines. The sad truth is that no one knows what occurred in the hundreds of towns and villages in Mozambique (and in thousands of villages worldwide like them) when the violence closed down the links with the NGOs, the administrators, the reporters, and the researchers. When we ask the questions, where are the girls? what is their experience of the war?, no answer is possible. Even the most concerned researchers cannot track the lives of girls in such towns under fire.

Following the plight of girls across time as well as across war zones complicates an already difficult task. The one million people killed in the fifteen years of war left some 200,000 to 300,000 orphans. During my fieldwork, I continually asked about the orphans: what became of them? Many simply shrugged their shoulders; local Mozambicans generally responded that someone took them into their own families. There is a strong tradition of such care in Mozambique. More than once I visited friends whose families had grown by a child or two from the last time I saw them: war orphans, they had taken them in.

But this is not the full story. Thousands of children were visible on the streets of the major cities. Virtually all of them were boys. I told people that not all children could have found homes, otherwise there would not be any street children. But when I asked where the girls are, the answers were vague. People claimed girls were easier to care for than boys, and thus they fit more readily into established families. Yet no one has followed the path of the hundreds of thousands of orphaned girls to find out what has really happened to them.

Although I met children who had been taken into caring homes, I also encountered girls who did not fare as well, and their stories are as much a part of war as the others. There is a great international network of illegal racketeering that is spawned in time of war and that we must recognize. One example of this occurred in 1991 while I was in Mozambique.

In the midst of a war where public violence is often associated with the armed forces, collective civilian actions stand out. In 1991, groups of civilians gathered in one of the suburbs of the capital city Maputo, then stopped and overturned certain vehicles and beat their occupants. The media explanations focused on *feiticeiria*, African medicine used for ill gain. For example, body parts, often of children, are said to be used in the more powerful and dangerous medicines of *feiticeiria*. The general word on these disturbances in Maputo was that children from the area were being kidnapped and killed to make these medicines. Many of the cars targeted in the attacks had South African registries. This happened when the South African apartheid government was aiding Renamo's war in Mozambique.

Having worked with African healers for over a year, I found this explanation to be false. When I examined the allegations of *feiticeiria* and the body parts racket, I found a different and more insidious truth behind these disturbances. A thriving international industry had emerged to sell Mozambican children into white South African homes as domestics or as sexual slaves. The attacks described by the media were actually launched against the people running children across the border. War orphans, refugees who had been separated from their families, the poor and the desperate were the targets of this trade in humans.

Curiously, while the stories of selling "body parts" in pursuit of "sorcery" were widely circulated in the media, the actual selling of living children was not covered. A handful of industrious journalists documented the sale of children into white South African homes and businesses, but the international media did not feature the stories. The reluctance to file the reports may have resulted from the rumors that news stories of such racketeering could ruin more than a journalist's career.

Networks that sell children internationally are not the result of the work of only a few amoral individuals. Business, government, and military officials worldwide have greased the wheels, and their own pockets, in such illegal enterprises, and blaming *feiticeiria* may be a safe way to discuss child disappearances. Lost are the links among war, network profiteers, illegal border transfers, and abusive labor practices. Exactly who did the selling and buying, and how, was not documented, either because the specifics were too difficult to obtain or too dangerous to print. As a result, the children's plight has not changed, and their experiences have remained largely unheard.

As a profound irony of war and peace building, young girls found themselves to be vulnerable to the sexual predation of the thousands of peacekeepers who passed through Mozambique in the two years between the 1992 Peace Accord and the 1994 elections. Each transient carried with him his own values about his rights as a soldier, as a peacekeeper, and (since most peacekeepers were male) as a man. Many peacekeepers were dedicated to their jobs and to the rights of the Mozambicans, but some also abused the rights of girls (and boys).

International justice systems tolerate the sexual exploitation of children; no U.N. soldier has yet been prosecuted for child rape or prostitution (Fetherston 1995).

Attitudes that appear to rationalize soldiers acting in this way only make matters worse. For example, the head of the U.N. mission in Cambodia, Yasushi Akashi, was asked about the physical and sexual violation of women and girls by U.N. troops. He responded by saying that he was "not a 'puritan': 18-year old, hot blooded soldiers had a right to drink a few beers and chase after 'young beautiful things of the opposite sex' " (Fetherston 1995: 23). Akashi left Cambodia to direct the U.N. peacekeeping mission in the former Yugoslavia where his attitudes, in that powderkeg of sexual violations, can have only fanned the flames of human rights violations.

These are international abuses, transcending different regions and peoples. While many nationalities were implicated in the sexual abuse of children in Mozambique, the Italians were considered the worst offenders (Fetherston, 1995: 23). M. Poston, who studied these abuses, claims that while local Mozambican officials knew about the Italian soldiers, they were afraid to make complaints about U.N. personnel—a clear indication of the power relations at work.

A report was made, and some soldiers were sent home, though the numbers of soldiers discharged and their nationalities were kept quiet. The report stated that while the sexual trade in children did exist, it was not restricted to the U.N. soldiers. To many, this constituted a whitewash. But it points to a deeper injustice: the sexual abuse of children is a human rights abuse racket that extends across societies and nationalities. Young prostitutes in Mozambique told the BBC's Barnaby Phillips that there is no shortage of foreign clients. "They come from lots of different countries. But they are usually white. It is white men who like young girls best" (Phillips, 1994).

A Cautionary Note

We must be cautious against "othering" violence against children. The United States Advisory Board on Child Abuse and Neglect just finished a two-and-a-half-year nationwide study, and found levels of fatal abuse and neglect far greater than even experts had previously estimated. The report, entitled "A Nation's Shame: Fatal Child Abuse and Neglect in the United States," found abuse and neglect in the home a leading cause of child deaths. Possibly more shocking, most abused and neglected children are under the age of four. This abuse, claiming the lives of at least 2,000 children and seriously injuring more than 140,000 each year, has been declared a public health crisis.

In some cases, the level of abuse that children suffer in "peaceful societies" may rival, or surpass, that in countries at war, as the above report shows. We should not look at the abuse of children in war, in another country, in another culture, in a different context, as if that were somehow different, more barbaric, than the patterns of abuse that characterize our own everyday cultures, in peace or in war. What people tolerate in peace and in the domestic sphere configures what takes place in war. Rather than seeing "war abuses" or "child (s)exploitation" as "outside" the rules and boundaries of "average" or "normal" society, we should instead be asking what makes such behaviors possible wherever they are found, what patterns of in/tolerance link them, and how they can be changed.

Following Girls' Stories Globally

The silence about Mozambique is not unique. Consider the following:

- Approximately 2 million children have died in wars in the last decade; 4 to 5 million have been physically disabled; over 5 million have been forced into refugee camps; and more than 12 million were left homeless (UNICEF, 1995: 2).
- More children are killed in wars today than soldiers (UNICEF, 1995: 2). Twenty-eight million minors lived in war zones in 1995.
- 70 to 80 percent of the world's refugees are women and children (Lang 1995). Children account for half of all refugees. Upward of 80 percent of girl and women refugees are sexually assaulted (United Nations, 1995: 47).
- One hundred million anti-personnel mines have been sown in about sixty countries. Girls suffer land-mine casualties in the greatest numbers as their traditional labors—fetching water and firewood—expose them to greater injury (U.N. Economic Commission for Africa, 1995).
- The number of children under age eighteen involved in prostitution probably exceeds 2 million.
- About one million children globally will be infected with HIV by the year 2000 (UNICEF, 1995).
- There are 100 million street children in the world. Many of these children "disappear, are beaten, illegally detained and confined, sexually exploited, tortured and systematically killed by agents of the state" (Millet, 1994: 294).

As of 1995, 168 countries—home to 90 percent of the world's children—have endorsed the Convention on the Rights of the Child, making it the most widely ratified human rights convention in history. Children are thus forced to live at the epicenter of the following irony: the major civil and human rights abuses children face are perpetuated by adults, yet children must rely on adults to protect their rights.

Children have no direct access to United Nations forums and decision-making consuls; nor to direct representation in courts of law; nor to state policy-forming committees; nor to NGO grants. In fact, children may find it difficult to elicit police protection, to find a hospital on their own, or to learn what rights they have in the many local, national, and international laws and conventions. They are bound by laws made without their input, and governed by institutions they cannot control, which may or may not protect their rights. A child who faces abuse at the hands of an adult learns that not all adults uphold the laws of the land; yet they also learn that only adults can rectify the situation.

War/Peace Time?

What are normally considered "war accounts" and "problems of peacetime" have been juxtaposed here to show that the distinctions between war zones and peace zones are not only blurred, they are interfused. The profiteering institutions that abuse children are not isolated to countries or to regions, to "war" or to "peace." The networks that make such trafficking possible are multinational industries with global linkages. Any hard and fast divisions between "war (zones)" and "peace (zones)" is not only misleading but also dangerously wrong. Such divisions obscure the processes by which abuses of power and privilege—and by extension the solutions to these abuses—can be carried out. Only by understanding how abuses are constructed across social and political settings can we work to dismantle them.

International systems that exploit children are carefully constructed and consciously used by people, maintained within societies, and often tolerated in legal practice despite actual laws. They exist, even flourish, across divisions and zones of contention. These systems of abuse put billions of dollars into specific people's pockets. These people benefit, or think they benefit, from exploiting or ignoring the exploitation of children.

Challenging the belief in the naturalness of separating "war (zones)" and "peace (zones)" helps clarify the mechanisms that support these systems of abuse. Social habits move fluidly across conflict zones; they are put into place by people whose actions resonate across war and peace. To put this point bluntly: would we as readily accept the physical and sexual abuse of children in war if child prostitution did not flourish in many countries, if domestic violence and incest were not tacitly allowed simply because these crimes are very difficult to formally uncover and prosecute?

Many of those who take sex tours to take advantage of under-age girls and boys are unlikely to find the abuse or exploitation of children in war, or in peace, a significant cause for concern. Those who are encouraged to use physical and sexual violence against noncombatants and youths in war also have families and personal lives themselves—and a number carry these kinds of abusive actions back home into their communities with them. Studies show that domestic violence (physical and sexual) increases dramatically during war, and that people in uniform show significantly higher rates of domestic and sexual violations in war and out (Nordstrom, 1996). That legal systems have so rarely prosecuted violators of children's rights, and in fact have often persecuted the victims themselves in peace or in war, shows that this is not idiosyncratic but rather a system of social practices that permeate civil, judicial, governmental, and military structures (Asia Watch, 1993:1).

This should not be overgeneralized: many people work diligently for human rights, and they have created institutional systems that help rectify the injustices perpetuated in the contemporary world. When we can answer the question of "where are the girls" with hard facts and not a few anecdotes, we will know these workers are succeeding.

Solutions

Ending the silences and gaps in the empirical data on the plight of girls in war and in "peace" is a major avenue for beginning to solve these problems. Nowhere is it more true that what is not known cannot be solved.

Sadly, we do not have adequate information on what happens to girls in war and out. In war we need to ask: what percentage of casualties are girls? How many are tactically targeted for torture or terror-warfare? How many girls, as well as women, are in rape camps? What do they face, if they survive, when they return home? And because statistics on social and political violence are more political discourses than accurate accountings (how many armies readily admit that more children are killed in war than soldiers, or that children are tortured in political prisons?), we must do direct fieldwork and not rely solely on secondhand data.

We must follow these questions out from war to map the international systems of child exploitation: What children are "bought" by whom and sold to whom for what purposes? What governmental, business, and legal and illegal networks make this possible, and what are their interrelationships? Who benefits, and how? If public opinion continues to see the exploitation of children as the random product of antisocial fragments of society and not as a well-developed transnational industry, the mechanisms by which this industry can be dismantled will not become evident.

Finally, we must ask girls to tell their own stories of war, its impact on them, and ask for potential solutions rather than assume the right to speak for them. If people misrepresent girls' experiences and opinions, the latter have little recourse to correct any misinformation: they have virtually no access to publishing, media, public presentations, and formal organizations. It is woefully easy to silence children's own words and realities.

Children often have a well-developed moral, political, and philosophical understanding of the events in their lives and worlds. Years of research on the front lines of war have taught me that even very young children have profound opinions on conditions of justice and injustice, violence and peace in their lives. Children fight and are fought against. UNICEF broke ground in the survey it sponsored in southeast Rwanda after the recent genocidal conflict. It found that almost 56 percent of the children interviewed had seen children kill people, and 42 percent saw children kill other children (UNICEF, 1995: 28). And on the other side of the equation, children worldwide have been involved in sophisticated peace building efforts. From Youth for Peace in Northern Ireland to the peace-building work of the YWCA of Sri Lanka and the youth groups of South Africa, children have been working to forge viable platforms for peaceful coexistence (Abitbol and Louise, 1993). As adults, we have a real obligation to support these initiatives.

Examples worldwide show children to be far more politically aware, more morally developed, and more actively involved in conflict and its resolution than most portrayals suggest. Adults do not necessarily impart responsibility to youths in a one-way process. Responsibility can flow from youths to adults as well. But who holds the reins of power?

ACKNOWLEDGMENTS

This article comes from a larger research and writing project undertaken for the Life and Peace Institute of Sweden on "Girls and War Zones." I am most grateful to the institute for the support they extended for this project. I am particularly grateful to Dr. Lucia Ann Mc-Spadden, whose encouragement, support, and insights made this research and writing possible. She commissioned this work as part of a larger project on Women and Nonviolence, which she will publish as an edited volume.

NOTES

1. Given the (few) excellent studies incorporating the stories and voices of children that do exist, the silence of nonadults in generalized presentations becomes all the more politically loaded. To give but a few examples: Veena Das's inclusion of children's realities during the 1985 rioting in India, "Our Work to Cry: Your Work to Listen," in *Mirrors of Violence: Communities, Riots and Survivors in South Asia,* V. Das (ed.) (Oxford: Oxford University Press). Ed Cairn's work on children and political violence in Northern Ireland, *Children and Political Violence* (London: Basil Blackwell, 1995). See also his *Caught in the Crossfire: Children in Northern Ireland* (Belfast: Appletree Press; and Syracuse: Syracuse University Press). Marcelo Suarez-Orozco's study of the strategies of torture directed specifically at children, "The Treatment of Children in the 'Dirty War': Ideology, State Terrorism, and the Abuse of Children in Argentina," in *Child Survival,* N. Scheper-Hughes (ed.) (Boston: D. Reidel, 1987). Neil Boothby's work with unaccompanied children in conflict conditions in Everett Ressler, Neil Boothby, and Daniel Steinbock, *Unaccompanied Children: Care and Protection in Wars, Natural Disasters, and Refugee Movements* (Oxford: Oxford University Press, 1988). R. W. Connell's book of children's voices describing their political identities, *The Child's Construction of Politics* (Melbourne: Melbourne University Press, 1971). Dorothy Allison's recent novel, *Bastard Out of Carolina,* based on her own childhood of severe physical and sexual abuse, throws open the question of how much experiential separation really exists between what is called war and peace in terms of human rights violations and the suffering of children. See also Dorothy Allison's *Skin: Talking about Sex, Class and Literature* (Ithaca, NY: Firebrand Books, 1994).

REFERENCES

Abitbol, Eric, and Christopher Louise. 1993. *Up in Arms: The Role of Young People in Conflict and Peacemaking.* London: International Alert.

Asia Watch and The Women's Rights Project. 1993. *A Modern Form of Slavery: Trafficking of Burmese Women and Girls into Brothels in Thailand.* New York: Human Rights Watch.

Cairns, Ed. 1995. *Children and Political Violence.* London: Basil Blackwell.

Connell, R. W. 1971. *The Child's Construction of Politics.* Melbourne: Melbourne University Press.

Enloe, Cynthia. 1989. *Bananas, Beaches and Bases.* London: Pandora.

Enloe, Cynthia. 1993. *The Morning After.* Berkeley: University of California Press.

Fetherston, A. B. 1995. "U.N. Peacekeepers and Cultures of Violence." *Cultural Survival Quarterly* 19:1, 19–23.

Fetherston, A. B., and C. Nordstrom. 1995. "Overcoming *Habitus* in Conflict Management: U.N. Peacekeeping and War Zone Ethnography." *Peace and Change* 1:94–119.

Hammer, Richard. 1971. *The Court-Martial of Lt. Calley*. New York: Coward, McCaan and Geoghegan.

Lang, Hazel. 1995. "Women as Refugees: Perspectives from Burma." *Cultural Survival Quarterly* 1:54–58.

Millett, Kate. 1994. *The Politics of Cruelty*. New York: W. W. Norton.

Nordstrom, Carolyn. 1996. "Rape: Politics and Theory in War and Peace." Working Paper No. 146, Peace Research Centre. Canberra: Australian National University.

Phillips, Barnaby. 1994. "Mozambique: Teenage Sex for Sale." *BBC Focus on Africa*, vol. 15, no. 2 (April–June).

Ressler, Everett, Neil Boothby, and Daniel Steinbock. 1988. *Unaccompanied Children: Care and Protection in Wars, Natural Disasters, and Refugee Movements*. Oxford: Oxford University Press.

Scheper-Hughes, Nancy (ed.). 1987. *Child Survival*. Boston: D. Reidel.

UNICEF. 1995. *Annual Report*. Paris: Author.

United Nations. 1995. *The World's Women 1995: Trends and Statistics*. New York: United Nations.

United Nations Economic Commission for Africa. 1995. *Statement of the First Regional Consultation on the Impact of Armed Conflict on Children*. Addis Ababa, Ethiopia, 17–19 April.

Chapter Nine

Gender, Militarization, and Universal Male Conscription in South Korea

Seungsook Moon

The growing corpus of literature on women and war highlights differential impacts of war and/or war preparation on women and men, as well as the ways in which gender structures such impacts (Elshtain, 1987; Elshtain and Tobias, 1990; Enloe, 1983; Reardon, 1985; Turpin and Lorentzen, 1996). This essay examines the ways in which war preparation militarizes society and thereby contributes to the maintenance of gender hierarchy in South Korea.[1] The Korean Peninsula is one of the world's most militarized regions by any measure (see table 9.1) due to the peculiar historical circumstances of national division and hostile confrontation between North and South since the Korean War (1950–1953).[2] Moreover, the Cold War persists in the post-Cold War era and is expediently used by the political elite even after the recent transition from military authoritarian rule to civilian rule. By militarization I refer not only to military buildup measured in terms of the absolute and relative size of the armed forces and the amount of military spending, but also to the increasing or continuous influence of military practices and values on the larger society as a result of war preparation.[3] I argue that the system of universal male conscription, integral to societal militarization, constitutes a crucial mechanism to perpetuate dominant notions and practices of femininity and masculinity in South Korean society.

Scope of Militarization: Historical Legacies and Military Buildup

In order to understand fully the consequences of universal male conscription on gender hierarchy in South Korea, we must look at the historical context of militarization leading to the prevalence of military values and practices in the society. Throughout the twentieth century, until the 1970s and before the rise of economic conglomerates, the military had been the single most powerful institution. In contrast to the Confucian past of Korea, the military had become the central influence on politics throughout Japanese colonial rule (1910–1945), United States Army Military Government rule (1945–1948), the Korean War, the acceleration and con-

TABLE 9.1
Militarization of the Korean Peninsula

	South Korea	North Korea
Population	43,100,000	21,400,000
Active Armed Forces	650,000	1,040,000
(soldiers/population)	(1.5%)	(4.8%)
Reserves	4,840,000	5,540,000
(soldiers/population)	(11.4%)	(25.3%)
Military Service	2.5 years	5 years
Military Spending, 1987		
% of GNP	5.2	10.2–25.0
% of Public Budget	32.8	40.0

SOURCE: Quoted from Philo Kim (1992: 158–61, 163).

NOTE: It is difficult to evaluate exact amounts of military spending due to the secrecy surrounding military information. There are discrepancies among estimated amounts. While the U.S. government has quoted high percentages for North Korean military spending—25 percent of the GNP—such private research centers as the International Institutes for Strategic Studies (IISS) and Stockholm International Peace Research Institute (SIPRI) have provided statistics that match official North Korean statistics.

tinuation of the Cold War even after its demise elsewhere, and three decades of military authoritarian rule (1961–1992).

During Japanese colonization, the repressive state apparatus was extended through society because Japan, like other colonial powers, operated primarily by coercion and imposition. The police, as well as the armies that acquired modern weapons and organizational structure, were intimidating symbols of Japanese power, images still held by older Koreans.

The military continued to be the most powerful institution in postcolonial Korea on the basis of its human and material resources and its organizational structure. The Armed Forces of the Republic of Korea were created and expanded by the United States Army Military Government (USAMG). The euphoria of independence soon evaporated with the beginning of the USAMG rule and the subsequent division of Korea into North and South. On its arrival in the Korean Peninsula, the USAMG proclaimed that it was the only lawful authority in the southern part of the peninsula and suppressed spontaneous political movements emerging in urban and rural areas.[4] Threatened by popular protests against the trusteeship of postcolonial Korea and widespread mass movements with leftist tendencies, the USAMG prohibited any kind of militia and established the South Korean National Constabulary in January 1946. Since then, the size of the Korean military has increased rapidly with the birth of the Republic of Korea (1948), which accelerated this buildup (S. Kim, 1971: 37–40).

The military buildup was further facilitated by the Korean War. The South Korean military multiplied from 100,000 strong at the outbreak of the Korean War, to its current size of 650,000 in 1954. In the midst of the escalation of the Cold War, the United States actively supported this expansion by granting various forms of military aid throughout the 1950s and 1960s. The United States pumped in approximately $2 billion during the 1950s (S. Kim, 1971: 66) and $1.22 billion during the period between 1964 and 1970 (C. Kim and Hong 1996: 295). The resulting expansion and modernization of the Korean military directly contributed to the rise of military elites that dominated Korean politics for three decades.[5] These years, especially the 1970s, were decisive to the spread of military values and practices in civilian social life.

Scope of Militarization: Societal Militarization

There is a close link between military buildup and societal militarization in South Korea, especially during the 1970s. This is quite different from the "postmilitary" societies in the West discussed by Martin Shaw (1991). According to Shaw, the ascendancy of nuclear and other high-tech weapons in the arms race has separated military buildup as an exclusive arena of elite politics from the rest of society. Therefore, in "postmilitary" societies, military buildup continues even though the system of universal conscription is abolished and society is generally demilitarized. After the Nixon Doctrine, Park's regime (1961–1979) accelerated military buildup by promulgating the idea of a "self-reliant defense" (*chaju kukbang*).[6] In 1971 the regime founded the Research Center for Defense Science (*kukbang kwahak yonguso*) in order to utilize military technology transferred from the United States. In 1974 it launched a long-term, systematic military buildup plan (*yulgok saop*), which was supported by heavy industrialization begun in 1973 (C. Kim and Hong, 1996: 297, 290). Since March 1978, the Team Spirit—coordinated military exercises between South Korea and the United States—has been a routine.

In the 1970s, Park's military regime established mechanisms to mobilize the entire population for war preparation. This mobilization had the effect of militarizing the larger society beyond the exclusive elite politics. In 1971, the regime instituted monthly civil-defense training (*minbangwi hullyon*) for the first time since independence from Japan. During the period between 1975 and 1991, it also levied a defense tax (*pangwise*) in order to repay soaring military loans obtained primarily from the United States.[7] Furthermore, from 1973 to 1988, military regimes engaged in a campaign to encourage students, workers, and housewives to donate to a defense fund (*pangwi songkum*) (C. Kim and Hong, 1996: 298).

Universal male conscription has been the most significant mechanism of mass mobilization for war preparation implemented since 1957. Park's regime sanctified military service as the most patriotic duty of Korean (male) citizens. Furthermore, it incorporated more men into the military mechanism for longer duration by creating the Homeland Reserve Force (*hyangto yebigun*) in 1968 and the Civil Defense Corps (*minbangwidai*) in 1975. After the completion of mandatory service in the standing armed forces, men are automatically transferred to these reserve forces, which train them annually (C. Kim and Hong, 1996: 82, 83).[8]

Clearly, societal militarization is not a uniform and monolithic process without resistance or unintended consequences. Not all social relations are shaped by military values and practices in an identical manner and to an equal degree, even in the heavily militarized society of South Korea. Some institutions are more militarized than others. This essay focuses on two major institutions that shape men's and women's lives before and after mandatory military service and display extensive incorporation of military values and practices: schools and business corporations.

The influence of military values and practices on civilian life is reflected poignantly in the militarization of schooling in several ways. First, specific military practices were blended into educational processes. Throughout the 1970s and 1980s, military drills were incorporated into formal curricula for male students in secondary and tertiary education after a new subject, educational training (*kyoryon*), was created in 1969. Mirroring the gendered division of labor in the larger society, female students were trained in emergency nursing care. Weekly morning meetings (*chohoe*) for both female and male students in secondary schools consisted of military review or parading. Typically, these ceremonies involved straight lines of students in uniform, positioned by military rank, a brass band playing marching music, and the national flag and school flags held high by specially selected students.[9]

A second reflection of military values and practices is the hierarchical interaction between teachers and students. Classes are usually conducted in a top-down command mode of communication. The regulation of students' behavior and appearance often involves intrusive surveillance and punishment for noncompliance. The method of punishment commonly resembles military discipline—e.g., collective punishment or such physical punishment as push-ups, running while squatting, kneeling, and sometimes beating (Chon, 1991: 22). Although modified in recent years, these aspects of school militarization persist after the more blatantly military practices discussed earlier were abolished.

The war metaphor also permeates the ways in which studying is conceptualized, particularly in relation to the college entrance examination. Each student is at war with other students as well as him or herself. Fiercely competitive college entrance, especially to prestigious institutions, is often depicted as a life-and-death battle. Students are bombarded by pseudo-aphorisms revealing this militarized attitude. To give a few examples: "If sleeping, you will perish" (*cholmyon chungnunda*), or "four rise, five fall," (*sadang orak*), which means that if one sleeps for four hours, one will succeed in passing the entrance exam; sleeping for five hours will cause one to fail. The underlying message to young students is that they, just like soldiers at the war front, have to conquer their basic desire for sleep in order to survive in the battlefield of college entrance. In fact, mass media tend to exacerbate this extremism by sensationally adopting such headlines as "No Friend in Entrance Examination Front" (Chon, 1991: 22).

Business corporations, especially the large and prestigious ones owned by economic tycoons (*chaebol kiop*), are another sphere of intense societal militarization. Ironically, corporations have emerged as the most powerful institution controlling massive resources and bureaucratic structures in rapidly industrializing Korea, thus weakening the historical dominance of the military. This shift in power may facilitate demilitarization of society. Yet they continue to exhibit military practices and values. Business corporations, like schools, have appropriated certain military practices as a way to discipline workers. During orientation periods, for example, groups of new recruits are sent away for training. This involves camping and such quasi-military training as marching and singing in uniform, acting as a unit, and inspections (Janelli, 1993: 141–43). This type of overtly militarized practice has been recently modified in response to popular criticism and the slowly growing number of female recruits in some companies.[10]

Second, again like schools, business corporations display a strict ranking system, a command mode of communication, and punishment for noncompliance. Young male workers in *chaebol* companies relate disturbing similarities between their military experience and that of employment (An, 1995: 36; Janelli, 1993: 43; Pak, 1995: 141). Punishment sometimes involves naked force. As a way to control defiant workers organizing democratic unions (as opposed to company-sponsored ones), companies organize "save our company" corps (*kusadae*) manned by hooligans skillful in the martial arts and fighting (Ogle, 1990).

This convergence of the military and business firms in their *modus operandi* is predictable in Korean society, since both institutions share similar organizational structures—rationalized bureaucracies with specific goals. The only difference is their goals—for one it is profit and for the other war victory. This difference collapses, however, when competition for profit-making is seen as waging a war. It is not accidental that a chairman of a *chaebol* company is often called a commander in chief (*ch'ongsu*).

Militarization of schools and business corporations has been directly or indirectly challenged and resisted by students, teachers, parents, and workers since the mid-1980s, when civil society began to be reactivated in South Korea under the overarching rubric of the democratization movement (Chong, Kim, and Yu, 1995). Some male college students, especially student activists, demanded the elimination of military drills and refused to take part in military training. A small but significant number of teachers and parents have been involved in movements aiming at the democratization of education. College-educated white-collar workers, as well as blue-collar workers, organize unions indirectly to question militarized practices and values in corporate life. However, these contentious activities cannot suddenly eradicate societal militarization. This will require not only continuous grassroots movements but also the unification of Korea after which an inflated armed forces on both sides would no longer be needed.

Gender Hierarchy and the Institution of Universal Male Conscription as a Source of Merit

The idea of universal male conscription was introduced to Korea by the promulgation of the Conscription Law (*pyongyokbop*) in 1949. Since its extensive revision in 1957, mandatory military service has been the single most important duty of South Korean (male) citizens. Currently, all able-bodied young men between the ages of nineteen and thirty-five are required to serve in the military for up to twenty-seven months, although there are certain restrictions based on the level of education (above middle school), and economic situation (he should not be the only provider for his family).[11]

Although this institution is not unique to Korean society, the ways in which it is integrated into the nation's political economy seem peculiar. In Western Europe the institution of universal male conscription was central to the masculinist construction of the political sphere in that the mass conscription of men was accompanied by women's exclusion from the modern politics of mass electoral democracy (Charlton, 1989: 25). However, this gender discrepancy resulted in the unintended consequence of mobilizing women for suffrage movements. Consequently, the blatant link between male soldiering and men's political prerogative was challenged and uncoupled. In South Korea, universal male conscription has never been tied to exclusive male suffrage because women's voting rights were given by the Constitution of South Korea as an element of equal citizenship. Instead, military service has been a source of men's economic superiority.

Mandatory military service in South Korea is unequivocally integral to societal militarization.[12] Furthermore, its continuity with employment has serious consequences for gender hierarchy in several ways. First, the state organizes the national economy around men's military service by institutionalizing its completion as a precondition for employment. Reflecting this arrangement, until recently all newspaper and magazine recruitment advertisements specified that an applicant had to complete military service (*pyongyokp'il*). This suggests that women are not even allowed to apply because they cannot meet the requirement. Women's organizations protested against this blatant sexual discrimination at the entrance level of employment and succeeded in eliminating this conventional practice of printing such a requirement. Now, technically, women can apply for any job, although this cosmetic change has not led to the elimination of military service as a prerequisite for employment altogether.

Second, military service is treated as a source of merit. Male applicants who have completed military service gain extra scores in employment tests or interviews. The state and its male citizens thus exchange military service for privileged access to the labor market.[13] From the state's point of view, this arrangement ensures continuous loyalty from men and reduces discontent arising from sacrificing one's youthful years. However, from the point of view of women, the practice seriously undermines their equal access to the job market.

Third, military service is considered valuable work experience. Hence, from the beginning of employment, male workers are entitled to higher pay than their female counterparts working in comparable jobs.[14] Officially, they are placed in a higher rank on the elaborate pay scale used by Korean companies than female workers with comparable or identical qualifications, except for the military service. The idea of military service as work experience highlights societal militarization, in particular militarization of business corporations. In the militarized context, military service and civilian employment are interchangeable and viewed as productive work. Like extra points given to male applicants, this monetary reward also serves as a mechanism intended to secure the smooth working of the conscription system. Women's unequal access to the labor market is thus compounded by the requirement of military service for men and its use as the source of merit in employment. This link between employment and universal male conscription unequivocally delegitimizes women as equal workers.

In addition to the devaluation of women as applicants and workers in the labor market, universal male conscription contributes to the maintenance of gender hierarchy by stabilizing dominant notions and practices of masculinity and femininity in Korean society. Newly industrialized Korea has adopted the Western middle-class notions of gender identities constructed around the woman as housewife and the man as provider. Reflecting this historical change, a new term, *chubu*, literally meaning a master's wife, was popularized during the 1960s, when society was rapidly being modernized by state-directed economic development. The first women's monthly magazine, named *Housewife's Life (chubu saengwhal)* targeting the growing section of young, urban, and educated women, was founded in 1965. This magazine, like others published later, contributed to the construction of the housewife by instructing women about marital life, housekeeping, and child rearing, along with other practices of modern womanhood. Man's identity as a provider was clearly codified in family law enforced between 1960 and 1990, which specified that a man as the head of household (*hoju*) was required to support family members. In return, he as husband/father was entitled to exercise authority over family members (Moon, 1996).

As Maria Mies (1986) has argued, "housewife" is historically a new category of woman that emerged with capitalist industrialization, transforming the majority of women from producers to primarily reproducers and consumers. Certainly, the "housewifization" of women on a global scale does not take place in an identical manner. In South Korea, this process superseded the Neo-Confucian gender ideology, which assigns women and men to the "inside" and "outside" of the household, respectively. This gender ideology of separate spheres is well illustrated by terms referring to husband and wife still widely used by older couples—i.e., sir outside (*pakkan nyangban*) and inside person (*ansaram*). Clearly, the majority of women and men in preindustrial Korea could not afford to live up to an ideology that confined women to the domestic sphere and reproduction. Peasant women and other lower-class women had to work inside and outside the household. Industrialization has increased the possibility for more women and men to conform to the gender arrangement in modern forms. By generating a sizable urban middle class whose family consists of housewife, husband-provider, and unmarried children, capitalist industrialization has popularized the Confucian version of gender roles that only upper-class *Yangban* families could afford previously.

The significance of economic privileges tied to military service cannot be over-emphasized in commercialized society. Paid employment is the material basis of men's domestic authority in contemporary Korea. As economic growth has been the paramount goal of national development, men's financial ability has become the measure of masculinity and domestic authority. Unfortunately, fathers/husbands are respected so long as they are capable of supporting families, and the majority of married men see this as their primary responsibility.[15] The failure to provide family support results in the loss of respect and authority as well as of self-esteem. Therefore, men's superior position in employment based on mandatory military service reinforces their dominance as husbands/fathers. This masculinized practice of supporting families goes hand in hand with women as dependent housewives, or at best as supplementary income earners. Women's secondary position in the economy significantly curtails the possibility of financial independence in highly commercialized South Korea. Financial insecurity makes marriage based on the asymmetrical gender arrangement a reasonable option for women, or even a necessity.

Conclusion

The exigency of war preparation in divided Korea has led to the militarization of South Korean society beyond the enclosed circle of elite politics associated with military buildup. Universal male conscription has been a crucial mechanism through which the population is incorporated into the military. As I have shown, miltary service occupies the transitional time from schooling to employment. In the militarized society it constitutes a critical apprenticeship during which men are prepared not only for soldiering but also for work in militarized business corporations. Furthermore, military service is directly translated into economic merit and thereby contributes to hierarchical gender relations based on the normative arrangement between male-provider and female-housewife.

In criticizing universal male conscription, I am not advocating women's equal access to mandatory military service. Gender equality often implies that women should emulate men. This interpretation, when applied to mandatory military service, results in the problematic integration of women into the war machine instead of its elimination. Although women should be able to pursue military careers as professional soldiers if a military force were to be preserved, I envision feminist transformation of society through gradual and progressive demilitarization. Certainly, this does not imply any essentialized notions of women-pacifists and men-aggressors, even though they tend to be socialized as such. What is needed is to abolish the practice of translating military service into economic merit and to create alternatives to military service, such as community service, for both women and men.

NOTES

1. This context-specific analysis enables us to avoid ahistorical and essentialist discussion of militarization and gender criticized by bell hooks (1984).

2. The war, which resulted in over three million casualties, did not end but has been postponed by the cease-fire agreement between the United States and North Korea.

3. This definition is based on discussions of militarism and militarization by Schofield (1994), Shaw (1991), and Galtung (1985).

4. Bruce Cumings (1981) documented the militant and brutal crackdown on indigenous political movements during this period.

5. The body of literature on political development in Latin America points to the parallel phenomenon of the "overdeveloped" military vis-à-vis other institutions. See Masterson (1991), Stepan (1988), and O'Donnell (1973).

6. The Nixon Doctrine signified a shift in the strategic relationship between South Korea

and the United States from recipient-patron to client-arms dealer. See C. Kim and Hong (1996: 294).

7. Annual military loans increased dramatically throughout the 1970s, from $15 million in 1971 to $275 million in 1978. Consequently, the amount of repayment has exceeded that of the loan since the 1980s. Defense tax was imposed as a way to mitigate this problem (C. Kim and Hong, 1996: 297–98).

8. The length of training has been shortened over the decades, from twenty-eight days in 1957 to two nights and three days in 1994 (*Pyongmu* 1995: 29). This change appears to reflect the ascendancy of economic activities over nonproductive military training in the decades of economic expansion, as well as the increasing significance of high technology in warfare.

9. This aspect of militarization of schooling has historical parallels elsewhere. British public schools training the British elite to administer colonies practiced military ceremonial and military drills. They also inculcated the ethos of "leadership/service/sacrifice" in students. However, unlike the Korean case, these practices were largely isolated from the society. The British military, throughout its imperialist expansion, remained segregated from the society. See Shaw (1991: chap. 4).

10. Interviews with new female recruits of *chaebol* companies in the summer of 1996.

11. The increase in the young adult male population has decreased the duration of military service from three years since the late 1980s.

12. This intimate link is not observed in some "postmilitary" societies in the West where the military is civilianized. For instance, soldiers in Germany and the Netherlands are allowed to form unions even if both preserve the system of universal male conscription (Shaw, 1991: 88).

13. There are historical and contemporary parallels for this type of exchange between the state and male citizenry. The earliest example would be the pact between the ancient Greek *polis* and the propertied free male citizens who were required to perform soldiering in exchange for their political participation. A more contemporary example can be seen in the United States immediately after World War II. All male immigrants who served in the armed forces during World War II were granted citizenship after the war (Kerber, 1990).

14. Some *chabol* companies have begun to hire female college graduates with male graduates since the early 1990s.

15. I examine the construction and subversion of this masculinity elsewhere. See Moon (1997).

REFERENCES

An, Chong-ok. 1995. "Hoesanun hoesail ppunida" (A company is merely a company). In *Hoesagamyon chungnunda: kyongjejuuitamnonui pip'anul wihan pild stodi (If you join a company, you're dead: A field study to criticize economistic discourse)*, P.-j. Cho and S.-t. a. Hong (ed.). Seoul: Hyonsil munwha yongu.

Charlton, Sue Ellen. 1989. "Female Welfare and Political Exclusion in Western European States." In *Women, the State, and Development*, S. E. Charlton, J. Everett and K. Staudt (eds.). Albany: State University of New York.

Chon, P'ung-ja. 1991. "Hangug sahoeui kunsajuui munhwawa yosong: hahkyo kyoyukui ch'ungmyoneso" (Militaristic culture and women in Korean society: Schooling). In *Yosong. pyongwha (Woman Peace)*, C. w. p. academy (ed.). Seoul: P'yongwhawa.

Chong, T'ae-sok, Ho-gi Kim, and P'al-mu Yu. 1995. Hangukui siminsahoewa minjujuuiui chonmang (Civil society and the prospect of democracy in South Korea). In *Siminsahoewa siminwundong (Civil society and citizens' movement)*, P. a.-m. Yu and H.-g. Kim (ed.). Seoul: Hanwul.

Cumings, Bruce. 1981. *Origins of the Korean War*. Vol. 1. Chicago: University of Chicago Press.

Elshtain, Jean B. 1987. *Women and War*. New York: Basic Books.

Elshtain, Jean B., and Sheila Tobias, eds. 1990. *Women, Militarism, and War: Essays in History, Politics, and Social Theory*. Savage, MD: Rowman and Littlefield.

Enloe, Cynthia. 1983. *Does Khaki Become You? The Militarization of Women's Lives*. Boston: South End Press.

Galtung, Johan. 1985. "Global Conflict Formations: Present Developments and Future Directions." In *Global Militarization*, P. Wallenstten, J. Galtung, and C. Portales (eds.). Boulder, CO: Westview.

hooks, bell. 1984. *Feminist Theory: From Margin to Center*. Boston: South End Press.

Janelli, Roger. 1993. *Making Capitalism: The Social and Cultural Construction of a South Korean Conglomerate*. Stanford, CA: Stanford University Press.

Kerber, Linda K. 1990. "May All Our Citizens Be Soldiers and All Our Soldiers Citizens." In *Women, Militarism, and War: Essays in History, Politics, and Social Theory*, J. B. Elshtain and S. Tobias (eds.). Savage, MD: Rowman and Littlefield.

Kim, Chae-il. 1996. "Hyangt'oyebigun opmu pyonch'on" (Change in the homeland reserve force's tasks). *Pyongmu* 32 (Winter): 80–83.

Kim, Chin-gyun, and Song-tae Hong. 1996. *Kunsinkwa hyondaesahoe (Mars and contemporary society)*. Seoul: Munhak kwahaksa.

Kim, Philo. 1992. *Two Koreas in Development: A Comparative Study of Principles and Strategies of Capitalist and Communist Third World Development*. New Brunswick, NJ: Transaction.

Kim, Se-Jin. 1971. *The Politics of Military Revolution in Korea*. Chapel Hill: University of North Carolina Press.

Masterson, Daniel M. 1991. *Militarism and Politics in Latin America: Peru from Sanchez Cerro to Sendero Luminoso*. Westport, CT: Greenwood Press.

Mies, Maria. 1986. *Patriarchy and Accumulation on a World Scale: Women in the International Division of Labor*. London: Zed Books.

Moon, Seungsook. 1996. "Modernization of Gender Hierarchy in South Korea: Politics of Family Law Reform." *The Journal of Modern Korean Studies* 6 (November):19–43.

———. 1997. "The Production and Subversion of Hegemonic Masculinity: Reconfiguring Gender Hierarchy in Contemporary South Korea." Unpublished manuscript.

O'Donnell, Guillermo. 1973. *A Modernization and Bureaucratic-Authoritarianism: Studies in South American Politics*. Berkeley: University of California Press.

Ogle, George E. 1990. *South Korea: Dissent within the Economic Miracle*. London: Zed Books.

Pak, Sam-ch'ul. 1995. "Chulkwa sont'aikui sai" (A gap between a line and a choice). In *Hoesagamyon chungnunda: Kyongjejuui tamnonui pip'anul wihan pild stodi (If you join a company, you're dead: A field study to criticize economistic discourse)*, P.-j. Cho and S.-t. a. Hong (eds.). Seoul: Hyonsil munwha yongu.

Pyongmu. 1995. "Pyongmuch'ong ch'angsol 25 nyon palchach'wi" (A 25-year history of the office of military manpower). *Pyongmu* 31 (Fall): 16–33.

Reardon, Betty. 1985. *Sexism and the War System*. New York: Columbia University Press.

Schofield, Steve. 1994. "Militarism, the U.K. Economy, and Conversion Policies." In *A World Divided: Militarism and Development after the Cold War*, G. Tansey, K. Tansey, and P. Rogers (eds.). New York: St. Martin's Press.

Shaw, Martin. 1991. *Post-Military Society: Militarism, Demilitarization, and War at the End of the Twentieth Century*. Philadelphia: Temple University Press.

Stepan, Alfred. 1988. *Rethinking Military Politics in Brazil and the Southern Cone*. Princeton, NJ: Princeton University Press.

Turpin, Jennifer, and Lois Ann Lorentzen (eds.). 1996. *The Gendered New World Order: Militarism, Development and the Environment*. New York/London: Routledge.

Chapter Ten

Militarization, Conflict, and Women
in South Asia

Anuradha M. Chenoy

The incidence of war and sectarian conflicts in South Asia, and women's suffering as victims of these conflicts, has not lessened today. Threats of wars between states and the reality of secessionist, communal, ethnic, and regional divides leading to civil conflicts threaten the South Asian region. These conflicts damage and distort civilian processes and affect women in a variety of ways. The pernicious impact of these conflicts and the state's response to them is evident in the process of militarization that has taken place throughout South Asia.

Concepts of Militarization and Militarism

Militarization is the process that emphasizes the use of coercive structures and practices. Militarism is the ideology that valorizes and glorifies such a reliance and practice. The most extreme form of militarization is a total reliance on the military and its structures as the basis of political rule such as ruthless military dictatorship. Militarization underlies wars and conflicts. It is a larger phenomenon than war. It can be practiced during times of peace and be part of institutions and structures not directly concerned with war. Militarization is a social process, while militarism is a worldview. Militarism glorifies practices and norms associated with militaries. Patriarchy and particular constructions of "masculinity" shape militarism's mindset. Rigorous discipline, obedience and hierarchical forms of decision-making, in contrast to democratic, inquisitive traditions, often become the accepted norms.

Given the sweep of democratization in the twentieth century, militarism as an ideology has been subject to popular criticism. As a consequence, practices promoting militarism have taken new forms. Civilian controlled forms have replaced those dominated by the military. In the developing countries, militarization has in some instances developed without militarism being overt or strident. Here, defense and social expenditures compete for budgetary allocations. Due to the secrecy of defense budgets, and due to civilian control, militarism is often not overt.

Moreover, in some Third World systems, militarist responses became essential for preserving sovereignty, as, for example, Vietnam's militarization was forced upon the country. But because the nationalism to which it was harnessed was extremely deep rooted and strongly progressive, this greatly tempered and qualified the militarism that existed. Militarism is thus often woven with nationalist ideologies in variable and complex ways.

The primary site for militarist behavior is the state, but militarism as an ideology has multiple sources. Thus civilian structures can be promoters of militarism, even if this is occasional rather than constant. At times of interstate or even intercommunity conflict, the media, civic groups, and others have called for military intervention and promoted militarism. For instance, a consensus approach emerged in India against the signing of the Comprehensive Test Ban Treaty (CTBT). Any dissenting voice was classified as "betrayal of a national cause." The use of the Indian Peace-Keeping Force in Sri Lanka was supported widely by the Indian media, and military excesses by this force against civilians, especially women, were not given proper coverage.

The state is both a major actor in the process of militarization as well as a site for its consolidation. But non-state actors are also sites and agencies for militarization. Movements which are secessionist, communal, or sectarian can advocate and pursue militarist methods and practices. These movements impose militarist discipline, strict hierarchies, and chain of command within their organizations. Democratic structures and functioning are virtually ruled out. Women often remain outside the leadership, or are utilized at the lowest level in these hierarchies. The Rashtriya Svayamsevak Sangh (RSS) in India and the Jamat-i-Islami groups in India, Pakistan, and Bangladesh display some of these characteristics.

Patriarchal attitudes and values are, unsurprisingly, embedded in the ideology of militarism, just as patriarchal practices will be manifest in the process of militarization. As such, they are a feature also of movements in society outside the domain of the state. Thus Punjabi and Kashmiri militants in India and religious fanatics in Pakistan and Bangladesh insisted that women revert to traditional dress codes and cover their heads (use of veils, etc.) when these movements were at their peak (Women's Initiative, 1994).

Protecting or promoting the "national interest" is repeatedly used as a legitimizing refrain or slogan by militarized states. But it has little or partial connection to the protection of real national security and sovereignty, which includes economic and social security. Defense and genuine social security are not seen as synonymous needs. In many states, including in South Asia, national security considerations are used to justify policies that go beyond issues concerning the protection of national sovereignty. It is often used to legitimize the regime in power, for example the emergency regime imposed by Indira Gandhi in India in 1975–76.

The slogan of national security is often used to maintain the status quo in the face of antigovernment protests. It is used to perpetuate the rule of the elite and the dominant ideologies, whether these are class or caste based, patriarchal or feudal. The suppression of the democratic movement in Nepal and ongoing oppression in the former East Pakistan are examples. National security considerations have also been used in South Asia to justify the oppression of minorities, as for example, in the eviction of ethnic Nepalese from Bhutan, and in regard to the Sri Lanka's treatment of the Tamils.

Militarization also exists in select and isolated regions within states at specific times, coinciding with normalcy elsewhere. This is the case, for instance, in the northeast and in the Kashmir Valley in India; in Baluchistan in Pakistan; in North East Sri Lanka. Sri Lanka did not even possess a military until 1971. It was after the JVP (Jathika Vimukti Perumuna) rebellion against the Srimavo Bandarnaike regime that the government created a significant military structure and resorted to its widespread internal use.

The degree of militarization varies with regimes. It is overt when the military controls power, such as in Pakistan, which witnessed military or quasi-military rule for twenty-five of its fifty years of statehood; or, in Bangladesh, with fifteen years of direct military rule since 1971. But militarization is not specific only to authoritarian systems. Militarized societies cover a wide spectrum. They differ with respect to form and content. Democratic systems like India may make selective use of militarist methods, internally and externally, and continue to be described as democracies. Democratic societies may also carry out or induce militarization outside their own regimes, as in the case of the United States in Vietnam and the Philippines.

Analysts of militarism and militarization from Lenin to Rosa Luxemburg have linked militarism and militarization to the development of capitalism and imperialism. Variations of this theory conceive of militarization as part of the postwar international system (Melman, 1974; Kaldor, 1981). Other explanations argue that since force is necessary to guarantee the success of nation states, war-making is linked to the growth of national states. Thus state-sponsored violence is viewed as legitimate (Tilly, 1985). Some theories give statist causes for militarization, or explain it in terms of bureaucratism (Adams, 1981; Bok, 1984).

These theories restrict the analysis as well as the phenomenon of militarization to state structures. Feminists criticize these theories for not taking patriarchy and its structures into account, relying as they do on economic or statist factors. Feminist theorists have convincingly established the linkages between militarism, masculinism, and patriarchy. It has been systematically shown that the subjugation of women for the sake of sustaining male privilege or patriarchy is a feature of militarization, and that forms of masculinity also link the military to industry (Enloe, 1983; Elshtain, 1982). Feminists thus link the militarization of state and economic structures to patriarchal civil and social structures.

Militarization in South Asia is particularly linked to the colonial experience and to the continuation of colonial structures and mindsets in the postcolonial period. Remnants of feudal society linger. Entrenched patriarchal systems of power and social relationships remain, as does a dependent capitalist path of development. The deepening of ethnic and religio-political identities exists throughout the subcontinent, with roots traceable to the colonial era. State power is used to maintain the status quo.

Security managers in South Asia play a lead role in safeguarding the national security-militarization paradigm. These managers are the top army commanders, select senior bureaucrats, a few civilian policy advisors, and key cabinet members. These managers are almost exclusively male. In Pakistan, the recent formation of a

Council for Defense and National Security, heavily supportive of the armed forces, has given more militarized content to security policies.

While objectively speaking national security needs have become broader, and the importance of military structures lessened worldwide and in South Asia, this change has not been clearly recognized by the South Asian elite, which remains a prisoner of outdated mindsets. Reality has changed; threats to the territorial integrity of states have decreased, and the military is less and less capable of addressing problems, both old and new. The old male-oriented and dominated militaristic approach, however, has not changed. It is this issue that must be addressed by the women's movement.

The South Asian Experience of Militarization

Militarism was part of the ideological practice of the colonial state in South Asia. Militarization was necessary for maintaining the colonial state and the communal/ethnic/caste divisions within these societies. These divisions were used to strengthen colonial rule and give it legitimacy. The anticolonial movement in India was led by a nationalist elite devoted to the establishment of modern states along the European model of democracy, secularism, and capitalism.

The attempt of the nationalist movements was not only to modernize these societies but also to assert cultural identities suppressed under colonial rule. Though women participated in these movements, the nationalist agenda took primacy over women's issues. Some reforms and education were directed at women, but the question of women's specific oppression remained largely neglected. While the nationalist movements were by and large nonviolent, the formation of the independent states of India, Pakistan (1947), and Bangladesh (1971) was accompanied by large-scale violence.

The communal nature of the violence during the partition of India and the ethnic violence in the formation of Bangladesh revealed the militarization of both the new state regimes as well as the societies involved. Besides large-scale genocide, gendered crime was a common feature of these events. Rape was a frequent form of meting out humiliation to the "other" community. Hundreds of thousands of women on both sides of the Indo-Pak border suffered sexual violence. They also suffered the violence perpetuated on them by their own families in order to "save their honor." In the rehabilitation that followed, it was easier to rehabilitate men, who were given jobs, property, and so on, whereas women were not easily accepted back into normal life. Even in the politics of recovering abducted women (50,000 Muslim women in India and 35,000 non-Muslim women in Pakistan), women received little justice or understanding (Menon and Bhasin, 1993).

Similarly, in Bangladesh, inquiries from the International Court of Justice revealed that an entire generation of Bengali women was raped or forced into prostitution (Chouduri, 1972; Hasanat, 1979). Once the state was established, it concerned itself with the rehabilitation of men and the duties of nationhood. Old patterns of gender biases and patriarchy were resumed. Laws and property rights continued to ensure patriarchal norms. In all three instances, nationalist and sub-nationalist ideologies were reflected both by the communities and by states involved. The links between chauvinism, patriarchy, and militarism were established and found expression through militarization of conflicts.

The postcolonial states of South Asia inherited and willfully retained militarized structures and ideologies from their past no matter what their political orientation. The national security paradigm in all states is a militaristic and patriarchal one. Militarization in postcolonial South Asia has an interlinked external and internal dimension.

The External Dimension

The key axis of militarization due to interstate security in South Asia is the India-Pakistan relationship. Here, a mutually competitive and hence militarist notion of security, centering on territorial dispute and the question of Kashmir, has institutionalized a tension-filled relationship. The militarization of both states can be attributed in part to this. The national security managers of both states manage this relationship, rather than transform it. Of course, both India and Pakistan cite a variety of threats as reasons to increase their military arsenal. This includes, for India, an unresolved border dispute with China, a perceived threat from Chinese nuclear power, and American-led nuclear hegemonism. Pakistan cites the instability in Afghanistan and the regional issue with the northwest as potential problems.

The other countries of South Asia maintain armed forces ostensibly for maintaining territorial integrity but use them primarily for domestic purposes. Defense expenditures in all of South Asia have spiraled, at the cost of forgoing much-needed social expenditures. Defense expenditures of all South Asian states double that of expenditures on health (Sivard, 1996). Surveys such as the Human Development Report (U.N.D.P., 1996) show that it is primarily women who have been hit by such lopsided expenditures and policies.

The external relations of South Asian states are based on "realist" doctrines of national security. This realist vision incorporates a masculinism that is hostile to feminist and democratic consciousness. Even women leaders heading security-making apparatuses have reflected taken-for-granted national security perspectives. This is evident in the behavior of Indira Gandhi, Benazir Bhutto, and Srimavo Bandarnaike, all of whom have relied heavily on the military for maintaining their regime and have held statist views of politics. Thus, democratization and feminization of the national security paradigm itself and of its underlying structures are the only possible ways of combating militarization.

The Internal Dimension

The project of nation-state building in South Asia has led to some positive developments, but it has also been marked with conflicts promoting internal militarization. These conflicts include secessionist movements that challenge the states. India faces secessionist movements in Kashmir and in the northeast and the Khalistan movement in Punjab. Pakistan experiences secessionist pressures in Baluchistan. In Sri Lanka there is the Tamil Elam movement. All these movements have specific causes, demands, and trajectories with uneven popular support. Local militants, often with mass support and sometimes with the support of external forces, have resorted to armed action leading to an unending spiral of militarized violence between the state and the militants.

In this process, large numbers of civilians have been killed. Reports from local and international groups show that both the militants and the state have been indiscriminate in their use of violence (Human Rights Commission, 1990). The armed forces deployed in these regions have used rape as a weapon of control (Women's Initiative, 1994). Rape is used as a symbol of humiliation and threat against an entire community. These conflicts have led to displacement, refugee movements on a large scale, gendered crime, and prostitution for women. Again, rehabilitation and compensation for women, whether in material or emotional terms, have been negligible in all cases.

Other movements exist which seek greater space within nation states. All these conflicts/movements display similar characteristics. Generally, complex issues of oppression and justice are involved. The states or regimes in power almost uniformly resort to militarist solutions to curb these conflicts. Thus, when interethnic violence occurs, such as the recent killing of nontribals by tribals in Tripura (*Asian Age*, 17 February 1997), the state intervenes militarily. The real issues of scarcity of resources, alienation of land, and so forth, get relegated to the background. Reports repeatedly reveal that these interventions include all the consequences of militarization, from unaccounted killing to rape.

The response to state terrorism in many instances has been one of further militancy from local groups, with even greater popular support because of the state's military excesses. Militant groups often replicate the state to counter repression. They procure arms, organize themselves along military lines, and have acted either against the military and state, against the civilians of the "other" community, or against those belonging to the opposition. This results in the further militarization of the conflict and social structures in that region.

The role of the LTTE (Liberation Tigers of Tamil Eelam) demonstrates the trajectory sketched above. The LTTE started as a movement for Tamil liberation in Sri Lanka in the 1980s. Within a few years their military machinery grew disproportionate to their political structures. Groups within the LTTE challenged one another's leadership. Dissenting opinions were suppressed. No concrete proposals were made in their program for minorities like the Tamil Muslims. Women were called to arms on the basis of military myths like the "valiant mothers" who either went to war, or sent their sons, lovers, and husbands to war. The influence of the LTTE women's wing was marginal and reinforced gender biases (Hoole et al., 1988). On the other hand, the Jaffna Mother's Front members who demonstrated and fasted for negotiations between India and the LTTE were more effective.

In many instances, the state has made use of the conflict between communities to arm one civilian group against the other. One blatant example is in the northeastern Indian state of Manipur. Here, the armed forces have used the Kuki tribe's old rivalry against the Naga to curb Naga insurgency by arming the Kukis. Militant action has in most instances helped the state to legitimize its own militancy and to conduct counterinsurgency directed both at militants and ordinary civilians. In this process, the national security paradigm is strengthened, society is militarized, gendered crime is retained,and patriarchal privileges are reinforced.

Religio-political movements flourish in four of the South Asian states: Islamic fundamentalism in Pakistan, Bangladesh, and India; Shia-Sunni clashes in Pakistan; Hindu communalism in India; and Buddhist nationalism in Sri Lanka. All these religio-political movements are very specific in their injunctions regarding the family, women, and education. Organizing the family is the method used to mobilize women in ways that reinforce patriarchy (Chenoy and Vanaik, 1996). None of these religious systems have liberatory or antipatriarchal impulses.

Martyrdom for religious and nationalist causes and a false heroism based on violent forms of action in support of religious causes are revered by these religio-political movements. Controlling female sexuality, for example enforcing and extolling the chastity of women and promoting sacred and traditional codes, are the basis for religious teaching and mobilization. These values are the norms for organizations like the RSS in India (Mazumdar, 1995; Sarkar, 1994). Muslim fundamentalists are strictest when it comes to codes for controlling women.

Yet women have been and are part of these fundamentalist groups. They have supported violence. For instance, in India, the *sadhvis* (Hindu priestesses) of the Rashtriya Swayam Sevak Sangh openly called to Hindu men during the Babri Masjid movement (1993–94) to take "revenge" on Muslims. Women are adversely affected with the rise of these movements and must reach women within communal groups, since women have an objective interest in opposing such fundamentalism.

In India between 1983 and 1995, ethnic and political violence led to 37,000 mostly civilian dead. Ethnic violence in all of South Asia resulted in more civilian killing than cross-border wars (Sivard, 1996). In almost all instances of communal/ ethnic clashes, rape occurred. Rape was used against women demonstrators for Uttrakhand (1995) and during post-Babri Masjid communal violence in India and in Bangladesh. In the Mohajir-Sind clashes in Pakistan, rape was a common way to treat the wives and sisters of the "enemy" (*Frontier Post*, 1993, 26/3). Gendered crime is common in all interethnic and communal conflict. The assumption is that "our" women have to be protected and "their" women are to be humiliated. In both instances, women's bodies are treated as territory to be controlled by both offenders and defenders.

The structural adjustment policies (SAP) followed in South Asia since the 1980s as part of the World Bank and IMF's globalization policies have meant the establishment of economic, political, social, and ideological relations that promote the new mobility of capital. SAP has led to the further redistribution of resources from the weaker sections of society to the already dominant ones. Inequalities in health, income, mortality, education, and social security resulted (World Development Report, 1994). Consequently, inequalities of social power in class and gender equations increased. SAP in South Asia has been grounded in gender ideology, which is exploitative of women's time, work, and sexuality. Thus, as global mass communications promote the ideology of consumption (Wilkin, 1996), and private power takes the space of the public realm, the economic and power imbalances in society as a whole and between men and women increase.

Women are victims of militarism even though they have no role in the decision-making structures that lead to militarization. Women suffer during civil strife, and their suffering continues afterwards. Conflicts brutalize society and destroy infrastructures. Families lose their economic productivity. In many cases families must leave their homes and livelihood and become refugees. More than 80 percent of these displaced are women and children (Bennett, Bexley, and Warnock, 1995). Women have to take over as heads of households. Compensation and rehabilitation are rare and can never match the loss. The South Asian experience has repeatedly shown that there is little support from either state or society to women affected by violence.

Women victims of violence must negotiate years of suffering, sometimes with a disabled husband, traumatized children, and no means to rebuild lives. This is often in addition to their personal trauma, which scars women and communities. A great effort is required to recover. Women's suffering and responsibilities increase—facts that are not recorded in manuals of war.

A related issue arises. Does militarization have any links with everyday violence against women? In regimes like Pakistan, direct military intervention in everyday life and laws discriminatory to women prevail. The Pakistani Law of Evidence, for example, makes it virtually impossible to prove a charge of rape, thereby promoting gendered crime. Patriarchal structures provide the link by which the ideology of militarism can negatively influence the problem of domestic violence.

Data sheets from India show, for example, that there is a rape every 54 minutes, one molestation every 26 minutes, one kidnapping/abduction every 43 minutes, one dowry-related death every 1 hour and 42 minutes, and one act of cruelty every 33 minutes. The situation has not improved over the years (*Times of India*, 8 March 1997). This violence continues due to the underlying patriarchy that leads to callous responses from society, governments, courts and the state. When state agencies or even antistate or intercommunity movements freely use gendered violence, acts of individual violence against women in society tend to be overlooked.

In South Asia, militarization is not restricted to militaries or military regimes. Ethnic, communal, economic, and gender relations have a militarized component. Militarization as a process has been shaped by the specific history of this subcontinent. It has been aggravated through the particular choice regarding development. It is women who consistently lose.

Militarism as an ideology coexists with other ideologies, and militarized structures exist alongside other cultural, political, and economic relations, without necessarily dominating them. Militarism is part of the wider web of social relations, between state and society, between groups, and between men and women. Militarism is compatible with and has interacted with patriarchy, capitalism, fundamentalism, communalism, colonialism, neo-colonialism, regionalism, and other chauvinisms and subnationalisms.

Despite its pervasiveness, militarism with all its interconnectedness can be challenged. Ideologies and movements that uphold democratization, feminism, secularism, and sustainable development have to question militarization, just as they must question patriarchy and injustice. The women's movements must throw their strength behind this wider agenda. It is only then that a more positive peace process will replace the process of militarization.

ACKNOWLEDGMENTS

I am grateful to Dr. Kamal Mitra Chenoy and Achin Vanaik for their comments and support.

REFERENCES

Adams, G. 1981. *The Iron Triangle, Politics of Defense Contracting.* New York: New York Council on Economic Priorities.

Amnesty International. 1990. *Report.* London: Amnesty International.

Bennett, Olivia, Jo Bexley, and Kitty Warnock, eds. 1995. *Arms to Fight, Arms to Protect: Women Speak Out about Conflict.* London: Panos.

Bok, S. 1984. *Secrets.* New York: Vintage.

Chenoy, Anuradha, and Achin Vanaik. 1996. "Promoting Peace, Security and Conflict Resolution: Altering the Gender Balance in Decision Making Structures." Paper presented at the expert group meeting on "Political Decision-Making and Conflict Resolution: The Impact of Gender Difference," United Nations Division for the Advancement of Women, Santo Domingo, 7–11 October 1996.

Chouduri, Kalyan. 1972. *Genocide in Bangladesh.* Calcutta: Orient Longman.

Cypher, J. M. 1982. "Ideological Hegemony and Modern Militarism: The Origins and Limits of Military Keynesianism." *Humanities in Society* 1/2: 45–65.

Elshtain, Jean B. 1982. "Women as Mirror and Other: Towards a Theory of Women, War, and Feminism." *Humanities in Society* 1/2: 29–44.

Enloe, C. H. 1983. *Does Khaki Become You? The Militarization of Women's Lives.* Boston: South End Press.

Hasanat, Abdul. 1979. *The Ugliest Genocide in History.* Dacca: Swadeshi Bangla Sahitya Parishad.

Hoole, R., et al. 1988. *The Broken Palymyra: The Tamil Crisis in Sri Lanka — An Inside Account.* California: The Sri Lanka Institute.

Jalal, Ayesha. 1990. *The State of Martial Rule: The Origins of Pakistan's Political Economy of Defence.* Cambridge, U.K.: Cambridge University Press.

Jayawardena, Kumari. 1986. *Feminism and Nationalism in the Third World.* New Delhi: Kali for Women.

Kaldor, M. 1981. *The Baroque Arsenal.* New York: Hill and Wang.

Mazumdar, Sucheta. 1995. "Women on the March: Right-Wing Mobilization in Contemporary India." *Feminist Review* (London), no. 49, Spring.

Melman, S. 1974. *The Permanent War Economy.* New York: Simon and Schuster.

Menon, Ritu, and Bhasin, Kamala. (1993) "Recovery, Rupture, Resistance: Indian State and Abduction of Women during Partition." *Economic and Political Weekly*, 24 April.

Sarkar, Tanika. 1994. "Educating the Children of the Hindu Rashtra, Notes on RSS Schools." *South Asia Bulletin* vol. 14, no. 2

Sivard, R. L. 1996. *World Military and Social Expenditures*. Washington, D.C.: World Priorities.

———. 1995. *Women: A World Survey*. Washington, D.C.: World Priorities.

Tilly, C. 1985. "War Making and State Making as Organised Crime." In P. B. Evans, D. Rueschemeyer, and T. Scocpol, eds., *Bringing the State Back In*. London: Cambridge University Press.

Times of India. 1997. New Delhi/Bombay, 8 March.

U.N.D.P. 1996. *Human Development Report*. London: Oxford University Press.

Wilkin, Peter. 1996. " New Myths for the South: Globalisation and the Conflict between Private Power and Freedom." *Third World Quarterly* 17, no. 2.

Women's Initiative. 1994. "Women's Testimonies from Kashmir: The Green of the Valley Is Khaki." New Delhi, report from The Women's Initiative.

World Development Report. 1994. Oxford: Oxford University Press.

Chapter Eleven

Militarism and Cypriot Women

Ninetta Pourou-Kazantzis

Cyprus—the cornerstone between the East and the West—has always been the military base of the powerful, from which they controlled surrounding countries and sea routes. The historical course of Cyprus and its civilization through the centuries has been determined, to a great extent, by its geographical position and strategic importance. There were times of independence and peaceful exchange, but also times when the island was under the yoke of foreign conquerors during the 9,000 years of its civilization.

The multiplicity of influences does not change the nature of the long and stable Cypriot relationship with the Greek and Byzantine world. Through the centuries, Cyprus has assimilated foreign influences to become a Hellenic civilization with its own peculiarities.

In 1572, Cyprus was occupied by the Ottoman Empire, which acted with great cruelty toward the defenders of the island. The period after the conquest is characterized by regression and the impoverishment of the people. And for the first time, there was the physical presence of Turks on the island, who came to Cyprus as soldiers with their families. Their descendants, together with the Islamicized Christians during the three centuries of Ottoman rule, constitute the present-day Turkish Cypriot minority.

The relations between Greeks and Turks were in general good, while on certain occasions revolts took place against the excesses and the repressive measures of the Ottoman administration.

In 1878, the Ottoman Empire ceded Cyprus to the British, a move that kindled hopes among Cypriots that the island would eventually be handed over to Greece, thus fulfilling their age-long quest and dream of unification. Unfortunately, their hopes were dashed by the British, and the Greek Cypriots were forced to seek their freedom through an armed struggle.

Cyprus emerged as an independent country in 1960 after a five-year guerrilla war against the British occupation. The Treaty of Establishment allowed three different forces to be on the island, namely: the Greeks with a Training Force of 950 men; the Turks with a Training Force of 650 men; and the Cyprus Army of 2,000 men.

At the same time, under the Treaty of Alliance, both Greece and Turkey would have guarantor forces on the island.

In 1964, after the first intercommunal troubles, Turkey bombarded the island, and the U.N. Security Council Resolution No. 186 called for a U.N. peacekeeping force to be present on the island; the force is still there today.

On July 20, 1974, Turkey undertook a military invasion of Cyprus which caused extensive destruction. On August 14, the Turkish invasion was completed with the second assault that culminated in the occupation of 37 percent of Cyprus. The Turkish troops destroyed any hope that the end of the Second World War meant phasing out the horror of war from Europe. Even worse, the extent of the destruction and the barbarity and plundering that have continued for twenty-two years are reminiscent of the dark days of the Middle Ages. The misdeeds of the Turkish Attila are very similar to the scourge and destruction of the notorious King of the Huns: 200,000 refugees; 1,619 missing persons; orphans, widows, devastation; and 45,000 Turkish occupying forces in the northern part of Cyprus. It was inevitable that the Cyprus Army would expand so that it could defend itself in the event of further moves by the Turkish forces. It has until today been impossible to find a just and lasting solution based on respect of the sovereignty, independence, territorial integrity, and nonalignment of the Republic of Cyprus.

The political solution of the Cyprus problem is a matter of urgency. A solution guaranteeing permanent peace and security for all is possible. Since 1974, the world has changed dramatically. We have all been witnesses to an unprecedented acceleration of history. The Cold War, superpower confrontation, the division of Europe—all have become things of the past and have given place to increased cooperation, which is necessary in order to meet the new challenges that lie ahead and to face the threats to world peace and security.

At the same time, we have witnessed a dramatic crisis which has increased our awareness of the dangers that we will have to face in this new era of transition and on the urgent need to bring about a new system of security based on the primacy of international law in the political conduct of states. The Gulf crisis enhanced our awareness of the danger that regional problems can present in this new era of world peace and security and that the urgent need to solve these problems is a priority if a new world order is to be established and maintained.

The last few years brought about major changes in the world, especially in eastern Europe. There has been progress in, and even resolution of, what appeared to be intractable problems in places such as Namibia, Afghanistan, and many others. Cyprus, unfortunately, has yet to be the beneficiary of the new developments and of the trend toward resolution of regional conflicts. In fact, not only has no progress been made on the key issues, but there have been no new developments in the purely humanitarian issue of missing persons. More than sixteen hundred persons are still unaccounted for.

All these changes have rendered the anachronistic character of the status quo on the island even more apparent and the need for a political solution even more urgent. Such a solution will put an end to the hardships of the people of Cyprus as well as increase the chances for peace and stability in the whole region, by eliminating a source of tension and acting as a catalyst and example for other regional problems around the world.

All people are affected by the situation of war, but what is the impact on women specifically? A woman's role has been and continues to be, even when there are careers outside the home, the protector of her children, the care giver, the harmonizer, the vessel of moral and ethical values, and the maintainer of the culture of the community in which she was born and raised. Preserving tradition is mainly a woman's job.

Grandmothers sing lullabies to newborns, put small children to sleep with traditional stories and tales, and recite old poems on occasions such as birthdays, religious holidays, funerals. Mothers cook traditional food and sing songs while cleaning or doing other domestic work. Women weave, embroider, knit, and paint in their free time. Mothers bring language to the young child, and by role playing they make tradition a daily fact. In a society—as in Cyprus after the 1974 Turkish invasion—where grandmothers are left behind, enclaved, where mothers no longer sing because the father is a missing person, where the community is no longer intact and has no chance of interacting—preserving tradition is a difficult task. People need their roots. They need to know where they have come from in order to know where they are going. They need to have continuity in linking the past to the present, and thus plan for the future.

War is the most venal threat to all of these things. In former times, a woman was likely to lose adult male relatives, husbands, fathers, sons. Nowadays, with more and more civilian populations involved, she loses her babies, her own life, or ends up a displaced person within her own country or a refugee outside it. Militarization in the Mediterranean, militarization of the world, has been the key producer of refugee populations, of which 80 percent are women and children. All of our countries have produced or received refugees. The refugee woman is a dramatic statement of what is wrong with our world. Her very existence makes a dramatic statement about war, economic hardship, religious persecution, racism, environmental degradation: in other words, about human rights violations in her native land. The refugee woman's situation is highly exploitable, dependent as she is on others for the basic necessities of life. Women workers in the United Nations High Commission for Refugees (UNHCR) have recently been stressing the need for special consideration of the female refugee's problems. One simple example is that for years now, the distribution of food was turned over to a male committee within the refugee populations. Many of the men used this power to elicit sexual favors. When women walked to the camp latrines at night, built some distance from the shelters, men would take another opportunity to sexually abuse them. In general, the militarization of the world has strengthened commercial prostitution as well as other forms of sexual slavery.

We could go on with more descriptions of women as victims of war. None of us is unaffected. Violence against women is pervasive and constant. It is not limited to geographical areas or certain political systems. It is structural and institutional.

Laws dehumanize women as "property," and economic systems exploit women as cheap labor. It is vicious, from wife beating to genital mutilation to bride burning to shooting, raping, and killing.

In Cyprus, we are refused access to our homes, access to our properties, access to our birthplaces. We are refused the basic human right of belonging, the basic human right of living in one's homeland. We have been refugees in our own country for more than twenty-two years now. This is an original statement from a Cypriot Refugee woman made at the AWMR Conference in June 1996:

> From Dherynia village, my home is only 4 km away. I can see my house, my old school and the Church clearly from there. I always try to show these places to my child and try to explain to him that our roots are there and that we have a place where we come from like everyone else. For the children these places are just pictures which, as time goes by, will fade. But for us they are—and always will be—vivid in our memory, and we shall not cease to struggle to go back to the places where we were born.

And as I stated at the same conference:

> We marched in peace this summer—all of us unarmed—and reached the so called "border," the dividing line. . . . We wanted to silently protest for the division of our country. . . . We stood there staring at our lost homes. . . . Two of us were brutally murdered, the one literally kicked to death by the Turkish Occupation Forces. The whole world was shocked by the scenes of these two murders. Yet they remain silent. Our greatest crime is silence. Disaster threatens as militarism combines with the technological and scientific communities. We whisper when we should shout and our voices are not heard.

The military presence on Cyprus has been escalating over the last years—the Turkish Occupying Forces expand, the Cyprus Army has to keep up in armaments to make sure it can defend the people—and this is a grave concern. Armaments take up an enormous amount of capital that would otherwise have been used for social development. Productive years of the youth are wasted, economic growth is hindered, people's welfare is overlooked, "quality of life" becomes a phrase unknown.

Recent developments cannot be ignored. The Cyprus government has decided to buy the Russian ground-to-air-missile-system S-300, which by definition is "defensive." Cyprus—being small as it is—cannot be offensive toward other countries. Cyprus—having the culture it has—does not wish to be offensive, war is not its aim. The people do not like having to spend huge amounts of capital on armaments—yet we must defend ourselves. Turkey has threatened to take military action against Cyprus if it decides to install the S-300. The United States and Britain have protested against the S-300 because they say, incredibly, that they do not wish the military balance in the area to be disrupted.

We can understand the U.S. standpoint that no escalation of tension is desirable in our area—or anywhere else, for that matter. But we must remember that 40 percent of Cyprus has been occupied for twenty-two years, and the United States did not at any point impose pressure on Turkey to withdraw its troops from the island. The United States has been, and still is, the major supplier of armaments to Turkey. Turkey used arms that were given to it as a NATO ally to invade Cyprus.

The same soldiers are still on the island, threatening constantly to take military action against us. It is time that the United States take political action against Turkey if it sincerely wishes to settle the problem and ensure peace and security in the region. It is time that the U.N. Resolutions on Cyprus be implemented.

We strongly believe that the only solution to our problem would be the total disarmament of Cyprus, the withdrawal of all foreign troops, and the disbanding of the Cyprus Army. The Security Council Resolutions have called upon this solution for several years and they should be implemented as soon as possible.

The Mediterranean is a sea that binds us all together. The peoples here have, through the ages, been people of peace, friendship, and high cultural achievement. Women of the Mediterranean are quite rightly preoccupied by the serious problems and conflicts in the region. They are claiming a serious and important role in the process of conflict resolution, and need to become well informed about these problems. They must join forces and set up a common front and a common struggle aimed at solving the regional problems. Cyprus, Lebanon, Palestine, the former Yugoslavia, have all gone through the same bitter experience of armed conflict, aggression, and ethnic cleansing with all their terrible repercussions. We can all start from one common ground and build a common future of peace and cooperation.

Part III

Women in the Military
and War Complex

Chapter Twelve

Feminist Perspectives on Women Warriors

Francine D'Amico

That we even need to talk about "women and war" underscores the gendering of our construct of war. War has been perceived as men's domain, a masculine endeavor for which women may serve as victim, spectator, or prize. Women are denied agency, made present but silenced. Perhaps that is why so many feminist researchers, like myself, focus on the subject of women and war. Perhaps our scrutiny is a fascination for the forbidden. Perhaps we need to reclaim an erased identity, to legitimize our ability to speak, to tell our own "war stories," to claim an "authentic voice." Must we have participated in war to claim that voice? Do we seek to challenge the powerlessness and the lack of control over our lives by embracing the "warrior mystique," to seek power over others?

These questions framed my thinking as I witnessed the Gulf War unfold. The war highlighted women's military roles in many countries. Several of the states that provided Gulf coalition forces had numbers of women in their armed forces: the United States (11%), Canada (9.2%), the United Kingdom (5%), and France (2.7%). After the war, several states revised or abandoned policies of exclusion based on gender and sexuality. Was the Gulf "the good war" for women? Did women's participation challenge traditional gender constructs and constraints, and open possibilities for renegotiating established gender lines? I think not.

While 11,000 United States servicewomen were posted in Saudi Arabia, the United States media focused on "war orphans" (children whose parents had both been sent to the Gulf), and on the capture and release of POWs Melissa Rathbun-Nealy and Major Rhonda Scott Cornum. They also emphasized the deaths of Beverly Clark and Christine Mayes—who were among the twenty-eight soldiers killed in the missile attack on the U.S. Army barracks in Dhahran, Saudi Arabia—and of Major Marie Rossi, who died when the helicopter she was piloting crashed on a supply mission. These reports highlighted the competing obligations of parents and soldiers, and the contradictions in the U.S. "combat exclusion" policy for women. They have implications beyond the United States or the Gulf crisis. The increasing reliance of state and nonstate militaries on "*woman*power" makes these questions vital for military planners and feminists alike. But focusing on these questions alone distracts us from more fundamental questions about the use and control of military power itself.

The image of the woman warrior has been viewed as distressing, intriguing, and compelling. Antifeminists decry the image as unnatural and warn us that women's increased military participation destroys both the family and the fabric of civil society while also impairing military efficiency. Their argument assumes inherent and natural gender differences.

Radical feminists see the image of the woman warrior as representing women's potential for power, as lingering evidence of an ancient matriarchy or woman-centered and woman-governed society. They embrace the image as a symbol of solidarity and sisterhood, and argue for a separatist philosophy of empowerment. Some see military means as necessary for liberating and defending women from patriarchy. In this view, as with the antifeminists, gender differences are seen as natural and immutable, and as barriers to gender equality within any community. But while antifeminists would maintain the current gender hierarchy, radical feminists would either reverse it or disengage from it via separation.

In contrast, another group of feminists touts the image of the woman warrior as evidence of women's equality with men: "See, we can do it, too." This "me-too" variety of liberal or equal rights feminism argues that women may prove their worth, may earn equality, by assuming social roles ascribed to men. In this view, the goal of women's militarization is women's equality, which they define as sameness with men. Some liberal feminists also argue that women's entry into the military will gradually transform it into a less hierarchical, more democratic and egalitarian social institution.

A third group of feminists warns us of the dangers of the woman warrior image: it draws from a "warrior mystique," promoting martial and masculine values rather than redefining gender-based social values and hierarchical power structures. These critical feminists argue that the woman warrior image subjects women to greater manipulation by those controlling military institutions, thus allowing women to be militarized but not empowered. Thus, women's militarization provides no substantive "feminization" of the military as a social institution. Military institutions and their needs (not women's needs) determine women's role in the armed forces. Women's military participation reinforces rather than undermines the gendered structure of the military and the broader society.

To evaluate these perspectives, let's examine the United States' experience. United States women's participation in the Gulf conflict built upon a pattern of expanded participation evident since 1973, with the end of the draft, and intermittent since World War II, when women's role was regularized. The Gulf War as well as recent interventions in Grenada (1983), Libya (1986), and Panama (1989) reveal the contradiction between the United States military's operational needs, which depend upon the expanded participation of women, and the military's patriarchal foundation, which denies that women or anything womanly has a place in the institution. The Grenada and Libya interventions showed that women are a "critical mass" in the U.S. forces that cannot be "left behind" when their units are deployed. The Panama invasion showed that women not left behind are liable to "cross the line" into combat, because the scope of women's participation cannot be controlled on a fluid battlefield. The Gulf War affirmed women as both integral to the proper functioning of the armed forces and as vulnerable to "the horrors of war" as POWs and casualties.

This example shows that women—in limited numbers and with the requisite skills—are good for the military. Is the military good for women? Antifeminists and radical feminists answer negatively, but for different reasons. Antifeminists want to maintain gender boundaries; women's entry into men's domain transgresses these boundaries. Radical feminists reject the integrationist strategy of women's entry into men's domain in favor of a separatist strategy of empowerment.

Liberal feminists, on the other hand, say that the military is good for women, and argue that military service has various payoffs. They see economic benefits from women's military participation in the form of higher wages, better benefits, and more educational opportunities. In many countries, military service carries the additional benefits of land or housing grants and employment training and placement, such as the "veteran's preference" in the United States civil service system. The political benefits of the military include the end of women's "second-class citizen" status; they can achieve full civil rights by fulfilling the same civil obligations borne by men. Thus, liberal feminists encourage women to believe the "warrior mystique," founded upon the martial power and political independence of the "citizen-soldier."

The record of women's service thus far does not support the arguments for economic and political payoffs from women's military participation. Because of exclusion practices, few women qualify for tangible benefits such as land parcels or job preferences; those who do qualify often do not claim these benefits, in part because program administrators may consider women's contributions as marginal, and in part because the veterans themselves believe the programs apply only to their male counterparts. Women who have served, therefore, often fail to benefit proportionately.

If war is simply politics by other means, as Clausewitz has suggested, it is a form of politics that marginalizes women. In highly militarized states, where the military is the government, women's exclusion from military participation effectively blocks them from political participation as well. In moderately and intermediately militarized states, the political impact of women's exclusion from martial occupations may be less apparent but no less significant.

Conventional wisdom holds that the battlefield provides the appropriate place to demonstrate one's capacity for leadership in the political realm, as seen in the cases of United States generals Washington, Grant, and Eisenhower, or of revolutionary leaders such as Cuba's Fidel Castro, for example. Women who seek political posts appear to suffer a decisive disadvantage from military exclusion, even when military service is not a legal prerequisite for governing. In fact, women who have served in their country's armed forces have sometimes been the targets of vituperative slander campaigns, where they are labeled either as unfeminine or unnatural, as "whores or lesbians" who have defied social conventions regarding gender roles. Military service may thus be more of a political liability than an asset for women.

In countries where women's military participation is substantial, their admission to the military ranks has seldom opened doors to national decision-making processes. For example, no woman has yet served on the Joint Chiefs of Staff or as Secretary of Defense or Commander in Chief in the United States. Women who commanded military units in Nicaragua during the civil war were given "political rather than military" assignments in the Sandinista government, in tasks deemed more appropriate for women, such as in the Ministries of Health and Education.

In countries where individual women have attained political prominence and a choice over issues of war and peace, such as Margaret Roberts Thatcher in the United Kingdom and Golda Mabovitch Meir in Israel, it has not been as a reward for military service to the state. Since women are excluded from military service in just over half of all state militaries and participate only marginally in other state militaries, they are perceived as amateurs in matters of national security and defense. In countries where women serve, a woman candidate's military service record is usually not a campaign issue; a man's record frequently is, as the 1988 and 1992 presidential races in the United States illustrated. Clearly, the political payoff for military service for women is limited.

Critical feminists argue that the liberal feminist fascination with the warrior image is dangerous, since the military reflects the racism, sexism, and heterosexism of the larger society. Further, the military insulates these practices behind the wall of "national security," constraining incursions by civil rights activists. The military as an institution successfully resists changes in personnel practices that privilege the dominant racial-ethnic gender group unless military planners recognize that such changes benefit the military mission itself. They then use the language of "women's liberation" to meet the institution's needs and employ gender categories to control women's participation.

A critical feminist perspective sees the expanded military participation of women as a symptom of the militarization of society, not as evidence of women's achievement of "equality." While some women may benefit from the educational or employment opportunities the military service provides, women's increasing presence in the military does not change the institution's fundamentally gendered structure, which at its core is coercive, hierarchical, and patriarchal. In fact, the increasing presence of women helps legitimize the institution by giving it an egalitarian façade. When women accept the "warrior mystique," they soften the military's image as an agent of coercion and destruction, and help promote the myth of the military as a democratic institution, as an "equal opportunity employer" like any other, without reference to its essential purpose: organized killing for political objectives.

In the Gulf War context, the media advertised the "equality" of United States women and men, evidenced by women's military participation, as compared to the "inequality" of Saudi women and men, represented by the veil, by mobility restrictions, and by women's lack of formal political rights. Much was made of the "liberalizing effect" that uniformed United States women would have on gender relations in Saudi Arabia; this further obscured the unequal gender relations in the United States military and the wider society. In the military, these include structural barriers to women's entry and advancement, such as higher recruitment standards, enlistment ceilings, and occupational specialty restrictions based on a rule of "combat exclusion," as well as institutional practices that celebrate masculinity and criticize femininity.

Descriptions of the Desert Shield and Desert Storm operations by United States public officials invariably referred to "our men and women in the Gulf" or "our brave servicemen and women." Servicewomen are thus useful to the military not only because they perform jobs necessary to the military mission, but also because they legitimize that mission. From military planners' perspective, servicewomen are also valuable because they boost the morale of male troops with their "nurturant socialization" and their availability for sexual service: they therefore make war more possible, the killing machine more efficient.

The militarization of any society is a gendered process. The essence of military training consists of the subordination of the individual to the institution, a desensitization to violence, and a dehumanization of the potential opponent. For male recruits, it also includes a process of masculinization where female and feminine are defined as "other" and as unworthy. The military seeks "to make a man out of you" or "to separate the men from the boys," and from the women. Military service constitutes a quintessentially male activity, a confirmation of masculinity, a proof of manhood. The military as an institution is thus sustained by this gender differentiation. The military milieu celebrates and privileges maleness. The marines are still "looking for a few good men."

The only place for women in this environment is that defined by this gender distinction: support and service in traditional female occupations and roles. Within this context, military planners define equality as allowing some women to do some of the important jobs men do (but not all the important jobs—hence the policy of combat exclusion, which maintains the male protector/female protected gender distinction) while simultaneously denying women's ability and worth. The standard to which women must measure up is men; military equality is gendered equality.

The specific training given to men and women, and the particular tasks they are assigned, reinforce gender differences. For women recruits and draftees in most state militaries, training in feminine rather than martial arts prevails. For example, Israeli women soldiers are taught the "regulation way" of applying makeup and how to comport themselves as "an officer and a lady." Even in militaries where women receive weapons training, they are rarely assigned to job specialties that require them to carry and use arms. Generally, weapons and physical training are emphasized as self-defense preparation in the event the unspeakable should happen, that is, that male soldiers could fail to protect them and women might come face-to-face with the enemy.

Like their sisters in the civilian labor force in most countries, servicewomen predominate in clerical, administrative, and support medical specialties such as being a nurse or technician. Unlike their civilian counterparts, military women have not, for the most part, been able to use litigation to protest their exclusion from certain occupations, especially those with the highly contested designation of "combat." Recent challenges to combat exclusion policies in the United States, Canada, and

Israel have redrawn rather than erased the gender boundaries separating military jobs. For example, although after the Gulf War the United States Congress rescinded those sections of the United States Code barring women from combat, United States servicewomen are still excluded from ground combat, submarine billets, special forces, and other assignments. While one court upheld a woman's challenge to the Israeli policy prohibiting women from serving as combat pilots, most military and political officials support continued combat exclusion.

The formalization of women's relation to the military, that is, the shift from auxiliary to regular service, has not secured equal rights or equal treatment for women in any country. Yet the formalization of women's role in the armed forces gives military officials direct control over women as personnel resources; they may use women's skills, talents, and energies as the military deems appropriate. When the boss/officer, usually a man, is one's military "superior," the potential for the abuse and sexual harassment of the employee/soldier, usually a woman, differs from that in the civilian employer-employee relation. His power over her has multiplied not only because of his gender and job title but also because of his rank. She has little immediate recourse: she cannot just quit because that would subject her to prosecution for insubordination or desertion. She may request a transfer but he must approve the request. And she may be frightened into silence by his threat to initiate discharge proceedings against her on the charge that she is a lesbian. If she attempts to lodge a complaint she will likely be told that she will ruin the career chances of a "fine officer" by making such a charge, and will be accused of having initiated the sexual contact.

In militaries where personnel policy excludes gays and lesbians, periodic witch hunts help keep military women in their places: "troublemakers," that is, those who reject male soldiers' sexual advances, who report harassment, who advocate changes in policies considered "women's issues," or otherwise engage in subversive solidarity and "buck the system" are targeted in these roundups. Military personnel policymakers attempt to justify the exclusion of gays/lesbians on the grounds that their presence in the ranks constitutes a national security risk and has a chilling effect on morale and recruitment. These rationalizations mask the heterosexism and homophobia of the policymakers and give them a tool to determine the number and kind of women who will be permitted to serve.

Thus, whether she is straight or gay, the servicewoman's sexuality becomes a weapon the military establishment uses to control her. A military career can hardly be considered, therefore, as a vehicle for women's empowerment, as the liberal feminists have argued. Instead of expending our energies on "making women equal" within the state military apparatus, feminists must work to dismantle the structure of the military institution and the destructive foreign policy it carries out.

We must begin by publicly challenging the myth of the egalitarian military and by working to provide women, especially working-class women and women of color, with real alternatives to military service as a way "up and out." The "easy victory" in the Gulf War will make these tasks more difficult, but the war's devastation has touched the lives of many, and the urge to heal these wounds brings hope. For the many unidentified women who were among the "collateral damage" of the precision bombing and Iraqi occupation, the effort comes too late. But we can and must deconstruct the "warrior mystique" and build in its place a positive concept of citizenship and equality.

Chapter Thirteen

Women Munitions Makers, War, and Citizenship

Angela Woollacott

In this century women in many nations have moved from being completely excluded from the armed forces (apart from a few military nursing units) to being included, if not equally, in the military. While technical issues remain about women's exact participation in combat, women have essentially gone from noncombatants to warriors.

For many who believed that women are more inclined than men toward pacifism, and that this would help secure the peace, women's inclusion in the armed forces has been a disturbing historical development. As democratic states have linked citizenship to war participation, women have embraced that participation to show their patriotism and to promote their bids for citizenship.

Abundant evidence from Britain's role in the First World War supports this case. Evaluating this historical episode compels us to consider the relationships among gender, citizenship, and war participation in a democratic state. The massive recruitment of civilians for the total effort of World War I opened up direct war participation in Britain (and elsewhere) far beyond the bounds of the regular armed forces. In the process, the gendering of patriotic involvement became negotiable. While the primary, heroic, mythical figure of the soldier remained resolutely male, the introduction of women's paramilitary organizations (the Women's Army Auxiliary Corps, the Women's Royal Naval Service, and the Women's Royal Air Force) in the war's final years raised questions about the masculine domain of soldiering.

As women approached (in more than one sense) the battle zone in their supportive roles, clerical and transport functions were no longer exclusively masculine preserves. At some remove from the battle front, but far more numerous and even more directly involved in propagating the war, women and their role in making the munitions of war transgressed notions of war as a masculine enterprise. Much as the working men of Britain were expected to join up and go off to fight for king and country, sacrificing their lives if necessary, so too were working women expected to join up, go off, and lay down their lives if necessary in the critical jobs in industry.

The poster that proclaimed "On Her Their Lives Depend" sought to draw women into munitions factories by glamorizing the munitions worker's patriotic importance. But its message became more than hyperbole, particularly in the wake of the May 1915 "shells scandal" when the press attacked the government for providing the army with an inadequate supply of munitions. The roughly one million women munitions workers were on the production frontline of the war: they made the guns, shells, explosives, aircraft, and other materiel that supplied the war at the front. Such workers found it difficult to embrace the pacifist opposition to war that was available to some nurses, VADs (Voluntary Aid Detachment workers), and ambulance drivers.

Women munitions makers were utterly implicated in the "making" of war. Most of them were probably comfortable with their direct involvement in propagating war; most were not pacifists. Besides earning a far better wage than most other women workers, munitions workers had the satisfaction of directly helping the armed forces by providing them with critically necessary ammunition, weapons or equipment. "My husband is fighting at the front, and I should like to make cartridges for him," one soldier's wife wrote to *The Daily Telegraph* in March 1915 (*Daily Telegraph*, 1915:777). Another worker, interviewed by the *Sunday Times* in July 1916, said: "Dad's in the Navy, and I applied for work in a danger room, where I tie the cordite, for I feel that with every day I work I am helping him. Lots of the girls whose men are out there want to do work that will help to kill Germans and end the war" (Moore, 1916).

Some enjoyed thinking about the firing of the weapons they were creating, such as the "Detonator Plug Girl" who in *The War-Worker* in September 1918 imagined the life span of a detonator plug she made, calling it "a dear little thing," describing "his" creation in quasi-sexual terms, and indicating in the end that she foresaw for "him" a situation where "many were sent to their last, long rest" and where "what remains of him lies alone unknown and forgotten in a foreign land" (Detonator Plug Girl, 1918:66).

Such belligerence is not surprising, since women had been imbued with the imperialist and nationalist moral code of the Edwardian and prewar years, just as had the men who went off to fight. Most of the working class in this period expressed an imperialist patriotism that easily lent itself to militarism.

For a working-class woman, munitions work provided a means of patriotic participation. The conscription of men into the armed forces began as a highly controversial political issue in Britain, yet when conscription was finally introduced in January 1916, the possibility of an equivalent system for women was also raised. This idea never gained currency largely because it was unnecessary. Women had entered industry, shifted to munitions jobs, took up charitable works, and joined the paramilitary forces with resolution and energy.

Economic forces, patriotic propaganda, and the loosening of employer prejudices and trade union restrictions successfully allowed the massive entry of women into wartime industries. The power of imperialist and nationalist discourses was so strong that there were many more women who viewed the war as an opportunity than women who opposed it.

In some ways, the women munitions workers' experience did resemble the military. The hostels built to house them near the factories resembled barracks. Women worked long hours on regular shifts six and sometimes seven days a week, were disciplined by various agents of authority, wore uniforms, and were surrounded by calls to work harder, to increase production, and thus to help to win the war. At least at Woolwich Arsenal in Southeast London, women workers were known to the office by their number rather than by their name. All over Britain, the factories in which women worked were often unheated, deafeningly noisy, full of noxious fumes and other dangers, located either in industrial urban areas or in remote countrysides, and surrounded by fields of mud.

Many women munitions workers received the Order of the British Empire for their bravery during explosions or accidents, and for injuries they suffered. On 20 April 1918 a special service for London munitions workers was held at St. Paul's Cathedral, during which the "Last Post" was played for those who had died. They were recognized in the charitable works of middle- and upper-class women, who would knit for the troops and sell flowers in order to build huts for women workers.

This all adds up to a female experience of war, a war endured and fought in the close, grinding confines of the factory. Women's participation in war has been underimagined because it has lacked the visibility and traditional veneration associated with warriors. Women's work as munitions makers has usually been viewed by historians as an aberration from normal employment patterns rather than as concrete involvement in war.

To the extent that feminist scholars have embraced pacifism and its interrelationship with feminism, we have been hard-pressed ideologically to evaluate women's work in munitions factories. Making the munitions of war was not a liberating or inherently good process for women. Women's increased participation in war should not be a feminist goal. Nevertheless, making munitions is what working women did as part of the war effort, replete with its dangers, discomforts, moral problems, and gender transgressions.

A connection existed between women's work in munitions factories and their claim to citizenship. This particularly involved the right to vote, which was partially awarded to them in 1918, but also other legal and economic goals as well. In the June 1916 *Ladies Home Journal*, H. G. Wells recognized the connection:

> And in the munitions factories, in the handling of heavy and often difficult machinery, and in adaptability and inventiveness and enthusiasm and steadfastness, their achievement has been astonishing. . . . They have revolutionized the estimate of their economic importance, and it is scarcely too much to say that when in the long run the military strength of the Allies bears down the strength of Germany it will be this superiority of our women . . . which has tipped the balance of this war. Those women have won the Vote. Not the most frantic outbursts of militancy after this war can prevent their getting it. The girls who have faced death and wounds so gallantly in our cordite factories—there is a not inconsiderable loss of dead and wounded from these places— have killed forever the poor argument that women should not vote because they had no military value. Indeed, they have killed every argument against their subjection. (Wells, 1916:60)

Women munitions workers did not themselves explicitly link their work to claims of citizenship, but they did valorize their contributions to prosecuting the war and the military value of their work.

To cheer themselves during the long monotony of their shifts, especially at night, women munitions workers sang the songs of wartime popular culture. Some of the songs were the same as those sung by soldiers while marching. Women munitions workers also made up songs, set to well-known tunes, where they placed themselves as the heroines of the lyrics. They did so partly to commemorate their own work group, to distinguish themselves from the women workers in the next shed or factory. Their invented lyrics often portrayed themselves as performing a direct, heroic role in the business of the war, in the bloodshed and vanquishing of the enemy. They indicate the women's vivid awareness of the nature of their work and of the war at the front, along with their desire to valorize their own role in it.

To some of them, the danger in their work helped prove their courage and patriotism. Caroline Rennles, for example, recalled in an oral history interview recorded by the Imperial War Museum that despite being severely discolored from their work with TNT, she and her friends blithely disregarded the physical injury the work was doing to them. Even when the train conductors on their way to work would direly predict that they, the young women workers, had only two years to live, they would reply: "Well, we don't mind dying for our country" (Rennles n.d.: 9–10).

To underscore for workers the direct connection between the shells they made and the war at the front, factories displayed posters of aerial photographs of German trenches on the western front before and after bombardment, with the caption "Munitions workers see the effect of your work!" By repeatedly assuring women munitions workers of the national importance of their work, such propaganda was critical in forging their sense of participation in the war effort. They increasingly believed they were playing an important public role.

The wider reading public was also led to believe that munitions workers were performing a central role in the war effort. In March 1917 the journal *The Englishwoman* published a one-act play entitled "The Munition Worker," the dramatic tension of which centered on "Tina," a skilled shell worker who is dying of consumption but who refuses to be placed in a rest home. She explains that when she heard she could work in a munitions factory,

> God was talkin' to me, and He'd never done that before, 'cos of course I'm too poor for the likes of Him, and He said, "Tina, you must go along and make shells for your country, and never think you won't have the strength," He says, "I'll give you the strength," and to this day He's given it to me, Matron, and there's nothing you can say to me—nothing—for my country wants me! (Holmes, 1917:264)

A doctor and a matron urge Tina to take a spell at the rest home for munitions workers, but she refuses because there is nothing in the world she wants to do more than to keep turning out as many shells as possible, and thus help the men at the front to kill the enemy. Finally, they resign themselves to the fact that she "will die as surely on the battlefield as any of our heroes," but comfort themselves with the thought that Tina's "spirit is the spirit of a whole nation soaring towards Heaven."

For some women, munitions work was a way of proving their strength. Miss O. M. Taylor related her feeling that "though small I considered myself equal to any man, having carried, occasionally, sacks of wheat weighing eighteen stones. . . . I had always wished I had been born a boy and never more so than at this period. I really wanted to be a soldier" (Taylor, 1914–18:1). After working in munitions for a while, she joined the Women's Army Auxiliary Corps (WAACs), an option that became available only in 1917.

Only a minority of women in munitions factories actively sought the franchise. Yet women munitions workers believed themselves to be discharging their duty to their country and, in so doing, to be pulling their weight as well as any man. Such equality of participation in the national effort, they assumed, established some claim that their interests be considered in the future. The blatant rebuttal of this claim during the war's demobilization and the immediate postwar period later angered many women who had been munitions workers.

Women knew that they had undertaken jobs considered "men's work," that they had performed these jobs creditably, and in so doing had made a significant contribution to a war effort that could, therefore, not be considered solely the undertaking of men. They knew they had performed critical work under some considerable danger.

In song lyrics, women munitions workers represented themselves as "the girls with yellow hands" (reflecting the jaundice caused by TNT poisoning) who were "in the fighting line," "willing to do or die." One song equated the "boys smiling though they rush against a barb'ed trench" with the "girls smiling though destruction hovers o'er their bench" (Percival, 1967:25; Kinnaird, 1925:162). Thus these women staked a claim, not only to their equal contribution but also to their equal courage and patriotic fearlessness. Women munitions workers saw themselves as vitally linked to their men at the front.

By exploring the options newly opened to them by the war's demands and dislocations, and by valorizing their own involvement in waging the war, women munitions workers participated in World War I in ways that undermined assumptions that war was men's exclusive domain. By playing an important, publicly acclaimed role in Britain's first nationwide war, where distinctions between the armed forces and the civilians at home were more blurred than ever before, women workers laid a claim to citizenship and more equitable treatment in the work force.

These experiences raise questions about the relationship between war participation and citizenship in the modern industrial democratic state. Since the eighteenth century, constitutional states have made the bearing of arms to protect the state an integral part of a citizen's duties. While women were excluded from joining military forces in Euro-American states before the twentieth century, the subsequent mechanization of "total" wars demanded more extensive popular involvement.

During the same time period during which women have first been drawn into making munitions, then into paramilitary organizations, and eventually into regular military forces, they have also been gradually (even if not yet equally) incorporated into legal, electoral, and economic citizenship. One of these processes could not have occurred without the other. The munitions workers of the Great War show us that even immediately prior to gaining the vote, women's direct involvement in war helped them make claims to legal and economic citizenship.

Rather than clinging to now discredited notions that women are somehow essentially pacifist, and worry therefore that women's inclusion in the armed forces will undermine pacifist hopes, we should instead consider the equation between citizenship and war service. It should hardly surprise us that women have followed the same roads and embraced the same symbols in pursuing citizenship that men have.

REFERENCES

Cooke, Miriam, and Angela Woollacott (eds.). 1993. *Gendering War Talk*. Princeton, NJ: Princeton University Press.

Daily Telegraph. 23 March 1915. In *Common Cause* 6, 26 March 1915, p. 777.

Detonator Plug Girl. 1918. "Fuze 106: The Adventures of a Detonator Plug." *War Worker* 2, no. 4 (September 1918).

Gould, Jenny. 1987. "Women's Military Services in First World War Britain." In Margaret Higonnet et al. (eds.), *Behind the Lines: Gender and the Two World Wars*. New Haven: Yale University Press.

Holmes, Alec. 1917. "The Munition Worker: A Play in One Scene." *The Englishwoman*, 33 March.

Kinnaird, Emily. 1925. *Reminiscences*. London: John Murray.

Moore, Mary Macleod. 1916. "Women as Munitions Workers." *Sunday Times*, 23 July.

Percival, Arthur. 1967. "The Faversham Gunpowder Industry and Its Development." In *Faversham Papers*, no. 4. Kent: The Faversham Society.

Rennles, Caroline. n.d. Interview. Department of Sund Records, London: Imperial War Museum, 000566/07, pp. 9–10.

Summers, Anne. 1988. *Angels and Citizens: British Women as Military Nurses 1854–1914*. London: Routledge and Kegan Paul.

Taylor, Miss O. M. 1914–18. "Recollections of the Great War, 1914–1918." Department of Documents, 83/17/1, London: Imperial War Museum.

Wells, H. G. 1916. "The Women and the War." *Ladies Home Journal*, June 1916, p. 60.

Woollacott, Angela. 1994. *On Her Their Lives Depend: Munitions Workers in the Great War*. Berkeley: University of California Press.

Chapter Fourteen

Women Warriors/Women Peacemakers
Will the Real Feminists Please Stand Up!

Ilene Rose Feinman

Right wing opponents to United States women's progress in the armed forces consistently point to feminist agitation as the cause of that progress, citing the success and visibility of women soldiers as one more example of feminist conspiracies to undermine the patriarchal nuclear family and the patriarchal state. Yet, there is no strong feminist presence in the push to get women in the forces' ranks, and feminists have traditionally been silent about or even hostile toward women's presence in the forces. Feminist antimilitarists have an opportunity to take advantage of this rhetoric to question the socially constructed and institutionally protected masculinity of the forces. However, there is a slight problem. Feminist antimilitarists and right wing opponents to women in the forces share some rhetorical ground.

Feminist antimilitarist opposition to the Persian Gulf War was redolent with rhetoric associating militarism and masculinity. Demonstration placards, for example, read: "War is a dick thing," "Fighting for peace is like fucking for virginity," "No more missile envy please," "Real men pull out early," "Read my labia, no war for oil."

Right wing response to women's presence in the Gulf War is most aptly summed up by Phyllis Schlafly, arch conservative antifeminist. Asked to respond to the numbers of women deployed in the Gulf War she said: "Have we lost our manhood?"

I have spent much of my activist life arguing that the military is saturated with destructive versions of masculinity. In my work teaching nonviolence preparations and participating in nonviolent direct action I have readily, albeit ironically, used the powerful symbols and stories of women as nonviolent. I have contributed to the myth that women are the antithesis to the culture of militarism as gunboat masculinity. In short, I have identified myself, through my practice, as a feminist antimilitarist.

During the deployments for and enactment of the Persian Gulf War, in 1990–91, I was organizing antiwar demonstrations and teaching both nonviolence preparations and a class on Gender and Politics. I found it increasingly difficult to use the framework of an automatic, easily recognizable linkage between feminism and antimilitarism in the face of women's increased presence, pride, and visibility in the United States' armed forces.

Women comprised 12 percent of the activated forces and yet they were all over the media (Becraft, 1991). To this day, the rage over women in the forces is not about the numbers of women (yet to exceed 15 percent overall), but about the challenge women pose to traditional masculinist military culture. This challenge, because of the centrality of martial citizenship to full citizenship claims, also reflects a challenge to the larger social and political culture in the United States.[1]

Feminist antimilitarists are faced with an opportunity to rethink movement strategies and rhetorical frameworks that have previously relied upon models of femaleness, however ironically deployed, as symbols for peace. This opportunity holds promise for a deepened understanding of how United States citizens envision themselves as a political community, freed from the constraints of particular and binary role models, and the redefinition of citizenship based on social justice and peace.

Two central conditions shape my analysis of women in relationship to the armed forces. The first is that for women of all colors in the United States the prospects for independent financial prosperity are slim to none: women still comprise the majority of adults below the poverty line, white women can still expect to earn, at best, between 67 and 72 cents for every dollar earned by a white man, and women of color fall 15 to 20 cents on the dollar below white women.

The military has been suggesting to women that they can trade time in the forces for a wage-earning skill and a sense of belonging and importance in the nation's political economy. Women's aspirations for equality in economy and citizenship are being utilized by the forces to fill the ranks that young white men have been abandoning since the close of the draft in 1974.[2] Women are specifically targeted as recruits, with the lure of high-technology training and a heightened sense of accomplishment and mastery, if the recruitment ad messages are to be believed. Over 85 percent of the armed forces' jobs are now—technically speaking—open to women, and yet, in the 1990s the Defense Department is in the process of personnel downsizing. The areas hardest hit by this reduction in personnel are the least technically advanced, and largely in the army, which is where the highest proportion of women of color are employed/deployed (Moore, 1991).

This job attraction has another serious downside. Even though sexual harassment is technically against the law, women in the forces still experience a great deal of harassment (as we have seen in the recent revelations from army training camps). While obvious harassment is being addressed in the law, albeit unevenly between men and women, a more subtle form of sexual harassment goes unchecked. This form of sexual harassment is structured in the forces' policies against lesbians that are frequently used to target and discipline women of any sexuality whose accomplishments are not properly contained by traditional notions of femininity, i.e., gals cannot really cut it, so if they do succeed they must not be *real* gals (Bennecke and Dodge, 1990).

The second condition that shapes my work is the further democratization of citizenship. Civil rights activisms begun in African American civil rights claims from the 1950s on are bedrock for the possibilities of democratizing citizenship. Subsequent civil rights activisms, for racial and ethnic groups, for women of all colors, and for lesbian, bisexual, and gay citizens have contributed to understandings of, fueled public debate about, and generally challenged the military with varying degrees of democratizing effect on policy. Racially hierarchized citizenship was contested in the forces as early as the Civil War, and more directly in World War II with the subsequent desegregation of the forces.

Since the mid-1970s and early 1980s, the U.S. military has been a central arena for contesting the extent of women's citizenship, most visibly with women's inclusion as volunteer soldiers and their admission to the military academies. Women's participation has also been contested in an odd format through a challenge to the draft's constitutionality via its exclusion of women in Rostker v. Goldberg (453 United States 57, 1981), first brought in 1971 as an act of draft resistance and revived in 1981 as a response to women's renewed exclusion from the draft (President Jimmy Carter had proposed that the draft be reinstated to include women). The propriety of men as draftees was affirmed by presiding justice William Rehnquist, who decided that the Fifth Amendment concerns of equal protection were overruled by strong government interest: discrimination to have a combat-ready military was acceptable.

My analysis of women's relationship to the military is informed by the assumptions upon which United States citizenship has been founded. In the framing of the Constitution and the debates surrounding it, martial service was seen as one of the linchpins of citizenship. Centerpiece to a host of rights and responsibilities, martial service was the ultimate form of patriotism and critical to male prestige and honor.[3] Tied to notions of liberal republicanism, martial service was one of a citizen's several primary duties which he exchanged for the rights of a fully franchised citizen.[4] The martial citizen had as his mandate the protection of the interests of the state, including the safety of its women and children. Martial valor and sacrifice were men's ultimate proof of worthiness for the rights of citizenship.

This sense of patriotic and moral proving ground for citizenship is one of the main draws for women joining the military. To fully achieve the logic of "equality" as citizens with men, women feel drawn to engage in the same contract of rights and responsibilities. This raises the issue of what equality means for women, why women should or should not want it, and how much the term can be extracted from its creation in relation to male models of citizenship as *public* that have relied upon female models of citizenship as *private*.

Martial valor remains the quintessential moment of citizenship, as the recent film *Independence Day* reminds us with its veteran Gulf War pilot, turned heroic president, fighting again to restore Peace. This film was about heroic men—a black male soldier and a Jewish scientist save the day. Curiously, in its representation as a future history, there are no women combat pilots, and no women pilots at all, even in the urgent final scenes where the forces recruit any and all pilots, resorting to a drunk male Vietnam War veteran (who dies as a martyr). Both citizenship and martial valor retain a strong impulse of masculinism. The important task for feminists interested in the military and citizenship is to develop our understanding of their linkage and participate in reshaping it. The struggle to define women's roles as citizens via the drafting of women (or not) and the assignment of women to combat both signify an interruption in what was previously considered uniquely masculine terrain. Feminist antimilitarists need to step in here and enlarge the terms of the debate.

Right wing opponents to women soldiers are correct in worrying that masculine martial citizenship is eroding, but it is eroding very slowly. Certainly public opinion, activism, and policy changes encouraging women soldiers are eroding this connection, as are the growing networks of communication around topics of women in the armed forces. These networks are participating in the current debates and producing women's military histories through a proliferation of biographies, autobiographies, and archival research. On-line networks such as the MINERVA listserv and H-WAR are creating instant information and debate arenas with a mixture of active duty, reservist, veteran, and nonservice-member scholarly participation. However, this is not antimilitarist work. These networks mainly support the development and distribution of information about women in the forces, recovering and validating women's long participation in the forces, and serving as conversation nets over current issues.

The Persian Gulf War generated a wide-ranging response to women's increased visibility as soldiers. Feminist antimilitarist analyses of the war complicated feminist responses to women soldier pilots who were lobbying Congress for combat positions. Congress's formal response illustrates my point that the language of social conservatives and the language of feminist antimilitarists can, and has, dangerously converged over assigning the martial to the male.

After the Persian Gulf War, women's war performance and extensive lobbying by veteran women pilots gave Colorado Democratic representative Pat Schroeder the necessary support to successfully attach a bill to the Defense Appropriations Act for 1993, which ended the exclusion of women pilots from combat missions. The bill, PL 102-190, passed with an addendum that a commission be convened to study the ramifications of the change. The Presidential Commission on the Assignment of Women in the Armed Forces was convened in 1992, appointed by President Bush. Its mandate was to determine whether the congressional vote to repeal the ban on women combat flyers should stand.

The formal report that emerged from the commission's research symbolizes what is at stake in the debates over women in the armed forces. Feminist antimilitarists can learn much from its pages (Presidential Commission on Women in the Armed Forces, 1993; hereafter PCR). Coming on the heels of the Persian Gulf War and the Tailhook sexual harassment investigations, and in the midst of the furor raised by Clinton's broken promise to lift the ban on lesbian and gay soldiers, this commission was embedded in one of history's most extended challenges to military culture. The report itself was published in the wake of George Bush's loss of the presidential election and a shift of the presidency to the Democratic Party for the first time in twelve years.

The Presidential Commission's report displays a clear struggle over the terms of social organization keyed to the register of "traditional family values." Concerns over family values are deeply inscribed in the report. Several of the members of the commission have histories with organizations promoting "family values," such as the Center for Military Preparedness, Concerned Women for America, and the Heritage Foundation. In the report, the language of feminist antimilitarism converges with the language of social conservatives. This intersection carefully reinscribes the differences between women's and men's social roles: men are warriors, women are peacemakers, men are self-sacrificers protecting the women and children, women are homemakers and reproducers. The thread of "family values" ties together the struggles over women and combat with the struggles over lesbian and gay soldiers openly serving in the forces. The presumptive family in this scheme is organized around particular models of family—typically heterosexual, nuclear, and white. It also places the women at home in a proper family. Thus, any woman deployed is not a real woman (read mother).

Commissioner Sarah White, in her statement of opposition to women in combat, highlighted the central theme for the conservative members of the commission. She wrote:

> I also believe an element of why men assume the combatant role is that, contrary to the opinions of some women, men take on that brutal responsibility out of self-sacrifice; it is because they do respect, and truly care for women. It is the ultimate act of love and self-sacrifice to lay down one's life for another. Along with millions of other women, I am grateful for the roles men selflessly assume. In no way do we consider ourselves second class citizens, or of less value to society, just because we do not participate as combatants in our Nation's wars. (PCR, 1993:121)

The commission's hearings included walkouts by conservative members when they did not approve of testimonies, and conservative dismissal of pro-women in combat testimony, claiming they were coerced by a few ambitious career military women. In one instance, on live telecast, Elaine Donnelly set up a tower of jenga blocks to represent the armed forces and proceeded to pull out one block after another in an attempt to demonstrate the weakening of the forces by women's presence. The tower refused to fall (Matthews, 1992). This proved to be an ominous foreshadowing of Donnelly's inability to stop the legislation giving women access to combat jobs.

Some commissioners expressed disillusionment with their service on the commission due in part to the preceding antics. Mary E. Clarke, Major General, USA (ret.), submitted a separate commissioner's statement in the commission report in which she recounts:

> Early on in the deliberations, it became clear that a number of the Commissioners had come with a set agenda and no amount of facts or testimony would change their minds for expanding opportunities for women in the military. This was evident in their questioning techniques of those whose testimony they thought might support women in combat, absenting themselves when they knew testimony would not support their views, and their insistence upon using equal opportunity as a red herring rather than recognizing women's capabilities and contributions to the military services. . . . (PCR, 1993: 98)

Political pundits, such as David Horowitz, testified that the repeal of the combat exclusion was simply to appease women due to Tailhook, and was bowing to radical feminists and a small group of aggressive career-minded women soldiers (the flyers who lobbied Congress for the repeal). Horowitz, who writes extensively on the feminist attack on the armed forces and other institutions, is an ex-New Leftist and current president of the Center for the Study of Popular Culture in Studio City, California (see especially, Horowitz, 1992). He states for the record: "*Without statistics and without detailed reporting from the field* . . . American ability to wage war has already been seriously weakened by the deployment of relatively large numbers of women troops to an overseas battlefield, even without sending them into combat" (PCR, 1993: 59–60) [italics mine].

Rather than acknowledge the actual changes in training and expertise that were the groundwork for repealing the combat exclusions, those opposed sought to demean the policy shift, insisting that women's full inclusion could result only from lowered standards. As former Secretary of Defense Richard Cheney was quoted in testimony: "We're not a social welfare agency" (PCR, 1993: 43).

Martial sacrifice is held up by White and other conservative panel members in their dissent to indicate men's valiant martial citizenship as unique and inherently heterosexually masculine. This is the traditional perspective of the circumscribed role for both men and women in martial service. Even with the process of structural and broader social change that has brought women into the forces in greater numbers, the belief that martial service is "a guy thing" is still quite strong—on both sides of the fence. However, feminist activists should be careful about associating themselves with right wing analyses that rely on notions of the traditional nuclear family and the "naturalness" of masculinity and femininity.

As the conservative commission members put it in their concluding statements:

> Those skeptical about assigning women to combat . . . have primarily focused on the needs of the military and combat effectiveness, as well as *deep-seated cultural and family values millions of Americans hold and are still teaching their children* . . . those values can be summed up in one simple phrase: Good men respect and defend women. (PCR, 1993: 46)[italics mine]

The Presidential Commission voted 8 to 7 against women as fighter pilots and 10 to 4 against women in ground combat. Yet, it did not become the guiding document for policy changes regarding women and combat. Instead, the report underscored the deep divisions and obstacles remaining for women in integrating themselves to the forces.

On 28 April 1993, under the new Democratic president, Defense Secretary Les Aspin presented his formal response to the Presidential Commission with his "Memorandum on the Assignment of Women in the Armed Forces." The Secretary instructed that all except direct ground combat positions be opened to women consistently across the reserve and active forces. By September 1995 (Department of Defense, 1995) women comprised 12.7 percent of all active-duty forces. Female officers were 13.2 percent of all officers. White women officers were 78.6 percent of all female officers and 55.1 percent of enlisted women. African American women were 13.2 percent of all female officers and 34 percent of enlisted women. Hispanic women were 2.9 percent of female officers and 5.8 percent of enlisted women. The category "Other Unknown" reports 5.4 percent female officers and 5 percent enlisted women.

Until and unless we as a nation move beyond martial politics, women have just as strong a set of rights and responsibilities to bear martial service as do men. Feminist antimilitarists in the United States need to participate in the debates about women soldiers. We must account for the economic and citizenship incentives to join (as more than false consciousness or a poor draft), argue for the explicit recognition of women's equal responsibilities as citizens to become conscripted members of the forces, and oppose right wing attempts to keep women out of the service by reinscribing women's need for protection and propensity for peacemaking. These understandings are critical if we are to build conversations across the divide of women soldiers and women peace activists and to develop a more nuanced approach to antimilitarism.

More particularly, those of us who are feminist antimilitarists need to insist that the debates over women's roles be more than questions of equal opportunity/responsibility but that they be questions regarding the very construction of democratic citizenship and the further realization of citizenship activated through social justice and peace.

NOTES

1. I treat this analysis at length in my dissertation manuscript, "Brutal Responsibilities and Second Class Citizens: Women Soldiers, Martial Citizenship, and Feminist Antimilitarism" (University of California, Santa Cruz, 1997).

2. See Martin Binkin and Shirley J. Bach, *Women and the Military* (Washington, DC: Brookings Institute, 1977), for the classic study of the changed demographics of personnel in the All Volunteer Forces and the logic for recruiting women.

3. For a careful history of the causal links between soldiering and citizenship, see Linda Kerber, " 'May All Our Citizens Be Soldiers, and All Our Soldiers Citizens': The Ambiguities of Female Citizenship in the New Nation," in J. Challinor and R. Beisner, eds., *Arms at Rest* (New York: Greenwood Press, 1987), 1–21. Also see Linda Kerber, *Women of the Republic: Intellect and Ideology in Revolutionary America* (Chapel Hill: University of North Carolina Press, 1980). Cynthia Enloe has done extensive work to demonstrate the connections between soldiering and citizenship in the contemporary period, and especially to uncover the enormous work that goes into constructing masculinity in martial practice. Her analysis undergirds much of my understanding of gender and the military. See especially *Does Khaki Become You? The Militarization of Women's Lives* (Boston: South End Press, 1983); "The Politics of Constructing the American Woman Soldier as a Professionalized First Class Citizen: Some Lessons from the Gulf War," *Minerva: Quarterly Report on Women and the Military* 10, no. 1 (Spring 1992): 14–31; and *The Morning After: Sexual Politics at the End of the Cold War* (Berkeley: University of California Press, 1994). For studies of the masculinist culture of the armed forces, see Kenneth Karst, "The Pursuit of Manhood and the Desegregation of the Armed Forces," *UCLA Law Review* 38, no. 3 (1991): 499–581; and Bennecke and Dodge 1990.

4. My initial understandings of martial citizenship have come from Gwendolyn Mink in the process of teaching with her on the development of democratic practice in the history of the United States.

REFERENCES

Becraft, Carolyn. 1991. *Women in the Armed Services: The War in the Persian Gulf.* Washington DC: Women's Research and Education Institute.

Bennecke, Michelle, and Kirsten Dodge. 1990. "Military Women in Nontraditional Fields: Casualties in the Armed Forces War on Homosexuals." *Harvard Women's Law Journal* 13 (Spring): 215–250.

Department of Defense. 1995. "Distribution of Active Duty Forces by Service, Rank, Sex, and Ethnic Group" (DMDC-3035).

Horowitz, David. 1992. "The Feminist Assault on the Military." Studio City, CA: The Center for the Study of Popular Culture. Reprinted in *National Review* 44, no. 19 (October 5, 1992): 46.

Matthews, William. 1992. "Don't Expect Sweeping Changes for Women," *Navy Times* (November 2).

Moore, Brenda. 1991. "African American Women in the U.S. Military," *Armed Forces and Society* 17, no. 3: 363–384.

Presidential Commission on Women in the Armed Forces. 1993. Report to the President. Washington DC: Government Printing Office (November 15).

Chapter Fifteen

The Expanding Role of Women in United Nations Peacekeeping

Janet Beilstein

Since 1987, United Nations peacekeeping missions have expanded, become increasingly complex, and now account for the largest share of the U.N.'s expenditures. Today, peacekeeping missions include nonmilitary components for preventive diplomacy, conflict resolution, peacemaking, and post-conflict peace building. These civilian components have broadened the range of personnel and skills beyond those of the traditional "blue helmets." Women have taken advantage of expanded opportunities and are serving in new roles, as legal and political advisors, civilian police officers, election and human rights monitors, information specialists, and administrators. They have promoted national reconciliation and democracy, repatriated refugees, and delivered humanitarian assistance. Women have served as team leaders and decision makers, supervising international and local personnel.

The greatest presence of women in peacekeeping has occurred in the twelve missions established after 1989. In contrast, those with the fewest women were established more than fifteen years ago and had limited participation by civilians. In 1993, eleven of the nineteen U.N. peacekeeping missions had significant civilian participation in which one-third (33%) of the mission staff were women (Women 2000, 1995: 4). In comparison, from 1957 until 1991, women comprised 5 to 23 percent of the international civilian staff for which data are available (United Nations, 1994). Further increases in women's participation will occur if the Secretary-General's 1995 recommendation to the General Assembly of 50 percent women in U.N. civilian peacekeeping posts is fulfilled (United Nations Economic and Social Council, 1995).

In 1995, the highest percentage of women (48.7%) was in the election-monitoring and human rights mission in Guatemala (MINUGUA). Many mission applicants from outside the United Nations were women lawyers who were concerned with human rights, were well informed about indigenous issues, and related well to Guatemalan human rights workers, the majority of whom were women. Another human rights monitoring operation, the International Civilian Mission in Haiti (MICIVIH), featured 39.2 percent women in comparison to 12.9 percent in the military-observer mission (UNMIH). The multipurpose U.N. observer mission in El Salvador (ONUSAL), with human rights monitoring, police, and military mandates, had 37 percent women (United Nations Division for the Advancement of Women, 1995: 8).

The percentage of women civilian staff in twenty-six U.N. peacekeeping and observer missions seems to be rising; however, they do not show the same level of women professionals as the general service staff. One mission for which an indication of the level of women's participation is available is the United Nations Preventive Deployment Force (UNPREDEP) in Macedonia. While the percentage of women civilian mission staff has risen to 57.9 percent in 1996, they are serving mainly in administrative, public relations, information, and secretarial positions. Very few women occupy positions that deal with high-level professional, substantive, and policy matters, which are still very much a male domain.

Out of twenty-five special representatives of the Secretary-General in peacekeeping missions, Margaret Anstee (of the U.K.) has been the only woman. She headed the United Nations Angola Verification Mission (UNAVEM II) in February 1992, coordinating U.N. activities in conjunction with Peace Accords and serving as chief of mission until civil war erupted in October 1992, in the wake of elections (Information Notes, 1995: 24). Angela King (of Jamaica) has been the only other woman to serve in a senior leadership position, as chief of mission and later as deputy special representative in the all-civilian United Nations Observer Mission in South Africa (UNOMSA).

Cases of Women's Expanding Contributions to Peacekeeping

The first and best example of an operation in which women played significant roles was the U.N. Transition Assistance Group (UNTAG) in Namibia from 1989 until 1990. UNTAG's mandate included military and civilian functions, such as demobilizing armed groups, repatriating refugees, releasing political prisoners, monitoring police activities, and supervising voter education and elections (UNTAG, 1991). In the mission selection process, there was a deliberate policy of recruiting women at all levels (United Nations Division for the Advancement of Women, 1995). The Secretary-General's special representative to Namibia, Martti Ahtisaari, was from the Nordic region, where women have played a prominent role in political decision making and where significant progress has been achieved toward gender equality. The special representative enabled more women to participate and engage in decision making. Consequently, women comprised 60 percent of UNTAG's professional staff (Stiehm, 1994: 8), five served at the director level, and three were regional directors (United Nations Economic and Social Council, 1995: 20). One director at a strategic border post in the northern Namibia region supervised eight hundred peacekeeping troops and found that being female gave her the element of surprise when interacting with South African police (Stiehm, 1994: 8).

In comparison with UNTAG, women's participation in the U.N. Mission/Transitional Authority in Cambodia (UNAMIC/UNTAC) was disappointing. From 1991 until 1993, UNAMIC/UNTAC had a multipurpose mandate including administration, human rights and electoral monitoring, military peacekeeping and civilian police functions, and refugee repatriation and rehabilitation (Stiehm, 1994: 8). Of the 22,000 UNTAC personnel, the vast majority were male peacekeepers. Although there were many women among the civilian international staff, none held decision-making positions. Men held all the senior decision-making posts, namely, seven at the "Director-2" level, and thirteen regional directors at "Professional 5" and "Director-1" levels (United Nations Economic and Social Council, 1995: 20). The lack of women in high-level positions drew criticism, particularly from professional women within the U.N. system.

Few women served in the military and civilian police contingents of UNTAC. Allegations of sexual abuse and mistreatment of women and children by male military and police personnel were made by Cambodians. Protests were made against the mistreatment of Cambodian women as prostitutes. The U.N. responded by creating a Community Relations Office. Particularly important in UNTAC were the civilian police monitors who were the only semblance of a police and administrative system in the country. Cambodians, especially women and children, might have regarded the police as allies if a much greater number of female police officers had been assigned to UNTAC. According to a woman in the Board of Inquiry Office, the presence of more female military and police peacekeepers might have changed the image of the U.N. in Cambodia as "an army of occupation" (Banerji, 1994).

The only completely civilian U.N. mission was the U.N. Observer Mission in South Africa (UNOMSA) from 1992 until 1994. Women constituted 53 percent of the fifty observers in peace-building and peacemaking structures. Angela King, Chief of Mission, appointed women to half the team leader positions as regional coordinators (Cubiero, 1994:4). Women were charged with supervising two regions, Natal and the eastern Rand, which experienced most of the pre-electoral violence. In 1994, the percentage of women declined to 21 percent, when the mandate expanded to include election monitoring and 3,500 monitors were dispatched by their respective governments (United Nations Division for the Advancement of Women, 1995).

In the U.N. Protection Force (UNPROFOR) in the former Yugoslavia, from 1992 until 1995, very few women were in military peacekeeping contingents. For example, Sweden, which has one of the best records regarding women in peacekeeping, sent only forty-four women (3.3%) to UNPROFOR out of the 1,300 nationals who served from 1992 to 1994 (National Report of Sweden, 1994: 33). One bright spot of UNPROFOR was in Civil Affairs, where gender parity prevailed, when a majority of women served at the Director D-1 level in 1993. They performed a wide range of functions, especially in political affairs, including negotiations at the government and local authority levels, as well as in public information, legal, liaison, and humanitarian work. Another highlight was the visibility of a female military officer from France who served as a U.N. media spokesperson in Sarajevo in 1995 (Peyard, 1995).

After UNPROFOR ended, U.N. missions in Bosnia, Eastern Slavonia, and Macedonia continued the pattern of underrepresentation of women. For example, out of 1,902 police monitors now deployed, only thirty-eight are women, with the largest contingent of eleven from the United States (United Nations Office of the Spokesman for the Secretary-General, 1996).

Women in "Blue Helmets": Where Are They?

Almost no women have served in the military contingents of U.N. peacekeeping operations, even though Article 8 of the U.N. Charter calls for equal participation of men and women in the work of the organization. Between 1957 and 1989, there were very few women "blue helmets." The number of women rose to only 255 between 1989 and 1992, representing little more than 1 percent of U.N. military personnel, and women comprised only 1.7 percent of military contingents in the seventeen peacekeeping missions active in 1993 (United Nations, 1994).

Women peacekeepers were not requested by the U.N. until 1994, when officials first indicated to member states that the U.N. would welcome more women soldiers. However, the selection of peacekeeping units is beyond U.N. control. After member states approve participation in a peacekeeping mission, the highest-ranking military authority, generally the Chief of Staff of the Armed Forces, decides which units are selected and trained as peacekeepers. Women are barred from military service in many countries, and they constitute more than 10 percent of military personnel in only five out of twenty-five reporting countries (United Nations Division for the Advancement of Women, 1995). In most nations, women are prohibited from combat roles and thus are largely denied the opportunity to serve as "blue helmets."

Change is occurring, as more women pursue military careers and are permitted to train for combat and for peacekeeping duties.[1] A breakthrough in women's participation came in the Western Sahara operation (MINURSO), where they comprised 10.2 percent of military personnel in 1993. The member states which contributed troops to MINURSO included France, the United States, and Australia, which had higher proportions of women among their peacekeeping staffs. The presence of a large medical unit in MINURSO composed of mainly female nurses and doctors underscores the fact that most women in military peacekeeping missions still serve in noncombat roles.

A few nations now actively recruit women as peacekeepers. For example, Sweden began to recruit women on an experimental basis in 1979, when forty-two out of more than 4,000 applicants were selected (National Report of Sweden, 1994: 33). After completing basic training, Swedish women soldiers today may apply for peacekeeping duty on the same basis as men. Sweden has suggested to the United Nations that the participation of women in U.N. peacekeeping operations be increased and that such an action would raise the awareness of U.N. peacekeeping personnel to the vulnerable situation of women civilians in armed conflicts.

A few other member states have taken the initiative and have contributed more women soldiers to U.N. peacekeeping missions. U.S. women soldiers, assigned with more than 3,600 troops to six U.N. peacekeeping missions, have served in a variety of noncombat and nontraditional roles, including medical and administrative jobs, logistics and supply, and military police (National Report of the United States, 1994: 95). An infantry company from Ghana, composed of men and women soldiers, served in refugee camps with the U.N. Assistance Mission in Rwanda (UNAMIR). Australia's first women peacekeepers were assigned to UNTAC in Cambodia in 1992 (Enloe, 1993: 35). While women comprised 12 percent of the Australian

National Defence Forces in 1994 (*Military Balance*, 1994/1995), they still comprised only 3.2 percent of Australia's contribution to peacekeeping operations in 1993 (National Report of Australia, 1994: 24). British women soldiers have served in support roles in the U.N. Force in Cyprus (UNFICYP) and in UNPROFOR (National Report of the United Kingdom, 1994: 10). Danish women have served in U.N. peacekeeping operations in the Balkans from units that were drawn from the Home Guard and the Armed Services (National Report of Denmark, 1994: 66).

Potential Unrealized: Women in Civilian Police Forces

Civilian police components of U.N. peacekeeping operations could be readily increased, as there are more women officers in civilian police forces than there are women in the military. Women constituted 11 percent of the civilian police forces in thirty-three nations in 1986, and 22 percent in Finland, 21 percent in the United States and 21 percent in Portugal (Women's Indicators and Statistical Database, 1995). In contrast, only 0.7 percent women were in U.N. civilian police forces in 1993, as many U.N. police officers are drawn from military police units, an occupational category where women are largely underrepresented (The World's Women, 1994). If member states would shift to contributing civilian police, this could result in rapidly increased female participation in U.N. peacekeeping operations.

Female Military Officers at U.N. Headquarters

In January 1994, the first female military officer was posted to U.N. Headquarters, after more than thirty years during which no women officers had been assigned. At that time, a Dutch officer was assigned to financial duties in the Field Administration and Logistics Division (FALD) in the Department of Peacekeeping Operations (DPKO). In 1995, three more women officers were appointed, along with a noncommissioned officer,[2] bringing the total to five women (4%) out of a total of 122 military personnel in the U.N. Secretariat (United Nations, 1995b). Three out of the sixty professionals (5%) in the Military Advisor's Office, including the Office of Planning and Support, were women. There were only two (4.2%) women out of the forty-seven military officers on loan to the FALD in DPKO (United Nations, 1995b).

Guidelines for U.N. Forces and the Code of Conduct

From 1948 until 1995, no formal code of conduct for peacekeepers existed, but U.N. peacekeepers were expected to act as model citizens and in conformity with U.N. norms, such as the Universal Declaration of Human Rights and the Standards of Conduct for International Civil Servants. However, in 1996, a new and comprehensive code of conduct for U.N. peacekeepers, which includes guidelines on the human rights of women and children and gender issues, was under preparation at U.N. Headquarters. In October 1995, a set of "Guidelines for Conduct of Personnel in U.N. Peace Keeping Operations and Related Missions in the Field" was circulated (Guidelines for Conduct, 1995). One guideline stipulates that "U.N. personnel must not abuse or exploit individual members of the local population, in particular, women and children." Another states that "in their private life, U.N. mission personnel must ensure that their conduct will not discredit the mission and not damage its credibility, effectiveness and image." In a related set of "Guidelines for U.N. Forces Regarding Respect for International Humanitarian Law," it stipulates that "women and children shall be the object of special respect and shall be protected in particular against any form of indecent assault."

Conclusion: Women Making a Difference in Peacekeeping

The increased presence of women in the civilian, military, and police components of U.N. peacekeeping has resulted in the establishment of good relations and trust with local communities, elements essential to the success of peacekeeping and peace building. Further increases of women in U.N. peacekeeping, particularly in decision-making positions and military and civilian police contingents, could deter the abuse of power by male peacekeepers and could minimize, if not eliminate, incidents of sexual harassment, exploitation, and rape.

A feminist perspective on conflict resolution asserts that women are socially conditioned to be more peaceful and less violent than men. The pacifist orientation of females is attributed to their roles as mothers who give birth to and nurture future generations and who act as conciliators in the family and in local communities. Their intermediary role within the household and community has provided women with well-developed negotiating skills that should be extended into conflict resolution and peace talks at local, national, and international levels. The Platform for Action of the Fourth World Conference on Women in Beijing in September 1995 recommended that national governments

> strengthen the role of women and ensure equal representation of women at all decision-making levels in national and international institutions which may make or influence policy with regard to matters related to peacekeeping, preventive diplomacy and related activities and in all stages of peace mediation and negotiations. (United Nations, 1995a: 64)

Feminist theorists assert that the presence of women results in differences in the content and priorities of decision making, as well as changes in management style, group dynamics, and organizational culture (Dahlerup, 1991). Women's leadership may also contribute to peacekeeping that is less military oriented. When women join organizations or decision-making bodies in sufficient numbers and create a "critical mass," they engender mutual respect, a more collaborative and less competitive environment, and consensus rather than "winners and losers." Instead of simply stating their positions, women focus more on resolving problems. Women's aptitude for consensus building, problem solving, and conciliation are valuable instruments that are also useful in peacemaking, preventive diplomacy, peacekeeping, and peace building. Evidence on women's contributions to U.N. peacekeeping operations suggests that the "critical mass" theory and the hypothesis that women's participation results in new values and perspectives are valid.

NOTES

1. Belgium, Canada, Denmark, France, Luxembourg, the Netherlands, Norway, Sweden, United States, Venezuela, and Zambia allow women to participate in some combat situations.

2. One major [Norway] in Air Operations in the Field Administration and Logistics Division, one lieutenant colonel [USA] in the Situation Centre, and one major [USA] who serves as military adviser to the United Nations Mission in Haiti (UNMIH) and the International Civilian Mission (MICIVH), a combined military/ civilian human rights mission in Haiti, based on information supplied by the Field Administration and Logistics Division/Department of Peacekeeping Operations, 22 May 1995.

This chapter is based on material researched by Janet C. Beilstein and published in *Women 2000*, December 1995, by the Division for the Advancement of Women, Department of Policy Coordination and Sustainable Development, United Nations, New York. The views presented in this paper are those of the author and not those of the United Nations.

REFERENCES

Banerji, Margaret. 1994. "Notes on a Personal Experience of a Women in Peacekeeping." Unpublished paper.

Cubiero, Antonia. "Women as Agents of Change in Peacekeeping Operations: A Voice from the U.N. Peacekeeping Mosaic—a UNOMSA Perspective." Unpublished paper.

Dahlerup, Drude. 1991. "From a Small to a Large Minority: A Theory of a Critical Mass Applied to the Case of Women in Scandinavian Politics," in Hem Lata Swarup and Sarojini Bisaria (eds.), *Women, Politics and Religion*. Etawah, India: A. C. Brothers.

Enloe, Cynthia. 1993. *The Morning After: Sexual Politics at the End of the Cold War*. Berkeley: University of California Press.

"Guidelines for Conduct of Personnel in United Nations Peacekeeping Operations and Related Missions in the Field." Unpublished document, October 1995.

"Guidelines for U.N. Forces Regarding Respect for International Humanitarian Law." Unpublished document, no date.

The Military Balance, 1994/1995. 1994. London, International Institute for Strategic Studies.

National Report of Australia. 1994. Submitted to the United Nations (Division for the Advancement of Women/Department of Policy Coordination and Sustainable Development) for the second Review and Appraisal of the Nairobi Forward-looking Strategies.

National Report of Denmark. 1994. Submitted to the United Nations (Division for the Advancement of Women/Department of Policy Coordination and Sustainable Development) for the second Review and Appraisal of the Nairobi Forward-looking Strategies.

National Report of Sweden. 1994. Submitted to the United Nations (Division for the Advancement of Women/Department of Policy Coordination and Sustainable Development) for the second Review and Appraisal of the Nairobi Forward-looking Strategies.

National Report of the United Kingdom. 1994. Submitted to the United Nations (Division for the Advancement of Women/Department of Policy Coordination and Sustainable Development) for the second Review and Appraisal of the Nairobi Forward-looking Strategies.

National Report of the United States. 1994. Submitted to the United Nations (Division for the Advancement of Women/Department of Policy Coordination and Sustainable Development) for the second Review and Appraisal of the Nairobi Forward-looking Strategies.

Peyard, Michel. 1995. "Moi, Myriam, commandant à Sarajevo." *Paris Match*. 15 June.

Stiehm, Judith. 1994. "Peacekeeping: Men's and Women's Work," consultant's report prepared for the expert group meeting on "Gender and the Agenda for Peace" 5–9 December 1994, Division for the Advancement of Women/Department of Policy Coordination and Sustainable Development, New York, p.8.

United Nations. 1996. *Information Notes: U.N. Peacekeeping*. Update: United Nations Publication DPI/13065/Rev. 4 (February).

United Nations. 1995a. Report of the Fourth World Conference on Women, Beijing, 4–15 September 1995, U.N. document no. A/CONF.177/20, 17 October.

United Nations. 1995b. Women's Indicators and Statistical Database (WISTAT). Version 3, CD-ROM, United Nations Publication no. E.95.XVII.6.

United Nations. 1994. *The World's Women: Trends and Statistics*. New York.

United Nations Division for the Advancement of Women. 1995. *Women 2000*. New York.

United Nations Economic and Social Council. 1995. "Peace: Women in International Decision-making," *Report of the Secretary-General*, 9 January, E/CN.6/1995/12.

United Nations General Assembly. 1995. *Improvement in the Status Of Women in the Secretariat, Report of the Secretary-General*. U.N. document no. A/50/691, 27 October.

United Nations Office of the Spokesman for the Secretary-General. 1996. Daily Press Briefing. 11 June.

UNTAG in Namibia: A New Nation is Born. 1991. New York: United Nations.

Chapter Sixteen

War and Gender
What Do We Learn from Israel?

Uta Klein

During the last few decades, women's integration into the armed forces, especially in combat roles, has been a predominant discourse of gender equality policies in many Western countries. Some streams of feminist policies consider the armed forces the "last bastion" for women to conquer. Liberal and equal rights feminists argue, for example, that women's military participation leads to legal and social equality for women. Political subordination of women—so the argument goes—has been legitimized by their nonparticipation in one of the "duties" of citizenship. Thus, to attain women's full legal and social equality, the duty of national defense must be shared.

The connection between citizenship and participation in defense in history certainly exists. Yet I am convinced that women's inclusion in the armed forces cannot dismantle the basic idea of militarism: the fear and the rejection of the "other" is linked to sexism. This sexism consists of both rejection of and violence against the female other.

Is the existence of a female warrior really a sign of a more egalitarian society? Is the message, brought to us by CNN during the Gulf War, that American women soldiers evidence egalitarian American society while veiled Saudi women represent backward Arab society, true? Or should we talk about the whole context of militarism and gender in society? Might we explore the construction of masculinity and femininity in militaristic thinking, practice, and values?

Militarism and war affect women and men in different ways. Israeli society provides an interesting case study for investigating the military/gender connection and the preceding questions. First, the state of Israel participated in six wars since its foundation.[1] Second, due to frequent wars and a history of persecution of the Jewish people, the armed forces in Israel are central in the Jewish population's consciousness and daily life. Third, men and women[2] are conscripted, making Israel unique. This uniqueness not only led to the myth of the woman soldier fighting shoulder to shoulder with her male comrade, but served as a role model for armies around the world. I am not going to analyze the gender distinction in the Israeli Defense Forces (IDF). Rather, I am interested in showing how national duties are gendered in times of conflict and war, and how wars sharpen the split between genders.

Times of Conflict and War: National Duties of Men and Women

We find a striking equivalence between maternal and military service and an analogy between childbirth and war in literature and mythology throughout history. "Rites of passage" in different cultures often reflect the maternal/military analogy. At the final stage of some rituals the boys may be called warriors whereas girls become brides. Nancy Huston notes that in Sparta it was forbidden to inscribe the names of the dead upon their tombstones, except for men who had fallen in war and women who had died in childbirth.

The same "division of labor" can be recognized in Israeli society. The fighter in Israeli culture has always been male, whereas women are responsible for reproduction. The roots for this dichotomy derive from Israeli society prior to statehood. The main desired characteristics of the "new Jew" the Zionist movement wanted to create were physical strength and readiness to defend honor by fighting. The Diaspora Jew was perceived as passive and effeminate, whereas the heroes of the Zionists were fighters for Jewish history. "The Maccabeans will rise again," Herzl proclaimed. The ethos of using force as a tool for Jewish national sovereignty became the dominant discourse beginning in the late 1930s.

Gender equality for the Zionist women did not have the major impact on women's roles that is often believed. Although women participated in Jewish military groups during the prestate period and were involved in the War of Independence, most women held limited auxiliary roles unless a dire emergency demanded further mobilization.

After the establishment of the state of Israel, the Defense Service Law established the conscription of men and women. During the Knesset discussion about female conscription, Ben Gurion expressed how Zionist men viewed women's tasks:

> Now, for the question of women in the army. When one discusses the position of women, two factors must be taken into consideration. First, women have a special mission as mothers. There is no greater mission in life, and nature has decreed that only a woman can give birth to a child. This is a woman's task and her blessing. However, a second factor must be remembered; the woman is not only a woman, but a personality in her own right in the same way as a man. As such, she should enjoy the same rights and responsibilities as the man, except where motherhood is concerned. (Quoted in Fuchs, 1987)

Zionism made an *expansion* of women's roles possible, but it did not affect the link between manliness and the role of the fighter and between womanliness and the role of a mother.

Military service in Israel is a dominant part of adolescence. The Israeli Army, one of the main mechanisms for building a *national* identity, has become the basis of a *male* self-image and a source for *male* social mobility. For Israeli Jewish males, military service is an inherent part of maturation, a rite of passage to male adulthood. Military service fulfills typically male adolescent desires for intense thrills, adventure, and peril, and is perceived by war and military veterans as an essential phase in the formulation of masculine identity. The symbolic differentiation between immigrant and "Sabra" (one who was born in Israel) is whether she or he has lived in the country during a war or not.

Security and *reproduction* are strongly connected concerns regarded as necessary for the survival of states during conflicts and war. We know from many examples that nationalist projects in times of conflict or war view women as biological reproducers of members of ethnic collectivities. The Israeli state, being in conflict and at wars with Arab neighbor states, tried from its inception to enlarge the Jewish population by mass immigration and by natural growth. Reproduction has been connected to national survival and security. We must not forget that reproduction is viewed vis-à-vis the Holocaust, the annihilation of the majority of European Jewry. High birthrates are seen ideologically as a "compensation" for Jewish children murdered in the Shoah. The rate of birth per Jewish Israeli woman is 2.6 (1995), higher than in Catholic European countries like Ireland (2.2) or Spain (1.4). Israel also shows the highest amount of in vitro fertilization clinics. The Jewish birthrate is discussed widely in the media. Parts of the country that have an Arab majority are still the politicians' cause for concern.

Some might ask themselves why the presence of female soldiers, the conscription of Israeli women, does *not* lead to another understanding of societal roles. First, women are excluded from the army not only when they give birth but as soon as they are married, showing us that the *raison d'etre* of marriage, according to the state, is reproduction. Second, women are not allowed in combat roles. Due to this prohibition, men are identified as the protectors and women as the protected. The notion of combat is fundamental to the concepts of manhood and male superiority. Combat is a key dimension in defining manhood and masculinity. In Israel it takes on a special dimension because Israel has experienced six wars since the establishment of the state. The exclusion of women is significant, because the experience of combat and war is an important, if not *the* important, ingredient of prestige and career in the political and other public spheres in Israeli society. The symbolic function of the exclusion is to maintain the stereotype that women are inferior and dependent on men for protection. Furthermore, men are called to reserve duty regularly, generally once a year for several weeks. During that period the woman remains behind, taking care of the home and children.

Whereas entrance into the society of men means passing a test of strength, force, and power (participation in the military), women are defined through their relation to the male members of society. Their task, as wives, mothers, or sisters of soldiers, is the female role in a process of initiation. This connection was shown in the speech of then Israeli premier Rabin when he signed the Oslo Agreement. He began his speech by saying, "We, the soldiers who have returned from battles stained with blood; we who have seen our relatives and friends killed before our eyes . . ." and continued to describe the Israeli-Jewish collective: "We have come from a people, a home, a family that has not known a single year, nor a single month, in which *mothers* have not wept for their *sons*" (quoted in Laquer and Rubin, 1995: 5; Sharoni, 1995).

Times of War: The "Homefront" and the "Battlefront"

The split between gender sharpens during times of war. Some researchers have stressed the observation that women can "gain" from wars, especially by expanding their roles in the labor market. The Israeli example shows that it is doubtful whether this means more than a temporarily limited expansion. The sexual division of the labor market has never changed as a result of war.

Bar-Yosef and Padan-Eisenstark show how the separation of the (male) "battlefront" and the (female) "homefront" worked during the Yom Kippur War (1973). Most of the men between ages eighteen and fifty-five were mobilized. Factories, businesses, schools, and universities were closed, public transportation nearly stopped. The civilian area turned out to be the area of female activity, but, as the Emergency Committee was an exclusively male group, women were excluded from decision making concerning the needs of the civil arena. Traditional sex roles were strengthened, as the well-being of the male members of the family became the central interest of civilians. Mass media presented men and women in images characterized by only a few basic attitudes: "The masculine attributes focused upon the instrumental combat roles and the feminine ones on the supporting expressive roles" (Bar-Yosef and Padan-Eisenstark 1977: 135). In every war women become traditionalized. They represent the "homefront" and are expected to stick to traditional roles, to cook, to stay more at home, and to nurture. They are the supporters who have to maintain stability in times of crisis.

Women are (in all societies) usually "punished" for staying at home during wartime in a most subtle way. Esther Fuchs finds, in an analysis of Hebrew literature, that the generation of Statehood (writing in the late 1950s and early 1960s) presented women as conjugal and national enemies, showing a deep-seated suspicion of women's roles in wartime. On the other hand, the literature also shows a deep-seated distrust of women soldiers. Women soldiers intrude in a male domain and undermine the myth of the male protector causing a threatened virility and a phallic anxiety (Fuchs 1987).

Another war experience, the Gulf War, demonstrates what happens when men cannot fulfill their roles as protectors. As Israel didn't join the war, Israeli men for the first time were spared the stress of participating in combat. On the other hand, they were deprived of weapons and deprived of defending and so forced into "passivity." They had to stay at home with their women and children, which undermined the male identity. Reports show that the number of sexual offenses and domestic violence increased during the Gulf War.

A common assumption exists that war brings members of a society together, that war unites and increases solidarity and cohesiveness. Vice versa, the state is dependent on the public consensus to gather the necessary resources for the use of force. Israeli Jewish women live in ambivalence. When their husbands, the soldiers, come home, women's duty is to comfort them and they are relieved that nothing happened to them. The taboo not to complain about the burden of the centrality of the armed forces has been successful, because every family in Israel has someone in the armed forces.

It is the *centrality* of the military that ensures the support of Israeli Jewish women and men. And it is the belief of the ever existing threat against Israel's existence that ensures the centrality of the Israeli forces and their necessity. Military service is more than legal obligation. Military service is connected to the right to belong to the collective. This belonging is defined along national lines. The very core of the collective is the community of "defenders." Male Jewish members of the society receive this message during their childhood.

The Dominance of "Security"

In times of conflict women's issues are always given low priority. This holds true for Israeli women. Armed forces become essential to Israeli collective identity, and war serves as a point of reference. In a society like Israel's, everything revolves around war. As I mentioned before, most Jewish men are called to reserve duty regularly. The woman remains behind taking care of the home and the children. Although reserve duty demands an interruption of the reservists' lives, as well as an element of risk, the motivation of individuals to bear this burden is still high. Through participation in the reserve they show their integration into the Israeli value system.

Those who do the most dangerous jobs gain in the military sphere as well as in the civilian sphere. Due to the centrality of the military in Israeli society, service is crucial for a civilian career. Service in the higher echelons of the army serves as a pathway toward positions of public influence. This holds true for men, as the IDF are a steppingstone to civilian careers for most senior officers. Groups not incorporated in the IDF—Moslem Arab Israelis of both sexes, female Druze Arab Israelis, and female Bedouin Arab Israelis—face automatic discrimination. Jewish Israeli men gain from their military service by establishing professional contacts. Since even the peace talks are run by army representatives or former army officials, women are not represented in peace negotiations.

We must recognize that Israel is indeed "unique." Its history of persecution culminating in the Holocaust forms the collective memory of the Jewish people and especially of the Jewish people in Israel. The permanent state of conflicts with its neighbors is an objective basis for daily life anxiety. But we also know that "anxiety" rarely exists in a purely objective form. Anxiety can be provoked and turned into an instrument useful for political interests. Israeli policies, and especially Israeli military policies, often use the Holocaust to justify military operations and to prevent criticism from the population. The Holocaust is a mighty force; anyone from the Jewish Israeli collective protesting against military procedures or a dominance of military attitudes may feel like a traitor. Opposition in Israel has often been marginal for understandable reasons.

Generally, when security and military policies dominate a society, the population is made to agree through brute force (in dictatorships) or by shaping a consensus that the policies are necessary and good. Israeli women internalized this support and it is difficult for them to express the ambiguity they might feel. A struggle for increasing women's status or even addressing discrimination has often been felt to be somewhat subversive.

Consequences

Anybody approaching the question of gender equality in Israeli society encounters a real paradox: on the one hand, the strong ethos of gender equality in the prestate period is an admirable part of Israeli history; on the other hand, the exclusion of women in Israeli society from powerful spheres remains troublesome. To give only one example: the percentage of women in the Knesset since the establishment of the Israeli state has never exceeded 10 percent. Regarding the legal status of women, Israel shows severe discriminatory elements, especially in the sphere of marriage and divorce.

These facts conflict with theories that argue for the integration of women into the armed forces, claiming improvements for women's status in society. The Israeli example shows that the conscription of women does not have a positive effect on the status of women in the broader society.

Cynthia Enloe rejects the argument that wartime experience is a liberating force on women's roles. The Israeli example strongly supports her argument that wartime experience only demonstrates the extent to which women's lives are controlled by male elites. Only in relatively demilitarized political systems, so her argument goes, do women who don't see themselves as masculinized politicians have a chance to run the government.

This definitely holds true for Israel. In spite of women's conscription in the Israeli Defense Forces, the "business" of war and conflict is an exclusively male one. As the concept of "citizenship" is associated with the right and the duty of defending the country, military service in feminist discussions is seen as a way to achieve political rights. The Israeli example shows that the exclusion of women from politics, from "first class citizenship," is maintained in spite of women's participation in the defense forces. They do not have control of the use of force. In other words, the inclusion of women in the military allows them to be militarized but not to be empowered. On the contrary: the "security question" is used to keep women quiet, to exclude them from far-reaching political functions.

NOTES

1. If we include the Gulf War, in which Israel did not fight.

2. As only *Jewish* men and women as well as Druze men are conscripted and Christian Arab and Bedouin Israeli men (not women) are "allowed" to serve in the army, the Israeli Defense Forces becomes a marker of ethnic boundaries.

Uta Klein thanks the Berliner Wissenschaftskolleg and the Van Leer Jerusalem Institute for their support for this research.

REFERENCES

Bar-Yosef, Rivka, and Dorit Padan-Eisenstark. 1977. "Role System under Stress: Sex Roles in War." *Social Problems* 25: 135–145.

Fuchs, Esther. 1987. *Israeli Mythogynies: Women in Contemporary Hebrew Fiction.* New York: SUNY Press.

Klein, Uta. 1997. "The Gendering of National Discourses and the Israeli-Palestinian Conflict." *European Journal of Women's Studies* 4: 341–351.

Laquer, Walter, and Barry Rubin (eds.). 1995. *The Israeli-Arab Reader.* New York: Penguin Books.

Sharoni, Simona. 1995. *Gender and the Israeli-Palestinian Conflict: The Politics of Women's Resistance.* New York: Syracuse University Press.

Stiehm, Judith Hicks. 1992. "The Protected, the Protector, the Defender." *Women's Studies International Forum* 5, no. 3/4: 367–376.

Part IV

Resistance Movements and Literature

Chapter Seventeen

Broken Dreams in Nicaragua

Diana Mulinari

Pre- and Post-Revolutionary Nicaragua: Our Time and the Time of the Rich

Doña Celia, a seventy-year-old woman, used to tell her grandchildren stories about her life. When asked about the time of a certain event, she had two possible answers: "During the time of the rich" or "our time." My work, as well as most research of women in Nicaragua, is about Doña Celia's time, the time of the revolution.

The time of the revolution is not a homogeneous time. My fieldwork was done in 1988 and 1989 at a time when the United States economic blockade and the war against the "contras" were pressing households harder than ever. In this context, "before" was related to the first years of the revolution: "That was fun—now it is hard." Women and children did in fact enjoy the benefits of the revolution during the first years, but in the late 1980s, in the context of the contras war, they experienced the hardships of the economic crisis. The Sandinista revolution was not defeated overnight.[1] When visiting Nicaragua in 1988, I heard many comments that began with "of course I am Sandinista but. . . ." These were the voices of Sandinista women who reacted to the constraints of an economy of war ("we only eat rice and beans") or military service ("I have two sons in the mountains. I do not want to send my last son").[2] As Angela expressed it, "You know I am Sandinista, but I am so tired."

Latin America and Violent Conflict

David Slater (1994) asserts that in the study of social movements there is the supposition that the "West" acts as the primary referent for theory and philosophical reflection. Often the "South" is presented as an absence, whereas the "North" is thought of as a self-contained identity. Representations of violence are central to this construction of the South's "Otherness." Explanations provided in terms of continuous civil wars, revolutions, and ethnic conflicts obscure global forms of power and domination. On the other hand, human beings are represented as passive victims of violence rather than as subjects who both reproduce and transform their worlds. In this context it is important to distinguish between "Northern" discourses that represent Latin America as ontologically violent and Latin American women as passive victims, on the one hand, and the structural violence embedded in the hierarchical forms of domination, on the other—as well as the forms that subordinated groups develop to contest this violence.

Latin American Women and Violent Conflict

According to Sharon MacDonald (1987), sexual representations are central in the creation of boundaries when women erode what are often represented as male arenas: warfare, guerrilla struggle, "insurrection," and "revolution." Political change provided new ways of conceptualizing the meaning of being a Nicaraguan. Many of them may be traced to metaphors of gender. Metaphors of national identity were strongly woven into metaphors of sexuality. Many of the (male) narratives re-create masculinity, such as this one, told by a fifty-year-old male member of the Sandinista workers' union:

> I tell you, I saw it. I was there. I saw it. He was all alone, he was not even physically strong, he had been so poor that he never had enough to eat. And then they came, they never came alone; they have no "*hombria*."[3] But you know the courage of our men. He was fourteen years old but he fought like a man. He fought until he did not have any bullets left. Then, they nearly blew the house and left him in the middle of the street. That is how we are, the men in Nicaragua /*Se dio verga*/ He did fight back. Ask your mom. She and other women fetched the body afterwards.

Darse verga means to fight back. And it is used to describe the political struggle of both men and women. But *verga* is also one of three hundred words for the penis. *Darse verga* then indicates the assumed aggressive power of masculine sexuality.

Let me give another example. Most Sandinista women who supported the military service and sent their children to the mountains (as they put it) nevertheless respected other women's decisions to hide or send their children abroad when military duty called. To inform on the deserters was unthinkable for them. Yet a young man, Osvaldo, looked at it differently. "Only *cochones* desert," he firmly asserted.[4] For him, as for many other young men, the military service was central to his notions of masculinity. Young men who avoided military duty were not labeled as traitors but rather as females and homosexuals. Sexual politics in Sandinistan Nicaragua was grounded in a "revolutionary" discourse that rejected gender hierarchies and preached equality in the armed struggle. Yet the most valued virtue of resistance appealed to men's notions of heroism where the weak was symbolically represented as female. "Women fought as men" (*las mujeres pelearon como varones*) was a proud comment of older Sandinista men when remembering the insurrection period.

The heroism of males (adults) dominates narratives constructed from active armed resistance. The heroism of women, however, who were very active as soldiers and commanded military actions, is remembered mostly as passive resistance. The images of women show them imprisoned, raped, violated, and noncollaborative, or as providing care within the struggle. Heroism was linked to suffering for the revolution—the loss of children. Women do not perceive their actions as violent but rather they see themselves as defending their children (an expansion of their nurturing role).

The symbols of this new Sandinista identity were masculine in character: Sandinista hats and uniforms, Sandinista military display. The construction of Sandinista national identity used images stemming from familial or kin ideologies. Women became both the "the mothers" and the girlfriends of the revolution. One of the posters of a Nicaraguan women's association shows a young Nicaraguan woman smiling at the camera with a gun in one hand and a baby in the other. This is a common image of revolution. The young guerrilla, despite the gun in her hand, recalls notions of peace, of home. Many men had a dual relationship with women in the revolution that can be traced to the metaphors provided by Sandinista discourses. On the one hand, women were idealized as pure and powerless, with men as their defenders; on the other hand, the revolution demanded that women be strong and independent (as they always had been).

In the summer of 1988 three Sandinista discourses (with corresponding images) described women and the revolution. These definitions of the feminine may be traced to the insurrection period, and consisted of images of the woman guerrilla fighter, the woman mother, and the woman revolutionary. As Natalia, a Sandinista feminist put it:

> They can say what they want, they can write what they want, but we know women are equal until they get pregnant, or women are equal to men after they have made the decision of leaving their children with their relatives in order to continue their political praxis. Because in revolutionary Nicaragua, fathers do not leave their children, it is the mother who abandons them for the struggle.[5]

Leftist Latin American armed resistance movements have argued that the revolution's special conditions make gender differences unimportant (Lobao, 1990). As was commonly expressed in the seventies: "With a gun in your hand there are no sex differences." In the Nicaraguan revolution, many women occupied high ranks. As a result, some women began to think of themselves as militants, claiming that being male or female was irrelevant. Many of these high-ranking women in the Sandinista leadership view themselves as examples of gender equality. While in the beginning men did resist being under their command, this gradually disappeared and was replaced by a deep sense of comradeship where sex was not important. The word "earned" is commonly used by this group of women to describe the respect they generated.

My field work shows that these women revolutionaries are role models for young Sandinista women. They have been socialized within a gender-neutral discourse, and are critical of their mothers' discourses of difference and motherhood. In Sandinista political representations these are the mythical, powerful women—loyal to their people and to Sandinism, and critical of feminism. They appeal to traditional notions in Nicaraguan gender culture of independent and autonomous women who sacrifice themselves for their children. Many of the women in leadership positions in the Sandinista movement had been active in the struggle from its beginning, and were married to another militant or were related to important male leaders.

Even though feminism and revolution had been integral to the lives of many of these women, discourses about woman militants emphasize their love for their country and people, their capacity for self-sacrifice, and their immense courage. They are the "sisters" of the revolution. According to women I met in Managua, holding feminist beliefs was not the key to political advancement within the Sandinista movement. While the movement voiced questions about machismo, its political discourses nevertheless excluded Sandinista feminists. Gender sameness in revolutionary theory makes the real differences between men and women invisible. Yet the child-bearing and rearing responsibilities assumed by most women were not shared by their men in struggle.

The "morality" of the sisters of the revolution is central to understanding the politics of gender within the political leadership. A link existed between women's political credibility and their sexual activities. To be taken seriously, women must act "morally correct." In the words of Andrea, "They have to respect you as a sister, a *companera*. You cannot go to bed with any of them. If you do so . . . they do not respect you afterwards."

There are boundaries between women militants (members of the Sandinista party) and women who actively participate in the grass roots organizations but do not have a political career. In Managua these are boundaries of class and ethnicity. On average, most women "militants" are "white," educated and urban, and in their late thirties. Women from my neighborhood drew lines between themselves and their "revolutionary work" and those women who were "organized." The representation of women militants (as well as their self-perception) as "politically" constructed reinforces the realm of women of the neighborhoods as "apolitical," as the "other." A political discourse whose aim is to "organize" and "mobilize" housewives and mothers involves an ambivalent relationship through which women from the neighborhoods are made visible.

The gender-neutral discourse reappears in relation to young women. Alejandra is seventeen years old and a passionate Sandinista. She was ten years old when the revolution "triumphed." As with many in her generation, her childhood memories emphasize the neighborhood resistance. Young women were appealed to in genderless ways, and they strongly identify themselves with the young Sandinista. We must not forget that these young women participated in the literacy campaign when they were thirteen and in the militia when they were fourteen. Like their brothers, these women were socialized in the revolution and in the formal aspects of equal conditions. In my neighborhood these young women were the first generation to have access to college education. They represented the "New Nicaragua."

Sandinista discourse becomes gendered again when appealing to those who fed the family and supported the revolution: women activists in the communities. Despite

Sandinista ideology describing the revolution as women's hope for full integration into Nicaraguan society, women in the country have always worked.[6] For the neighborhood children the guerrilleras are some kind of mythical older sisters who, according to the songs my little friends taught me, were unbounded and free. Their mothers, in contrast, were neither unbound nor free. The women activists are "the revolutionary women" who must support their Sandinista men in the struggle, and take men's place in fields and factories when the men are sent to the mountains. They are expected to provide a higher level of productivity, to raise the "new revolutionary generation," to be active in neighborhood activities, and last, but not least, to broaden their political consciousness to include the women's struggle. In the 1982 "Frugality Campaign" or the campaign to support the war effort (*Todo a los frentes de combate, todo a los combatientes*) as well as in ration campaigns, only women were responsible. They were asked to sacrifice "the Family" for "the Nation."

Within Latin American patriarchal ideology, motherhood is reified while the praxis of mothers of flesh and blood is simultaneously devalued and made invisible. Nicaragua had no maternity leave before the revolution and one of the highest mortality rates for mothers and children in all of Latin America.[7] Real mothers are abandoned and battered. Within this gap between a discourse of motherhood and a devaluation of motherwork, the Sandinista discourse on mothers developed. Through social programs, Sandinistas did try to ease the burden of mothering. Many women I met discussed the gains of the revolution in terms of mothering, such as their greater access to higher education and improved health and housing standards for their children. The revolution meant, for many of them, a better future for their daughters.

A striking official rhetoric praising the role of women as "Sandinista mothers" prevailed. In practice, however, this referred not to all mothers and women with small children but rather primarily to older women—to grandmothers, who have always held a strong position within Nicaraguan culture. Sandinista discourse on mothers was woven into a class discourse. Sandinista mothers are women from the popular sectors who have lost their children during the insurrection or in the "contra" war. These mothers had their status transformed after the death of their son or daughter. Their contribution to the revolution was acknowledged in terms of their "sacrifice." They were given minimal material resources, and their channels to the Sandinista leadership were better than for other women.

In Sandinista discourses, mothers are by definition altruistic and self-sacrificing. Sandinistas usually speak of *el dolor de una madre* (mother's pain). Sandinista discourse on motherhood does not break traditional notions of gender but rather deepens them. In my neighborhood some of the organized mothers also functioned as the guardians of "revolutionary morality" (keeping young women faithful to their fiancés while they were in military service).

Discourses of Sandinista motherhood, as well as pronatalist policies, were reinforced by the contra war. The Sandinistas praised women as reproducers. A slogan painted on one of Managua's walls reads, "Holy the womb that gave birth to a Sandinista" (*bendita la panza que parió un Sandinista*). Women's high fertility rates were given a new "revolutionary" meaning.

Many Sandinista women workers present themselves as the mother of a son (or daughter) killed in the insurrection. These women were active in the revolution in different ways but they tend to emphasize their maternal roles. The sacrifice of their children represented their highest political credentials, particularly when these women were making demands upon the Sandinista government. Maternal sacrifice served as a strong political symbol.

Whether guerrilla fighter, revolutionary, or mother, images of women in Sandinista discourse linked national identity and gender. Rarely did these metaphors concretely promote increased gender equality.

NOTES

1. Several researchers suggest that in the period prior to 1983 with no military aggression, the average Nicaraguan enjoyed an improved standard of living. While some of the Sandinista economic policies contributed to the deterioration of the country's finances, the United States-sponsored contra war that had been waged against Nicaragua since 1982 had a serious effect on the national economy. In 1986 war damages amounted to 60 percent of Nicaragua's export earnings and defense took up half the national budget.

2. According to AMNLAE (Sandinista women's organization), over 11,000 women in Managua, the Nicaraguan capital, are mothers of children killed or disappeared in the war.

3. *Hombria* is derived from the word *hombre*: man. *Hombria* covers the qualities of hegemonic notions of masculinity. In the context of this narrative, the focus is on courage.

4. *Cochones* is the popular representation of passive, feminine homosexuality. Lancaster (1992) provides one of the best analyses of notions of masculinity in Nicaragua.

5. Note that Natalia uses the verb "leave" in relation to the children in the first part of her argument and "abandon" in the second.

6. According to the 1963 census, 20 percent of all households nationally and 25 percent of the households in Managua were headed by women. The 1979 labor force statistics from OEA showed that Nicaragua had the highest rate of women in the work force of any Central American country.

7. According to Bossert (1985), during the period 1974–77 infant mortality was somewhere between 120 and 146 per 1,000 live births.

REFERENCES

Bossert, Thomas John. 1985. "Health Policy: The Dilemma of Success." In T. Walter (ed.), *Nicaragua: The First Five Years*. New York: Praeger.

Collins, Helen. (ed.). 1990. *Women and Revolution Nicaragua*. London: Zed Books.

Lancaster, Roger N. 1992. *Life is Hard: Machismo, Danger, and the Intimacy of Power in Nicaragua*. Berkeley: University of California Press.

Lobao, Linda. 1990. "Women in Revolutionary Movements: Changing Patterns of Latin American Guerrilla Struggle." In G. West and R. Blumberg (eds.), *Women and Social Protest*. New York: Oxford University Press.

MacDonald, Sharon. 1987. "Drawing the Lines—Gender, Peace and War: An Introduction." In S. MacDonald and S. Ardener (eds.), *Images of Women in Peace and War*. London: Macmillan.

Mulinari, Diana. 1996. *Motherwork and Politics in Revolutionary Nicaragua*. Lund, Sweden: Bokbox Publications.

Murguialday, Clara. 1990. *Nicaragua, Revolucion y Feminismo (1977–1989)*. Madrid: Editorial Revolucion.

Perez Alemán, Paola. 1992. "Economic crisis and Women in Nicaragua." In Beneria L. Feldman and S. Feldman (eds.), *Unequal Burden: Economic Crisis, Persistent Poverty and Women's Work*. Boulder: Westview.

Slater, David. 1994. "Power and Social Movements in the Other Occident: Latin America in an International Context." *Latin American Perspectives* 81 (21): 11–37.

Chapter Eighteen

Zapatismo
Gender, Power, and Social Transformation

Mariana Mora

On January 1, 1994, the Ejército Zapatista de Liberación Nacional (EZLN) revealed itself to Mexico and the world by declaring war on the Mexican government and taking over the colonial town of San Cristóbal de las Casas in the southeastern state of Chiapas. In the darkness signaling the New Year, Major Ana María, the major who headed the military maneuver, recovered the national flag from the town's municipal palace, symbol that the struggle had begun, and declared, "The flag has been recovered."[1] Later, during the daylight, curious onlookers talked to Subcomandante Marcos, the voice of the rebel army, and watched as Zapatista soldiers—their faces covered with red bandanas—held the town's square. Few people noticed the number of women insurgents present, and no reporter asked the woman major, who stood alongside Marcos, any questions. However, that day, two EZLN documents appeared in their newsletter, *El Despertador Mexicano*: one, *The First Declaration of the Lacandon Jungle*, issued a declaration of war and a list of demands; and the other, *The Women's Revolutionary Laws*, detailed women's fundamental rights.[2]

As time went on, the covered faces of Zapatista women became well known, as did their public appearances: Comandante Ramona, a tiny Tzotzil woman dressed in an intricately embroidered *huipil*[3] outside San Cristóbal's cathedral during the first peace talks; Comandante Trini, an elderly Tojolabal woman in La Realidad speaking in front of several thousand national and international participants of the first Intercontinental Encounter in July 1996; thousands of Zapatista women, from all parts of the state, marching down the cobblestone streets of San Cristóbal on International Women's Day; the anonymous faces of women and children defending themselves after the Mexican military intervention in February 1995.

Long before the EZLN became public, the indigenous women in its territory participated in the movement. This essay examines some of their history by considering the following questions: How have these women participated in the struggle? How have they defined the movement, and how has the movement structured women's roles? And what are some of the challenges presented to the movement and to the role of women in the process?

The point of departure in answering the preceding questions lies in the relationship between the way Zapatista ideology created space for women to claim their rights as well as how women helped shape the ideology. This section focuses on the first point. The second section of the paper explains the construction of alternatives in the EZLN territory. The third section examines the Women's Revolutionary Law as an example of how women have shaped the struggle and power relations in the community. We then detail the forms of women's participation and the challenges presented. Finally, this paper addresses low-intensity warfare as the main obstacle for the continuation of the movement.

Zapatismo, Giving Power to the Voiceless

Zapatismo, both as a movement and as a set of ideas, breaks from the traditional revolutionary model that embraces the taking of power. Instead of adhering to this objective, the EZLN calls for a reconceptualization of power by constructing it from below—at the individual, family, community, and organizational level. Power, they say, begins with self-representation and through the construction of local nuclei in which the most marginalized of society, especially women and indigenous people, create channels for their voices to be heard.[4] As these nuclei solidify, power is redistributed from a vertical structure to a horizontal base, and the current institutions eventually shatter and are slowly replaced by local forces.

Globalization and the neoliberal economic model, the Zapatistas argue, are The Enemy because they lead to the global political-economic concentration of power and capital as well as the elimination of cultural, political, ecological, and economic diversity. "Globalization of the markets signifies erasing borders for crime and economic speculation and multiplying them for humankind. . . . It doesn't turn countries into one country but rather countries into many countries," explained Subcomandante Marcos in his speech during the Intercontinental Encounter against Neoliberalism and for Humanity in July 1996.[5]

Rather than allowing neoliberalism to dismember humanity, Zapatismo instead calls for the construction of spaces in which all members of humankind can participate and reclaim control over their own lives in order to "create a world in which all worlds can fit."[6] This construction of power focuses on the "forever dead," that is to say, those sectors of society eternally labeled "the other," which in Mexico have historically been indigenous peoples and women.

By building local forces based on self-representation, the Zapatistas hope to carve spaces for the voices of those who, up to this point, have been silenced and to assure that these voices actively participate in constructing the future.[7] By creating a force from below, Zapatismo breaks from a pattern that is advantageous to those who already have access to power. In revolutions focused on taking power, it is men, in this case mestizo men, who are more likely to secure power and create new institutions so that the rest of society can benefit. In the case of Zapatismo, the objective of the revolution is realized through the revolutionary process and therefore creates the space for Mexico's indigenous groups, women, and other marginalized sectors of society to define how that process evolves while at the same time empowering them.

The Struggle for Autonomy, the Construction
of Regional Alternatives

Within the EZLN territory, Zapatismo seeks territorial autonomy. The Tzeltales, Tzotziles, Tojolabales, Choles, and Mames who make up the EZLN do not intend to separate themselves from the nation-state but rather cause its transformation through the inclusion of their cultural, political, social, and economic traditions as well as those of the fifty-two indigenous ethnic groups making up Mexico. As a pivotal issue, the question of autonomy was central in the first round of peace talks entitled "Indigenous Rights and Culture," held in February 1996 in the fog-covered highland community of San Andrés Larrainzer Sacam Ch'en de los Pobres. In the Indigenous Forum organized by the EZLN to gather the opinions of Mexico's indigenous groups prior to the peace talks, the Mixe Indians of the state of Oaxaca presented a document in which they define autonomy as "the collective form in which we practice self-representation. We don't want to separate ourselves from the Mexican nation, but rather we are only demanding spaces of liberty in order to: possess, control, and manage our territories, take control over our political, economic, social and cultural life, as well as intervene in national decisions because they affect us" (Servicios del Pueblo Mixe, 1996: 19).

The EZLN territory—composed of the canyons in the Lacandon Jungle, the Chiapas highlands, and the northern part of the state—is now divided into autonomous municipalities. Some of these, such as 17th of November (remunicipalized from what used to be the region of Altamirano), already have their own parliamentary structure and commissions overseeing the thirteen points of autonomy, such as land, education, health, women's rights, and agricultural production. Each commission is responsible for ensuring that the municipality self-administers its territory. For example, the commission on education is responsible for the creation of a methodology to train local teachers, develop a bilingual curriculum, and create educational materials based on their indigenous culture and practices.

The nation-state, according to the EZLN objectives, would still have to channel funds and fulfill its constitutional obligations, but the municipality would administer those funds and, in the case of educational funds, how the population is taught. Thus the EZLN creates a new type of relationship to the nation in which the municipality acts on the principle of self-determination without segregating itself from the rest of society.

The First Revolution within the Revolution: Focusing on Gender to
Reconstruct Local Power

The relationship between the autonomous regions and the nation-state is analogous to that between women and the community. The movement attempts to transform the nation-state by redistributing power, recognizing differences within equality and creating mechanisms for self-representation. Likewise, it attempts to transform gender relationships within the community by breaking with traditions that subordinate women, creating spaces for their individual rights and providing equal participation in the decision-making processes of the family, the community, and the Zapatista movement. Thus, Zapatismo attempts to create autonomy for women within the community without separating them from the collective whole. By transforming gender relationships, women are not only empowered in their own space, but the entire social fabric is strengthened.

The focus on women's rights puts into practice the Zapatista concept of power in communities. In order to do this, Zapatistas have radically transformed traditions that made women the invisible within the invisible. The first cracks fractured the traditional community structure early in the movement as women began to incorporate themselves among the military ranks. It was their high level of participation that allowed for a series of small cracks to follow as they decided that a document outlining the rights of women needed to be written. As Comandante Susana, the main instigator of the document, explained in an interview with journalist Guiomar Rovira, "I decided that things would be better if there was a Law of Women, so we began to organize in each community so that there would be such a law. . . . The women, my *compañeras*, saw that there isn't any respect, that is why we wrote the law, so that there would be respect. . . . We went to all the villages, in each one we held an assembly and collected the opinions of the women. Later we met with the men and joined together everyone's ideas" (Rovira, 1997: 73).

The law was approved in March 1993 in an assembly described by Subcomandante Marcos in a letter published in the Mexican newspaper, *La Jornada*,

> Comandante Susana, of Tzotzil ethnicity, is angry. A little while ago other members of the Indigenous Revolutionary Clandestine Committee (CCRI) were teasing her for being responsible for the first uprising of the EZLN in March 1993. "I'm furious," she says. ". . . The compañeros say that it is my fault that the Zapatistas rose up last year." . . . Later I discovered what it was about: in March 1993, the compañeros discussed what later became the "Revolutionary Laws." Susana was in charge of visiting dozens of communities to talk to the women's groups and, through their thoughts, draft the "Law of Women." When the CCRI met to vote the laws into effect, each commission had their turn: justice, agrarian law, war taxes, rights and obligations of communities in the struggle, and women. Susana read the proposals that synthesized the thoughts of thousands of indigenous compañeras. . . . The law of women, that Susana had just finished reading, meant for the indigenous communities a true revolution. While the men looked at each other nervously, the women applauded and spoke amongst themselves. Needless to say, the law of women was unanimously approved. . . . This is the truth, the first EZLN uprising happened in March of 1993, and was headed by the women. There were no casualties and they were victorious. Such are things in these lands. (*La Jornada*, January 30, 1994: 1)

The Women's Revolutionary Law creates a framework for the construction of women's rights in the family, in the community, and in the revolutionary movement. It has become a channel for creating dialogue among the women Zapatistas and the population in general, not just as a way of ensuring that its contents are practiced but also to create a discussion about the role of women within the struggle and in society (Millán, 1996). The text, as published in *El Despertador Mexicano*, on January 1, 1994, is as follows:

> In the just struggle for the liberation of our people, the EZLN incorporates women into the revolutionary struggle, regardless of race, creed, color or political affiliation. The only requirement is to make the demands of the oppressed people one's own and the commitment to accomplish the laws and regulations of the revolution. Taking into account the situation of the working woman in Mexico, her just demands for equality and justice are incorporated into the following Women's Revolutionary Laws:
>
> 1) Women, regardless of race, creed, color, or political affiliation, have the right to participate in the revolutionary struggle in the space and to the degree which her capacity and desire determines.
> 2) Women have the right to work and receive a just salary.
> 3) Women have the right to decide the number of children they want and can take care of.
> 4) Women have the right to participate in matters of the community and to have "cargo" responsibility if they are elected freely and democratically.
> 5) Women and children have the right to medical and nutritional attention.
> 6) Women have rights to education.
> 7) Women have the right to choose their partner and not be forced into marriage.
> 8) No woman can be beaten or mistreated by a family member or stranger. Those charged of rape or attempted rape will be severely punished.
> 9) Women can take positions of leadership in the organization and have military rank in the revolutionary armed forces.
> 10) Women have all the rights and obligations as signaled in the revolutionary laws and regulations.

The Women's Revolutionary Law represents the determination of women to participate in defining the movement. The fact that this document was voted into place and unanimously approved is also representative of Zapatismo as an ideology that embraces new forms of thinking and acting when the traditions no longer respond for the collective benefit of the community. Yet it simultaneously revives and strengthens those cultural traditions that will guide the future. By far the three points in the law that represent the most significant changes are the right to own land, the right for a woman to choose her partner, and the right to choose the number of children she wants. These three points completely redefine the way a woman is viewed both in the family unit as well as within the community structure. Now that such a document exists, the challenge lies in ensuring that not only are the rights put into practice but that the dialogue that initially created it continues.

The Participation of Women, from the Mountain to the Community

As has been the case in other revolutionary movements, women explored their rights while integrating themselves into the military ranks. Those women that held military positions came down from the mountains to work and raise consciousness among the civilian support base. Comandante Christina,[8] a young Tzeltal woman from the region of Altamirano, explained how women first became involved in the movement: "When there was first talk about the clandestine organization, it was only the men that participated. They were the first to go to meetings and some agreed that women had to become involved as well. Little by little, women started participating because we realized that in order to struggle, everyone had to be involved, men can't do it alone" (interview, June 1997).

The recruitment of women into the organization occurred in a number of ways and for various reasons. In some cases it was through the family unit, as this was the primary structure that allowed the EZLN's support base to grow during the 1980s and the beginning of the 1990s. The older son would begin to participate and explain the struggle to the mother and father. In other cases it was the daughter, or even the mother who, for the future of her children, became interested in the organization. In the ten years undercover, beginning in 1984, the EZLN incorporated more and more women into its military ranks. At first, only two, Major Ana María, now maximum military authority in the highland region, and another compañera, participated. Later, as they became visible, others decided to integrate themselves. As the major explained,

> Many women decide to do this [enter into the EZLN as insurgents] because they see that they have absolutely no rights in their community, they don't have rights to education, or any sort of preparation; they keep them there as if they had a cloth around their eyes without learning about anything; they are mistreated, and exploited. They are exploited much more than the men because they are much more marginalized. (Rovira, 1997: 73)

It was during the training in the mountains where women experienced, for the first time, a level of equality and where they explored their rights as women. As part of their military duties, the EZLN women insurgents had to perform certain recruitment and consciousness-raising duties in the support base communities. These insurgents faced difficulty because of the lack of space in which they could freely speak. They found the answer by organizing women into production collectives in the communities (Rovira, 1997). Although initially set up in some areas by women insurgents for strategic military purposes, women's collectives now function in the vast majority of the support base and are completely run by civilian women.

"Now that we are organized in collectives, more and more women are beginning to awaken," explained Comandante Christina.

> For example, here in the community, we have a collective of women artisans, bread making, a vegetable garden, and a collective *milpa* [land in which to grow corn, beans, and squash]. Working in the collectives not only gives women a chance to provide food to the community or to sell products and earn some money, but, more importantly, it is a space in which women can learn about their rights. I remember when the only *milpa* was for men and women, we would all have to go together. The men would make fun of us because we would bow our heads and not speak a word. They would say we were dumb and didn't know how. Once we decided to have our own *milpa*, apart from the work we do with the men, everything changed. We laugh, we joke, we

never stop talking! It is here where we learn from each other, where the women that have "awakened" talk to those that are still "asleep" and where those that have fears are guided by those that have found their voice. It was in a space similar to this where I first learned about my rights, and learned to lose the fear of my silence in order to speak. (Interview, April 1997)

The Changing Role of Women in the Community

Women now comprise over one-third of the EZLN military. In addition to participating in the military, women also form part of the Zapatista political leadership both in the form of overseeing appointed responsibilities in the villages and as members of the Indigenous Clandestine Revolutionary Committee (CCRI), the highest political body. With women participating at all levels of the organization and in all of its parts, concrete changes, albeit slow and plagued with challenges, have taken place.

Ofelia, a Tzeltal elder from the region of Altamirano, explained "how things used to be" when describing her marriage to her husband:

I was basically traded for several jugs of *posh*,[9] soda, cigarettes, and corn. My parents and my husband's parents prearranged the marriage from the time we were children. I wasn't allowed to even meet him until the day of the marriage. It didn't matter if I loved him or not or if he was a drunk and beat me, as was the case; what mattered was the agreement our parents made. Life was much more difficult then, for everyone in the community. We suffered much more than we do now. It was worse so for the women. But we weren't aware of our suffering, we just thought that is how things were supposed to be. (Interview, July 1997)

Herminia, a younger woman standing next to her, nodded her head in understanding, "Women still do more work than the men," she said, " but things have changed. Not only do we now choose our own husbands but we have found our voice and responsibility in the community. Our work, the work women do, strengthens the communal tasks. Like the work in the women's collective *milpa*, what we harvest is for the benefit of the community" (interview, July 1997).

The most significant change in women's lives and in the family occurred when men, under EZLN law, quit drinking. Herminia said:

Now that the men—our husbands, fathers, and brothers—don't drink, there is less violence in the family. Some men are still confused and don't understand the rights of women, but many have stopped beating their wives. Some men in the community completely support us, and they help talk to the men who still don't understand. Under the Zapatista Laws, the community has to support the woman if she is beaten, so now more women have less fear of speaking out because they know they will be backed up. Not only has violence lessened but we have found that men are much more willing to listen to us and understand what we have to say when they are not drunk.

Although the initial spaces have been carved for the transformation of gender relationships in the communities, many obstacles limit progress. Perhaps the greatest

obstacle is changing the attitudes, not just of men, but of women as well. Comandante Magdalena, a Tzeltal women from the municipality 17th of November talked
about the barriers that exist in the region she oversees: "Not all women, or even the
majority of women participate, but some women do. Even though other women or
men don't understand and speak badly of them, they don't care. They are committed
and continue with their struggle, what they know is correct, with what they know
needs to change. But it is difficult to change the ideas that other people still carry with
them" (interview, July 1997). Some men, primarily those who have also received military training, support and actively encourage their wives or daughters to participate.
Comandante Christina's husband, for example, who is also a comandante, takes care
of their child, cooks, and cleans the house when she is away. For the most part, however, the women have actively pushed open spaces for other women and supported
their efforts to take part in the public space of the community.

Comandante Magdalena went on to describe the various types of spaces she
helps to create so that women can begin to participate.

> We work a lot with the *muchachas*, the younger women, because they are more willing
> to learn new things. With them, we plan various activities to help them lose their fear.
> Not only do we have discussions while working in the collectives, but we also plan
> basketball tournaments, like the men do on days of festivity. They learn to play and
> participate, even if it is in their dresses and plastic shoes, in front of the eyes of the
> community. We also plan theater pieces and songs so that the women can express
> themselves during the cultural events on the days of fiesta.

At the April 10 celebration of Zapata's death, in the Diez de Abril community,
men, women, children, and elders participated in the festivities.[10] In the center of
the community, the elders danced to traditional songs, while later in the evening
adolescent girls, dressed in flowered dresses and wearing ribbons in their hair, sang
a song composed during a municipal women's meeting titled, "No One Ever Takes
Us into Account." In between giggles, but with their backs very straight, they sang,
"As girls, no one ever takes us into account/ Not when it's time for school/Not
when it's time to talk/ Not when it's time to play/ We are only taken into account
when it's time to cook/ When it's time to carry water/ When it's time to take care
of our younger brothers."

Cultural events are something fairly new and part of most EZLN support base
communities since it is a conscious strategy to maintain cultural practices while
incorporating new traditions into their history. Local leadership attempts to re-
create the history of the struggle and remain firmly rooted in their past by ensuring
that traditions along with recently created pieces are integrated through cross generational participation and through the voices of both genders.

The Threat to the Vision: Low Intensity Warfare, the Reagan Doctrine

The main threat to the future is the low-intensity warfare first launched by the
Mexican government immediately following the January 1 uprising. Although the

fighting lasted only twelve days, the communities have been subjected to a war of attrition for the past three years. The impact of low-intensity warfare according to the Fray Bartolomé Human Rights Center's book, *Ni Paz Ni Justicia,* is stated as follows: "This war of attrition is one in which the objective is not to physically eliminate the enemy but rather undermine, delegitimize, and isolate him until he is no longer considered a valid and stable alternative for the people" (Centro de Derechos Humanos Fray Bartolomé de las Casas, 1997: 167).

Low-intensity warfare undermines the social fabric and psychologically demoralizes the community to achieve its objectives. It severely alters the daily life of the community and doubly affects women, as those whose role has traditionally been one of resource reproduction and of weavers of the extended family structure (Jiménez, 1997a; Jiménez, 1997c). For that reason, women have become central targets in this counterinsurgency operation. The territory is saturated by Mexican soldiers who declare their presence in places that are most intimidating to women: the washing and bathing spots in the river, the areas where women walk to fetch wood, or other spaces primarily occupied by women and children.[11]

Comandante Magdalena described the pressure women feel under this source of tension:

> With the heavy presence of the Mexican military everyone—men, women, children and elders—suffer, but in some cases, the women more so. When the military increases their patrolling and surveillance, the men can't leave the community to go work in the *milpa,* they can't harvest the beans or the corn. They suffer knowing that the family is suffering. But the woman has to find the way for the family to survive. She has to find a way to make tortillas when there is no corn, find something to eat when there is no food. She has to take care of the children when they get sick because they can't eat, she has to continue fetching water and carrying wood even if the military patrols in those very spots. (Interview, July 1997)

Besides being targeted under low-intensity warfare as the reproducers of resources in the household, women are doubly affected as they often become targets of the frustrations of their husbands and fathers. An example of this was presented by Father John,[12] a priest from the parish of Ocosingo, as he spoke directly to the men about low-intensity warfare and gender dynamics during mass one morning in the community of La Garrucha. He said during his sermon that the diocese knows that the constant pressure, the threat of war, and the inability to maintain certain fundamental aspects of daily life stable sometimes leads men to go against the orders of "the organization" and return to *jaguar,* alcohol, or begin fights in the family. "But brothers," the priest said,

> That is exactly what the government wants you to do. He wants the poor to fight among the poor, brothers against brothers, and brother against sister. The women bear the brunt of your frustrations. For example, the woman raises pigs in the households, she finds the scraps of food to feed the pig, she makes sure that it gets big and fat, so that it can be sold at a decent price. But it is the man who takes the pig to Ocosingo to sell in the market, and it is the man who keeps the money.

The women turned to each other and smiled. "And if the man is upset, if he feels that things are too difficult, that the struggle is being lost, what does he sometimes do with the money? He spends it on *jaguar*. And what does the woman receive in return for her work? A drunken husband and no cents."

The priest ended the sermon by saying that even though the women suffer the most under these conditions, it is the entire community that ultimately feels the loss and disempowerment, because "if the brothers and sisters don't support each other, the community loses control, it gets weak, and the government wins another small victory."

The Impact of Low-Intensity Warfare on Women

Not only do women bear the weight of men's frustrations but they must also cope with their own fears and stresses. When women are asked about their fears in relation to the military, the main response is the fear of sexual assault and rape. During the last three years since the uprising, documented reports of rape have risen dramatically. Rape has become a central tactic in counterinsurgency (interview with Marta Figueroa, director of COLEM, March 1996). Although advisors to the EZLN and women in numerous forums on women's rights have demanded of the government and international organizations that rape in the conflict zone be considered a war crime, cries have fallen on deaf ears. Meanwhile, incidents of rape and sexual assault continue to take place.

An example of the impact of rape, not only on women but on the entire community, occurred in the summer of 1994. Three Tzeltal women from the village of Morelia were raped at a military checkpoint on their way to the nearby town of Altamirano. The crime was denounced by the San Cristóbal women's group, El Colectivo de Mujeres de San Cristóbal, COLEM, which independently attempted to help the women with their lawsuit but were prevented as the military intervened in almost every step of the process. The medical examinations were done by military doctors at a military camp, military officials handled the interrogations, and the women were so severely harassed and threatened that the community asked the women to relocate in order to protect its safety. The three women eventually dropped the case out of fear, left their community, and took on completely different names and identities.

Of the various forms of the psychological destruction of low-intensity warfare, that which weighs most heavily in the hearts of the women is not only survival, but the healthy survival of their children. Virginia, from the community of 10 de Abril, explains, "My son is only two years old, he barely speaks but already knows what is a helicopter. Whenever one flies overhead, he comes running to me, pulls on my sleeve, and points to the sky" (interview, May 1997).

During the Mexican army's military offensive on February 9, 1995, the communities fled to the mountains as the soldiers hunted for the EZLN leadership. The offensive took the Zapatista support bases by surprise and the women had to carry their small children up to prearranged hiding places in the mountains with limited food supplies. "I don't know what will happen if there is another offensive like in 1995," Virginia continued to explain:

> My son was barely five months old when we had to go into hiding for over two months. I wasn't the only one to carry a newborn to the *monte*, the mountains, some women even gave birth in our temporary refugee camp. Those times were really difficult for me. I felt guilty for having put my son through so much suffering. Since I hardly ate, my milk dried up, and if it wasn't for the courses on nutrition that I learned while working with the nuns at the San Carlos hospital, my son could have died. In 1995, we were lucky to have survived, but that wasn't a real war, we haven't seen real warfare. The next time there is an offensive, that will be war, and I know many, too many will die.

While the threat of full-blown warfare weighs on the minds of people living in the so-called conflict zone, frequent confrontations with the military provide a steady reminder of external pressures. Women often have to interact with the soldiers during such confrontations, since the men work in the *milpa* during the day or hide for fear of being taken when the military enters. A powerful example occurred in the Zapatista Center of Resistance Oventic when the Mexican military attempted to establish a camp in this highland community.[13] The men were away in the collective milpa, so when the community alarm sounded, the women and children quickly grabbed whatever makeshift weapons were most accessible—stones, sticks, a few machetes. Some covered their faces with red bandanas, the symbol of their identity, as they ran to block the road. The women, grandmothers, mothers, and young daughters firmly planted themselves in front of the armored vehicles, throwing stones and hurling insults in Spanish and Tzotzil. In one instance, a little girl placed her hand in front of a soldier's machine gun as he stepped down from his vehicle. Eventually the soldiers gave up, turned around, and the tanks rolled back down the road, followed by the women who accompanied them to make sure they were indeed leaving.[14]

Scenes such as this are a common occurrence in the communities. As those who have to show their masked faces to the enemy, women are forced to shatter their role as keepers of the private sphere and become the voices and protectors of the community. As Marina Jiménez, the director of Fray Bartolomé Human Rights Center, explains, "Women have had to confront their fears and the dangers of living in a context of war to become the subjects of collective security" (Jiménez, 1997b). In the continual demand for their rights and the rights of their communities, women not only defend their villages from the military but actively take part in demonstrations, marches, forums, and conventions. Since 1994, women's voices have had a dramatic impact, felt beyond the EZLN territory.

From the Jungle to the National Dialogue

Women are not only more active in the public sphere and in demanding changes in their private roles, but they have become an integral part of the national dialogue that surfaced after the EZLN cried "¡Ya basta! Enough!" on January 1. The active participation of Zapatista and non-Zapatista women created spaces for dialogue previously almost nonexistent in Chiapas and in the rest of the Mexican republic. The new national dialogue, of which indigenous rights and the rights of women play a central role, has become one of self-representation in the construction of a participatory democracy.

This is due in part to the inherent elements of Zapatismo. Compared to other revolutionary struggles, the EZLN is not telling women to wait until the revolution triumphs to become a priority, but rather includes women's rights as a central part of their objectives—the reconstruction and redefinition of power in order to include the excluded. Similar to other revolutions, women in the movement are not simply expecting Zapatismo to incorporate the transformation of gender relations into their discourse but are actively constructing spaces, for their self empowerment, for the strengthening of the community structure, and for the steering of the national dialogue. Thus the movement becomes one in which the objectives are defined through the process of their construction and whose spaces are not just for the benefit of women, or for the indigenous of Mexico but for the collective whole.

Contrary to the events of the past, those leading the discourse and shaping the discussions are the same people whose plight is being addressed. The traditional paternalism in which those in power address the needs of the "deep Mexico," the indigenous Mexico, as well as the needs of indigenous and non-indigenous women, has largely dissolved. The new national dialogue, and the transformation of those voices into the construction of alternatives, has become one of self-representation. The conceptualization of power, as understood and practiced in Zapatismo, has created the room for this process to take place precisely because it was constructed by those to whom it speaks, "the forever dead who had to die in order to live."

NOTES

1. Subcomandante Marcos, "Twelve women on the twelfth year (second of the war)."

2. In this document, the EZLN states the following demands: work, land, house, food, health, education, independence, liberty, democracy, justice, and peace.

3. A traditional embroidered blouse.

4. For a more detailed description of how the EZLN sees this taking place on a national scale, see The Fourth Declaration of the Lacandon Jungle.

5. The convention was held in the five Zapatista Centers of Resistance from July 27-August 3, 1996 in which over 4,000 people from 42 countries participated. In his closing speech, Subcomandante Marcos explained the ways in which the fragmentation of humanity takes place under neoliberalism: through the militarization of many aspects of daily life as a means of controlling any threat to the model, marginalization to the point of genocide of those sectors of the population who are "economically disposable," and the transferring of control from the nation-state to the virtual power of the market. This is manifested in the explosion of internal conflicts throughout the world.

6. A phrase commonly used by the EZLN when describing its vision of the world.

7. For that same reason, the Zapatistas have never claimed that they have the recipe for solutions and that it is up to the rest of society to learn what they know, but rather admit that all must participate in shaping Mexico's future through a process.

8. Names of all women comandantes have been changed.

9. Home-made liquor.

10. Emiliano Zapata, a hero of the Mexican Revolution, is a symbol for the land struggle and is known for the phrases, "Land and Liberty" and "Land for those who work it."

11. Although it is difficult to know the exact number of Mexican soldiers in the state of Chiapas, roughly 60 percent of the entire Mexican military is present in the state.

12. The Father's name has also been changed.

13. In January 1996, the EZLN formally declared five Centers of Resistance within their territory: Oventic in the highland, Morelia in the region of Altamirano, La Garrucha in the canyon of Ocosingo, La Realidad past the region of Las Margaritas, and Roberto Barrios 30 kilometers from the town of Palenque.

14. The powerful images were captured by San Cristóbal video documentalist, Carlos Martinez, February 1996.

REFERENCES

Centro de Derechos Humanos Fray Bartolomé de las Casas. 1996. *Ni Paz Ni Justicia*. San Cristóbal.

Holloway, John. 1996. "La resonancia del zapatismo." In *Chiapas 3*. Mexico: Ediciones Era.

Jiménez, Marina Patricia Ramirez. 1997a. "Resistencia Civil y la Participación de la Mujer en el Proceso de Paz en Chiapas." Paper presented in Los Angeles, California (January).

———. 1997b. "Mujeres y Resistencia en zonas rurales de México." Paper presented in Taxco, Mexico (June).

———. 1997c. "Militarización en México." Paper presented in Los Angeles, California (January).

LeBot, Yvon. 1997. *Subcomandante Marcos: El Sueño Zapatista*. Spain: Plaza & Janés.

Millán, Márgara. 1996. "Las zapatistas de mil del milenio. Hacia políticas de auto-representación de las mujeres indígenas." In *Chiapas 3*. Mexico: Ediciones Era.

Montemayor, Carlos. 1997. *Chiapas: La rebelión indígena de México*. Mexico: Editorial Joaquín Mortiz.

Rovira, Guiomar. 1997. *Mujeres de Maíz*. Mexico: Ediciones Era.

Servicios del Pueblo Mixe, AC. 1996. "La autonomía: Una forma concreta de ejercicio del derecho a la libre determinación y sus alcances." In *Chiapas 2*. Mexico: Ediciones Era.

Chapter Nineteen

Domestic Activism and Nationalist Struggle

Monica E. Neugebauer

Scholarship on the political roles of non-Western women within their societies has been limited and is often criticized from a Western-centric point of view. Western feminists sometimes seem mystified by the unwillingness of women in the developing world to engage in certain types of activity or in the pursuit of further gains within the context of a political struggle. Yet what is often overlooked is that our conceptions of what constitutes "political activism" may be different and other social conditions may preclude additional changes to women's status or their forms of expression. Western feminist strategies for activism may not be applicable; a separatist strategy of women's liberation has little room in the context of a national liberation struggle where strong links between segments of society have been carefully nurtured. Also, the view that the family is the principle site of women's oppression may not be viewed as comparable to imperialist or military occupation.

Analyzing the role of women in political conflicts, Rosemary Ridd acknowledges that women do have power in nonpublic roles, but this is usually depoliticized because this power (in the private sphere) does not give them the authority to legitimate their actions in society (Ridd, 1987). This is a limited view of potential influence; is women's activism only valid when it is outside the domestic sphere? This would tend to reinforce the public/private split which Western feminists abhor and maintains the view that participation in the military or formal politics are the only arenas for recognized "political" activism. The usual approach to women's activism that analyzes the activities outside of the home and family is based upon measuring women's status by their influx into the job market and government institutions. However, in doing so, domestic life has become devalued, or at the very least, not recognized as an arena of influence. In many developing countries, women do not work outside of the home and may not have access to political participation; this leaves them with the domestic sphere—one in which they may have ultimate control—as a means of empowerment.

In the Palestinian case, the context of activism is different due to two factors: the different composition of the family and society, and the length of the conflict. The organization of Middle Eastern society is much more fluid than in the West; kinship and community ties are still very strong. The extended family within Palestinian society is itself a social arena, and the domestic sphere is recognized as a site of action and power. The significance of the family must be taken into consideration. While it may be true that placing the interests of others, such as the husband, children, and community, above the self impedes women's interests, the woman's identity may be defined by these people and the very roles she plays in relation to each. She will seek to preserve this identity. Perhaps the reason Western feminists do not acknowledge domestic activism and advocate strategies of separatism is because Western women themselves are very autonomous individuals who do not relish interdependence, and because the structure of the nuclear family is very isolating, thus prompting Western women to seek forms of expression in more social formats like the business world, the military, or formal politics.

Another defining characteristic of the Palestinian conflict is its duration. Julie Peteet, an anthropologist who has conducted a great deal of research on the links between women and struggle, writes:

> The mobilization of the domestic sector during a protracted crisis disputes any facile dichotomy between formal and informal spheres, and domestic and public domains. When a community is under attack, . . . domestic boundaries are shattered, revealing the illusory character of domesticity as the realm of private familial relations distanced from the spheres of formal politics. (Peteet, 1986:22)

The "private" sphere of the Palestinian woman is far from apolitical; home demolitions, random imprisonment of sons and husbands, and refugee status are definitely within the realm of politics. Palestinian women feel their entire life is politicized; the majority of the population either experienced the debacle of the June 1967 war, or were born since and have lived their entire lives under Israeli occupation. They do not feel there is a split between public and private as described in the West.

The politicizing of domesticity consists of women baking the bread, preparing the food, and tending to the wounded. Reproductive politics is embodied in the "mother of the martyr"; the maternal sacrifice of a son is the supreme political act, and the mother becomes the symbol of the trauma of exile and resistance. It is her duty to educate her children to be nationalists. These forms of action do not challenge domesticity, but expand the tasks and political significance associated with them. Remaining in the domestic sphere may keep women from making certain contributions to public struggle, but it strengthens the bonds of cooperation among women which can be mobilized in a way that brings women into meaningful participation. It must be realized that discarding the private sphere may not be beneficial to all women. In developing societies this individualism leaves women very vulnerable because the infrastructure and economic and educational systems are not well enough established to offer alternative forms of support in place of the extended family or community.

The Palestinian struggle for an independent state has a long history, and the participation of women has been strong since the beginning. It has been characterized by the efforts of women to mobilize still more women. The women's movement has consisted of women capitalizing on their traditional roles as mother, caretaker, and educator, in order to increase the sphere of political participation and significance. The division between public and private is not being maintained; rather, domestic activism is taking the public into the private realm.

As early as 1917, Palestinian women acted on behalf of national aspirations. This early phase of activism was initiated by the wealthy, educated, urban women affiliated with the male leaders of the nationalist movement. Their actions consisted of raising consciousness by traveling to villages and making speeches and lodging formal protests against British occupation. The creation of Israel in 1948 marked a change in women's needs and strategies. Charitable organizations were founded in order to provide social services in the face of losses of homes and land, and upheaval due to the diaspora and the formation of refugee camps. Although the women were very active, it was always within the context of the national struggle. Yet the women realized that this was the only chance to break into the male public sphere.

The Arab loss of the June 1967 war was devastating to the Palestinians. The Israeli occupation of the West Bank and Gaza resulted in the complete confiscation of remaining Palestinian lands and increasingly harsh means of repression. The crisis destroyed traditional patterns of affiliation to land and kin and fueled a new sense of radicalism, also among women, many of whom had lost their means of livelihood with the confiscation of agricultural lands. Even nonactivist women could not escape occupation and had to live with the imprisonment of men, the imposition of social controls, the loss of income, and the destruction of their homes.

This era was marked by a flourish of institution building as protest movements consolidated their organizations and sought to extend their memberships. This extended to the women as well. The two most prominent organizations were the General Union of Palestinian Women (GUPW) and the Palestinian Union of Women's Work Committees. The General Union was formed in 1965 and unified several smaller charitable organizations. The formation of the Women's Work Committees in 1978 was representative of a new form of activism that emerged in the 1970s. New grassroots committees composed of trade and student unions and youth organizations engaged in volunteer work in order to involve the urban poor and rural populations. Activities included literacy programs, publishing leaflets, fundraising, crafts training for homework projects, aid to the families of prisoners, and health education. The goal was to raise consciousness and mobilize the population into the nationalist struggle. While these committees extended the avenues of activity, especially for younger, university women, the group soon split into different parties reflecting their affiliation with the four main factions of the PLO.

While work committees operated within the liberation movement, private women's organizations developed as well. The most famous were the *In'ash al-Usra* (the Society for Family Development) and the Arab Women's Union, which operated a hospital in Nablus. Both were motivated by charitable and nationalist sentiments. The society was founded in 1965 by Samiha Khalil, and at its height in the mid-1980s it had 152 full-time employees consisting of teachers, caretakers, clerks, and librarians. Its membership of 5,000 women were engaged in home-production activities such as embroidery, knitting, and sewing. It offered classes, day care, a dental clinic, a cosmetics institute, orphanage, library, and textile workshops. These organizations were the most effective way to mobilize the women because they operated in the same sphere. They brought the public realm into the private and appealed on the familiar level of a sisterhood.

What characterized the women's movement up to this point was a dedication of attention and activities to the nationalist movement. Prevailing gender ideologies were not challenged. Despite widespread memberships and the provision of important social services, these movements did not significantly change the status of women in Palestinian society due to several factors. Most importantly, the women lacked a broad-based coalition and the autonomy to promote their own agenda. The nature of the nationalist struggle meant formal integration into the liberation movement that fragmented their organizations across ideological lines and caused a sense of paralysis in their actions. Their potential autonomy to pursue women's issues and social concerns was diluted because they were part of a wider political movement that granted primary concern to the goal of independence. These women's groups did not challenge the patriarchy of nationalism or of the PLO, thus the leadership remained ambivalent to the issue of gender. Some factions, especially Fatah, did not want to confront social transformation due to a fear of alienating support. Private organizations faced Israeli repression and forced closure. And, women's groups also had far fewer resources, limiting their ability to attain widespread exposure. Their sources of support usually came from United Nations grants, membership fees, and some private contributions, which quickly dried up in times of scarce finances.

A major change occurred in the late 1980s that catapulted the women of Palestine into a new form of activism marked by direct confrontations with the presiding sources of oppression and an independence in their actions. This catalyst was called *intifada*.

The *intifada* was a unique moment in the Palestinian struggle. Previously, activities had been structured and planned by the PLO or its component factions. The emphasis had been on armed struggle, shuttle diplomacy, and limited mass action, all dominated and controlled by men. Yet the *intifada* was a spontaneous reaction to years of oppression, and was marked by mass insurgency and collective defiance. The *intifada* marked a shift from formal, centralized control of the liberation struggle by the factions to activism by local committees.

The numerous grassroots and neighborhood movements formed by the women extended participation and democratized the struggle. The *intifada* was distinct in that it was reliant upon the activism of village and refugee camp women, two groups that had been reluctant to participate so openly in the past. The women's organizations were nonhierarchical and sought horizontal integration; the lack of an overarching leadership structure allowed for decentralization; and the lack of a paramilitary as an outlet focused attention on social, economic, and legal concerns and activities.

Yet despite its revolutionary beginnings, the *intifada* is a story of gains and losses. The women feel alienated, because they believe that the committees they established during the struggle laid the foundations for the new system, and now they are being ignored. Women's activism and visibility were higher than ever before, yet they suffered continuous Israeli repression of their committees, closure of the universities, and an Islamic backlash. The results of the *intifada* were disheartening. Arafat's PLO had once again entered the scene and took charge of the grassroots protests and mobilized militant youth to confront the Israelis, pushing women to the sidelines of a battle they had started. At the same time, Islamic groups tried to enforce new dress codes, including mandatory veiling, sometimes violently, and secular parties acquiesced in order to avoid confrontation.

The post-*intifada* situation is still characterized by conditions that reinforce the subordination of women, but it is also one that has a strong potential to influence the emerging political organization.

The traditional liberation organizations cannot be counted on to promote women's development. The PLO positioned itself as a government-in-exile for decades, yet when the Palestinian authority assumed control over the self-rule areas, it had no clear plans for health, education, economic development, or social involvement. Rather, the multitude of women's organizations had served to meet these needs. PLO leadership never developed an acknowledgment of women's diverse roles and since 1982 reflected the belief that women's primary role was as the mainstay of the family and the vessel of Palestinian culture. This was due to the PLO's increasing insensitivity due to geographic isolation and an appeal to the growing number of Islamist (*Hamas*) supporters.

This represents the new threat to women's emancipation—a resurgent Islamist movement. The appeal of Hamas is due to the extreme economic conditions experienced by the Palestinians, especially those in the Gaza Strip and the refugee camps, where poverty and feelings of marginalization are at their worst. The Islamists attacked the PLO's status by focusing on its weakest link—the lack of cultural sensitivity and social programs—the two areas that involve women the most. The problem is that Hamas is not just a religious revival, but a political movement as well, which also strives to influence the current state-building process. This is something not realized by the traditional nationalists, who just view Hamas as another faction, yet it is frighteningly acknowledged by most women, who know that Hamas is their direct antithesis. It seeks to maintain the split between public and private law, and wants a total separation between Islamic courts, which would deal with issues of "personal status" such as marriage, divorce, and inheritances, and a new Justice Ministry, which would handle criminal and company law.

The Palestinian women are now left with a dilemma: Do they strive to influence the state-building process or do they act independently? The leaders of the women's movements believe that their best chances for preserving their status still involve the pursuit of full legal equality and access to positions of leadership, as well as continuing to shift consciousness in society toward the recognition of the rights of women.

The means for action consist of several components. The place of women's organizations remains strong. In the last five years, many new centers and research organizations have arisen to focus attention on legal rights, domestic violence, and the study of women's issues. These include the Center for Women's Legal Rights and Counseling in East Jerusalem, the Women's Study Committee in Ramallah, and the Women's Resource and Research Center. What is distinctive about these groups is that for the first time they are organized and run solely by women for the express purpose of addressing women's issues. The mission of these new research and resource centers must be on education and training, the gathering of data on the conditions of women, and efforts toward communication and publication. The Women's Study Center in Jerusalem publishes a women's magazine, and Women's Affairs in Nablus and Gaza teaches courses in the social sciences, methodology, English, women in development and Palestinan history, and publishes a journal. Bir Zeit University has created an institute for women's studies, only the second of its kind in the Arab world. Women's organizations must also encourage public discussion of violence and abuse against women and serve as advocacy groups to promote better access to health care and the need for the reform of family law. Like many of the women's groups before them, these new centers can serve as the foundation for a social infrastructure that may find a role in a new Palestinian state.

In the Palestinian case, the activities and gains of women were indeed limited by their subordination under a patriarchal liberation movement, and the practices of patriarchy in Palestinian society remain strong. Thus, this is where the crux of women's actions must be—a desire to change the thinking of society. The future Palestinian state will reflect the Palestinian society. The structure and organizations that grew up around the domestic activism during the liberation movement can now be utilized and expanded to promote consciousness-raising among the rest of the population and move toward social transformation. These groups must remain independent of political factions if they are to enact effective changes. The battle for an independent Palestine may be drawing to a close, but for the women many years of fighting remain.

REFERENCES

Abdo, Nahla. 1994. "Nationalism and Feminism: Palestinian Women and the *Intifada*—No Going Back?" in *Gender and National Identity: Women and Politics in Muslim Societies,* Valentine M. Moghadam (ed.). London: Zed Books.

Brand, Laurie. 1988. *Palestinians in the Arab World. Institution-Building and the Search for State.* New York: Columbia University Press.

Callaway, Helen. 1987. "Survival and Support: Women's Forms of Political Action." In Ridd and Callaway (eds.).

Danforth, Sandra. 1984. "The Social and Political Implications of Muslim—Middle Eastern Women's Participation in Violent Conflict." *Women and Politics* (Spring).

Develin-McAliskey, Bernadette. 1992. "No Patronage, Please, Sisters: Northern Ireland." *Connexions* (Summer).

Emerson, Gloria. 1991. *Gaza: A Year in the Intifada.* New York: Atlantic Monthly Press.

Fishman, Alex. 1989. "The Palestinian Women and the *Intifada*." *New Outlook* (September–October).

Fluehr-Lobban, Carolyn. 1993. "Toward a Theory of Arab-Muslim Women as Activists in Secular and Religious Movements." *Arab Studies Quarterly* (Spring).

Giacaman, Rita, and Penny Johnson. 1989. "Palestinian Women: Building Barricades and Breaking Barriers." In *Intifada: Political Uprising Against Israeli Occupation.* Zachary Lockman and Joel Beinin (eds.). New York: I. B. Tauris and MERIP.

Gluck, Sherna Berger. 1995. "Palestinian Women: Gender Politics and Nationalism." *Journal of Palestine Studies* (Spring).

Haj, Samira. 1992. "Palestinian Women and Patriarchal Relations." *Signs: Journal of Women in Culture and Society* (Summer).

Jayawardena, Kumari. 1986. *Feminism and Nationalism in the Third World*. London: Zed Books.

Joseph, Suad. 1986. "Women and Politics in the Middle East." *Middle East Report* (January–February).

Kawar, Amal. 1993."National Mobilization, War Conditions and Gender Consciousness." *Arab Studies Quarterly* (Spring).

Kuttab, Eileen. 1993. "Palestinian Women in the *Intifada*. Fighting on Two Fronts." *Arab Studies Quarterly* (Spring).

Najjar, Orayb Aref and Kitty Warnock. 1992. *Portraits of Palestinian Women*. Salt Lake City: University of Utah Press.

Peteet, Julie. 1986. "Women and the Palestinian Movement—No Going Back?" *Middle East Report* (January–February).

Ridd, Rosemary. 1987. "Powers of the Powerless." In Ridd and Callaway, eds.

Ridd, Rosemary, and Helen Callaway. (eds.). 1987. *Women and Political Conflict: Portraits of Struggle in Times of Crisis*. New York: New York University Press.

Sinora, Randa George. 1990. *Palestinian Labor in a Dependent Economy: Women Workers in the West Bank Clothing Industry*. Cairo: American University in Cairo Press.

Strumm, Philippa. 1992. *The Women are Marching. The Second Sex and the Palestinian Revolution*. Chicago: Lawrence Hill Books.

Usher, Graham. 1993. "Palestinian Women, the *Intifada* and the State of Independence: An Interview with Rita Giacaman." *Race and Class* (January–March).

Winternitz, Helen. 1991. *A Season of Stones: Living in a Palestinian Village*. New York: Atlantic Monthly Press.

Chapter Twenty

Torture as Text

Irene Matthews

This chapter reads civil warfare in the book *I, Rigoberta Menchú* as an extreme example of how the degradation of a mother's body represents some of the fundamental, archaic goals of warrioring—control and direction of the productive space, the implantation of ideology, and not incidentally, injuring the "enemy" and subjugating other (men's) women.

I will start with a quote, written by a man, that gives historical precedence to the procedure of state terrorism. Tsvetan Todorov's epigraph to *The Conquest of America* cites a report from the sixteenth century:

> As he fought the war of Bacalar, Captain Alonso López de Avila . . . captured a young, pretty and graceful, Indian woman. She, fearful that he might be killed in the war, had promised her husband to have relations with no man other than him; and so, nothing would persuade her not to take her own life, to avoid being defiled by another man; for which reason she was thrown to the dogs. (Landa, 1566:90–91)

This epigraph from observations made in the Yucatan province of Mexico suggests that war would normally seem to directly oppose conjugality. Yet four hundred years after *Conquest*, the way the Mexican Revolution was fought and written about betrayed it as a product of archaic, perhaps Latin, ideology and custom. Although its twin goals of restricted elective power and socialized land distribution are modern political concepts, in this, the first popular revolution of the twentieth century there were certain codes of behavior. Although they were often breached, they were equally often upheld: while huge numbers of the general population were involved in the war, civilian deaths were still often assessed either as "accidental" or as "murder." And men and women were treated differently (although not necessarily "better" or "worse").

Historically, most women's writing on war in the Americas also identified clear gender roles in the "involvement" of men and women in battle. In the second half of the twentieth century, however, civil war takes on a different perspective. It has become no longer a socially sanctioned open conflict but a diffuse and generalized violence, pitting unequal forces against each other: "overarmed militaries" on the one side, and traditionally unarmed civilian institutions on the other—oppositional political parties, workers' unions, the indigenous community, the Church, and the family. Jean Franco reminds us: "These institutions owe their effectiveness as refuges to historically based moral rights and traditions. . . . Homes were, of course, never immune from entry and search but until recently, it was generally males who were rounded up and taken away often leaving women to carry on" (1985:414).

While this is a somewhat optimistic (and class-blind) assessment of the historical inviolability of the domestic—women's space and women's continuity—it does point toward recent drastic increases in attacks on the home front (62 percent of the reported "disappeared" in Argentina's "Dirty War" were kidnapped from their homes, for example). The continual dismantling of forms of civic society in many countries is only the latest terrible example of the erosion of familiar inherited forms of private and public existence. Indeed, in Latin America the eradication of civilian institutions seems to have been an essential factor in the development and self-protection of militarized, authoritarian states. Traditionally, church and family were immediate, tangible rivals to "government." When the state was relatively weak, these were the principal functioning social organizations, and when the state sought to reaffirm hegemonic power, they were absorbed or coerced into subordination or collusion, or, if resistant, identified as "enemies" under a declaration of war.

The contemporary history of almost any country in Latin America might be culled for evidence of large-scale organized political violence as an alternative to other forms of civic persuasion, and for examples of women's involvement and resistance. Tsvetan Todorov chose to epitomize his ethical examination of *The Conquest of America* in terms of women's violation; his work is "dedicated to the memory of a Mayan woman devoured by dogs." After several hundred pages of exegesis on the semiotics of conquest, Todorov returns in his epilogue to the Mayan woman:

> A Mayan woman died devoured by dogs. . . . Her husband, of whom she is the "internal other," already leaves her no possibility of asserting herself as a free subject: fearing he'll be killed in the war, he seeks to ward off the danger by depriving the woman of her will; but war will not only be an affair among men: even when her husband is dead, the wife must continue to belong to him. When the Spanish conquistador appears, this woman is no more than the place where the desires and the wills of two men confront each other. To kill men, to rape women: these are at once proof that a man wields power and his reward. (1984:246)

Todorov's comprehension of the "tragedy of the other"—woman as the place of desire between two men—is interestingly ambivalent. The husband "deprives the woman of her will," yet choosing "to obey her husband and the rules of her own society . . . she places all that remains to her of personal will in defending [herself against] the violence of which she is the object." A hopeless defense if she has no will since it has been prohibited to her—and what sort of will-full "choice" weighs between rape and death?

The central aspect of the reference is, of course, not just horrible violence but the powerlessness of a woman not only caught between the "desires of two men," but unprepared to fight and therefore both choiceless and helpless when her "protector" is unavailable. Her protection is, in this instance as always, as much ideological—a projection of a masculinist ideal—as actual. In "civil" times (one hesitates to call not-war "peace" in our contemporary world), avoidance of rape and of death often depends on women being trained to defend themselves, physically and emotionally; on being capable of negotiating with their attackers; and, above all, on being scared enough and alert enough to avoid dangerous situations. In wartime, when many men are armed and in groups, when violence is sanctioned by the state and therefore not negotiable on a personal level, and when dangerous situations are usually unavoidable, survival is not so easy. Especially when "survival" is associated with degradation and betrayal.

In most areas of Central America today, still subject to violent oppression, women survivors are reluctant to classify violence against themselves as a projection of masculinist aggressions or goals: that in absolute terms more men than women have suffered torture and death in their countries mitigates or conceals the fact that it is primarily men who are the victimizers. It also conceals the fact that (relatively) more of the women victims of police and military violence are uninvolved unfortunates targeted as decoys and hostages for their family connections or punished for seeking information about other deaths and disappearances, or caught up incidentally in recurrent sweeps against the civilian population. And it also conceals the fact that among both "political" and "nonpolitical" prisoners, more than twice as many women as men are submitted to sexual torture, and virtually all women political prisoners are subject to massive and repeated rape.

The book *I, Rigoberta Menchú* makes no overt, direct connection between the continuing cult of machismo in the author's society and the reactionary violence inherent in militarized politics. Nor does the author reduce suffering to a single woman's experience. There exists, however, a strongly personal—and uncomfortable—identification between the individual woman who narrates and the perverse violence perpetrated upon the women who are narrated.

Rigoberta Menchú is the daughter of Vicente Menchú, an indigenous leader burned to death in the Guatemala City Spanish Embassy massacre, who gave his name to one of the leading associations for Christian solidarity and resistance. This "filiation" forged the first link in Rigoberta's chain of social consciousness: her father represented the most noble, the most social (and subsequently, the most revolutionary) aspects of her group life and traditions. Nevertheless, although Rigoberta Menchú seems always to have been, regretfully, more aware of her father's than her mother's social role, she also relates how, as a local leader and as one on call to attend the sick and aid in childbirths throughout the highland area, her mother developed close ties early on with the "*compañeros* from the mountain . . . the *guerrilleros*, as if they were her own children."

This mother had already lost two baby sons to the "normal" conditions under which the Indian families have to live and work, and she will also lose her surviving son to the state terrorism of public and publicized torture in the open assassination— burning alive—of a group of "subversives": an incredible "performance" that recalls Inquisitional tactics and objectives. This scenario, combining political obtuseness and sadistic impunity, serves to instill fear in the onlookers forced to witness the event, but it also serves to unite the people in their anger and in their will to organize. The revolutionary militant carries a twin soul: revenge for the ills of the people, and the conviction that he or she has nothing to lose. In the case of Rigoberta's mother, the death of her son incites in her the anger necessary for overt action: "She went straight to the women and said that when a woman sees her son tortured and burned to death, she is incapable of forgiving anyone and of ridding herself of that hatred, that bitterness" (Menchú 1984:196).

In reconstructing her mother's thoughts and aspirations, Rigoberta Menchú exemplifies women's special courage that gives them the strength to remain "behind the lines" and strengthen others. Rigoberta's mother proves to be as much a revolutionary as her father, her life is a *testimonio vivo*—a "living testimony"—to other women to show them how "they too had to participate, so that when the repression came and people had to suffer, it shouldn't be only the men who suffered . . . that any evolution, any change that women didn't participate in, would be no change and show no victory" (ibid., 196). Women's wartime spirit of community develops out of this sense of political responsibility: in order to be worthy of sharing a better future, the women must also directly share men's combat. So in Guatemala's "revolution" the classic structure of interstate warfare—where men are recruited to protect (ideally) the women and children who are left behind to weep—is radically inverted into the direct confrontation of the weak and the civil against the strong and the militarized. In *I, Rigoberta Menchú*, the Guatemalan women's willingness to confront the army is a deliberate attempt to "read" the "rules" of men's war: "It seemed as though the women and children might be shown more respect by the army because the army mostly kidnapped the men, precisely the leaders of the community. So in this case, the men should leave first and the women stay behind as the rearguard to confront the blows" (ibid., 127).

This nostalgic cooptation of the rules of "civilized" war does not, however, work in the diffuse violence of Guatemala's "low intensity warfare." Many armies are capable of massacring women and children, and this military was notorious for enjoying the spoils of war. When the women and children are left behind as the "rear guard," they run risks equal to those of their men: of capture and death; and of rape.

Organized rape plays a special role in a policy of ethnocide. It violates the rules and customs of the group, spreads fear, morally and physically disintegrates the family and the community, and submits women to the most monstrous evidence of the power of violence. Torture and rape also serve to initiate the unwilling conscript: one of the "training techniques" of modern militaries—particularly those in Central America, where they were likely to be involved in conflicts with guerrillas— is to brutalize new recruits through self-torture and, more often, through forcing them to collaborate in the abuse of captives and civilians. Dissension and mistrust "in the ranks" is quashed through group ritualization of torture, particularly of rape, thus "guaranteeing to the company the solidarity required to sustain it as an effective . . . unit." Torture and rape also reward, or appease, the professional warrior. When Rigoberta's mother is captured, she is raped by the "military chiefs of the town" (ibid., 224). She is tortured almost to death, resuscitated and raped again. It is easy to read into this torture scene an instance of "gang rape taken to its pathological conclusion, where the torturers are competing with one another over who has control of the victim's body and what they do to it" (Wilden, 1985:70). And the logical conclusion, as happens here, is a God-like control over not just woman's body—her life—but also over her death. One of the particular refinements of the technology of intelligence and oppression in modern Latin America, and particularly in Guatemala, is the extent to which the victims were tortured to death.

Additionally, the forces of "conquest" (or control) in Central America were often comprised of young men coopted from the indigenous population itself—although usually from groups or regions other than the ones allocated in the army, many of them orphans taken in off the streets or raised in harshly authoritarian institutions. The outraged body in *I, Rigoberta Menchú* is not that of just "any" Indian woman (although it might be almost every Indian woman). Nor does it represent, as the sixteenth-century versions of conquest did, the common commodity exchange of women's marital fidelity versus the military ethic of rewarding the conqueror. In a country where women are still doubly colonized by their sex and their ethnicity, they are now also punished not because of their chastity, nor to intimidate or humiliate their menfolk, but for the public nature of their own actions: for their assumption of a voice—unprecedented and unwelcome and insistent "noise" against the oppressive monologue of the warfare of state terrorism. This mother's body was punished for daring to stray away from her secondary identity and her home.

Despite Hegel, Nietzsche, Freud, Adler, Levi-Strauss, Bataille, and Theweleit, it takes a special stretch of the imagination to "explain" the (apparently) aberrational nature of male cruelties against the mother. (And I borrow here from Bataille's definition of "cruelty" as one of the forms of organized violence.) Theorists have attempted to isolate the male tendency toward aggression through rereading classic philosophical and psychological parameters and studying girl and boy children. Nancy Chodorow's neo-Freudian analysis of individuation and separation is based on her argument that the asymmetrical "practice" of parenting projects masculine socialization through repression of the female and its relegation to the domestic sphere, in other words, the devaluation of woman-as-mother. In turn, Jessica Benjamin suggests how not merely separation but independence or self-identity requires a confrontation with an other that needs to be "created" in the unwilling domination that physical violence expresses, most often borne out (in a heterosexual and patriarchal society) as male-master and female-victim. If we combine and project these two masculinizing scenarios of empowerment and identification inside the military, we see how the debased woman, and particularly the debased mother—insufficient in her self to fulfill a "real man's" identification needs—"serves" under rape for men to recognize other men's manhood. So, woman in war, or perhaps women and war, becomes the embodiment of what Benjamin calls "the erotic of patriarchy."

We don't have to accept this model (based on Hegel and Bataille), of course, but it seems as though the Guatemalan military did. Imitation and secondariness are almost inevitable characteristics of an army that was a vital but precarious linchpin in a society tottering interminably on successive schemes of dependent development—economic, political, and military. The soldiers in the Guatemalan army were themselves positioned very precariously on the ladder of social and sexual security. Klaus Theweleit observes that the most common sign of upward social mobility is acquiring a woman from the social stratum to which the man has risen. Given Guatemala's complex history of *mestizaje*, that may be the second step; the first is the denigration of the women in the soldier's own social stratum: the indigenous peasant women who don't speak Spanish (but who give birth to soldiers). The capturing and torturing of this mother's body, then, might fill varying categories of "otherness" that conflate the imperialistic, masculinist, racist, and professional inversions of an "orphaned" military based on often reluctant recruitment and socialized into "selfhood" through techniques instilling fear, obedience, alienation, objectification, and brutality.

But just as torture cannot and should not be reduced to mere military methodology or some sort of "torturology," this mother's body is not "merely" a cipher of deathly transcendence nor an abject symbol of repudiated ethics. Her daughter's text re-presents a living, breathing, maternal body that is inflicted with pain and humiliation and done to death as it is used to call her own *biological* children to present themselves morally and actually to the scene. The torture scenario is converted, deliberately, into a timeless scene of sacrifice. The mother's clothes are put "on display" as a record of the event (her capture) and proof of her helplessness, her nakedness. Her family is invited to expose themselves in order to cover up their mother's "shame." In turn, her daughters (in consultation with an absent brother) must agree not to submit themselves to a certain death just like their mother's: "We had to guard that suffering to ourselves, as a testament. . . . And so we had to accept that my mother was going to have to die, in any case. . . . The only thing left for us to hope was that they would kill her quickly, that she would no longer be alive" (Menchú 1984:199–200).

This terrible ethical dilemma involving the daughter's sacrifice of her own mother in wartime, announced as the account of a mother's courageous struggle against violence, is also, perhaps particularly, the story of the daughter's encounter with futility: "I never thought my mother would meet a worse death than my father's" (ibid., 210). The daughter's denial of a normally "attentive" response, her refusal to comply with the torturers' demands that she present herself, may have been the only way to break the cycle that was destroying her family—her father, brother, and now her mother—and her people. If the daughter had only consented (to her own certain death), might her mother have been spared? We are reminded of the terrible futilities of the "family dilemmas" in Holocaust reports, extinguishing indiscriminately the noblest gestures of love and martyrdom. This daughter will never know the truth of her choice but lives on in "panic" of emulating her mother: "I don't want to be a widow woman, and I don't want to be a tortured mother, either" (ibid., 225). *I, Rigoberta Menchú*, and its evidence of and on "participating mothers," underlines how complex is the nature of mothering, and daughtering, in wartime, when the ultimate goal of war—injuring—strains and ruptures forever the closest of all emotional and physical bonds.

While the very public nature of Guatemala's state terrorism against the populace emphasized the devaluation of individual life, it also confirmed the impunity enjoyed by those who perpetrated the official violence. Violence specifically directed against women would seem to have little political import in this climate of virtually total control. Once again, however, I would supplement Todorov's interpretation that widespread rape is a signal to raped women's menfolk, to argue that it is an act of triumph and bonding among the "conquerors" and a signal of contempt to other women. I read *I, Rigoberta Menchú* as the exposure of a conflation of racist and sexist ideologies, many inherited virtually unmediated from the early Spanish agendas compensating for the disappointments of an expected encounter with great civilizations and with gold. Guatemala's political stability is still fundamentally subservient to economic and ideological demands, now from the United States. Like much of Central America, Guatemala is not "underdeveloped" but a construct of *dependent development*, producing seasonal export monocrops for "First World" markets, where often the most heavily labor-intensive but delicate work—the harvesting—can be and still is done best and cheapest by women and children. This essential but secondary population—old people, women, and children—was transplanted to "ideal villages" controlled by institutionalized patriarchy: small teams of male "civil patrols" and the army. A few of the captive population were permitted to preserve their ethnic identity and archaic cultural production in favor of the other foreign currency earner in Guatemala—international tourism for the picturesque (especially women and children in traditional costume) and the purchase of artifacts (handmade primarily by women).

In this system, where traditional paternal and group protection was usurped literally by the presence of the army, where women's submissive production was essential, and where "conquest" was reaffirmed through both violence and seduction, women leaders, and particularly women leaders who themselves birthed a generation of subversives, were a particular anathema. And yet in the history of almost five hundred years of occupation, Guatemalan women have learned how to maintain their own will, how to revive ancient abortion techniques for young women impregnated during rape, how to arm themselves and defend themselves and to propagate power: rape alone is not enough to discourage women's empowerment.

In the years following the worst moments of military-political violence, the mothers and the grandmothers and the families of the disappeared have bravely paraded the two-dimensional faces of lost husbands and lost sons and daughters, like a "moving cemetery," around the Plaza de Mayo in Argentina, in Uruguay, in Chile, in El Salvador. There are few photographs of the indigenous women lost to violence over the centuries; but now, in contemporary Guatemala, strong resistance groups have formed independently of the mainly male-led peasant and workers' unions: El Grupo de Apoyo Mutuo (the Group for Mutual Support) and Conavigua, the Committee of Guatemalan Widows. And the hopeful militancy responding to the litany of savagery inside Rigoberta Menchú's text has brought the Nobel Prize, the world's greatest acknowledgment for peace work, to its author: celebrating—or denouncing—exactly half a millennium since *The Conquest of America*.

REFERENCES

Franco, Jean. 1985. "Killing Priests, Nuns, Women, Children." In Marshall Blonsky (ed.), *On Signs*. Baltimore: Johns Hopkins University Press.

Jonas, Susanne. 1991. *The Battle for Guatemala. Rebels: Death Squads and United States Power*. Boulder: Westview.

Landa, Diego de. 1566. *Relación de las cosas de Yucatan*. Mexico: Truay, 1938. [Diego de Landa's Account of the Affairs of the Yucatan: The Mava, ed. and trans. A. R. Pagden. Chicago: J.Philip O'Hara Inc., 1975. I have translated and cited the Spanish version; available in English in Pagden, pp. 90–91.]

Lovell, W. George. 1988. "Surviving Conquest: The Maya of Guatemala in Historical Perspective." *Latin American Research Review*, 23 (2): 25–57.

Menchú, Rigoberta. 1984. *I, Rigoberta Menchú: An Indian Woman in Guatemala*. Trans. Ann Wright. London: Verso.

Millett, David L. 1995. "An End to Militarism? Democracy and the Armed Forces in Central America." *Current History* (February): 71–76.

Todorov, Tsvetan. (1982) 1984. *The Conquest of America. The Question of the Other*. (I have revised the translations.) New York: Harper and Row.

Wilden, Anthony. 1985. "In the Penal Colony: The Body as Discourse of the Other." *Semiotica* (54.1/2): 33–85.

Chapter Twenty-One

Women's Prison Resistance
Testimonios from El Salvador

Lois Ann Lorentzen

> All you, are part of the game
> interrogators, detectives, officials,
> class, agents, prison guards, administrators,
> doctors, infirmary workers,
> and also the builders . . .
> All sustain this hell.
> which isn't from Dante.
> Some are more dangerous, others indifferent
> but, all play, the victim is my people.
>
> (Díaz, 1993: 167)[1]

Salvadoran political prisoner Nidia Díaz wrote "combat" poetry from her prison cell as resistance to the gendered domestic militarization found in the "secret" prisons of El Salvador. This paper explores women's prison writings from El Salvador as resistance in themselves, as well as accounts of resistance strategies that demystify the hegemonic history represented by the prison. Like Salvadoran liberation theology, they provide strategies of autonomy and emancipation.

Women, Testimonios, and Liberation Theology

Women's *testimonios* are the primary focus of this chapter. *Las cárceles clandestinas de El Salvador* (El Salvador's Secret Prisons) tells the story of the capture, torture, and imprisonment of Ana Guadalupe Martínez by the Salvadoran army in 1976. Her account of seven months in a "secret" National Guard prison was first published in Mexico and distributed clandestinely in El Salvador. *Nunca Estuve Sola* (I was never alone) by Nidia Díaz tells of 190 days in prison after her April 1985 capture by a United States' military advisor. Both are examples of the *testimonio* or testimonial genre.

The *testimonio* as a genre developed out of Latin America's history of military dictatorships. Anyone wishing to study popular resistance in El Salvador must study *testimonios*. The *testimonio*, generally told by the actual protagonist or witness, chronicles a life episode such as imprisonment. The narrator is generally not a professional writer, and may even be illiterate. Often an intermediary records, interviews, transcribes, or edits the *testimonio*. The protagonist claims to speak for or in the name of a group. Ana Guadalupe Martínez, for example, says her story was repeated thousands of times in the decade after her imprisonment (Martínez, 1992: 454). Nidia Díaz, in an interview, states, "Although I was physically alone and disadvantaged, tortured, wounded, I had the conviction that I was part of a collective force" (Ueltzen, 1993: 65).

Women's *testimonios* further reflect the specific circumstances of *women* in prison. The emphasis on rape, sexual violence, sexual torture, and women's family roles distinguish women's *testimonios* from earlier accounts such as Cayetano Carpio's 1952 *Secuestro y Capucha*. Martínez and Díaz speak for both the Salvadoran people and the women of El Salvador.

Liberation theology is clearly linked to *testimonio*. Nearly every Salvadoran woman I know who has been imprisoned considers radical Catholicism, or liberation theology, an important part of her lineage. Ex-comandante Rebeca Palacios claims that "most women of the front come from religious sectors as part of the 'boom' of liberation theology" (Ueltzen, 1993: 4). Nidia Díaz worked with Catholic Student Youth and was influenced by both Paolo Freire and liberation theology. The Committee of Mothers and Relatives of Prisoners, the Disappeared, and the Politically Assassinated of El Salvador, Monsignor Oscar Arnulfo Romero (COMADRES), was a direct outgrowth of liberation theology. The group, founded in 1977 under the direct oversight of the archdiocese of San Salvador and Archbishop Romero, maintained close ties to Christian base communities. Alicia, of COMADRES, says, "Most of us at this time were from Christian base communities. . . . Monsignor Romero would read our public letters out loud in his Sunday homily in the Cathedral so that the COMADRES became known nationally" (Schirmer, 1993: 36).

Although Martínez's *las cárceles clandestinas* is not about liberation theology per se, she begins and ends her book by placing it in the context of liberation history. Martínez dedicates her book, in part, to "catholic priests, Rutilio Grande, Alfonso Navarro Oviedo and various members of the brave progressive Church of El Salvador which the dictator brutally assassinates" (Martínez, 1992: 13). The epilogue honors Romero as "our Bishop martyr." And, the book ends by recounting lessons learned from Ignacio Ellacuria, one of the six Jesuits assassinated at the University of Central America. *Cárceles clandestinas'* final sentence reads, "Ignacio is a martyr of the negotiated revolution in El Salvador, together with his brothers and the two women, who for us signify the innocent people martyred in this long transformation process" (456).

Martínez claims that her decision to fight with the People's Revolutionary Army stemmed from her Catholic faith. In a 1992 interview she states: "That mixture of Christian influence and Bolívar was decisive in my joining the people's struggle in

El Salvador. Being a Catholic was important to me, and when I was able to understand what solidarity was, and what a Christian should be for others, I thought: 'Well, why not fight for the people who need it?'" (Best and Hussey, 1996: 188).

Opposition movement women and the texts they write are framed here as being part of the history of liberation theology in El Salvador. Many women describe liberation theology and involvement in Christian base communities as a life transformation that led them to resistance, and in many cases, to prison.

Women's Prison Strategies and Counterstrategies

Early in *Las cárceles clandestinas*, Martínez gives a brief history of political interrogation in El Salvador. Imprisonment and disappearance of political prisoners generally resulted in death for the captured. As the need for information grew, however, political police refined their techniques in the hope of demoralizing prisoners and forcing them to collaborate (Martinez, 1992: 23). Martínez's *testimonio* narrates her imprisonment and looks at the combination of methods used in the prison, as well as prisoner counterstrategies. We will first look at strategies and counterstrategies within the prison, looking later at the characteristics of *cárceles* as *testimonio*.

Salvadoran prisons employed a variety of well-known strategies. Nidia Díaz experienced total sleep deprivation for weeks. Martínez went for three weeks without eating. Food regularly appeared with cockroaches. As her hunger increased, so did obsessions about food. The prisoners depended on their torturers for all basic needs. As Kaminsky notes, "In the experience of arrest and internment in a prison, power is stripped from the victim and invested in the interrogators . . . the victim depends on them for all of life's necessities, food, clothing, shelter . . . the torturers exercise power over the victim's body in the functions of sleep, elimination, movement, sight, speech . . . they have power of life and death" (Kaminsky, 1993: 56).

The sense of isolation prisoners experienced was exacerbated by sensory deprivation. Both Díaz and Martínez wore the famous *capucha* or hood throughout the months of their internment. Martínez's permanently closed eyes developed serious infections. Silence was an additional part of the violence used to demoralize the captured. Speech itself became an offense, and as Kaminsky notes, "under these conditions language is a highly valued commodity . . . for the victim to put the experience of disappearance and torture into language is to exercise a form of control over that experience . . . this articulation is not a private affair" (1993: 56–57). When Martínez was finally able to speak with other political prisoners, she notes, "At times the only thing that distinguished us from animals was the possibility of talking among ourselves" (Martínez, 1992: 128). Her captors even offered her a television program, hoping to exploit her need to speak. On the other hand, refusing to speak to one's interrogators, thus controlling one's discourse, became an important resistance strategy. As Martínez notes several times, "*Quien habla, colabora*" (who speaks, collaborates) (116).

Skilled at physical torture, interrogators beat prisoners with fists, boots, wooden paddles, whips, chairs, and the like. Martínez describes electricity as the worst torture. Probes were placed on different parts of her body, including in her vagina, water was splashed on her, and she was shocked. She writes, "What is it possible to say about people who can discharge electricity in this way on a human body?" (Martínez, 1992: 115). Observing and/or hearing the violence inflicted on others was another common strategy. Martínez writes, "How many times did I hear the shouts of pain of some patriot who suffered indescribable torments at the hands of the same ones who were in that moment torturing me" (112).

In addition to physical violence and numerous discomforts and humiliations, the interrogators waged psychological warfare. With Díaz, they successfully made her feel guilty, nearly convincing her that papers she carried caused her companions to fall. Traitors were flaunted before the prisoners. In Martínez's case she was confronted by Valle, the colleague who turned her in to the National Guard. She admits to being demoralized by his defection and the [alleged] betrayals of others. Torturers also exaggerated internal conflicts within the resistance movement. Guards, many of whom were members of the death squads, enjoyed congregating outside prisoners' doors to discuss which leaders had been killed or defeated (Martínez, 1992: 91).

This psychological war was waged, according to Díaz, to "alter the emotional direction of the prisoner" and the most effective aspect was the conscious destabilizing of the prisoner. Physical aggression and terror were altered with apparent calm. The hatred of the interrogator reversed and he become someone "who offers a friendly hand, who speaks in a paternal tone . . . the man who only wants the best for you" (Díaz, 1993: 81). Martínez's primary interrogator becomes her savior who "rescues" her from electrical torture. She writes, "Each time the door opened, you wonder what torture the interrogators would think of next" (Martínez, 1992: 51). Interrogators regularly stripped prisoners. Of the month she spent without clothes, Martínez writes: "Being without clothes leaves you feeling disempowered, feeling unprotected and more exposed to whatever abuse they want at that moment" (51).

Prisoners developed counterstrategies in this context of physical violence, sensory deprivation, and psychological warfare. One of my favorites is the counterinterrogation strategy employed by both Díaz and Martínez. Although, as I have noted, prisoners would generally refuse to answer questions, some would interrogate the interrogators. Díaz was repeatedly asked who she was. The interrogators would ask, "You are Maria Marta Valladares?" to which she would respond "Who do you think?" They asked, "How are you?" to which she would answer, "How do you want me to be?" (Díaz, 1993: 54). Martínez's captors were also obsessed with forcing her to say her name. Interrogators persistently told her they knew her name and she should say it aloud. Martínez asked again and again, "Why do you want me to say it?"

Interrogating and counterinterrogating exposes the battle for information and "truth" waged within the walls of the political prison. Harlow writes: "The interrogators waged a different discursive battle in the attempt to extract information from the prisoners and to introduce destructive disinformation" (1992: 172). The torturers used personal information as part of their psychological warfare, showing Martínez documents about the movement, including a file on Martínez with pictures and descriptions of how she walked and combed her hair (Martínez, 1992: 40). Prisoners however, waged a counter discursive battle through watching and witnessing. As Harlow notes, "The witnessing of torture by the tortured yields another kind of information that is the testimony of the political prisoner who survives" (1992: 26). A COMADRE tells the story of being tortured, beaten, raped, shocked, and of being thrown naked in a dark room. As she felt around the room she detected shattered bones and picked up a human finger. Her mother writes, "But what she saw in that room and what they did to her is to witness what goes on in the military garrisons" ("Alicia" quoted in Thompson, 1995: 42).

Martínez describes how she and Ana Gilman listened to telephone conversations and peered through a little hole in the door to see who was walking by. As listeners, watchers, and witnesses, they were, as Harlow puts it, " 'semiologists' of the prison system, whose collective discursive strategies of resistance served as a continuous renovation of the circuits of communication" (1992: 172). Díaz not only witnesses the torture of others, but upon hearing violence, shouts for the torturers to be quiet, claiming torture "is not allowed here" (Díaz, 1993: 225).

Prisons, as battlegrounds over information and knowledge, became actual training grounds for resistance. Marbel tells an interviewer, "Before I was captured, I hadn't participated in any organization, but the experience of being a political prisoner soon changes your mind. Through COPPES (a prisoners' organization) I learned a lot about the political situation of our country" (Thomson, 1986: 107). Harlow writes,

> Penal institutions as part of a state's coercive apparatus of physical detention and ideological containment, provide the critical space within which, indeed out of which, alternative social and political practices of counterhegemonic resistance movements are schooled . . . Prison education, unlike much university instruction professed in the Western academy, functions to undermine the very walls and premises that contain it. (Harlow, 1992: 5, 23)

The act of writing and creating becomes subversive within the prison. Díaz wrote poetry and drew. Her poem, "Playing the Blind Chicken," with which I began this chapter, refers to a children's game in which all are blindfolded. The drawing illustrating the poem depicts a woman facing the "players" who are blindfolded. This reversal, in poem and drawing, depicts her captors as the blind, imprisoned players of a destructive game. A drawing of Díaz and her interrogators is yet another reversal. A blindfolded, wounded woman stands erect as flying demons surround her, but don't touch her.

Bonds that developed among prisoners and bonds remembered with loved ones outside the prison walls sustained captives. Díaz writes in order to "record those days, to see my pain alive, which is yours" and claims she learned to survive in the enemies' jails through hearing "the voices of a people who sing better than I" (Díaz, 1992: 162, 167). Martínez's prison friendship with Lil Milagro Ramirez led to the development of new tactical strategies of the resistance movement (Martínez, 1992: 285). Yet all friendships and emotions remain, of necessity, imprisoned. Díaz writes, "One can't manifest anything personal to your captors and interrogators." Clandestine emotions and a "camouflaged" heart were necessary resistance strategies (Díaz, 1992: 8). The most common response to all interrogations was, "*Yo no se nada*" (I know nothing). Yes, I act like the dumb woman, the *puta* (whore) you want me to be, and in so doing I resist.

Gender and Prison

Martínez and Díaz were not merely political prisoners. They were *women* political prisoners. As such, their experiences disclose the ways in which domestic militarism (local police forces, prisons, etc.) is gendered. In these "secret" women's prisons, captors, guards, and torturers were all male. Prisoners were female.

Sexual violence, notes Martínez, was the "primary way women suffered" (51). Sexual assaults, gang rape, mutilations, and the constant threat of rape were methods used against women political prisoners. As Harlow notes, "The sexual violence unleashed against women political prisoners is seen as the key in controlling them" (1992: 170). Constant references to rape and sexual abuse were the most demoralizing aspect of imprisonment, according to Martínez (1992: 51).

Martínez was kept naked with her head covered during most interrogations. On many occasions she heard other prisoners being raped. Captured COMADRES often watched guards rape fellow COMADRES. Most women were addressed as *puta* (whore). During her first interview, Martínez's captors commented, "*Bonita esta puta*" (this whore is pretty). Controlling and repressing the bodies of women political prisoners clearly was central to interrogation strategy. Kaminsky notes that these strategies reverse the insight of North American feminists that the personal is the political. She writes that this insight "rarely led to its corollary: the political is the personal—that the official and unofficial structures of power and authority of the state get expressed in our day-to-day experience. Of Argentina in the 1970s she writes, "National politics was played out on the field of the body in the form of physical and psychological torture, and life was indivisible from politics" (Kaminsky, 1993: 50). The same statement could be made of El Salvador in the 1980s as state policies were played out on the bodies of women prisoners.

Women political prisoners, in addition to being seen as especially vulnerable sexually, were perceived in light of gendered family roles. Threats against prisoners' children and other family members were made repeatedly. Harlow notes that interrogators' "particular stratagems practiced against their women victims" included "the suggestion that their children too will be made to suffer for the 'subversive' activities of their mothers, who, according to the militarized patriarchal customs of the society, do not know their proper place as women in the home" (1992: 162). She concludes that "family as a contested sociopolitical institution is thus central to the issue of political detention" (1992: 233).

The interrogators consciously manipulated this orientation toward family, calling themselves the only hope and family for the prisoners. To Martínez they said, "Here we are the only ones who can do something for you" (Martínez, 1992: 101). To Díaz, "We know that the FMLN is not going to help you. Only we are able to help you. From now on, we are your mother, your father, your husband, your child. We are your world, know it. . . . We will help you" (Díaz, 1993: 43). Díaz, in an interview says, "I understood that the first objective of my interrogators was for me to feel alone and to feel that they alone were my mother, father, and brother" (Ueltzen, 1993: 69). As Harlow notes, one of the purposes of the actual isolation, coupled with the constant reminder of the solitude, is "isolation of opposition leadership from its base of popular support in the larger community" (1992: 19).

Women political prisoners found themselves in a unique position to pose a counterdiscourse to the family language of the state. Interrogators asked Díaz, "Where does your family live?" She responded, "Go to the front, there is my family" (Díaz, 1993: 35). Martínez writes, "How would they be able to understand the friendship and love that one is able to feel for her compañeros" (1992: 103). New conceptions of family itself were articulated by women within the prison setting.

COMADRES most clearly demonstrates the reorganization of the traditional family brought about by the prison experience. Many of Ilopango's (the women's prison) political prisoners were there due to their participation in COMADRES (or because of accusations of participation). Women often entered the political/public arena because of their family roles. COMADRES cofounder Raquel Garcia became involved when, in 1980, her fifteen-year-old son was captured. Death squads killed two nephews in 1985.

COMADRES at one point visited all the jails and military barracks in El Salvador, inquiring about young people who had "disappeared." Schirmer reports that "in every place the soldiers would tell them, 'They haven't been captured, they aren't here. We don't know anything [about it]' " (Schirmer, 1993: 37). The state claimed that the children never existed, that these mothers never had children. The COMADRES battle was one of "seeking to know who claims the truth about the disappearance of their relatives" (Schirmer, 1993: 31).

In the process of battling with the state over truth claims, these peasant women gained knowledge of national and international law, protest and resistance strategies, and public relations. As COMADRE Alicia notes, "Now there are COMADRES who can't read or write but who can debate the socks off a lawyer about international law and war" (Alicia quoted by Schirmer, 1993: 30). According to Schirmer, they have also "come to question the acceptance of violence against women, and have made a theoretical leap: they have connected their experience and analysis of political violence (disappearance and torture) to personal violence against women (rape and battering)" (31). As Mercedes Canas notes, "The same type of torture that was practiced in the secret prisons was practiced by men in their homes" (Ueltzen, 1993: 154).

The prison experience, whether their own or that of their relatives, politicized motherhood. A COMADRE mother became a truth seeker, subversive, threat to the state, political analyst and strategist, and eventually one who challenged traditional patriarchal family structures.

Testimonio as Liberation Text

Testimonios not only chronicle resistance strategies within the prison, they also self-consciously serve as part of a larger revolutionary struggle. As René Cruz writes of *Las cárceles clandestinas*, "The book is an initial effort to write the history of our revolution from the trenches of combat" (Martínez, 1992: 21). *Testimonio*, as perhaps the "dominant contemporary form of narrative in Central America," serves, as Beverly and Zimmerman note, as a "cultural aspect of the overall struggle for hegemony linked to the impulse to displace or overthrow both elites and elite cultural modes" (Beverly and Zimmerman, 1990: 172). The purpose of *testimonio* coincides with that of theologies of liberation. The word itself suggests witnessing as a religious term.

The narrators, as noted earlier, place themselves self-consciously within a liberation lineage. Martínez later finds it significant that her clandestine book was eventually published by the Jesuit University of Central America, encouraged by Ignacio Ellacuria and Ignacio Martín Baro. The agendas coincide concretely in an urgently expressed need for the taking of sides. Liberation theologies and *testimonios* both serve as ideological criticisms clearly on the side of the "most oppressed." In these texts, the "most oppressed" are women. For liberation theologians, such as the Jesuit Jon Sobrino, faith commitment is expressed in praxis, or struggle with and for the poor. God is seen in the faces of the poor and the oppressed. Jesus may be symbolized as a *campesino* (peasant) struggling for land or as Archbishop Oscar Romero, who was killed for his criticisms of the Salvadoran government and military. The stations of the cross adorning the chapel walls at the Jesuit University of Central America depict peasants being tortured and/or killed. These "suffering servants" are the focal point of the liberation gospel. One's faith commitment is judged by how one stands vis-à-vis the poor.

Testimonio and liberation theology share the same subject and struggle to bring this subject to visibility. Leonardo Boff writes, "It [liberation theology] starts from a definite practice of liberation focused on the poor themselves as subjects of change" (Boff, 1995: 123). *Testimonio* records the voice of a subject we are meant to experience as a real person, yet a person who stands for a group as speaking subject. It is, as Beverly and Zimmerman claim, "the mark of a desire not to be silenced or defeated, to impose oneself on an institution of power like literature from the position of the excluded or the marginal" (1990: 175). That which is repressed, that which is forbidden, that which was literally imprisoned claims a voice through *testimonio*. The significance of the liberation-oriented University of Central America's press publishing *Las cárceles clandestinas* was, to Martínez, that "it wasn't a pamphlet, it was a reality, la UCA publishes reality" (Ueltzen, 1993: 67). In these *testimonios*, the "invisible" subject is the powerful speaking woman.

Martínez, as a woman, self-consciously makes not only herself present, but other women as well. She interviews other prisoners, some of whom were later killed. Thus, these female victims exert political claims on the reader. This presence becomes a "political claim which declares the existence of the individual not as a coherent psychological subject but as a potent political subject" and is "claimed in a situation in which some dominant force deliberately denies it" (Kaminsky, 1993: 54).

As Beverly and Zimmerman note, *testimonio* cannot affirm a self that is "separated from a group or class situation, marked by marginalization and oppression and struggle" (1990: 177). The narrator has taken sides and is part of an ongoing social struggle. And just as the protagonist remains involved in social struggle, the reader is called to praxis. Kaminsky writes, "Taking testimonial writing seriously, which means paying attention to its call for action in society, means a return to the concrete" (1993: 54).

The praxis demanded by both theologies of liberation and *testimonio* is social transformation. The Christian and the church are called to change unjust social and economic structures. Jesuits, such as the murdered Ignacio Ellacuria noted in Martínez's book, consistently denounced the structural violence and injustice witnessed in El Salvador. The popular church in El Salvador provided the ideological critique and motivation that helped radicalize many Salvadorans, including the COMADRES and Martínez.

History is contested ground for both *testimonio* and theologies of liberation. *Testimonios* use the prison experience to articulate the dominant history, which is then challenged by a counterhistory of revolutionary struggle. The *testimonio* view of history is remarkably similar to that found in theologies of liberation. Leonardo Boff writes,

> The same logic that destroyed the "witness cultures" of Latin America in the sixteenth century has continued its devastating course to the present. . . . Today in the name of modernity, Latin American governments are bringing the logic of domination up to date through the grandiose schemes of multinational corporations from Japan, Germany, Italy, and the United States. The cost of this and of a foreign debt that cannot be repaid is more and yet more deaths. (Boff, 1995: 101–2)

René Cruz's prologue to *Las cárceles clandestinas* similarly places the text in the context of global capitalism and North American imperialism's role in "sustaining the edifice of exploitation and dependency of America" (Martínez, 1992: 17).

The narrating of this history occurs in very concrete ways in *testimonio*. Díaz knows her captor is a Yankee when she sees his blond hair, athletic body, and RayBan glasses. She writes, "This Yankee was a symbol of Reagan, he was one of the 300 advisors in El Salvador" (1993: 15). When her interrogators ask her, "Where do the arms come from?" she answers, "From the United States. Reagan sends them to you" (40). In a later interview Díaz says, "I knew that I fought against the United States" (Ueltzen, 1993: 69). The blond captor stands for Reagan, who stands for the United States as the embodiment of the history of dominance thrust on El Salvador.

When Martínez was released from prison, her former jailers and torturers became her bodyguards, charged with insuring her safe release. She reflects on the irony of this, asking, "What power changed their roles like this? The only power which came from being members of the class that held the political and economic power of the country" (Martínez, 1992: 321). She further notes that the political police, horrible as they were, were merely a means of repressive control against the popular movement, an "instrument of the dominant classes . . . in almost all parts of the world they are used . . . above all in Latin America, where the Imperialist Yankee" encourages repressive control (363). The political police, like the prisoners themselves, are represented as mere pawns in the grand history of domination and dependence.

Testimonios, however, spend more time articulating the counterhistory of revolutionary struggle than the history of dominance. This understanding mirrors the liberation perspective of the one "real history," which consists of "the defense of the rights of the poor, punishment of the oppressors, a life free from the fear of being enslaved by others, the liberation of the oppressed. Peace, justice, love, and freedom are not private realities; they are not only internal attitudes. They are social realities, implying a historical liberation" (Brown, cited in Tilley, 1995: 126).

Díaz views her book as a "small piece of the prolonged history of the fight of the Salvadoran people" (Díaz, 1993: 9). Prison provides a story within which larger revolutionary history is told. As Harlow writes, "Texts written out of political detention" are an "important dimension of the history and theory of organized struggle and dialogue between political detainee and the state's prison apparatus" (1992: 178). Díaz's references to Reagan under interrogation demonstrate that "the most ordinary of daily encounters between victim and victimizer managed by the prison apparatus and its routines are remodulated into a historical struggle" (Harlow, 1992: 16).

Both Martínez and Díaz self-consciously place their texts in the line of prison narratives and revolutionary struggle. Martínez begins her *testimonio* with a reference to Cayetano Carpio's 1952 prison narrative, *Secuestro y Capucha* (1992: 11). Díaz writes that she remembered the earlier prison books *Secuestro y Capucha* and *Las cárceles clandestinas* while in prison (1993: 46). This linear historical progress reflects an attempt to articulate an alternative national narrative of social struggle, "leading to some kind of socialist salvation" (Beverly and Zimmerman, 1990: 116).

Testimonios as liberation texts share a common lineage, are on the side of the "most oppressed," call the reader to praxis, demand social transformation, bring the poor to visibility as political subjects, and articulate the "real" history of engaged struggle over and against the history of domination.

For Martínez and Díaz, this liberation struggle is also gendered. As women prisoners they struggle against male prison guards and police—caught in a gendered domestic militarism. The dangerous "game" played by the many actors Díaz identifies in her "Blindfold Chicken" poem warns of the high price of subjugation and any and all forms of totalizing. As texts of liberation and women's resistance, these *testimonios* demand a dismantling of prison in its many forms.

NOTES

1. All translations by Lois Ann Lorentzen.

REFERENCES

Algería, Claribel, and Flakoll, D. J. 1993. *No me agarran viva: La mujer salvadorena en la lucha*. San Salvador, El Salvador: UCA Editores.

Best, Marigold, and Pamela Hussey. 1996. *Life out of Death: The Feminine Spirit in El Salvador*. London: Catholic Institute for International Relations.

Beverly, John, and Zimmerman, Marc. 1990. *Literature and Politics in the Central American Revolution*. Austin: University of Texas Press.

Boff, Leonardo. 1995. *Ecology and Liberation: A New Paradigm*. Maryknoll, NY: Orbis Books.

Cooey, Paula M. 1994. *Religious Imagination and the Body: A Feminist Analysis*. New York: Oxford University Press.

Díaz, Nidia. 1993. *Nunca Estuve Sola*. San Salvador, El Salvador: UCA Editores.

Harlow, Barbara. 1992. *Barred: Women, Writing and Political Detention*. Hanover, NH: Wesleyan University Press.

Hicks, Emily D. 1991. *Border Writing: The Multidimensional Text*. Minneapolis: University of Minnesota Press.

Kaminsky, Amy K. 1993. *Reading the Body Politic: Feminist Criticism and Latin American Women Writers*. Minneapolis: University of Minnesota Press.

Larsen, Neil. 1991. Foreword to Hicks, Emily D., *Border Writing: The Multidimensional Text*. Minneapolis: University of Minnesota Press.

Martínez, Ana Guadalupe. 1992. *Las cárceles clandestinas de El Salvador*. San Salvador, El Salvador: UCA Editores.

Pottenger, John R. 1989. *The Political Theory of Liberation Theology: Toward a Reconvergence of Social Values and Social Science*. Albany, NY: State University of New York Press.

Rodríguez, Guadalupe. 1994. *Marianela*. San Salvador, El Salvador: Editorial Guayampopo.

Schirmer, Jennifer. 1993. "The Seeking of Truth and the Gendering of Consciousness: The COMADRES of El Salvador and the CIBAVUGYA Widows of Guatemala." In Sarah A Radcliffe and Sallie Westwood, eds., *'Viva': Women and popular protest in Latin America*. London: Routledge.

Sobrino, Jon, S.J. 1985. *Christology at the Crossroads: A Latin American Approach*. Maryknoll, NY: Orbis Books.

Thompson, Martha. 1995. "Repopulated Communities in El Salvador." In Minor Sinclair, ed., *The New Politics of Survival: Grassroots Movements in Central America*. New York: Monthly Review Press.

Thomson, Marilyn. 1986. *Women of El Salvador: The Price of Freedom*. London: Zed Books.

Tilley, Terrence W., with C. Bradley Morris. 1995. "Gustavo Gutiérrez and Praxis in Christian Communities." In Terrence Tilley, ed., *Postmodern Theologies: The Challenge of Religious Diversity*. Maryknoll, NY: Orbis Books.

Ueltzen, Stefan. 1993. *Como Salvadoreña Que Soy: Entrevistas con mujeres en la lucha*. San Salvador, El Salvador: Editorial Sombrero Azul.

Chapter Twenty-Two

Imagining Peace

Elaine R. Ognibene

> A line of peace might appear
> if we restructured the sentence our lives are making
> revoked its reaffirmation of profit and power, . . .
> . . . peace . . .
> might pulse then
> stanza by stanza into the world. . . .
> (Denise Levertov, "Making Peace," 1988)

Throughout history, women working for peace have always imagined that it was more than the absence of war. Virginia Woolf did, and in *Three Guineas* (1938)— a brilliant response to a question about how to prevent war—she raised important questions about the relationship of war to women's situation in society. For Woolf, patriarchy meant hierarchy, competition, aggression, violence, and finally war. The private and public were intimately connected; in Woolf's ironic analysis, fascism began in the family. Hope for a tolerable future, therefore, relied on extending to the public realm "female" visions, virtues, and skills: peace, justice, nurturance, integrity, and concern for others. Woolf suggested that if women were granted equal opportunities, the separation of public and private life—and the male domination of both—would come to an end. The final results would be a nonviolent transformation of social structures and values, producing a more just and peaceful world.

Woolf's suggestions for peace reappear in fiction written by women, the "outsiders" who can imagine a world that males might not see. These outsiders tell their stories not by repeating the words or following the methods of the patriarchal power structure but rather by finding new words and creating new methods.

Several contemporary women writers do just that; their fictional responses to war appear not as linear descriptions of military events but rather as personal stories set in the context of public historical moments: Vietnam, Nicaragua, Castro's Cuban revolution, the civil rights movement, the fights for oil on tribal land in Oklahoma. In their stories, contrary points of view often interrupt each other, as authors shift time frames, locales, and the meaning of words like silence, speech, freedom, and power. Connecting the private and the public, the personal and the political, they challenge traditional assumptions about war. Imagining peace, they show how we can restructure "the sentence our lives are making."

Bobbie Ann Mason's *In Country* (1985) provides a coming-of-age story about Sam Hughes's search to discover who her father was and what the Vietnam War was about. It also provides a story about the futility of war, its searing legacy of confusion, and the human yearning for reconciliation. In the narrative voice of Samantha, Mason tells a story about war's effects not only on those who fight it, but on those who survive it, like the veterans, her family, and Sam herself.

Demonstrating her growing knowledge and concern and frustrated "that it was so hard to find out the truth" about Vietnam, Sam has an argument with her boyfriend about the ethics of war:

> Well, then, if you go off to . . . a bad war, and you believe you're doing the right thing, is it your own fault if you get killed? If the war is wrong, then do you deserve to die for believing the wrong thing? . . . My mom said not to worry about what happened to Emmett back then, because the war had nothing to do with me. But the way I look at it, it had *everything* to do with me. . . . It was such a waste. (Mason, 1985: 71)

In a moral tale that connects private anguish with public history, Mason offers a fresh perspective on the Vietnam War; her art, like the monument Sam finally visits, challenges readers to heal the wounds and find a better way to live.

The public war in Barbara Kingsolver's *Animal Dreams* (1990) appears in the letters Cosima receives from her sister Hallie, who is working for a new social order in Nicaragua during the decade after the 1979 revolution. The private wars (e.g., the father-daughter conflict, the Stitch and Bitch Club's piñata sales to save the land) occur in Arizona, when Cosima goes home to care for her ailing father. Inside the broader story of Cosima's search for both personal identity and communal connection, Kingsolver places Hallie's letters about her work to help the people of Nicaragua survive poverty and violence.

Hallie's letters end, just before she is kidnapped by terrorists and shot in the head, with her trying to explain the ordinary, heartbreaking detail of war and rural life in the context of hope:

> I am not saving Nicaragua. . . . You're thinking of revolution as a great all-or-nothing. . . . Wars and elections are both too big and too small to matter in the long run. The daily work—that goes on, it adds up. . . . Good things don't get lost. . . . And the most you can do is live inside that hope. . . . What I want is elementary kindness. Enough to eat, enough to go around. The possibility that kids might one day grow up to be neither the destroyers nor the destroyed. (Kingsolver, 1990: 299)

Hallie understands what war is about; she bequeaths that knowledge to her sister. By the end of the novel, Cosima also understands. She empowers her students, with "a spirited development of a relevant curriculum," to question convention and to act for positive change.

*

These examples suggest the insights women's fiction can offer about war; a deeper examination of three more novels—Christina Garcia's *Dreaming in Cuban*, Alice Walker's *Meridian*, and Linda Hogan's *Mean Spirit*—illustrates more fully how characters, like Hallie, shape the contours of their lives in nonviolent ways even in the center of national wars. They develop a moral code based on the values necessary for peace, and work to establish justice.

Initially, the central characters in *Dreaming in Cuban* (1992)—three generations of del Pino women—appear radically different. Celia, the sixty-year-old grandmother, guards the north shore of Castro's Cuba and becomes a community leader in the socialist revolution. Lourdes, Celia's thirty-six-year-old daughter who escapes Cuba, rejects her mother and Castro; she establishes a chain of Yankee Doodle Bakeries in Brooklyn. Pilar, Lourdes's teenage punk artist daughter, argues constantly with her mother. All three females are rebels; but Celia and Pilar emerge particularly as models of nonviolent thought and action.

Garcia uses collective memory, dreams, magical realism, and interrupted time sequences to organize and interpret history. Celia remembers 1938 as the time of Chamberlain ignoring Czechoslovakia, the year Felicia was born, the time of near defeat for the Spanish republic, and the era of her lost Spanish lover. She counts all losses, public and private, present and past, in a single sentence.

Garcia collapses calendar time. Although the novel begins in 1972 and ends in 1980, the stories inside the novel begin in 1934, when Celia falls in love with Gustavo, the Spanish lawyer who leaves her to return to his wife. Celia's letters to Gustavo, interspersed ahistorically throughout the story, track the parallel progress of Celia's personal life and the sociopolitical life of her country over a twenty-five year period.

Celia's rebel nature moves her to become a public participant in Castro's revolution. Seduced by *El Lider's* promise of a better Cuba, Celia cuts sugar cane in the fields, sets tiles, operates construction lifts, inoculates schoolchildren, and serves as family court judge—all while nurturing her daughter Felicia through bouts of recurring madness, taking care of her grandchildren, and nursing her son Javier through a nervous breakdown.

In both the private and the public realm, her rebellion against social norms is gendered. Acting as civilian family court judge in the Ester Ugarte-Loli Regalado case (the postmaster's wife accuses Loli of seducing her husband), a case of domestic disagreement, Celia holds Postmaster Rogelio—a man who cannot keep his hands to himself—accountable for the public conflict between two women. Much to Rogelio's and the spectators' surprise, Celia orders him to do one year of volunteer work at the state nursery. The revolutionary nature of Celia's sentence is clear: she has not only sentenced a man, but she sentences him to do woman's work—changing diapers, washing linens, caring for children. Celia hopes to reform Rogelio by educating him to "women's" skills and values.

Celia's granddaughter, thirteen-year-old Pilar Puente, rebels against her mother by running away to Cuba. On a bus to Florida, Pilar reflects on the limits of history as taught in schools: "It's always one damn battle after another." If it were up to her, she would record other things such as "a freak hailstorm in the Congo" that led women to believe that they should rule, or "the life stories of prostitutes in Bombay." "Who chooses what we should know or what's important?" she asks (28). Besides challenging traditional education about war, Pilar's comments demonstrate her awareness of gender and cultural inequities; they also show her concern for outsiders.

Pilar's disregard for boundaries becomes clear in her rejection of traditional religion, her addiction to Lou Reed's "expectant, uncertain" music, her art, and her feminist perspectives about gender. Nowhere is this disregard more visible than in the Statue of Liberty painting Pilar creates for her mother's bakery. When, with great ceremony, Lourdes unveils Pilar's work, she finds "SL-76," a portrait of the Statue of Liberty, slightly off center, right hand covering her left breast, black stick figures floating in the background, and a safety pin through her nose. Pilar's painting symbolically critiques the fundamental hypocrisies in America's rhetoric of freedom and justice.

Pilar's personal attitudes affect her politics; her resistance to control is clear in both countries. In the United States, she "resent[s] like hell the politicians and the generals who force events on us that structure our lives." In Cuba, she sees through the false promises of Castro's billboard messages. Amidst chaos and destruction, she recognizes that to accomplish her goals, she must return to the United States: "I know now it's where I belong—not *instead* of here, but *more* than here" (236).

In *Dreaming in Cuban*, Garcia tells stories about women who suffer a sense of absence and oppression but who use their language—words, music, pastries, or art—to rebel nonviolently, renegotiating communal identities, and establishing a sense of power. In *Meridian* (1976), Alice Walker presents a young woman who is physically and psychologically abused, constantly in conflict with her mother, and engaged in a series of relationships that test her ability to endure. But she, like the del Pino women, becomes an agent of change. The novel opens in the seventies in the South, with Meridian demonstrating the effect of nonviolent resistance to the children of Chicokema, but the story of Meridian's adolescence occurs in the sixties within the context of the civil rights movement.

Central to Meridian's adolescent development is the conflict with her mother. In that stormy relationship Meridian's initial self-awareness and "voice" surface. At age thirteen, Meridian questions the logic of her mother's Christian beliefs and refuses to submit to her control or to that of a patriarchal church that fosters submission, inequality, and acceptance of oppression. Meridian sits "mute," refusing to accept Christ like the others and "be saved." This act drives Mrs. Hill to reject her daughter.

In response to her mother's rejection, Meridian engages in a wanton pursuit of affection, having sex to please her teenage lovers, "while enjoying it not at all." As a result, Meridian, at age fifteen, finds herself imprisoned in a life much like her mother's: pregnant, married, and unhappy. After two years of what Meridian considers a life of "slavery," she experiences a personal awakening that leads her to leave her child and volunteer in the Civil Rights Movement. Escaping traditional social constraints, Meridian breaks a maternal pattern, as well as a cultural convention, for the second time.

In contrast to her relationship with her mother, Meridian's relationship with her father is very positive. Meridian's compassionate father teaches his daughter about justice, Native Americans, and a life "ruled by its own spirit," not governed by convention. Meridian's father refuses to keep land that belonged to the Indians, returning "the deed to the sixty acres his grandfather acquired after the Civil War" to Walter Longknife, a Cherokee, "a wanderer, a mourner" from Oklahoma. Angrily confronted by his wife, he explains that even black families were "part of it," part of the disappearance of Native Americans.

Despite her father's efforts to transfer the deed, the county would offer only token payment for land they had already taken to convert into Sacred Serpent Park, which now ironically belonged to the public, and was, therefore, "of course not open to Colored." Meridian often visited the park with her father and learned about her great-grandmother Feather Mae's "strange spiritual intoxication" that lifted her from the confines of her world. This secret bond, shaped during adolescence with her father—shared information about injustice done to Native Americans and spiritual ecstatic moments that allow her to rise above conflict—helps explain Meridian's later behavior when she sets out to seek justice for the oppressed in her culture.

She begins by peacefully protesting a town's segregated hospital facilities, and learns that even singing in the wrong places can provoke violence. Beaten, trampled, and jailed, Meridian does not leave; she commits to the movement, but she will not agree to violent action. She types, teaches illiterates to read and write, demonstrates against segregated facilities, and keeps the movement house open when others return to school. Offered an unexpected gift, she goes to Saxon College and begins her search.

That search takes Meridian on an eight-year journey during which she discovers the power of her African American past, returns to her geographical roots, and commits herself to activities that demonstrate both nonviolence and justice. Nowhere is that behavior more visible than in her endless work for the people of Chicokema, who comprise her ancestral community. She registers people to vote, but only after she works with them, shops for them, and nurses them; even then she only signs them up in their own time and on their own terms.

At the beginning of the novel—which chronologically is the end of Meridian's story—she marches with elementary school children in nonviolent protest of a segregation that keeps the children from the equal opportunity of viewing "Marilene O'Shay: One of the Twelve Human Wonders of the World: Dead for Twenty-Five Years, Preserved in Life-Like Condition." Despite her frail body, Meridian's power radiates. The children fall into line behind her, "their heads held high," and press onward through the ranks of the arrayed riflemen up to the circus car door.

Obviously, Meridian teaches the children more than a lesson about the fraud of the O'Shay exhibit. She teaches them about the power of nonviolent protest and about courage; she models how to act on one's beliefs. She is a woman of incredible moral concern who acts in small but significant ways to change the world in which she lives—a model for us all.

Linda Hogan's *Mean Spirit* (1990), a novel about the Osage Indians' experiences in Oklahoma in the 1920s, also shows how outsiders keep pace with the changing realities around them, not by repeating the words or the methods of the greedy, white power society, but by developing new words and ways to establish peace. For Moses and Belle Greycloud's family, "harmony, balance and community" are the central values of their tribal community. The competition, greed, and violence of the white male society that attempts to destroy their tribe triggers personal and public wars. The protagonists embody what Woolf termed "female" virtues and skills: mental chastity, nurturance, "the art of understanding other people's minds," integrity, concern for others, and peace.

Early in the novel the Greyclouds' granddaughter, Nola Blanket—in psychic shock from having seen her mother killed for the family's oil-rich land—is taken from her family. At the Watona School, Mrs. Seward, a teacher "bewildered" by students whom she sees behaving as "animals going to slaughter," uses the legal system to impose a white man as Nola's guardian, thus robbing her of her natural rights to her mother's land. When the threat escalates and Nola's life is at risk, Belle brings her home, placing the entire family under observation and attack. Although Sheriff Jess Gold and his cohort try to murder Nola, the way they murdered her mother, neither the watchers nor the family who protect Nola use violence. They watch, guard, nurture, and hide Nola; they use silence as a form of power; but they never adopt the violent ways of the white society.

Michael Horse, the writer and keeper of stories—who always retells history in his own words—constantly reminds characters of their culture's values. As he moves into the hills and away from the violence of white society, his people follow. At the end of the story, Horse shares his Native American "Bible," saying that he has "added" what he thinks is missing from the pages of the traditional European Bible. He reads,

> Honor father sky and mother earth. Look after everything . . . on earth, every creature and plant wants to live without pain, so do them no harm. Treat all people in creation with respect. . . . Live gently with the land. We are one with the land. . . . The world does not belong to us. We belong to the world. And all life is sacred. . . . Remake your spirit so that it is in harmony with the rest of . . . the universe. Keep peace with all your sisters and brothers. Humans whose minds are healthy desire such peace and justice. (Hogan, 1990: 212)

Horse's words bring the novel and this essay full circle. The values that Linda Hogan saw as crucial to deflect the "mean spirit" governing Oklahoma in 1923 are the values we need to deflect the "mean spirit" threatening our world today. Those values—integrity, respect, equality, peace, and justice—although not exclusively "female," do appear in women's writing about war, fictional and factual, across diverse cultures. In the novels above, the authors demonstrate how, if characters act upon those values, peace does indeed "pulse then into the world." Their stories challenge readers to act likewise.

REFERENCES

Allende, Isabel. 1986. *The House of the Spirits*. New York: Bantam.

Garcia, Christina. 1992. *Dreaming in Cuban*. New York: Ballantine.

Giosoeffi, Daniela, ed. 1988. *Women on War: Essential Voices for the Nuclear Age*. New York: Touchstone.

Hogan, Linda. 1990. *Mean Spirit*. New York: Ivy Books.

Kingsolver, Barbara. 1990. *Animal Dreams*. New York: Harper Collins.

Levertov, Denise. 1988. "Making Peace." In Daniela Giosoeffi, ed., *Women on War: Essential Voices for the Nuclear Age*, 326–327. New York: Touchstone.

Mason, Bobbie Ann. 1985. *In Country*. New York: Harper & Row.

Walker, Alice. 1976. *Meridian*. New York: Washington Square Press.

Woolf, Virginia. 1938. *Three Guineas*. New York: Harcourt, Brace, Jovanovich.

Part V

Motherhood, Parenting, and War

Chapter Twenty-Three

"Woman of Peace"
A Feminist Construction

Sara Ruddick

In Ingmar Bergman's movie *Shame*, two musicians, Jan and Eva, husband and wife, have fled from city war to island refuge. The war catches up with them, then engulfs them in cruelty, fear, and brutalization. At the end of the film, which also appears to be the ending of life in the afflicted war zone, the couple drifts in a small boat, far from shore, without food or water. The concluding image of the war is postnuclear—crops are ruined, the rain is poison. But the war itself had the attractions of "conventional" battle: gun fights and explosions, interrogations and betrayals, bribery, execution, fear, bitterness, despair, and hunger. A "civil" war.

In the final words of the film Eva recounts a dream.

> I had a strange dream, it was absolutely real. I was walking along a very beautiful street. On one side were white open houses with arches and pillars. On the other side was a lovely park. Under the big trees by the street ran cold dark-green water. I came to a high wall, that was overgrown with roses. Then an aircraft came, roaring down and set fire to the roses. They burned with a clear flame and there was nothing particularly terrible about it, because it was so beautiful. I watched in the reflections of the water as the roses burned. I had a baby in my arms. She was our daughter, she was only about six months old, and she was clutching my necklace and pressing her face to mine. I could feel her wet open mouth against my cheek. I knew the whole time that I ought to understand something important that someone had said. But I had forgotten it.[1]

In war's iconography, as in Bergman's film, it is often women who retain the dream of peace; they are on the side of "life," and keep others alive when war surrounds them. But like Eva, women of peace are represented as, and remain, dreamers. They do not remember what they know, what their lives may have taught them. Instead they dream of walking down a beautiful street, of large sheltering houses and cool green water, of "trees" of life and a child's embrace, and of a war not too bad because it is beautiful. Eva's dream, if dreams can be false, is a false one. The war Eva lived through was tawdry, ugly, and bleak. The meager peace she made with her husband—he wanted no children, in the midst of war she is pleased they have none—meant hard negotiating work in cramped spaces.

From ancient times, and certainly in the wars of this century, many feminists have been drawn to the idea of a woman of peace and to the images of shelter, fertility, and embrace that she sets against the nightmare of destruction. But in the last decades feminists have also become increasingly suspicious of the dreamer and her dreams. They have wanted the woman of peace to speak and act, to remember what she knows, to be not only on the side of life but amidst life's politics and choices.

I want, in this chapter, to outline a "figure" of a "woman of peace" as she has been reconstructed by recent feminist work. A "figure" crystallizes real possibilities but she (or it, or he in other contexts) is a figment of analysis and imagination defined by her "identities." These identities are imperfectly and fluidly embodied in historical and contemporary women's lives. A "figure" can inspire, frighten, repel, or instruct. The "figure" of a woman of peace may have this psychological significance for men as well as women. But she is a feminine figure who expresses, and under feminist construction also resists, certain norms of "femininity."

In outlining the "figure" of a *woman* of peace I make no quantitative, much less competitive comparisons between women's and men's peacefulness. Someone might outline the "figure" of a man of peace with his identities, his partial embodiment in men's lives, his psychological and political effects on women and men. The difference between the feminine and masculine figures are qualitative matters of meaning. Certain behavior, for example weeping for war dead, will have a different significance if the mourner is a man or woman. Similarly the interpretation of a symbolic act often turns on the sex of the actor. The logo of the War Resisters League, to cite one example, shows a pair of arms and hands breaking a gun into two parts. The hands are a man's and cannot be changed into a woman's without change of meaning. In the United States a woman would either be breaking someone else's gun or a gun she has only recently acquired. By contrast, breaking the gun is part of men's history; were someone to outline the figure of a man of peace, it might well symbolize aspects of his identity.[2]

I say that feminism is reconstructing the "figure" of a woman of peace. But there are many feminisms, many ways to define who counts as a "feminist." In a general sense of the term, "feminists" believe that gender arrangements are damaging to women and perhaps to men, at least in the society in which a feminist lives and perhaps in most societies, and that therefore these arrangements should be changed. On this or any other reasonably inclusive[3] definition of "feminism," feminists may be militarists or antimilitarists, realists, just war-theorists, or pacifists. So, for example, some feminists in the United States fully support its military policies and work for women's equal participation in all aspects of fighting and command.

When I speak of "feminists" without modifying adjective, I allude to the writings and politics of any people or groups who profess general "feminist" attitudes. So, for example, I speak of "feminist" worries about the deleterious effect on women of the virtues of peacemaking for which they are praised. This concern for women may be shared by feminist pacifists or militarists, though in any discussion of these worries their divergent interests would become quickly apparent.

Most people who are feminists under any general definition of the term also have other, sometimes more primary, political allegiances and identities that "modify" or "hyphenate" their feminism.[4] There are capitalist and socialist feminists, for example, and feminists who would never separate their feminist from their national or ethnic or religious identity.

The feminist peace project within which I locate myself involves a modified, hybrid feminism that is partly constituted by its antimilitarism and commitment to developing nonviolent relationships. A feminist woman or man becomes antimilitarist partly because s/he sees that war is in some sense "masculine" and expresses and reinforces violence against women. Conversely, an antimilitarist woman or man becomes feminist because she or he recognizes in militarism an extended expression of the domination of women that feminists are committed to eradicating. Each commitment informs, and each can modify, the other. I refer to this hybrid feminism with which I ally myself as antimilitarist feminism or, alternately when stressing its commitment to nonviolence, as peace feminism. Although this hybrid feminism is committed to developing nonviolent relationships and resistances, it is not necessarily pacifist. On the contrary, for this antimilitarist and peace feminism the question of "just wars" has come to appear defining and troublesome.

A Woman of Peace: Three Identities

I outline the "figure" of a woman of peace by ascribing to her three identities: *mater dolorosa*, outsider, and peacemaker. These identities overlap—especially that of *mater dolorosa* and outsider—but are also sometimes discordant, especially the outsider and peacemaker. Each identity has its genealogy, "a history of ancestors of present-day concepts and practices."[5] Among the ancestors are "real life" representatives who most visibly enact one identity but also, typically, participate in others.

Kathe Kollwitz, for example, drew and sculpted protective, sorrowing mothers and became a mourning mother herself. And she also achieved something of an outsider's relation to war and was, intermittently, a peacemaker.[6] Virginia Woolf invented a particular version of the woman as "outsider" in her pacifist and feminist *Three Guineas* and also enacted this identity in her own life and death. Images of mourning were central in her rejection of war but she was no peacemaker (Woolf, 1938). The members of Women's Strike for Peace attempted to make peace, deploying maternal rhetoric against armament and for conciliation. They were not outsiders but insisted on chaining themselves to government buildings, entering government committee rooms, and negotiating with those in power. They did use images of anticipated mourning and loss as counterpoint to the "peace" they were hoping to make.[7] These women, two with roots in the First World War, one with roots in the Cold War, are but three particularly visible representatives of identities that recur, in recognizable but various forms, in different cultures and in response to particular wars and potential wars.

Of these identities, the most deeply rooted *within* war stories is the *mater dolorosa*, the mother of sorrows. The mother of sorrows not only mourns war's suffering, she also holds lives together despite pain, bitterness and deprivation. In refugee camps across the world, women appear as mothers of sorrow, searching for lost children, keeping living children alive, and giving birth once again in the hope of more lives to which they will then cling.

The *mater dolorosa* weeps for good reason. War and violence destroy all of "women's work"—mothering, feeding, sheltering, nursing the ill, tending the frail elderly, maintaining kin connections. Years of child tending are not only wasted by shots but also perverted. An Israeli mother is reported to have said: "I sent my son away a good man; he came back a killer." The soldier returning home, to mother and lover, is a familiar literary figure. Nearly unrecognizable and unrecognizing, he is mad, embittered, "crippled" in spirit and often also literally in body. Women themselves, and their daughters, are particular targets of war, victims of rape, sexual humiliation, radical social dislocation, permanent injury, and murder.[8]

It is a feminist task, generally, to transform dominant visions of the "world according to him" by including many women's visions. Anyone who looks at war through women's eyes and lives can see the ravages war wreaks on relationships and bodies of both sexes of all ages; conversely, the world seen through mourning women's tears suggests the blessings of peace. But the *mater dolorosa* is not yet a figure of peace. Actual weeping women are often too exhausted for any political response, or may be hungering for revenge. Whatever the politics of those who suffer, displays of suffering are notoriously unpredictable in their effects. People who witness suffering may respond with sympathy and help, but they may also turn away out of indifference, fear, or disgust, or worse, be strangely excited by the spectacle.

How can suffering be made effectively political? While there is no recipe for effectiveness, it is possible to look at women's protests of the last decades for some recurrent features of effective representations of suffering. For example, many effective protests display in public emotions that have been relegated to a "private," apolitical world. In particular, women's bodies and the artifacts of attachment are brought into public spaces where they were never meant to be. So, for example, women camping outside the Greenham Common missile base in England tacked familiar paraphernalia of British domestic life—pillowcases, diapers, and drawings— against the wire gate of a nuclear installation. The Madres of Argentina, protesting the "disappearance" of their children, paraded in the central square in front of the primary government building. As kerchiefs they wore diapers embroidered with the names of many disappeared children. They walked with photographs of their own children around their necks. These photographs "belonged" in a common family room or bedroom. Tokens of childhood, they were meant to capture events and stages of lives of children meant to live. Now these records of life are suffused with terror and policies of death.

Put generally, these effective representatives of suffering both deploy expectations of womanliness and violate them. They elicit the sympathies that mourning tends to elicit but in a context in which passive or sentimental witness becomes difficult. This dissonance is most politicized when the representatives of suffering are disobedient to their own state or social powers. Women of sorrow are meant to accept their suffering, protesting only against enemy aggressors. Women who act *as women* in public spaces transform the passions of attachment and loss into political action, transform the woman of sorrow from icon to agent.

The second identity included in the figure of a woman of peace, that of woman as outsider, is a stranger to *men's* wars. Virginia Woolf developed this identity in her feminist, antifascist, antiwar polemic, *Three Guineas*. Women, she said, speaking particularly of upper-class women, were outsiders by fate, lacking rights to property and political power as well, of course, as the right to fight in wars. Therefore, women have no country and, she urged, they should want no country.

But, as Woolf well knew, if women were outsiders by fate, they were not outsiders in spirit or by choice. Women thrilled to their empire, its wars, and the soldiers who fought them. In this time of multiplying nationalisms, it is increasingly clear that women not only have countries; they also act as "mothers" of the nation and mothers of its "martyrs," recruiting fighters and excoriating cowards. Woolf wanted women to claim an outsider's status, to learn to say, "As a woman I have no country, as a woman I want no country, my country is the whole world" (Woolf, 1938: 109). But she was well aware of the strength of nationalist and xenophobic impulses and of the appeals of violence.

One way that Woolf and later feminists encouraged women to assume an outsider status was by reminding us that war is men's business and that their business is repugnant. There is an evident sense in which war is still largely a masculine enterprise. But feminists, including Virginia Woolf, have wanted to insist not so much on the sheer fact of male presence but on a particularly repellent masculine character who makes and is made by war—a predatory, heterosexually bigoted misogynist, a "monstrous male, loud of voice, hard of fist" who finds a "naked hideous male gratification" in fantasies, and sometimes in acts, of looting, injuring, torture, and rape (Wolf, 1984: 74; see also Woolf, 1938).

Predatory sexual fantasies have been found in a variety of texts ranging from the literature of *Freikorps* death troops to boot camp training rituals, to graffiti on bombs and guns, the tough talk of generals, and metaphors of defense strategists.[9] Let me cite just one notable, disturbingly singable example of soldierly lust. In 1987 in England the "private" songs, lyrics, and fantasies of a squadron of USAF pilots was mistakenly put out for sale at an air force open-day picnic and fundraiser. It fell into the hands of feminist writer Joan Smith, who included it in a book entitled *Misogynies*, a series of revelations about men's hatred of women. These pilots imagined going off to war singing of the "Persian-pukes" they are ready to "rape," the faggot assholes they are ready to sodomize, the dead and diseased whore they are ready to rape. Time and again the lyrics represented women as enemies and agents of death; also as fat, disgusting, and smelly. Men and their assholes are another focus of excited aggression. And destruction itself is a sexual high. "Allah creates but we cremate," one songwriter exults (Smith, 1990).

In identifying a predatory, misogynist, heterosexually bigoted masculinity characteristic of war, feminists are not claiming that men as a group display this sexuality. The air force lyrics express fantasies; some pilots may have hated singing them. In action, some men are sexually excited by war's permission of brutal sexuality, but even some of these are later ashamed of their excitements and their acts.

In all war, on any side, there are men frightened and running, fighting reluctantly and eager to get home, or even courageously resisting their orders to kill. The peace-feminist's point is not that men are warlike but that war elicits and satisfies preda-tory, assaultive impulses. And despite their ever-increasing participation in actual battle, it seems that women are still far more likely to be targets than subjects of these impulses.

The repugnance of war's predatory, heterosexually bigoted, misogynist masculin-ity is not in itself sufficient to turn women from war. Unless she is a target of *her* soldiers' assault, or unless *her* soldier returns a killer or batterer, a woman may attribute predatory masculinity not to war but to enemy men only. She may then remain a lover of her war's men and their battles. The vulnerable but armed hero, just restrained protector and jousting boy are as sexually alluring as the predator is repugnant. Nor are women immune from a more general erotics of war and its weapons, which takes different forms in different kinds of battle and was vividly expressed, for example, during the Cold War. Here is Helen Caldicott, a passionate feminist and peacemaker, responding to a film of a missile launch. "I recently watched a filmed launching of an MX missile. It rose slowly from the ground, surrounded by smoke and flames, and elongated into the air. *It was a very sexual sight indeed. . . .* A sight sexual for women as well as men" (Held, 1993: 147, italics mine).

This erotic appeal of war is one aspect of what J. Glenn Gray calls war's "weird but genuine beauty" and which led Robert E. Lee to exclaim, watching a column of soldiers advancing to death, "it is good that war is so terrible—we would grow too fond of it" (Gray, 1970: 31). War's beauty appears in Eva's dream of burning roses and in many other dreams that belie the ugliness the dreamer has seen. Women, like men, are inside war and will not move out of it until we acknowledge its sexual allure, tribal passion, and strange beauties.

Once she acknowledges war's attractions, it is easier for a woman to *choose* to be an outsider, which means becoming disloyal to war plans and state aggressions. The increasing presence of women soldiers and their determination to fight and command fighters highlights the *choice* of remaining outside. Women can no longer understand themselves as peaceful by "nature." They are responsible for their atti-tude toward war and nonviolence. Choosing the outsider's attitude is also encour-aged by, or perhaps requires, allying with others—outsiders by fate or by choice. Woolf herself advocated a loose coalition of outsiders made of people "shut up and shut out" because they are women, or "because they are Jews, because they are democrats, because of race, because of religion," because (as she surely would have added today) of sexuality (Woolf, 1938: 103).

A steady realization of the predatory misogyny, not of men, but of masculinity in its most repellent guises, marks only the beginning of estrangement from violence. Like the gay man or lesbian who must "come out" again and again in different contexts with distinct inducements to hide or pass, the outsider must repeatedly, on many occasions, turn away from official violence as it is presented in desperate or patriotic guise. Only gradually can those who chose to be outsiders, along with those who have that status visited upon them, learn to hold fast to a steady suspicion of collective terror, enthusiasm, and patriotic exhortation—a steady suspicion of violence.

The third identity in formation, that of *peacemaker*, is rooted in the daily lives of many women. Unlike the *mater dolorosa* or outsider, the peacemaker takes responsibility for violence, her own and others', in her home, neighborhood, and country. She then counters violence nonviolently. A peacemaker may be a pacifist, someone who believes that war and other forms of deliberate, institutionalized violence are unjustifiable in principle. But such a general renunciation of violence is neither defining nor typical. Rather, the peacemaker is defined by a commitment to developing nonviolent relationships and ways of fighting, not by a principled or contingent attitude toward uses of military violence.

Making peace is not, as Eva dreamed, a matter of providing a haven—a beautiful, white house by a cool green stream—but rather a matter of creating *relationships* in which people, at the least, feel and are safe, where at best they feel and are respected. When there are painful rifts in relationships, or unresolvable and bitter conflicts, a peacemaker searches for ways for people to live without injuring, separately or side by side if physical distance is not possible. In stable times, a peacemaker aims to create relationships that can withstand difference, anger, and bitterness. Stable relationships are only occasionally without conflict, as any parent or community organizer can attest. But they are free of the *willingness* to injure and damage others in order to have one's way with them.

A story first told by Carol Gilligan is often used to illustrate the kind of inclusive solution peacemakers look for (Gilligan, 1988). Two children are having trouble agreeing on what game to play. He wants to play pirates, she wants to play neighbors. In this situation, either child might try to prevail through aggressive argument or by bullying. Or, if they were good children, they might take turns, each playing the others' game for equal amounts of time, a "fair" solution. The girls' solution, and the peaceful one, is to invent a game they can play together: "We'll play neighbors and you'll be the pirate who lives next door."

Charming as this story is, from a feminist perspective the inclusiveness it praises is troubling. A girl's ability to make up *some* game she can play with even the most pirate-like boys often does not serve her well. Put more abstractly, the virtues of peacemaking, like the ethics of care that honors them, are entwined with norms of femininity that are often destructive of the women governed by them.

Consider only one example: capacities for anger, aggression, conciliation, and restraint. Disciplined restraint of resentment and anger is often necessary in nonviolent protests and negotiations. Women have often learned disciplined restraint because they have "managed" their feelings in order to "feed the egos and tend the wounds" of others—demanding children, domineering spouses, tyrannical employers.[10] This managed restraint does not serve a woman well when she is treated with disrespect, but it does enable her to negotiate when others can only fight. Women are said, more than men, to experience anger as a sign of impotence and loss of control. This contrasts with an allegedly masculine tendency to experience anger as a license for violence and to experience violence as a means and expression of mastery (Campbell, 1993). The satisfactions and effectiveness of violence are routinely and overwhelmingly exaggerated. It is therefore a virtue to see, as women allegedly do, the sense of impotence from which violence often arises, a virtue to appreciate the loss of control to which violence often leads. The norms of femininity and the requirements of peacemaking overlap.

Yet it is also true that nonviolent protest requires fighting to get what one needs and to protect what one loves without damaging others or being damaged oneself. And this requires distinguishing anger and aggression from hate and violence in order to act aggressively. Similarly, women who suffer particular abuse must acknowledge legitimate anger and cultivate aggressive, self-protective tactics of defense.

I am not suggesting that "feminine" peacemaking and feminist consciousness are at odds. A critical, resistant feminist consciousness heartens women who do not yet trust their own independent critical judgment or who have not yet risked disobedience to familial or patriotic norms. An appreciative, constructive feminism identifies as praiseworthy relationships that do not sacrifice any participants to the well-being of others. Feminists have placed a high value on friendship—for example, a relationship that J. Glenn Gray described as quintessential antimilitarist, resistant to both the self-loss of collective bonding and to imperialist self-interest (Gray, 1970; On, 1996).

But the virtues of peacemaking in present circumstances of women's subordination may be linked with harmful habits of compliance and self-denial; it may even sustain them. No twist of feminist rhetoric will erase this complex heritage of femininity.

If peacemaking girls become women too willing to play with pirates, they also become women who can still see neighborliness in pirates, who can accord a "moral standing" to pirates. The refusal to demonize or racialize the enemy, once conjoined with a refusal to submit to his or her terms, is the central achievement of peacemaking. Piracy hurts and therefore we should not play pirates with anyone. But, to paraphrase Martin Luther King, Jr., the thing that hurts in our "enemy neighbor" is never all there is to him. It is possible to invent games other than piracy that even the pirate can play with us.

The Woman of Peace in Just Wars

For many years, it seemed unnecessary to ask what a "woman of peace" would do when asked to support violence in a so-called just cause. Feminists were preoccupied with "senseless" wars (the First World War was a favorite) or unjust wars (the U.S. war against Vietnam or the U.S.-sponsored Contra war against Nicaragua haunted many United States feminists). Nuclear war was and—far more than we like to admit—remains a terrifying possibility that buries all questions of justice.

With these wars in mind, the task of the woman of peace seemed clear. She should represent the potential sufferings of nuclear "exchange," the current economic, social, and psychological sufferings occasioned by nuclear deployment, and the actual injuries suffered by unjust aggression. She should disassociate herself from military rhetoric and plans, at the least adopting a skeptical stance toward them, at best an actively disgusted one. She should also make peace between enemy-strangers, at best creating mutually rewarding nonviolent relationships between them.

The antimilitarist, peace feminist's relation to the woman of peace was also clear. She should articulate more precisely the moral and cognitive capacities of peace-making associated with women and developed in their work and relationships. She should heighten a sense of war's repugnant and strange masculinity and underline the specific suffering that wars cause women both as caregivers and targets of masculine rape and violence. She should also bring women to acknowledge their own sometimes excited complicity with violence, the temptations of too long, or too familiarly, proclaiming victimization, and the deleterious effects of norms of femininity on peacemaking.

At least since 1990 the task of a woman of peace, and peace feminists' attitude toward her, is no longer clear. It seems impossible now *not* to address questions of the proper use of military force. Moreover, when seen retrospectively in the light of current military aggressions and massacres, the earlier clarity of peace feminists and women of peace seems partly a function of a safe distance from actual battle and military tyranny. The formerly confident "woman of peace" can appear to the antimilitarist feminists who constructed and honored her as naive, indifferent to suffering, an "appeaser."

How then *should* the woman of peace judge the use of military force in what others call "just causes"—defending one's own or another people against brutal violence or putting a stop to civil massacre?[11] Military action is only one way to stop violence. Its effects are unpredictable yet predictably damaging beyond the best intentions of the actors. Nonetheless there are some situations (Haiti, Bosnia, Rwanda come to mind) in which it *appears* to be impossible to stop aggression nonviolently. And in those same situations, even allowing for routine but often extreme exaggeration of the effectiveness of violence, it nonetheless *appears* that certain particular military measures are likely to be effective. It seems that the woman of peace must judge the use of military force in this kind of situation. Only then, someone might argue, will we know what her "peace politics" amounts to.

Despite all these circumstances, one possible, even characteristic, response of the woman of peace, and of the peace feminists who are constructing her, is to refuse to enter into discussions of the just use of military force. A woman of peace would not enter into cost-benefit analyses of particular military actions, though a woman inspired by her might maintain a more lively, concrete grasp of individual and social harms wrought by particular weapons and strategies. Nor would the woman of peace enter into diplomatic questions of whether, for example, Germany should have recognized Croatia before it had guaranteed the rights of minority Serbs, or whether the Dayton Peace Plan improves on the Vance Owen Plan. Actual women inspired by a woman of peace might address these questions, and diplomacy would be better for their presence. But a woman of peace, as a *figure*, is not a diplomat.

Just so, a woman of peace might remain outside the rhetoric of just war theory. There are historical precedents for this refusal among representatives of women of peace, women who acknowledged the justice of causes but refused the justice of war. Virginia Woolf and Simone Weil, who wrote their most profound antimilitarist work during the Spanish Civil War and the European war against Hitler, serve as exemplars. In their refusal of war's justice, Woolf and Weil developed a conception of war as seen from the position of a *moral* outsider. Their views are still common among peace feminists, though usually not so consciously expressed.[12]

Virginia Woolf's central concept is that war is not episodic, a matter of threat, invasion, battle, and cease-fire. Rather, war is a predictable expression of the culture in which it is waged. Military and civil worlds are inseparably connected; the tyrannies, servilities, conquests, and humiliations of the one reflect the structure and experience of the other. Looking at the patriarchal (her word) family, and particularly at education and professional life in early twentieth-century England, Woolf saw an ethos of male dominion and military domination in the making. People are taught "not to hate force but to use it" in order to keep their possessions, defend their grandeur and power, through varieties of economic, racial, and sexual violence (Woolf, 1938: 142).

The concept of a "war culture" directs attention away from battle to the cultural practices that fuel the desire for violence in assaulter and assaulted. It identifies "war zones" where the weapons and ravages of battle—injury, hunger, homelessness, chaos, despair—exist in the midst of peace and ferrets out violence concealed within order, including the global order.[13] The idea of a war culture is also a hopeful one. If war is within and among us, rather than visited upon us, we can begin to prevent war by changing our societies and ourselves.

When war is seen as an expression of a culture, then the rhetoric of just-war theory—like the rhetoric of patriotism and honor—is seen as a "fiction," an "old lie."[14] This view of war as "unreal" is not unlike "realism." War is an amoral expression of contesting parties attempting to assert or defend their interests. The constitutive business of war is to get one's way by threatening to harm or actually harming others. The winner is one who either terrorizes more effectively or actually "outinjures" the opponent.[15] Soldiers, even governments, may sometimes fight for "just" causes of rescue and, more likely, of immediate self-defense. But there is no conceptual or moral anchoring of a collective's ability to outinjure to the virtue of its cause. Only amoral capacities to arm and strategize determine winners or losers.

To this deconstructive, realist view of war, Simone Weil and many peace feminists who follow her add an explicitly antimilitarist sentiment that is also antimoralist. Whatever the justice or injustice of the cause it invokes, the activity of injuring leads to blood lust, cruelty, and a drive for revenge that overshadow virtues of loyalty and courage that collective outinjuring may also elicit. Winning itself is an illusion that discounts the sufferings and impermanence of victory. The injunction of the woman of peace is to leave "the cold brutality of the deeds of war . . . undisguised"; to remember that only "chance" separates by an abyss the good from the bad army or soldier, the comrade from the enemy (Weil, 1946: 32).

This amoralist, antimilitarist focus on the horrors of armed injury and terror represents a deepening rather than a transformation of the outsiders' stance. The *mater dolorosa* is similarly freer to represent the sufferings of victims as sufferings of war itself when the sense of war in no way derives from virtue. But the peacemaker, accustomed to taking responsibility for violence, remains troubled in the particular circumstances under consideration, where violence is unchecked and brutal yet might be checked by particular limited military action. War is a dreadful expression of a war culture; military actions will never create a culture of peace. But on this particular occasion, a peacemaker will still consider whether a particular use of military force can be made to serve as an instrument of the nonviolence she is seeking to create.

Some individual peacemakers are pacifists who reject the use of military force in advance on principle. Others, nearly pacifist, do not find in any particular instance a justification for military action. But some peacemakers find that in the circumstances of brutal aggression and likely military effectiveness, the use of military force seems obligatory. Can peace feminists imagine a peacemaker who calls for fighters— or joins a fighting force if she is young, able to be trained, and fit? Many (former?) peace feminists in the United States have supported the call for arms, bombing campaigns, combat, and occupation in Bosnia and forceful occupation in Haiti. Are they then revising the figure of a woman of peace, or are they abjuring the figure they have constructed and honored?

This is a question feminists will answer collectively and contentiously as they continue to respond in individual situations from their particular endangered or safe, embedded or distant, relation to violence. Here I can only suggest some directions they (we) will take. First, peacemaking is only one identity of a woman of peace. In other theoretical contexts, feminists have recognized that "identities" are often in conflict. Here too, the woman of peace, although a peacemaker, could remain an outsider who is alienated from, even disgusted by, the violence she recommends. As a *mater dolorosa* could continue to represent the sufferings of war, refusing to demonize an enemy even if, as a peacemaker, she subjected particular aggressors and their military apparatus to the violence whose effects she mourns.

Second, a peacemaker could continue to abjure moral language. The words of the British psychoanalyst D. W. Winnicott seem to the point. As London was being bombed in World War II, and as Winnicott himself supported defense efforts, he wrote: "If we fight to exist we do not claim to be better than our enemies. We should win a military not a moral victory" (Winnicott, 1986). But in alliance with the realist outsider and *mater dolorosa*, an antimilitarist feminist peacemaker would speak less easily than Winnicott of "victory," preferring instead the driest descriptions of deplorable, temporary tactics for stopping violence.

Finally, even if she endorsed a particular and limited use of violence, even if she petitioned for it, a peacemaker could keep her mind focused on the 'postviolent' peace that violence is meant to provide. There are many stories of nonviolent relationships created even in "wartime" among committed military opponents and enemy civilians. A peacemaker, freed from the excited or paranoid righteousness of violence, should be especially poised to notice and to create such moments of peace. Even more, she could continuously imagine in detail postwar relationships between war's enemies that could maximize safety and respect.

I see no likelihood that peace feminists will agree on particular limited deployments of military force in desperate situations. I am suggesting that they may none-theless continue to construct a woman of peace, and to be inspired by the figure they have constructed. Indeed, a peacemaker who does not resolve but instead expresses the conflicts she experiences may be a more fitting guide for actual peace-makers, women and men, who live in radically different relations to battle and everywhere disagree among themselves.

NOTES

1. Ingmar Bergman, *Shame* in *Persona and Shame*, tr. Keith Bradfield (London: Marion Boyars, 1972), 188–189. The published script differs from the film, which ends with the words I cite.

2. On "Breaking the Sword," see J. Glenn Gray, *The Warriors* (New York: Harper & Row, 1970), 225ff. Gray cites Nietzsche, *The Wanderer and His Shadow*.

3. Any general characterization of "feminism" will be rejected by some other feminists. I mean only to contrast a definition of unmodified feminism with hybrid peace feminism.

4. It was common in the late seventies and early eighties to speak of hybrid or hyphenated feminism. The term "modified feminism" comes from Catharine MacKinnon, *Feminism Un-modified* (Cambridge, MA: Harvard University Press, 1987). MacKinnon is critical of any modifications of feminism.

5. Claudia Card, *Lesbian Choices* (New York: Columbia University Press, 1994), 31. See, for Card's source, Nietzsche, *The Genealogy of Morals*.

6. On Kollwitz, see any catalog or reproductions of her work; for example, *Kathe Koll-witz*, ed. Elizabeth Prelinger (New Haven: Yale University Press, 1992). For a moving ac-count of Kollwitz's slow and painful turning against war, see Sara Friedrichsmeyer, " 'Seeds for the Sowing': The Diary of Kathe Kollwitz," in *Of Arms and the Woman*, ed. Helen Cooper, Adrienne Munich, and Susan Squier (Chapel Hill, University of North Carolina Press, 1989).

7. See Amy Swerdlow's marvelous history of this movement, *Women Strike for Peace* (Chicago: University of Chicago Press, 1993).

8. I heard the story about the Israeli mother at a conference convened by Women in Black in Jerusalem, December 1994. Two classic accounts of the return of the maddened soldier are Toni Morrison's *Sula* and Virginia Woolf's *Mrs. Dalloway*. The rape of women in war has often been a galvanizing issue, and was bitterly so in reference to Bosnian Serbs' rape of Bosnian Muslim women.

9. On the Freikorps, see Klaus Theweleit, *Male Fantasies*, vols. 1 and 2 (Minneapolis, University of Minnesota Press, 1987, 1990). On training rituals, see, for example, the film *Full Metal Jacket* and Tim O'Brien, *If I Die in the Combat Zone* (New York: Dell, 1979). On the sexuality of the language of defense intellectuals, see Carol Cohn, "Sex and Death in the Rational World of Defense Intellectuals," *Signs* 12, no. 4 (1987).

10. The phrase "feeding egos, tending wounds" and many of the critiques of norms of femininity can be found in Sandra Bartky, *Femininity and Domination* (New York: Rou-tledge, 1990).

11. I am assuming some familiarity with just-war theory. Just causes (*jus ad bellum*) include defense against murderous aggression, intervention on behalf of just but vulnerable defenders, and intervention to halt civil massacres. If there is just cause for military aggres-

sion, then nonviolent alternatives must have been exhausted and violence is the "last resort." The real aims of the aggressor must be the stated aims, the use of military force must be likely to achieve those aims, and the good of achieving the aim must be "proportional" to the harm suffered. In traditional theory, the war must have been called by a proper authority, but I leave these and other issues aside. A just war must be fought justly—roughly, with the right weapons, aimed at the right people (armed combatants are the paradigm case). The good achieved by each weapon and strategy must be proportional to the harm done. For an account of feminist critiques of just-war theory, see Lucinda Peach, "An Alternative to Pacifism? Feminism and Just War Theory," *Hypatia* 9, no. 2 (Spring 1944).

12. Woolf wrote *Three Guineas* during the Spanish Civil War in which her nephew was killed. She continued to write against militarism as well as fascism (the two were closely connected for her) until the end of her life during the bombing of England. See, for example, her last novel, *Between the Acts*, and her letters and diaries during the thirties until 1941. Simone Weil, finding it impossible to stay behind the lines when every day she hoped one side would triumph, renounced her previous pacifism and attempted to join the troops against Franco. But her experience there led her to reject the distinction between moral and immoral soldiers that she had only recently and reluctantly drawn. See her letter to Georges Bernanos, in the *Simone Weil Reader*, ed. George Panichas (Mt. Kisko, NY: Moyer Bell, 1977). She wrote *Iliad: Poem of Force* while awaiting passage to the United States, having fled Paris after the Nazi occupation.

13. Cynthia Enloe especially has shown the ways that a military culture combines with economic imperialism to shape and distort women's lives as service employees, low wage workers, and "comfort women" for soldiers. See her *Bananas, Beaches and Bases* (Berkeley, University California Press, 1990), and *The Morning After: Sexual Politics at the End of the Cold War* (Berkeley, University of California Press, 1993).

14. The phrase "old lie" comes specifically from Wilfred Owen's poem "Dulce et Decorum est." Woolf, who was moved by Owen's poetry, referred to war as a fiction, explicitly and implicitly, from the First World War on. "I become steadily more feminist, owing to the *Times*, which I read at breakfast and wonder how this preposterous masculine fiction [the war] keeps going a day longer—without some vigorous woman pulling us together and marching through it." See *Collected Letters*, vol. 2, letter 748, written to Margaret Llewellen Davies, 1916.

15. The word "outinjure" comes from Elaine Scarry, *The Body in Pain* (Oxford: Oxford University Press, 1985).

REFERENCES

Campbell, Anne. 1993. *Men, Women and Aggression*. New York: Basic Books.

Gilligan, Carol. 1988. "Remapping the Moral Domain: New Images of the Self in Relationship." In *Mapping the Moral Domain*. Carol Gilligan, Janie Victoria Ward, and Jill McLean Taylor (eds.). Cambridge, MA: Harvard University Press.

Gray, J. Glenn. 1970. *The Warriors*. New York: Harper & Row.

Held, Virginia. 1993. *Feminist Morality*. Chicago: University of Chicago Press.

On, Bat Ami Bar. 1996. "Meditations of National Identity." In *Bringing Peace Home*, Karen J. Warren and Duane Cady (eds.). Bloomington: Indiana University Press.

Smith, Joan. 1990. *Misogynies*. New York: Ballantine Books.

Weil, Simone. 1946. *Iliad: Poem of Force.* Pendle Hill Pamphlet, #91, Wallingford, PA.

Winnicott, D. W. 1986. *Home Is Where We Start From.* Harmondsworth, U.K.: Penguin.

Wolf, Christa. 1984. *Cassandra.* New York: Farrar, Strauss and Giroux.

Woolf, Virginia. 1938. *Three Guineas.* New York: Harcourt Brace.

Chapter Twenty-Four

Maternal Thinking and the Politics of War

Nancy Scheper-Hughes

Conventional ways of thinking about the gender of war and peace center on the too-comfortable view of women—and especially mothers—as embedded in particular ways of being-in-the-world that presumably make them resistant to wars and receptive to peacekeeping. Yet in many cases this theory doesn't hold true. Instead, aspects of the experience of mothering—especially under conditions of scarcity, famine, oppression, and political disruption—can both instruct and allow women to surrender readily their sons (and their husbands) to war, violence, and death. There's a maternal ethos of "acceptable death" without which political violence and wars of all kinds would not be possible.

A popular Irish ballad sung in pubs during the height of IRA gun-running in western Ireland goes like this:

> I. At a cottage door one winter night
> as the snow lay on the ground,
> a youthful Irish soldier boy
> to the mountains he was bound.
> His mother stood beside him saying
> "you'll win, my boy, don't fear":
> and with loving arms around his waist
> she tied a bandolier.
>
> II. "Goodbye, God bless you, Mother dear,
> I hope your heart won't pain,
> but you'll pray to God that soon you'll see
> your soldier boy again.
> And when I'm in the firing line
> it will be a source of joy
> to know that you're the mother proud
> of an Irish soldier boy."

Why would Irish mothers—or any mothers, for that matter—arm their sons and send them proudly, almost joyfully, into war? What of the perception that those who give birth are "by nature" less likely to support killing and war?

Sara Ruddick has made perhaps the most cogent statement of the putative relationship between gender and the politics of peace. She has written extensively about "maternal thinking," by which she means a distinctively "maternal" shape of moral and political reasoning and practice. Ruddick does not view maternal thinking as innate, as biologically driven, or as a projection of female somatic design. Rather, in the tradition of Wittgenstein and Habermas, Ruddick argues that particular ways of seeing and thinking arise from experience and the practices in which people engage.

Because women, Ruddick argues, are existentially thrust into the world as potential mothers and as those most often called on to care for the young, women tend to develop a moral commitment to social values that foster human growth, life preservation, and peacekeeping. *To protect, to nurture, and to train* characterize maternal thinking and practice. Maternal thinking, then, begins in a stance of *protectiveness*, "an attitude governed . . . by the priority of keeping over acquiring, of conserving the fragile, of maintaining whatever is at hand and necessary to the child's life" (Ruddick, 1980:350). It is, Ruddick continues, citing Adrienne Rich, an "attitude elicited by the work of 'world-*protection*, world-*preservation*, and world-*repair*'" (ibid.). Ideally, it should lead to an ethical commitment, to "a politics of peace."

Yet mothers worldwide have just as often encouraged, even willingly sacrificed, their sons in wars that risk the safety of their children and their world. Where, for example, were the voices of United States women clamoring for "world protection, world repair" during the Gulf War? Instead, we heard women and mothers claiming the right to fight on the front lines and the equal opportunity to master the tools of organized violence.

Ruddick notes the contradiction of women who take "authority's side" in promoting wars; she explains it in terms of women's relative political powerlessness. Women ineffectively press their moral visions of peacemaking because they live in a world where maternal values and thinking count for very little. Since their public thoughts are so rarely solicited, women abdicate their maternal authority and surrender their children to the war machine. Thus, even though women may hate wars in general and despise a particular war policy, they may still urge their sons to join the army because "the law" requires them to do so. Here, women's actions represent a perverse sort of "peacekeeping" through accommodation: "Don't make waves, don't buck the system, do what 'the man' says, son."

My feminist colleagues in Israel exhibited such thinking when I was a guest of the Israeli Anthropological Association in 1994 following the Hebron massacre. They defended Israeli women for helping their draft-age children face military service proudly and cheerfully. The draft functioned in Israel, they said, the way college did in other countries. The military created a strong peer group that would remain a primary source of social solidarity throughout the child's life. Israeli mothers were thinking "maternally," my feminist colleagues argued, by making sure their children were rendered "socially acceptable" by their participation in the draft and even in military actions.

But this experience makes me wonder about Ruddick's argument. In response, we should more closely explore the links between maternal thinking and military thinking, and between "maternal practice" and the practices of war. Ruddick evokes the powerful image of the *mater dolorosa,* the mother of sorrows, as the symbol for maternal peacekeeping. The grieving, sorrowing mother weeps over the body of her dead son and is left to nurse survivors, to rebuild homes, and to reweave the social connections that wars have destroyed. This image provides a great deterrent to the politics of war.

But in my research in Brazil, I learned how the frequent experience of child death in impoverished shantytowns shapes maternal thinking in a way that extinguishes maternal grief over premature death. Instead it summons another dimension of maternal thinking—one more congenial to military thinking: the notion of inevitable, acceptable, and meaningful death. When premature or untimely death is all too frequent, the loss of a small child can seem like a relatively minor misfortune. Maternal resignation or accommodation can often displace resistance and outrage. Following the death of a hungry infant, some shantytown mothers would say: "*Pois, menos um por meu poquinho de angu*" (less one for my little bit of gruel). Or they would comment philosophically: "*Melhor morrer menino do que um de nos mourrer*" (better a child die than one of us). Embedded in this kind of maternal thinking, the existential dilemma that emerges from the experience of chronic loss is resolved by "letting go."

Ruddick has identified "holding"—holding on, holding up, holding close, holding dear—as an essential element of maternal thinking. But maternal thinking under conditions of scarcity, political disruption, and violence can instead be guided more by this metaphysical stance of "letting go." If "holding" carries the double connotation of loving care ("to have and to hold") and of passive resistance ("holding back," a refusal of aggression), "letting go" also carries a double meaning. In its negative sense, "letting go" implies the letting loose of destructive maternal power, as in physical abuse. But among the poor women I met in the Brazilian shantytown, "letting go"—"*deixa, deixa pra la menina!*"—was invoked to summon a "peaceful" resignation to events they could not easily overcome.

Where infant mortality is high, maternal thinking often means knowing when to "let go" of an infant or small child who "wants" or "needs" to die. Here, mothering requires the inner resources to help mortally weak or sickly infants to "let go," to die quickly, peacefully, and well. This constitutes the existential commitment to the idea of "acceptable death." One form, rooted in the maternal experience of chronic infant death, "conforms" women to their fate and allows them to regain the hope necessary to attempt pregnancy and birth again . . . and again, if necessary. The other form, analogous to the first, is summoned up during times of political disruption and warfare, and allows mothers to surrender their adult sons to wars that put their sons and their entire communities at risk. The idea of acceptable death undermines the image of the sorrowful, grieving *mater dolorosa* as a deterrent to violence.

In the shantytowns of Brazil, I came to think of the "given-up" (i.e.. "offered up") angel-babies in the context of the ritual scapegoating and sacrifice discussed by René Girard. Girard built his theory of religion around the idea of sacrificial violence, and the need for an agreed-upon surrogate—the "generative scapegoat"—the one (like Jesus) whose suffering or death helped resolve unbearable tensions and material difficulties. The given-up, offered-up angel babies of northeastern Brazil had likewise been sacrificed in the face of terrible conflicts over scarcity and survival.

A question was posed at a community meeting in the Alto do Cruzeiro: "What does it mean to say that a baby 'has' to die, or that it dies because it 'wants' to die?" One woman, Terezina, replied: "It means that God takes them to save their mothers from suffering." "Yes," agreed Zephinha, "God know the future better than you or me. It could happen that if the baby were to live he could turn out a thief, or a murderer, or a good-for-nothing. And so they die, instead, as babies to save us from great suffering, not to give us pain. There are many reasons to rejoice for the death of a baby!" Luiza added: "Perhaps the first nine of mine had to die to open the path so that the last five could live."

"Letting go" requires a leap of faith most poor women found difficult to achieve. But "holy indifference" in the face of terrible adversity remained a cherished religious value for these mostly Catholic women. Here, maternal thinking and military thinking converge.

When angels (or martyrs) are fashioned from the dead bodies of those who die young, "maternal thinking" most resembles military, especially wartime, thinking. On the battlefield, as in the threatened homes of a Brazilian shantytown, an ethic of triage, thinking in sets, and ideas of the "magical replaceability" of the dead predominate. Above all, ideas of "acceptable death" and of "meaningful" (rather than useless) suffering extinguish rage and grief for those whose lives were unnecessarily lost or taken.

Just as shantytown mothers in Brazil consoled one another that their hungry babies died because they were "meant" to die or because they "had" to die, Irish mothers and South African township mothers consoled one another during political funerals with the claim that their "martyred" children died purposefully and well.

Accommodationist maternal thinking affects more than merely poor and uneducated women. The grieving mother of Amy Biehl, the American Fulbright student who was brutally stoned and stabbed to death by an angry, chanting mob in Guguletu during a national strike that swept South African townships in the summer of 1993, whispered to me conspiratorially during a break in the trial of her daughter's alleged killers in Cape Town: "Don't you think there was something destined about Amy's death? Don't you think that for some reason, perhaps not known to us here and now, that Amy had to die?" Later she told me,

> Amy was very competitive, a high diver and a marathon runner. The last photo I have of her is a newspaper clipping of Amy just as she came through the finish line in a South African marathon. Her face is full of ecstasy, pain, exhaustion, and relief. I like to think that this is what Amy looked like when she died in Guguletu—as if she was just breaking through another, her most difficult finish line.

One sympathizes with Linda Biehl's desire to memorialize her daughter's brutal death as a kind of final test, as her daughter's last marathon. It must have summoned all her Christian faith and taxed her maternal thinking to the extreme to be able to view Amy as a "martyr" in the tradition of Saint Stephen. Linda's refusal to condemn her daughter's killers was broadcast widely in South Africa.

She was not the only mother left to ponder the meaning of her child's death from the "Operation Barcelona" township strike that provoked the random attacks on suspected police collaborators and "suspicious" white cars. I think, for example, of Dolly Mphahlele of Tembisa township, the mother of fifteen-year-old Ernest who made the mistake of running with a street gang that had been terrorizing the community. When teenage vigilantes, emboldened by Operation Barcelona came looking for Ernest, Dolly knew that her wayward son was as good as dead. She respected the harsh "codes" that governed township life during the anti-apartheid struggle, and when the young "comrades" warned her that Ernest would be "disciplined," Dolly "peacefully" accepted the death sentence, adding only one request: "The one thing I won't stand for," she said, "is fire on my son. *You can kill him but do not burn him.*" Her modest maternal plea was ignored, however, and the next day Dolly buried the charred remains of young Ernest. Her handsome, strong, and, above all, resigned face filled the front page of the local newspaper under the headline "Horror Necklacing of Teenage Boy." Immediately, the story was picked up by Bill Keller (1993:A-3) for the *New York Times*.

"Maternal thinking" can be summoned during times of war, disruption, and political trauma to produce resignation, accommodation, and acceptance of horrible deaths. Wars and militaries cannot proceed without the idea of "acceptable death." The practices of mothering can actually help maintain this difficult moral stance. Women worldwide have been asked to face, with "cheery optimism," unwanted pregnancies, single parenting, the birth and rearing of sick and disabled children, and (in Third World shantytowns) the repeated experience of child death. These repeated expectations can push women to abdicate their fury and grieving over the death of their children.

It's a blind sort of maternal thinking that can exalt the production of Irish soldier boys, IRA gun runners, rifle-toting Israeli teenagers, and township warriors and "comrades" with matches in hand. It's an accommodationist sort of maternal thinking that can be summoned to accept the useless suffering and premature deaths of children as "meaningful" or necessary.

Beyond these prototypes, in what ways have women consciously used maternal claims as explicit political positions during times of political conflict? Many feminists argue that motherhood carries an implicit moral authority, and that when women speak from the position of their most "traditional" roles they often exercise extraordinary political power. But maternal identity has no essential position; instead it may be used ambiguously to structure very different, even antagonistic, political positions—from promoting peace to advancing war to mobilizing political resistance. Women have fought, sometimes fiercely, under the banner of motherhood and in the name of protecting the "female" domains of family, household, kindred, and community from a broad spectrum of political loyalties and ideologies.

Temma Kaplin (1994), for example, has noted the contrasting examples of Chile, Argentina, and South Africa. In Chile in the mid-1970s, conservative and mostly affluent women took their opposition to the Socialist government of Salvador Allende into the streets of Santiago, banging their "empty" kitchen pots and pans. Their children were hungry, the mothers protested, blaming the Socialist government and its redistributive policies. Yet the children of these women were quite well fed, and the women themselves left the "maternal" tasks of shopping, cooking, and serving food to their domestic help. The counterfeit revolt of the "mothers" of Santiago succeeded, nonetheless, in goading the embarrassed Chilean army into seizing the country by a military coup swathed in slogans of rescuing Chile's "abandoned" mothers and children.

In contrast, the Madres of the Plaza de Mayo confronted the Argentine military's "dirty war," which it waged against ordinary citizens suspected of harboring subversive sentiments. The "mothers" and "grandmothers" demonstrated, in the name of their disappeared children and grandchildren, in the heart of the financial district and main shopping center of downtown Buenos Aires. While other civil rights groups went into hiding during the worst phases of the "dirty war," Las Madres, contemptuously labeled "Las Locas" by government officials, broke the code of silence by publishing a full-page ad in *La Prensa* listing the names and political identification numbers of 237 "mothers of the disappeared." The Madres matched their maternal authority against the military's abuses of power. The military could not defend itself without confronting the sanctity of the family and motherhood, the values the *junta* claimed it was defending by its brutal attacks on citizens.

Appeals to motherhood were also invoked in South African political trials. Both prosecution and defense used images of motherhood in the trial of the three young men accused, and finally convicted, of the murder of Amy Biehl in Cape Town. The prosecution used Amy's grieving mother during a portion of the trial, evoking her maternal suffering. The coroner who prepared the report on Amy's body said he spared her mother the medical details of her daughter's painful death. Defense attorney Nona Gozo retaliated by calling her clients, even though they were young men in their early twenties, "children, beautiful children, like any other, were it not for the distorting effects of apartheid." Gozo later told me: "I feel sorry for Amy's mother. I am a mother myself, but Linda Biehl needs to understand the trauma these children [the defendants] have been through. They have been exposed to everything. Apartheid has reduced life to the extent that suffering and death count for very little" (personal interview).

The mothers of political prisoners held, like Mandela, on Robben Island used their "maternal" claims to demand visitation rights and the ability to wash their clothes, bring them food, and minister to their ills. They took advantage of visits made available to them "as mothers," and helped establish communications between the prisoners and their external political contacts. Objects going in and out of prison were carefully monitored, but laundry was exempt. Thus, mothers and sisters who washed the prisoners' dirty laundry were able to smuggle in messages in underwear and in the corners of sheets. The political prisoners' mothers also "read" the dirty laundry in order to diagnose prison conditions and to detect any signs of physical or psychological stress. One woman gathered material evidence of her son's torture while doing his prison laundry. "First of all you watch the clothes to see if there is any blood on them, and you also watch the condition the clothes are in. When Peter's clothes were nicely folded I knew he was still in a good state of mind."

In the end, it's simply not the case that men make wars and women make peace, or that mothering "naturally" opposes militarism. If that were so, mothers would raise sons to resist wars, and women would refuse to bury their war dead. But the experience of mothering can instead promote an accommodation to war, and an acceptance of premature and violent death. Women have just as often used the moral claims of motherhood to launch campaigns to support war as they have to support peace. Motherhood is, of course, as social and as fluid a category as fatherhood. Only by intentional design, rather than by any natural predisposition, do women devote the thinking and practices of motherhood to peacekeeping and world repair rather than to war making and world destruction.

REFERENCES

Chodorow, Nancy. 1978. *The Reproduction of Mothering*. Berkeley: University of California Press.

Enloe, Cynthia. 1995. "Is Militarized Masculinity Violent? Some Feminist Thoughts on Militaries and Militias." Paper presented at the International Conference on (En)Gendering Violence: Terror, Domination, and Recovery, at Zagreb, Croatia, 27–29 October.

Gilligan, Carol. 1982. *In a Different Voice*. Cambridge, MA: Harvard University Press.

Kaplin, Temma. 1994. "Gender Identities and Popular Protest." Paper presented at the National Humanities Center Conference on Identity: Personal, Cultural, and National, at Chinese University of Hong Kong, June 2–4.

Keller, William. 1993. "A Short, Violent Life in South Africa." *New York Times* (International), November 17:4.

Ruddick, Sarah. 1980. "Maternal Thinking." *Feminist Studies* 6:342–364.

———. 1989. *Maternal Thinking: Toward a Politics of Peace*. Boston: Beacon.

Scheper-Hughes, Nancy. 1979. *Saints, Scholars and Schizophrenics: Mental Illness in Rural Ireland*. Berkeley: University of California Press.

———. 1992. *Death without Weeping: The Violence of Everyday Life in Brazil*. Berkeley: University of California Press.

Chapter Twenty-Five

War, Nationalism, and Mothers in the Former Yugoslavia

Vesna Nikolić-Ristanović

In the autumn of 1991 women in Sarajevo protested against the war. "We are women—not nationalities, generals, or murderers!" they shouted. . . . A few days later hundreds of women from Croatia and Bosnia set off for Belgrade, where they were to be met by women from Serbia. They were all supposed to go together to the Headquarters of the (by then already former) Yugoslav People's Army. The women had only one weapon in their hands: little photographs of their sons. The generals, realizing for the first time that women after all amounted to half the population, roughly prevented them from meeting. Soldiers blocked the roads leading to Belgrade and the women returned to their homes humiliated. The very next day Serbian television showed pictures of weeping Serbian mothers joyfully sending their sons to the army. "This is the happiest day of my life," said one of them, wiping away her tears. On the third day other men, Croats, convinced their wives that they had no choice but to send their sons "to defend the homeland" for "liberty." On the fourth day, a group of women from Croatia was shown in a television shot in Germany, in an audience with a leading German politician. Instead of little photographs of their sons, this time the women were carrying large photographs of their president. It was a humiliating scene, no less humiliating than the one that was shown some months later when the man from the big photograph, the president, was handing out medals to the widows and mothers of brave Croatian knights who had laid down their lives on the altar of the homeland. On the occasion one of them gratefully kissed the president's hand. (Ugrešić, 1994: 135)

When the war in the former Yugoslavia began, women protesters from all regions and ethnic backgrounds united around their identities as the mothers of sons serving in the Yugoslav army. They joined together to save their sons from going to battle and from being sacrificed in a conflict that, at that time, made no sense to them. Their protest contradicted the nationalistic interests of their leaders and the historically deep-rooted patriarchal model of the proud mother of the soldier son. Thus, it was no surprise that protesting mothers were labeled as traitors and threatened, until at last their protest was transformed into support for official politics, thereby promoting the war.

Nationalist propaganda changed women's identities as mothers to those of citizens of a nation-state. As Claudia Koonz wrote in *Mothers in the Fatherland*,

"Women lost control of their choices and started to believe that sacrifices played a vital role in a greater cause" (Koonz, 1986: 6). The mothers' protests were transformed into mothers demonstrating to support nationalistic politics. Instead of asking their sons to remove their uniforms, they began to ask their sons to exchange their former Yugoslav army uniforms for those of the armies of their "new" nation-states. Hypocrisy became a part of the everyday lives of ordinary people.

Koonz suggests that "what you do is public, how you feel is private" (Koonz, 1986:418). In the case of women in the former Yugoslavia, this means sacrificing their sons to fulfill the most sacred duty to the fatherland. The nationalistic hypocrisy culminated in the 1995 Christmas message from the Patriarch of the Serb Orthodox Church, when he called on women to stop "killing" their unborn children, to bear more children despite economic hardship, and to learn from mothers who lost their only sons in the war and who now regret not bearing more sons who could bring them consolation ("*Politika*," January 6, 1995).

Women responded differently, however, to their leaders' nationalistic calls. Urban women, who are better educated and less traditional in their gender roles, resisted these calls. Some hid their sons to save their lives. Others sent their sons abroad into uncertain situations and did not see them for years. Many of these mothers were persecuted. They learned not to answer the doorbell or entry phone. They lived in fear and uncertainty about their sons' and their own future. But despite resisting the nationalistic hysteria, most women did not succeed in saving their sons.

Women on both sides of the nationalist fence were equally powerless to prevent their children's deaths. They viewed violence against their children as violence against themselves—a kind of violence that, according to one refugee woman I interviewed, affects women more than rape or any other form of violence aimed directly against them.

As mothers, women are given special status in the ideology of nationalism throughout the former Yugoslavia: they are "mothers of the nation," "protectors of offspring." During wartime, women's bodies—as soldier production units—become sites of political contention. The glorification of women as biological regenerators of the nation combined with a disregard for women as people produced a massive abuse of women's reproductive rights and maternal emotions.

Nationalism demands that women bear and care for sons who they will sacrifice for the "defense" and "self-determination" of their nation. Ironically, as many women who lost sons in the war point out, it is precisely in the role of mother that women suffer the most—directly contradicting the supposed veneration of motherhood that characterizes nationalistic societies.

As usual, when nationalism and militarism escalated in the former Yugoslavia, the glorification of women as biological reproducers of the nation began. And it began first with a restriction on the previously unquestioned right of women to abortion. Strong anti-abortionist movements, supported by the church and leading politicians, sprang up in Croatia, Slovenia, and Serbia. Even when the law on abortion remained unchanged, social pressure—especially from the church—was so intense that many women lost control of their own bodies.

In parts of Bosnia under Croat control, every obstetrical examination was witnessed by a nun who insisted the child be carried to term. The church did not distinguish between women who had been raped and those who became pregnant under "normal" circumstances. The pope, promoting the image of women as passive recipients of whatever injustice comes their way, publicly urged women who became pregnant from rape to "accept the enemy" by bearing the children they conceived, rather than seeking abortion.

Restrictions on abortion were followed by a shortage of contraceptives, forcing women to bear unwanted children under conditions of poverty, social disorganization, and inappropriate health care. But women were not only forced to bear unwanted children. Living in uncertainty, women were forced to delay marriage and face the trauma of bearing and raising children in wartime conditions. Many women died after giving birth in unsafe, unsanitary conditions, plagued by a constant shortage of medicines and medical equipment. Fetal defects and infant mortality also rose dramatically.

This occurred particularly during the great exodus of Serbs from the former Serbian province Krajina (Croatia). Pregnant women and women with newborns were helpless waiting in refugee lines. Women bore children in cars and tractors. On hot August days, without medical care and elementary hygienic supply, women died with their newborns and were left near the roads—they could not even be buried. Many pregnant women who survived bore children with defects that resulted from their ten-to-fifteen-day trips in horrific conditions.

In the war in the former Yugoslavia, however, restrictions on abortion and contraceptive shortages were not the only problems that forced women to bear unwanted children. Wartime interethnic rapes forced women to bear children who belonged to their enemy's ethnic group. In this war, rape has been used as a method of "production" of children for the rapist's nationality. The idea of rape as a method of ethnic cleansing, forcing women to bear the children of their enemies, derives from a deep patriarchal construction: that women are objects, "dishes" that passively accept a male's seed and add nothing original to it. Therefore the child's identity depends only on the man who "fathered" it, and thus women impregnated by their enemies give birth to children who belong to the enemy's ethnic group.

Wartime rapists try to send a message to husbands and other males from the enemy side: that their women are worthless since they gave birth to the enemy's rather than their own children. Sadly, the husbands of raped women and other men often accept this message: they reject raped women who bear children to the enemy.

In 1993, when people worldwide were talking about raped and impregnated women in the former Yugoslavia, almost nothing was said about these women as suffering mothers. The women's experiences were overshadowed by political and military discussions about wartime rape as a method of ethnic cleansing. But the maternal agony of women who bore children conceived from war rapes devastated women and had more serious consequences for their future than any other aspect of rape.

Milica, a Serbian woman raped by Croats, gave birth to a boy whom she gave up for adoption. After childbirth, she stayed in the Home for Unprotected Children.

Despite declaring, before childbirth, that she never wanted to see the baby, Milica had to share a room with the baby and the staff forced her to care for the child. Not surprisingly, this caused her to bond with him. She gave him a name even while she still rejected the thought of keeping the child. As with many women who gave birth to children conceived through rape in war, the emotional conflict caused horrible pain and trauma. A letter Milica sent me after she returned to her town best illustrates this:

> There is nothing new here. There is war. People are being killed. Nothing new, indeed. We can barely make the ends meet. I'm not feeling well. I feel so bad, depressed, irritated. I became withdrawn. My nerves went down the drain. I have nightmares. I don't know what to do. I only smoke and worry. I can't eat, I lost my appetite. I lost 10–12 kilos. The other day, I was given an infusion. I don't know what to do. (Nikolić-Ristanović et al., 1995:64)

Conflicting emotions, constant clashes between love and hatred, between acceptance and rejection, are even more dramatically expressed by women who decided to keep and rear children conceived through rape. Along with social ostracism, these women are faced daily with a painful reminder in the face of their innocent children, who often bear a physical resemblance to their father-rapists. We've seen this before. For example, consider the ambivalence of a Jewish girl raped in a concentration camp in World War II, as recorded in Simon Wiesenthal's book *Max and Helen*:

> You would probably like to ask: "Why did you give birth to a child of that evildoer?" That is the question I have often posed to myself too. The whole of my being strongly resisted the idea of abortion. In fact, what was the culpability of that little being in my womb? It did not beg anyone to come to this world. Of course, I could have left him in an orphanage or given him for adoption. But it was my baby, and I was his mother. . . . The child grew. It resembled more and more to Schultze. I thought I could not bear it. Will he also inherit his impulsiveness, his brutality? Will fear ever stop? (Wiesenthal, 1991:117)

Another woman I interviewed, Milena, was traumatized when she tried to live with a child conceived during seven days of rape by three Moslem soldiers. She arrived in Belgrade in the seventh month of pregnancy and stayed in the Home for Unprotected Children. She wanted first to have a Caesarean abortion in her seventh month. Doctors said it was better to give birth. While delivering the baby, the nurse covered Milena's eyes so she could not see it.

After recovering from childbirth, she returned to her town, but could not find peace of mind—she was torn between her desire for the baby and the terrible memories of rape. She decided to give the baby up for adoption, but then changed her mind and tried to live with the child. She could not bear it, and had to be hospitalized for psychological trauma; she could not care for the baby.

When the war ends, the International War Crime Tribunal should punish those who raped and impregnated women. But as Christine Chinkin has argued, the tribunal should also separately investigate and prosecute rape as a tool of ethnic cleansing, which consists of two war crimes: rape and forced impregnation

(Chinkin, 1993). The latter is an offense the international community and the International War Crime Tribunal still do not consider criminal. If forced impregnation in war were criminalized, then both the gravity of rape and the violent abuse of women's reproductive rights and maternal feelings would be emphasized, apart from their association with other tactics such as "ethnic cleansing."

The United Nation's culpability in the rise of unwanted pregnancies, pregnancy and labor complications, and maternal and infant mortality cannot be ignored. These are the direct effects of U.N. sanctions imposed on Serbia during the war. Not only in Serbia but also in other countries where these kinds of sanctions were imposed, mothers helplessly face the illnesses and deaths of their children. As the least powerful segment of society, women bear the brunt of scarcity. Just as nation-states forced women to identify themselves primarily as citizens of the nation regardless of their status as mothers, the United Nations punished them as members of the nation-state for crimes committed by their leaders—who already grossly violated women's elementary human rights.

One of the few Westerners who dared raise this issue publicly was French deputy Yves Bonnet, who wrote in *Le Monde* after visiting Children's Hospital in Baghdad:

> The young woman slowly unwraps the layers of cloth in which the little person is bundled. He is three months old, weight little over 4 lb., is emaciated, inert, unaware of the doctor's final verdict: condemned to die. I look at the mother, two large black eyes silently reproaching me; then I turn away, guilty, ashamed. . . . I am filled with shame and anger at myself, at my cowardliness, my silence, my complicity with those who, despite their claims to the contrary, have killed hundreds of thousands of civilians, without incurring the wrath of the (War Crimes) tribunal of the Hague, implacably going about their dirty, evil work. I think, too, of Serbian children no one speaks of, because they too are dangerous criminals. The sick, the bereft, the injured I've seen in Belgrade; the children of Baghdad: all guilty in the eyes of the U.N. sanctions committee, all refused care, medication, operations. (Bonnet, 1995)

As in any other war, in the war in former Yugoslavia, women, with their destinies interlaced with their children's, suffered more than men. But it's simplistic to claim that women are only victims. As the Serbian sociologist and feminist Marina Blagojevic has written: "Releasing women of any blame for the war and 'crises' would be another trap of patriarchal narcissism. Where there is no guilt, there is no complicity and therefore no subjectivity" (Blagojevic, 1994:475). Consciously or not, women's contribution to militarism is critical.

Women often participate through their roles as mothers and wives, even though, ironically, these are the roles that also cause their most tragic suffering. As Jeanne Vickers has suggested, women contribute to militarism through the early education of their children; they "accept that their sons and husbands go to fighting forces and feel that it is their duty to their country to support an operation which will decimate the population and destroy the very bases of civilized society" (Vickers, 1993:43).

When the war in the former Yugoslavia began, the spontaneous protests of mothers failed to unite women and others who opposed the war. As Slavenka Drakulić wrote: "The women needed to define their potential aims for themselves. Their common denominator should have been more than their shared desire to take their sons home, especially having in mind the strong patriarchal tradition which condemned such attitudes. It should have been a call for peace" (Drakulić, 1983:129).

But since this was not the case, women fell victims, not only to their nationalism, but to their lack of organization and political vision, or to their indifference—the products of their alienation from politics over the past forty years of life under communism.

REFERENCES

Blagojevi, Marina. 1994. "War and Everyday Life: Deconstruction of Self-Sacrifice." *Sociologija* (*Sociology*), October–December, 469.

Bonnet, Yves. 1995. "Sanctions That Should Shame the UN," reprinted from *Le Monde* in *The Guardian*, 10 June, p. 8.

Chinkin, Christine. 1993. "Peace and Force in International Law." In D. G. Dallmeyer, ed., *Reconceiving Reality: Women and International Law*. New York: Asil.

Drakulic, Slavenka. 1993. "Women and New Democracy in the Former Yugoslavia." In Nanette Funk and Magda Mueller (eds.), *Gender Politics and Post-Communism*. New York: Routledge.

Funk, Nanette, and Magda Mueller (eds.). 1993. *Gender Politics and Post-Communism*. New York: Routledge.

Koonz, Claudia. 1986. *Mothers in the Fatherland*. New York: St. Martin's Press.

Nikolić-Ristanović, Vesna. 1996. "War and Violence against Women." In Jennifer Turpin and Lois Ann Lorentzen (eds.), *The Gendered New World Order: Militarism, Development, and the Environment*. New York: Routledge.

Nikolić-Ristanović, Vesna, Natasa Mrvic-Petrović, Ivana Stevaziou, Slobodanka, and Konstantiwovic-Vilić. 1995. *Zene, Nasilje i Rat* (Women, Violence, and War). Belgrade: IKSI.

Ugrešić, Dubravka. 1994. "Because We're Lads." In *What Can We Do for Ourselves — East European Feminist Conference*. Belgrade: Center for Women's Studies.

Vickers, Jeanne. 1993. *Women and War*. London: Zed Books.

Wiesenthal, Simon. 1991. *Maks i Helen — istiniti roman* (Serbian edition). Novi Sad: Dnevnik. (Original title: *Max und Helen — ein Tatsachenroman*.)

Chapter Twenty-Six

Drafting Motherhood
Maternal Imagery and Organizations in the United States and Nicaragua

Lorraine Bayard de Volo

Although war is commonly represented with images of men in combat, wars are fought on a variety of "fronts" in explicitly gendered ways. This chapter explores the ways in which mothers are targeted by war propaganda in the cultural battle to capture citizens' "hearts and minds." Motherhood is critical to the study of war for several reasons. First, in light of the nearly universal portrayal of women as nurturers, peacemakers, and givers of life, we must wonder how a nation manages to convince women to support their sons' entry into war. Second, maternal imagery is emotionally evocative and thus a powerful symbolic resource in garnering public support for war. Finally, the construction of maternal identities for the war effort has implications for women's place in postwar societies.

Mothers are both subjects and objects of wartime maneuvers along the ideological front line. Maternal imagery is mobilized to garner support for the war effort. Furthermore, mothers of soldiers, of potential draftees, and of fallen combatants are themselves mobilized into various mothers' organizations to dampen their resistance to the war. In examining the wartime mobilization of mothers and maternal imagery, I draw upon the war experiences of two very different nations: the United States in World War I and World War II, and Nicaragua during the Contra war. A comparative analysis of these two cases has several benefits. These wars were relatively popular among people who might otherwise consider themselves pro-peace. When compared with the Vietnam War, for example, World War I and World War II can be considered large-scale "popular" wars supported by a wide spectrum of American society. Both of these wars were perceived as immediately threatening American democracy and "way of life." In the Nicaraguan Contra war, initiated by a U.S.-financed counterrevolutionary force in the early 1980s, the revolutionary Sandinista government was supported by leftists both within Nicaragua and internationally. At least from an anti-imperialist perspective, the Contra war also threatened Nicaragua's newly installed revolutionary "way of life."

Drawing on these three "good wars" to explore traditional maternal imagery demonstrates all the more starkly the conservative and manipulative nature of wartime mobilizations and propaganda aimed at women. Revealing the dominant gender imagery of such popular wars provides a foundation from which to contemplate the postwar implications for women. More pointedly, it emphasizes the importance of critically examining the process of cultural struggles in wartime and undermines the assumption that women's wartime entry into the "men's world," in the form of the United States' "Rosie the Riveter" or Nicaragua's guerrilla girls, will logically lead to peacetime gender progress. Fighting the "good war" in the context of unreflective patriarchy, even as women enter the "public sphere" in unprecedented numbers, does not necessarily translate into postwar expansion of options and identities for women. Despite the countries' obvious differences in size, wealth, and power, and despite the fact that the Sandinista government was defending a leftist revolution against a U.S.-financed army, I demonstrate that both nations employed surprisingly similar discursive and organizing techniques in mobilizing mothers to war.

Motherhood and War

In mobilizing a nation to war, differences are squelched as the individual voices of the citizens must appear to speak as one. Since a nation's way of life is to be protected, voices outside the mainstream appear as a threat. As with representations of ethnicity and race, the most traditional and extreme representations of masculinity and femininity are to be found during wartime (Cooke and Woollacott, 1993). Recent studies have examined the relationships among discourse, gender, and war and shown the dramatic dichotomies constructed between men/war/battlefront and women/peace/homefront.[1] Narratives of men and war reject all that is conceived of as feminine. In the Western tradition of war stories, women have been the "other"— patriotic mothers sending sons off to war, pacifist givers and protectors of life, or the civilian support network cheering on the soldiers (Elshtain, 1987).

In rallying support for the war effort, a key problem lies in mothers' opposition to the conscription and, not surprisingly, the death of sons and daughters. In part, this potential maternal opposition is checked through the drafting of maternal symbolism. Mothers as images are enlisted in propaganda efforts and posed in relation to hearth and home and all that is not war. This maternal imagery is linked to the protection of the homefront and national way of life—that for which the soldiers are fighting. Mothers are also more literally drafted into civilian organizations that engage women actively in supporting the war effort while at the same time remolding the dominant discourse of the "good mother" to fit wartime circumstances. This "good mother" does not resist her son's (and increasingly her daughter's) entry into the war but instead supports his or her ideals through a variety of volunteer activities. Finally, mothers are mobilized in a passive sense as they are honored for the sacrifices—their children's lives—that they have made for the "greater good." I begin with the U.S. case, looking first at the ways in which images of mothers were mobilized in World War I and World War II. I then trace several organizations through which women were mobilized. Next, I consider the Nicaraguan case in a similar manner, concluding that wartime priorities led to similar discursive strategies by these two very different states.

U.S. Spartan Mothers: Saying Good-bye with a Smile and a Prayer

Symbolic Mobilization

On the ideological front of the First World War, the American "Mom" was the dominant image of womanhood (Zeiger, 1996). Susan Zeiger has shown how maternal imagery in World War I was highly dichotomized. The representation of the "good" or "patriotic" mother involved obedience to the state and a willingness to sacrifice sons to war. Conversely, the "unpatriotic" mother included those expressing a "selfish," excessive attachment to their sons. These maternal representations were linked with the United States' first military draft, implemented in 1917. The Wilson administration, in establishing support for this new form of military recruitment, feared the potential of mothers to undermine its efforts.

In the three years before the United States entered the war in Europe, there was considerable public debate surrounding U.S. neutrality. A women's peace movement developed alongside the suffrage and reform movements of the era (Berkman, 1990). In 1915, one of the most popular songs was entitled, "I Didn't Raise My Boy to Be a Soldier." The lyrics were distinctly anti-war, telling of mothers grieving for sons sent off to kill and die in vain. The song became a center for controversy surrounding U.S. neutrality (Zeiger, 1996: 12). For example, a widow of the Civil War who lost a son in the Spanish-American War was appalled by the lyrics, exclaiming that it was shameful for a mother to dissuade her son from serving his country: mothers of sons in other wars deserved "the satisfaction of knowing that their sacrifice was not in vain, that the freedom their men died for [was] permanent" (Steinson, 1980: 266). Once the U.S. entered into the war in 1917, the anti-war sentiments noticeably ebbed and many peace movements dissolved. Still, the Wilson administration concerned itself with meeting the challenge of maternal war resistance. A conference on morale in 1918 elicited a warning that with the predicted high casualty rates, war bureaucrats should be prepared for active opposition from mothers. Accordingly, the anticipated maternal outcry was countered with a campaign to convince mothers not to impede the drafting of their sons.[2] At its most basic, the message was that mothers must not put "selfish," "unreasonable," and even "hysterical" emotional attachments to sons above duty to the nation.

Interestingly, Joyce Berkman reveals that some pro-war feminists rallied women through notions of women's protective responsibilities (Berkman, 1990: 151). The logic went that in order for women to be good mothers, the nation itself must be protected, and this could only occur through raising good soldiers and supporting a militarily strong state. Accordingly, women must serve and protect not only their families but also the nation.

As Leila Rupp persuasively argues, U.S. women in the interwar years continued to be portrayed primarily in traditional images of wife and mother (Rupp, 1978). The "good mother" offered her services to the nation in a variety of ways. One method was through bearing and raising citizen sons. However, Rupp reveals that the "good mother" also recognized maternal duties outside of the home and beyond her own children. This mobilizing identity, which Rupp terms "world mothers," was an extension of that described by Berkman in the World War I context. It entailed the notion that women had maternal responsibilities on a global level.

The advent of World War II challenged the dominant portrayals of women as mothers because of the new need for women to step into the factory jobs vacated by men enlisting in the military.[3] Nonetheless, as in World War I, maternal imagery was enlisted to rally the nation to war. During World War II, Mothers' Day was "an occasion," as New York mayor La Guardia put it, "to express our appreciation of the men in our armed forces and to their mothers who are willingly and gladly making this sacrifice" (*New York Times* May 10, 1942:1). This quote expressed a common theme running through appeals and homages to mothers—that mothers should actively, voluntarily send their sons to war. Rabbi Goldstein expressed this sentiment even more directly: "The nation is blessed whose women give their boys to the service not because the law demands it, but because they willingly recognize the need and rightness of the cause" (ibid., 42:5). A popular war required that mothers "send their sons off to war" through active consent rather than reluctantly through the force of law. This theme was popularly circulated with the phrase, "Mothers are saying good-bye with a smile on their lips and a prayer in their hearts" (ibid., May 2, 1942, 12:6).

Through such construction of active consent, maternal voices of resistance to the draft were hushed by the loud applause for the ultimate in maternal sacrifice—that of a beloved son. General Marshall, in paying tribute to American mothers, stated that "the hundreds of letters that have come to me from mothers who have lost their best beloved sons are my great inspiration. . . . The spirit of patriotic resolution that shines through their heartbreaks is a wonderful thing, a perfect example of pure patriotism and self-sacrifice" (*New York Times*, May 9, 1943, 10:1). Military leaders exclaimed that mothers were among the true heroes and the real sufferers in war, worthy of full recognition in the nation's halls of fame (*New York Times*, May 11, 1942, 10:1). Indeed, mothers of war heroes and generals were publicly thanked. Women of the Brooklyn Hebrew Home and Hospital for the Aged sent the following Mothers' Day telegram to Mary P. MacArthur, mother of General MacArthur: "Love from all 389 mothers in our home to a mother endowed with kindliness, patience, and courage who has given to the world a hero to free men the world over" (ibid.).

In a sermon, Reverend John S. Bonnell lauded the power of mothers in war: "[T]he most powerful influence in the life of any young man is the memory of a good mother. The mothers of America have behaved nobly in the present crisis and their influence and example have done much to keep resolute and steadfast the youths who are going out from our American homes to face the ordeal of battle" (*New York Times*, May 10, 1943, 13:4).

An "American Mother of 1942" was elected to serve as a "war spokesman" by the American Mothers Committee of the Golden Rule Foundation. This mother, Mrs. William Berry, was described as having thirteen children, with two sons in the military and a third about to enlist. As Rupp's notion of "world mothers" suggests, the American Mother's duties extended beyond the United States. This representative of "the best there is in motherhood" was to represent not only American moth-

244 LORRAINE BAYARD DE VOLO

ers but also serve "in the interest of widowed mothers and fatherless children in wartorn Europe and Asia" (*New York Times*, April 7, 1942, 25:8). From her post, the American Mother implored mothers everywhere to support America's fighting men. Said she: "They should encourage their sons, write to them real often, and pray for them" (*New York Times*, May 8, 1942, 42:2). Thus, the wartime "good mother" ensured that her son did not stray from his patriotic duty, opting to protect the greater good rather than shelter her offspring.

In discourse directed at mothers of fallen soldiers, a letter by Abraham Lincoln to a mother who lost five sons in the Civil War was often quoted: "I pray that our Heavenly Father may assuage that anguish of your bereavement and leave you only the cherished memory of the loved and lost, and the solemn pride that must be yours to have laid so costly a sacrifice on the altar of freedom."[4] Thus, in such discourse the loud, angry, and uncontrollable grief that we might expect from families dealing with such a loss was decentered, privileging instead a mother's silent, "solemn pride" softened with "cherished memories."

Enlisting Mothers: U.S. Wartime Organizations

Women were organized in numerous ways to support the war effort. In regards to redirecting mothers' anxiety and grief, several programs were developed. Following the sinking of the *Lusitania* in 1915, the Navy League took advantage of public outrage in order to shore up support for a defense buildup. In the interest of reaching many segments of the population, Navy League officials established a Women's Section of the Navy League (WSNL). The primary tasks of this organization were to both guard against possible invasion and stimulate feelings of patriotism among U.S. women (Steinson, 1980).

During World War II, the United Service Organizations, Inc. (USO) was formed in order to serve a double purpose of bolstering the morale of soldiers in new situations and giving civilians an opportunity to "do something" for U.S. military personnel (Ross, 1943). The USO was to be a "home away from home" for soldiers, and with this aim the USO organized an "Adopt-a-Mother" campaign. On Mothers' Day, 133 USO units held an "Adopt-a-Mother" breakfast so that servicemen might honor local mothers in tribute to their own mothers (*New York Times*, May 10, 1942, 42:1). The "Adopt-a-Mother" plan was to match servicemen away from home with mothers whose enlisted sons were stationed outside the United States.

The Navy Mother's Clubs of America were created in order to "promote a program of education, welfare and social interest between the parents of Navy men and the enlisted personnel, and to encourage contentment, efficiency, patriotism and pride among the men themselves" (Ross, 1943: 55). Their motto was: "America of Today Needs Mothers at Their Best."

Most notably, Gold Star mothers received high visibility in both wars. Gold Star mothers, introduced by President Lincoln at the conclusion of the Civil War, recognized mothers of fallen soldiers. Gold Star Mothers as an organization reached its peak during World War II.

Nicaraguan Mothers and the Contra War: Maternal Mobilizing Identities and Cultural Warfare

Although images of women in war are culturally distinct, I found strong similarities between dominant U.S. themes and those found in Nicaragua. The gendered imagery and women's active role in the Contra war also has implications for women's postwar position. As Miriam Cooke and Angela Woollacott wrote: "Women's inclusion as participants in wars of this century has blurred distinctions between gender roles in peace and war. War has become a terrain in which gender is negotiated" (Cooke and Woollacott, 1993: xi). Women's participation was essential to the success of the revolution, both as combatants and civilian supporters, and as such, traditional ideas of femininity were challenged and new opportunities were opened for women to demand greater rights as full citizens in Sandinista society. Did the new revolutionary government represent women in ways that might enlarge their arena of opportunities, as Sandinista discourse proposed? On the contrary, I submit that despite women's revolutionary experience and the Sandinista's considerable effort to improve women's socioeconomic position, the Contra war, along with a revolutionary party not fully committed to feminist ideals, led back to the safer, traditional images and identities for women. Crossing gender boundaries during exceptional circumstances such as popular insurrection did not secure women an equal position in the "New Society" nor did it fundamentally alter traditional notions of femininity.[5]

The wartime struggle to construct women's subjectivities centered on motherhood, notwithstanding the occasional photograph of women driving tractors and the articles about women taking over jobs vacated by men fighting in the war. These representations of women played a constitutive role in the structuring of Sandinista society and set the horizon of expectations for women's behavior.

Universal Mothers

As with Rupp's "world mothers" in the U.S. context, I found representations of women as mothering and protecting all Nicaraguan children—Universal Motherhood—in revolutionary discourse and practice. It was a common image put forth to recruit women into revolutionary tasks. For example, during the Contra war, women were encouraged to become "adoptive mothers" to soldiers hospitalized or stationed far from their own families. As an article in a Sandinista women's publication put it, "United by the universal sentiments of motherhood, we make each soldier another son. . . . Let us arise in war, joining forces with our children to gain peace in Nicaragua" (*Somos*, May 1984: 2).

Translation of revolutionary tasks and condemnation of Contra attacks in the language of motherhood was an effective means of mobilizing women, particularly middle-aged and older women not already mobilized as students or workers, into the revolutionary process. This appealed to many women whose own subjectivities prioritized their identities as mothers. If their positions as mothers could be broadened, if women came to see all Sandinista combatants, or all Nicaraguans, as their own children, this would boost their commitment to the revolution. Self-sacrifice and concern for others, as opposed to individualism, was an important revolutionary theme, but while young men were encouraged to sacrifice their lives at the battlefront in order to save the nation, women were encouraged to mother on a larger scale.

Combative Motherhood

As Contra attacks increased, the image of the mother was tied to protection, even armed protection, of the nation's children. The desire to protect one's children, even through the use of violence, was posed as a natural or divinely ordained maternal reaction. Women organized in committees of the Mothers of Heroes and Martyrs during the insurrection urged other mothers to form committees with the following argument: "From the moment of conception, the mother has the obligation to protect her child, and she who does not do this is breaking divine law. For this reason, NICARAGUAN MOTHER, reflect: your mission is too great to be stifled by fear. Do not be afraid to protect your child" (*La Prensa*, February 18, 1979, 7). Top Sandinista official Tomas Borge stated in a 1980 speech that the new government intended to develop "women's militias and give every woman a gun with which to defend her children. Women know how to organize themselves, especially to defend the generations that are now growing up."[6] In this way, the very logic which traditionally fed the image of women as natural peacemakers—givers and protectors of life— was used to mobilize women into the military and the revolutionary vigilance programs.

In analyzing the representations of Nicaraguan women, I found that protection of one's children was overwhelmingly the most common theme in Sandinista attempts to mobilize women into defense work. The caption under a photo of uniformed, armed women crossing a river, which appeared in a 1981 issue of the Sandinista newspaper *Barricada*, reads: " 'No more crimes against our children!' This is the combative shout of Nicaraguan women that was raised by thousands of female soldiers . . . in the reserve battalion. They, like many sectors of the population, are prepared for the defense of the country. And you, *compañera*? Have you joined yet?" (*Barricada*, July 8, 1981, 1).

Among the most arresting images of combative motherhood, copied countless times by Nicaraguan artists, is a photograph of a woman in military clothing, with a gun slung on her back and a baby at her breast.[7] This image was sometimes accompanied by a slogan, such as the following celebrating women's participation in neighborhood Sandinista Defense Committees (CDS): "The woman of the CDS, tender in love, fierce in battle!" This representation of motherhood gave the message that combat, especially in the name of one's children, did not conflict with traditional notions of motherhood. Women who joined the guerrillas or, later, the militias had to leave their children in the care of others for extended periods of time. In contrast to an interpretation of these women as bad mothers, Sandinista discourse stressed that military women were exemplary mothers willing to offer their lives for the defense of their children and the country—the epitome of the selfless, self-sacrificing mother. Thus, the apparent contradictory aims of motherhood and war were made complementary.

As with Universal Motherhood, Combative Motherhood was aimed at mobilizing women (Molyneux, 1985). It undermined the traditional notions that women were naturally nonviolent or passive and that war was an exclusively male realm. Instead, women were positioned as naturally fierce protectors of their children.

Patriotic Wombs and Sandinista Spartan Mothers

Once women were excluded from the draft in 1983, however, this image of Combative Motherhood faded, eclipsed by images of women bearing future soldiers and sending them off to war. Now, the good mother was sometimes depicted as the bearer of future soldiers—a "Patriotic Womb." One mother of a mobilized son exclaimed, "We will continue giving birth to children in order to defend the conquests reached at the cost of our blood" (*Barricada*, March 16, 1982, 6). A Sandinista official used similar imagery to praise mothers on International Women's Day: "We celebrate women, saying that today you are a thousand times mothers because you gave birth, leaving to the country so many children to defend it and liberate it from the oppressive yoke of tyranny. Because with this act, you participated in the birth of history when the womb contracted to give birth to the Sandinista Popular Revolution" (*Barricada*, March 8, 1982, 2). In 1984, the city of Rivas celebrated Mother's Day under the theme, "Blessed is the womb of the mother that gives birth to a combatant son" (*Barricada*, June 1, 1984, 4).

As the Contra aggression intensified in 1983, the Sandinista state focused on raising moral and economic support for the mothers of combatants, urging reluctant mothers not to impede their children's recruitment into the military (Randall, 1992). Toward this end, Sandinista media projected images of women as patriotic mothers who were prepared "to offer to the nation their lives' most valuable treasures, their sons and daughters, in order to obtain our liberty."[8] This representation of motherhood runs close to that of Plutarch's Spartan mothers who raised their sons to be warriors ready to die for the country.[9] One member of the Mothers of Heroes and Martyrs who lost two sons told the press, "I feel proud to have two Sandinista children and prouder to have given my children to this Revolution" (*Barricada*, June 22, 1983, 7). A mother who had already lost one child told *Barricada*, "I am ready to give all my children and die together with them rather than be under the boot of imperialism" (May 31, 1983, 1). Note that these "Spartan Mothers" were portrayed and saw themselves as taking an active part in the enlistment process. They did not simply support their sons' enlistment, they *offered* or *gave* their sons to the country. In the Sandinista narrative of motherhood and war, the act of sacrifice was more the mothers' than the sons'.

Although mothers seen as givers and protectors of life might evoke images of war as destructive, in Sandinista discourse over and over again mothers espoused an image of war as creative: "I'm proud of my son, because he gave his life for the life of the people. He . . . died to give a new life for his people" (Whitcomb, 1983:

10). At the funeral of one soldier, a mother was quoted as saying, "This is painful for all of us, but we know that each loss is a seed which will germinate and multiply into thousands of sons and daughters of our country who will know how to defend it" (*Barricada*, November 24, 1984, 6). In a 1968 letter by Sandinista founder Carlos Fonseca to Nicaraguan mothers on Mothers' Day, he wrote, "A salute to mothers of glorious martyrs who have offered their lives for the liberation of Nicaragua. . . . Let the best consolation for the mothers who carry a tortured heart be that their children are the honor of Nicaragua in these times. If in Nicaragua not everything is selfishness, avarice and darkness, it is because the martyrs have shed their blood (*Barricada*, May 30, 1988, 5). In this discourse, Sandinista blood was not spilled in vain but rather fertilized the revolutionary process, laying the foundation for the germination of "fruit": new combatants and a new society.

The mothers of the fallen were also enlisted to convince mothers not to stand in the way of the drafting of their children. The following is a typical plea by these mothers: "To mothers all over the country, I beseech you to not revert to the selfishness that at times characterizes us—don't cut off your children's dreams to go to the borders to fight for the country. Let them go" (*Barricada*, June 22, 1983, 7). Here, a mother's desire to protect her children is translated into "characteristic" maternal selfishness. In other words, if a youth is willing to sacrifice his or her life for the good of the country, the mother should also be so generous with that life.

Sandinista leadership at times presented an explicitly pronatalist stance, which was particularly pronounced in its arguments concerning reproductive rights. President Ortega told an audience of women that sterilization and abortion must be viewed in terms of U.S. imperialism, which involved halting the population growth in Third World countries "to avoid the risk of an increase in the population that could threaten a revolutionary change." Nicaragua had a small population and, he argued, was subject "to a policy of genocide" through the U.S.-supported Contra war. "The ones fighting in the front lines against this aggression are grown men," he continued. "One way of depleting our youth is to promote the sterilization of women in Nicaragua . . . or to promote a policy of abortion. . . . The problem is that the woman is the one who reproduces. The man can't play that role" (*The Militant*, November 19, 1987, 123). This speech offers a glimpse at the Sandinista logic behind the emphasis on women as Patriotic Wombs and Spartan Mothers—while men fought imperialism at the battlefront, women's primary role in defense was to ensure the supply of future soldiers. Because it denied women control over their own reproduction and restricted access to political and military ranks that conferred the highest status and power during the Sandinista regime, this way of thinking ignored women's history of guerrilla struggle and contradicted the Sandinista policies meant to ensure women's emancipation.

Las Continuadoras

Sandinista discourse supported the ideal of loyal and brave mothers keeping alive the memory and ideals of the fallen, thus continuing the struggle where their martyred children left off—Las Continuadoras. The most common mode of organizing in this identity and disseminating its message was through the Committee of Mothers of Heroes and Martyrs. As one member of the Mothers told the crowd during a 1981 protest against counterrevolutionary aggressions: "The Mothers of Heroes and Martyrs should be united as one fist ready to defend the Revolution and continue the struggle which our children began" (*Barricada*, May 25, 1981, 1).

Sandinista discourse and quotes from the Mothers of Heroes and Martyrs revealed that the symbolic survival of the heroes and martyrs depended upon the survival of the revolution. Just as the martyred Christ lived on in all Christians, martyred Sandinistas lived on in all free Nicaraguans. Dead combatants lived on particularly through their mothers in the struggle. As a banner carried by Mothers of Heroes and Martyrs read, "Heroes and Martyrs of 1970—you are present in your mothers" (*Barricada*, July 13, 1981, 1).

The Mothers were also effective in presenting the lives of their martyred children as brave and worthy examples to young men of draft age. One Mother who lost two sons during the insurrection made a call to all mothers to inspire their children to fight: "Our children aren't dead, they live on in our hearts and the pain fills us with the courage to inspire other children to avenge their deaths" (*Barricada*, May 15, 1983, 1).

Sandinista discourse of Las Continuadoras posed mothers who were resentful of their children's deaths, particularly those who blamed the state for the deaths, as acting against the wishes of their children, sullying the memory of their children, and even contributing to the destruction of that which their children had given their lives to protect. The implicit argument was that defense of the revolution would assure that these precious lives had not been given in vain. According to the logic this discourse entails, to truly respect these martyrs, one must carry on their struggle. This, in turn, presented a strong social constraint against mothers of the fallen who were not politically mobilized or who espoused anti-Sandinista views.

The Mothers of the Heroes and Martyrs

The Mothers of the Heroes and Martyrs were mothers of children killed or captured in the revolution or Contra war. With support from the Sandinista state (1979–90), the Mothers organized memorials for those who fell in the revolution, offered economic and emotional support to mothers, opposed amnesty for political prisoners, and campaigned for the safe return of those kidnapped by the Contras and an end to the Contra war. The Committee of Mothers of Heroes and Martyrs served as a moral resource of the Sandinista state against right-wing propaganda. They symbolized the sacrifices made and Nicaragua's obligations to uphold the revolution, and conducted propaganda work with mothers of draftees and war victims to deflect resentment away from the revolution. For its own members, the Mothers provided an economic and emotional support group.

On anniversaries of battles in various cities, the Mothers led marches and occupied the front rows of assemblies honoring those who died. Throughout the 1980s, committees of Mothers in various cities established permanent records of the sacrifices of their children by giving testimony of their children's deaths and constructing monuments and galleries containing pictures and mementos of those who died.

The Mothers also provided an effective counterattack against anti-Sandinista propaganda. For example, the mothers of counterrevolutionary prisoners in the Sandinista jails were well publicized by the anti-Sandinista press in the early 1980s, and in response to this campaign, mothers of fallen Sandinistas carried signs at rallies reading: "Mother of the National Guard, your son is in jail, and my son, where is he?" By 1981, the Committee of Mothers of Heroes and Martyrs were collectively denouncing counterrevolutionary aggressions and U.S. economic policies. They compiled testimonies on the deaths of their children and presented them to international human rights organizations. The announcement of this project in a *Barricada* headline as "Mothers Will Present Their Pain to the World" suggests the emotional response the mobilized mothers were meant to evoke nationally and internationally (*Barricada*, May 20, 1981, 1).

While their externally directed efforts served to undermine right-wing propaganda, local branches of the Committee of Mothers acted as mutual support groups where members could share their pain and work to overcome an often paralyzing grief. The Sandinista state supported these committees in order to integrate into the revolutionary process a sector that was difficult to organize—women over forty years old who did not work outside the home or worked in the informal economy—while ensuring that the mothers, in their grief, did not come to resent the revolution. These mothers were repeatedly exhorted to "not sit home and cry all the time but rather to remember [their dead children] by being fully integrated in the defense of the revolution" (*Barricada*, May 23, 1981, 7). The Mothers' committees raised funds to erect signs and monuments dedicated to fallen Sandinistas, to help families with funeral costs, and to support sick mothers and mothers whose primary means of support had been the child who died. Individual mothers also received pensions and supplies, and the committees received some government funding.

Mothers were mobilized into rear-guard defense work primarily through the Las Continuadoras mobilizing identity. One prominent Sandinista told the Mothers, "You should demand that the ideals of your children be carried out because you have sufficient moral authority to demand it, to criticize it, to direct this process" (*Barricada*, May 14, 1981, 10). Thus, the Mothers, armed with moral authority, became Las Continuadoras, stepping in where their children left off and defending the revolution on the ideological front.

Many Nicaraguan mothers individually resisted the drafting of sons. The Committee of Mothers of Heroes and Martyrs were enlisted for ideological work in solidifying the support of mothers of draftees and were held up as symbols identifying the proper revolutionary behavior for soldiers' mothers. Mothers of fallen combatants were also organized to do political work with these mothers of draftees, visiting them regularly to give moral and economic support as well as to raise their political consciousness by explaining the necessity of the draft and the ideological aspects of the war effort.

In the early years of the Contra war, the military recruited Mothers of Heroes and Martyrs to deliver the news of war deaths and to comfort the grieving family, hoping to lessen resentment and check counterrevolutionary propaganda. The Mothers, it was believed, had the moral authority both to give sympathy and do consciousness-raising with the family. The Mothers of Matagalpa explained this process in their 1984 report: "Each time that there are fallen *compañeros* we accompany the new mother of this movement in this difficult moment, but we also prevent the enemies of the Revolution from taking advantage of the family's grief. We work to rescue all the mothers whom we find isolated or resentful until we convince them that we confront problems better united" (*Somos*, May 1984). In the words of one member, Doña Nacha: "We went first to accompany her as other mothers and also to talk with her. When you lose your child it seems to you that you're the only one that this has happened to. And you ask 'Why? Why?' But later you begin to reflect and see that they had to die so that many things are gained" (ibid.).

Here we find the theme of losing in order to gain, which was key to Sandinista discourse on martyrdom. Doña Nacha touched upon the development of this political consciousness encouraged by reflection upon the meaning of the death. The Mothers of Heroes and Martyrs were an effective conduit through which to construct and disseminate the meaning of death in war in a manner conducive to Sandinista victory.

As such, in addition to emotional support, the aim of the visit was political as well. During the visit, the Mothers, as representatives of the state, helped the family make wake and burial arrangements and informed the mother about government benefits and pensions. If the mother of the dead soldier showed resentment toward the revolution—and many did—the visiting Mothers tried to refocus her anger on the Contras. As Doña Leonor recalled: "Some reacted badly. They would say, 'It's the [Sandinistas'] fault that my son fell.' In this work we would say to them that it wasn't the [Sandinistas] that was killing them. It was the Contra. If the Contra wasn't in the mountains, they wouldn't have died" (ibid.).

The Mothers infused their message of death with revolutionary-style sacrifice for a higher cause. The Mothers/messengers became the prototypes for future Spartan Mothers. Yet this task also involved a high emotional toll for the Mother/messenger. Such a difficult job, which many believed required maternal empathy, also involved a measure of self-sacrifice because the Mothers, in delivering the news of death, relived the day they received news of their own child: "We cried as much as she did." In 1984, the Combatant Support Regional Committee was created to take over this daunting task.

Conclusion

The campaigns in both the U.S. and Nicaragua were aimed at "educating" women with regard to the proper behavior of the "good mother" in the context of war. Ironically, those in charge of mobilizing a nation to war fear mothers; more specifically, they fear the potential for resistance based upon maternal love. This has been particularly acute in terms of the draft. In response, war mobilizers try to reframe definitions of good versus bad mothers and play off of maternal imagery meant to arouse sympathy for the cause of the fallen or to compel protective mothers to deliver their sons to induction centers. The mobilization of grieving mothers, both symbolically and literally, has been an effective method through which the state is able to deliver its pro-war messages. As demonstrated in these two divergent cases, it is important to recognize the ways in which maternal symbolism and mothers themselves are used to facilitate war. Such research not only gives insight into women's war experiences, but also suggests significant postwar cultural fallout to the extent that these wars were fought along the cultural front lines by shoring up traditional maternal imagery.

NOTES

1. See, for example, Jean Bethke Elshtain, *Women and War*; also *Women, Militarism and War*, ed. Elshtain and Sheila Tobias (Lanham, MD: Rowman and Littlefield, 1990); and *Gendering War Talk*, ed. Miriam Cooke and Angela Woollacott.

2. Zeiger argues that the motion picture industry produced a number of films geared specifically at promoting draft registration. See pp. 26–27.

3. Rupp presents a valuable analysis of the shift in gendered imagery as the United States entered World War II and required women's labor in industry.

4. For example, General Dwight D. Eisenhower quoted Lincoln in his 1943 address on Mothers' Day, (*New York Times*, May 9, 1943); see also Elshtain, *Women and War*, 106. Mary Steele Ross, *American Women in Uniform* (Garden City, NY: Garden City Publishing, 1943), 34.

5. It is important to note that after 1990 Nicaragua saw a marked growth in feminist organizing. The Sandinista loss of the 1990 elections and end of the war, in a sense, freed Sandinista women to shift the focus to themselves. Despite the traditional gender images described here, the revolutionary experience shaped these women (as they shaped the revolution) in radical and empowering ways.

6. Borge speech in Managua on March 8, 1980, translated and printed by WIRE.

7. Molyneux, "Mobilization without Emancipation?" See also Cynthia Enloe, *Does Khaki Become You? The Militarization of Women's Lives* (London: Unwin Hyman, 1988), 166–67.

8. AMNLAE article reprinted by WIRE from ISIS International Bulletin #14, Carouge, Switzerland.

9. Maternal war discourse stretches across national boundaries and through time. Note the similarities between U.S. Civil War and Nicaraguan Contra war maternal discourse: Confederate "Spartan Mothers": "I have three sons and my husband in the army. . . . They are all I have, but if I had more, I would freely give them to my country," and "The blood of the slain sons called for additional sons to battle for the vindication of those who had fallen." Quoted in Elshtain, *Women and War*, 100.

REFERENCES

Berkman, Joyce. 1990. "Feminism, War, and Peace Politics: The Case of World War I." In Jean Bethke Elshtain and Sheila Tobias (eds.), *Women, Militarism, and War: Essays in History, Politics, and Social Theory*. Lanham, MD: Rowman and Littlefield.

Cooke, Miriam, and Angela Woollacott (eds.), 1993. *Gendering War Talk*. Princeton, NJ: Princeton University Press

Elshtain, Jean Bethke. 1987. *Women and War*. New York: Basic Books.

Molyneux, Maxine. 1985. "Mobilization without Emancipation? Women's Interests, the State, and Revolution in Nicaragua." *Feminist Studies* 11 (Summer).

Office of the Mothers of Heroes and Martyrs of Matagalpa. 1984 (exact date unknown). "Information Sheet about the Movement of Mothers of Heroes and Martyrs." From the office files of the Mothers of Heroes and Martyrs of Matagalpa.

Randall, Margaret. 1992. *Gathering Rage: The Failure of Twentieth Century Revolutions to Develop a Feminist Agenda*. New York: Monthly Review Foundation.

Ross, Mary Steele. 1943. *American Woman in Uniform*. Garden City, NY: Garden City Publishing.

Rupp, Leila J. 1978. *Mobilizing Women for War: German and American Propaganda, 1939–1945*. Princeton, NJ: Princeton University Press.

Somos. AMNLAE publication, May 1984.

Steinson, Barbara J. 1980. " 'The Mother Half of Humanity': American Women in the Peace and Preparedness Movements in World War I." In Carol R. Berkin and Clara M. Lovett, eds., *Women, War and Revolution*. New York: Holmes and Meier.

Whitcomb, Riley. 1983. "The Committee of Mothers of Heroes and Martyrs." *Nicaraguan Perspectives* (Winter).

Zeiger, Susan. 1996. "She Didn't Raise Her Boy to Be a Slacker: Motherhood, Conscription, and the Culture of the First World War." *Feminist Studies* 22 (Spring).

Chapter Twenty-Seven

Moral Mothers and Stalwart Sons
Reading Binaries in a Time of War

Malathi de Alwis

At the height of the Sri Lankan government's first major offensive against the Tamil militants fighting for a separate state, in 1986–87, the Ministry for Women's Affairs issued a poster that depicted a woman—bearing the obvious cultural markers of a Sinhalese (the majority community)—breastfeeding her baby while dreaming of a man dressed in army fatigues. The Sinhala caption below read: "Give your life blood in breast milk to nourish our future soldiers." Juxtapose this image against that of a color photograph published on the front page of a leading Sunday newspaper at the start of the third major government offensive against the Tamil militants in July 1990: the photograph was titled "Defender of the Faith." It depicted a youthful soldier armed with a machine gun and a necklace of ammunition with the caption: "A lone soldier stands guard at a Buddhist temple on the Vavuniya border" (*Sunday Times*, July 1, 1990). Such idealizations of feminized sacrifice and masculinized valor, notes Cynthia Enloe, become especially exaggerated in periods of national crisis (Enloe, 1989: 197). In this paper, I push this insight further by questioning the very en-gendering of such a rigid binary. I will trace the contours of a particular ideological field that enables the production, dissemination and apprehension of such gendered images, and concomitantly, gendered practices. The rhetoric and practices that I focus on in this paper are those that are related to (civil) war and not other forms of national crises that might be defined by terms such as "riots" or "insurrections."

To ask what do women have to do with war[1] also behooves the question what do men have to do with it. In short, it is crucial that we understand and analyze the ideological practices that simultaneously socialize women as sacrificing mothers and men as heroic sons. It is the production of such subject positions that orient us toward a chronology of activity that "naturalizes" the assumption that these are our primary roles as patriotic citizens of the nation-state. The feminization of the nation-state further complicates this mother-son binary.[2] The nation-state, i.e., the Motherland, conceptualizes the citizen-subject through a particular configuration of "motherhood": nurturing and caring for her citizens in exchange for a similar reciprocity. In times of crisis such as a war or an uprising, such symbiotic relationships are especially highlighted: the heroism required of her male citizens foregrounded against the sacrifices of her female citizens. In addition, the female citizen is often perceived to embody the Motherland (they are both nurturant yet vulnerable); her rape or capture symbolizes the very desecration of the community/ nation/land.[3]

The first section of this chapter unpacks the production of this gendered binary by exploring a specific practice within a crucial "ideological state apparatus," the school, which primarily interpellates students into heroic sons and sacrificing mothers. I find Althusser's formulation (1971) of interpellation (which can be described, at the simplest level, as a ritual of ideological recognition) especially useful here because it enables the theorization of the material constitution of the subject through ideology. It is also my suggestion that students are not merely interpellated in terms of gender but also in terms of ethnicity, religion, and so on. In the context of Sri Lanka, which is a multiethnic, multilingual, and multireligious country, it is nevertheless a Sinhala and a Buddhist hegemony that is disseminated through the state educational structure.[4] Such interpellations are also constantly reiterated and reaffirmed in other aspects of Sri Lankan society, for example, through other ideological state apparatuses such as the media and national rituals.[5] While it is imperative to interrogate the interpellation of such a norm, it is also important to consider how such a normalization can be disrupted and countered. The second section of this chapter will briefly address this issue while also considering how such disruptions can be conceptually positioned in relation to the dominant binary of Moral Mothers/Stalwart Sons.

The Educational Space

"Gradually—but especially after 1762—the educational space unfolds," noted Michel Foucault, who went on to analyze in depth the disciplinary practices that molded the body and mind of the student through exercises, the timetable, the bell, and the examination (Foucault, 1979: part 3). In the same way that the age of the "examining" school "marked the beginnings of a pedagogy that functions as a science," argued Foucault, the inspections and endlessly repeated movements in the army "also marked the development of an immense tactical knowledge" (ibid., 187). Such "examinations" thus introduced "a whole mechanism that linked to a certain type of the formation of knowledge a certain form of the exercise of power" (ibid.).

The textbook, an essential commodity in secondary schools today, is a crucial repository of knowledge that can be "scientifically" and economically dispensed among students through practices of pedagogy. In Sri Lanka, textbooks are issued free to all students and are thus crucial catalysts in the transference of knowledge from teacher to student. Usually, each lesson in a textbook is explained within the classroom by the teacher who is often guided by a government-issued lesson plan but not circumscribed by it. The exercises that accompany each lesson are also explained by the teacher and can be completed during the lesson period or done as homework. Extracts from these lessons may also appear in the midterm or end-of-term examination, thus requiring the student to constantly read and revise his or her lessons and exercises, and thereby doubly reinforcing the ideological content of the lesson as well as training the student in the acquiring of a particular knowledge through a specific form of discipline.

Due to spatial limitations, I will focus here only on two extracts from the Sinhala reader *Kumarodaya*, used by eleven-year-olds in both public and private schools in Sri Lanka. First published in 1952, this reader was last reprinted in 1990 and continues to be used as a supplementary text in grade five Sinhala classes across the nation, thus amply affirming Laclau and Mouffe's assertion that every hegemonic formation is "constructed through regularity in dispersion" (1985: 142).[6] Interspersed with many folktales and folk poems, the *Kumarodaya* contains a variety of historic tales[7] that have been adapted from the fifth century Pali chronicle, the *Mahawamsa*, which was translated into English in the early nineteenth century by the orientalist George Turnour, who claimed that it contained a chronological, continuous, and "authentic" history of Ceylon extending from 500 B.C.[8] The two stories I will discuss here focus on the youthful King Duttugemunu (161–137 B.C.), the hero of the *Mahawamsa*, a text which has been crucial to the project of Sinhala Buddhist nation building in Sri Lanka (cf. Gunawardana, 1984). Duttugemunu is presented here as being the first Sinhala king to vanquish the Tamil rulers in the north and to unite all the kingdoms under his sovereignty. One would assume that a focus on Duttugemunu as a youth would enable schoolchildren to identify more closely with his character, thus making the pedagogy more explicit here. Another interesting feature of these two stories is that they appear in the form of play scripts, with an accompanying exercise requesting the student to act it out. Unlike the examination, the invitation to play/act makes acquiring knowledge and training the body and voice a more pleasurable exercise.[9]

Talking Peace

The first play, entitled "King Kavantissa's Palace," is set in the palace flower grove, where we encounter Kavantissa's[10] queen, Vihara Maha Devi, reading a *Bana potha* (a text containing the sermons of Buddhist monks). Because Vihara Maha Devi "has all the attributes of the *panchakalyani*,"[11] she does not "lack in beauty and youthful looks," notes the author of this text, and her youthful son, who sits pensively beside her, "has a handsome body that would stir any heart" (*Kumarodaya*, 1965[1952]: 39). The reader soon discovers that the reason for Gemunu's pensiveness is that his father has, once again, forbidden him to fight the "enemy," who has subjugated many of his countrymen who are domiciled in the north-central region of Lanka.[12] In order to placate her troubled son, Vihara Maha Devi defends her husband by pointing out that he values peace, at which point, Gemunu bursts out: "Of course, I too love peace. Who would not crave for peace, Mother? But this problem cannot be solved peacefully. If we do nothing about this, *our people will be unable to practice their religion, our race (jatiya) will be destroyed*" (ibid., 39–40, emphasis mine). Vihara Maha Devi remonstrates with Gemunu: "It is not right to get angry with your father. He forbids you to go to war because he loves you and does not want you to get injured," which leads to another outburst from Gemunu: "How can one protect a country without facing danger, Mother? *Am I a woman to be restricted to the kitchen all the time?*" (ibid., 40, emphasis mine).[13] Vihara Maha Devi too acknowledges that her one desire is to see "a united land where the Buddha dharma flourishes," but she warns her son not to be too impatient because of his youth. Instead of dissuading him completely of his ambition, however, she counsels him on how to prepare for battle: (1) Gemunu must send spies to the enemy—King Elara's kingdom—in order to ascertain the strength of his army and then try to increase the strength of his own army tenfold more. (2) It is essential that Gemunu reaches the acme of training in the arts of warfare because King Elara is more advanced in age, in war skills, and has superior troop strength. After eagerly listening to her advice, Gemunu gleefully exclaims that he cannot rest until he takes his revenge from Elara. Vihara Maha Devi then launches into a lengthy soliloquy wherein she chastises Gemunu for speaking of revenge: "I too encouraged your love for your race but I did not *train (puhunu)* you to speak or act like one who has been blinded by it" (ibid., 42, emphasis mine). She once again stresses that they must fight to protect their land and religion and not to seek revenge, for *the reason the enemy became powerful was due to the shortcomings of our own people* (ibid., emphasis mine). Therefore, if Gemunu cannot acknowledge an honorable characteristic in an enemy and learn to see the faults of those loyal to him, he will never be able to be a righteous (*dharmishta*) king.

After such a masterly exposition on military tactics and righteous government, the play smoothly reverts to more spiritual matters once again. Gemunu, after seeking forgiveness from his mother for speaking of revenge, leaves to join his younger brother, who is having a discussion on Buddhism with the Chief Priest at the temple, while Vihara Maha Devi gets ready to offer *Dane* (alms) to twelve mendicant monks. However, she is forestalled by the arrival of her husband, who has just returned from overseeing the construction of an irrigation tank. He is delighted to hear that Prince Gemunu is at the temple and hopes that "if Gemunu spends the majority of the day in the temple, he will forget his 'war craze' . . . though I suppose *if young boys learn war skills, it is natural that they should hunger for war*" (ibid., 45, emphasis mine). However, Kavantissa receives a bigger shock when he realizes that his wife too is quite insistent that he should wage war against King Elara in order to protect "what we have rightly inherited—our race and religion" (ibid., 46). Vihara Maha Devi, who had earlier gently defended her husband to her son like a dutiful wife, now freely argues with her husband and attempts to highlight his shortsightedness as a ruler. Completely cornered, the king accuses her of having planted incendiary ideas in their son's head and questions whether she does not fear her son dying in battle. Vihara Maha Devi's reply is a telling indictment on her husband as well: "If one goes to war or not, one has to die some day. If my son, who is the heir to the throne, cannot sacrifice his life for his country, he is not fit to be a king" (ibid., 47).

Planning War

The other story, entitled "King Gemunu's War Parley," is set in a slightly later time period, as by this time, King Kavantissa has died and Gemunu,[14] after battling his brother for the throne, has finally attained the coveted position and is on the verge of achieving his ambition of fighting the Tamils. The scene is set in the palace where four ministers and Pussadeva, Gemunu's prime minister, have gathered for the war parley, which Gemunu refuses to begin until his mother arrives. Immediately after her arrival, they begin to discuss war strategy, with Pussadeva pointing out that it is essential to produce and store large quantities of food before going to battle. Vihara Maha Devi then reminds them that there is a second task that needs to be attended to as well: "Go to Tissamahrama and ask the Chief Priest to provide you with a large contingent of Buddhist monks to accompany you in battle" (ibid., 99). Gemunu, absolutely astonished, points out that it is a great distance from the Ruhuna to Anuradhapura and that this journey would be very hazardous and exhausting to the monks, especially since he and his retinue would be too busy with the tasks of war to attend to them adequately. Pussadeva adds that this plan will not only be injurious to the monks but will impede the progress of the troops as well. However, Vihara Maha Devi shrugs off their dissent as mere short-sightedness:

> From here to Anuradhapura, you have to pass many villages and though they are the serfs of King Elara, they once were Sinhala Buddhists. Therefore, the best way to regain their loyalty is to leave a few monks at each village rather than depleting your troops by stationing a few of them at each village. This way, not only will the villagers accede to us but they will surely come forward to care and pay obeisance to the monks. (Ibid., 100)

Delighted with this plan, Gemunu exclaims: "This will ensure our victory as well as our protection," and invites his mother to accompany them in battle because she is the best adviser of them all. Though Pussadeva seconds Gemunu's invitation, as Vihara Maha Devi's presence would surely boost the morale of the troops in the battlefield, he worries that she will be "much inconvenienced." To which the Devi replies: "At a time when we are required to sacrifice our life for the sake of *our country, race and religion (rata daya samaya),* it is not seemly for people like us to worry about our comforts" (ibid., 101, emphasis mine).

Interestingly, the foci of both these stories are not some of the better-known events of Gemunu's youth (see the above notes) but rather they are primarily oriented toward inculcating what I would call a "military zeal" and a "racial/religious passion" in the reader. The fact that Gemunu features twice in this reader is also no accident, for as Gananath Obeyesekere has pointed out, the mythic significance of Dutugemunu as the savior of the Sinhala race and of Buddhism has been developed into one of the most powerful instruments of Sinhala nationalism in modern times (Obeyesekere, 1979: 285–86). Over and over again we are reminded in these two stories that what is at stake is *rata, deya, samaya* (country, race, and religion), and that we must regain it. Race here of course denotes the Sinhala race, and religion,

Buddhism, in collocation with Lanka the "country." Thus, "what these terms are directed toward is the identification of patriotism with a sectional loyalty to one race and religion—that of the majority" (Siriwardene et al., 1982: 13). Moreover, since both stories focus on the Tamils as villains, the hero's loyalty to this trinity of "country, race, religion" is also "defined through opposition to and struggle against the Tamils" (ibid.). Even in contexts where the textbooks refer to "other" invaders such as the Portuguese or British, the heroism of those who struggle against them is always coded as only being Sinhala (ibid., 20–21, 24–25, 27).

To sacrifice one's life for one's "country, race, religion" is valorized here not only as a marker of patriotism but as the ultimate essence of masculinity and heroism as well. The juxtaposition of the impetuous but heroic Gemunu against that of his peace-loving father who prefers to build tanks rather than wage war emasculates and feminizes Kavantissa, whose humiliation is complete when he cannot even beat his wife in debate. The characterization of Vihara Maha Devi as an extremely articulate and clever woman is quite unusual in comparison with the depiction of other women in the *Mahawamsa* as well as in Sinhala folklore and idiom (cf. Obeyesekere, 1963; Schrijvers, 1985; Risseeuw, 1988). However, she is also a "woman without blemish" (Seneviratne, 1969: 20), having earned this reputation by never forgetting her place as a woman. She is an example to all Sinhala mothers in the way she has nurtured her son to be a "true" nationalist and patriot despite the "negative" influence of her husband; when her husband dies, she willingly abdicates her throne in favor of her son, despite obviously being more skilled in military tactics and governance. As a reward for such exemplary behavior she is treated with much deference and respect in the *Mahawamsa* and continues to be feted as the Moral Mother of the Sinhala nation.

Moral Mothers and Stalwart Sons

I want to pause here to explain my usage of "Moral Mother" and "Stalwart Son," which are two concatenated subject positions that also denote the two opposing poles of a gendered binary. I use the adjective "stalwart" here not merely for its alliterative efficacy but because it contains within it a sense of physical strength along with a resolute and uncompromising nature.[15] The combination of strength and dependability are important here, for they suggest a capacity for brawn as well as brains, a willingness to fight in an intelligent and principled manner (important attributes that had to be inculcated in the defiant and impetuous Prince Gemunu before he could take on the mantle of king and warrior). It is also such attributes that are the hallmark of a hero, thus my previous usage of "heroic/heroism" and "valor" which I would like to continue to retain within the term "Stalwart Son" especially since the most common Sinhala word to describe Sri Lankan soldiers is *veera*, which is best glossed as heroic or valorous. However, it is not that "stalwart" is not in usage as well, as the following excerpt from an English poem by Kamala Wijeratne well attests:

> Don't ask me to forget Duttugemunu
> Dear brother of the North,
> For I cannot and will not;
> You are asking me to forget my dreams
> My glorious youth and twenty hundred years
> of gold-inscribed history.
> The time we stalwart, brave
> Faced the world unflinching
>   (Quoted in de Mel, 1996: 177)

The term "Moral Mother" has hitherto been used to discuss a primarily American phenomenon. Micaela di Leonardo (1985), who borrows this phrase from Ruth Bloch (1978),[16] describes the Moral Mother—in the context of an increasingly militarized society—as someone who primarily speaks for peace, who is "nurturant, compassionate . . . the sovereign, instinctive spokeswoman for all that is living and vulnerable" (602).[17] However, di Leonardo is also quick to point out that the ideology of the Moral Mother can be used for both antimilitarist and militarist ends (611, 605). Nevertheless, since the materials she discusses do not actually address the mobilization of the Moral Mother for militarist ends, she does not discuss the latter phenomenon in any depth. It is this lacuna that I hope to address through my formulation of Moral Mother, analyzing the portrayal of Vihara Maha Devi in the *Kumarodaya*.

While Vihara Maha Devi embodies all the characteristics of the Moral Mother delineated above, her relationship to the concepts of "life," "vulnerability," and "peace" have to be formulated differently; she speaks for peace and for life through a call for violence that is nevertheless framed as being Moral and Right. Unlike in the American examples that di Leonardo cites (the American Moral Mother's critique is addressed to a Superpower that is both militarily and economically dominant), the construction of Vihara Maha Devi as Moral Mother is enabled by the positioning of the Sinhala race, the Buddhist religion, and the Motherland (i.e., the land of the Sinhalese) as victimized and vulnerable. Her call to arms is thus framed in terms of patriotism, not violence. This doubled identity of woman and patriot is also what enables her espousal of violence without reducing her femininity and vulnerability. The reason she refuses to worry about her comforts and is even willing to see her son die is because of her commitment to a greater good—the unification of the country and the protection of her race and religion.[18] It is this double identity that also enables her to retain the moral high ground (as well as her articulateness) in her encounters with her overly militant son and pacifist husband. In another well-known incident from her life (also featured in textbooks), she once again epitomizes morality by sacrificing herself to an angry sea to appease the wrath of the gods vented on her people after her father rashly and sacrilegiously kills a Buddhist monk due to his rage at the discovery of his wife's continued adultery. Vihara Maha Devi is not only an example to her fickle mother and impetuous father but to the general populace as well; despite her youth and privileged birth, she is willing to take responsibility for her parent's actions and to sacrifice her life for the sake of her people. The *Mahawamsa* is quick to stress that it is as a reward for such exemplary behavior that the gods decided to spare her life and safely guided her vessel to the kingdom of her future husband.[19]

What is most interesting about the narratives of Vihara Maha Devi and Duttu-gemunu is how the narratives themselves are constructed, presented, and read at different moments in Sri Lanka's history. I am sure that the two lessons I analyzed above would have produced very different resonances in a student studying it in the early 1950s (when no ethnic riots or wars had occurred) than in a student studying them in the present context of civil war and post-1983 ethnic riots. Though Vihara Maha Devi is popularly understood today to be a historical figure rather than a mythic one, she is perceived as an ideal type, a symbol of a past Golden Age, an epitome of patriotic and moral womanhood that contemporary Sinhala women can always aspire to emulate though will rarely succeed.[20] Excerpts from a contemporary Sinhala poem entitled "To My Son on the Battlefield . . . ," which was published in a women's magazine, movingly captures this:

> When her son Gemunu went to battle
> The venerable queen did not shed tears
> I cannot do likewise my son
> For warm tears are cascading down my face
> Even if you die upon the battlefield, beloved son
> Lay not your rifle upon the earth, hand it over to another
> That is the way I'll know you are my eldest son for sure
> Tomorrow I'll send my heroic younger son to battle.
>   (*Birinda*, October 25, 1993)

In this poem, the weeping mother comes across as more human than Vihara Maha Devi, but her militaristic zeal is more than a match for the queen; she beseeches her dying son not to let his firearm go to waste, and then she triumphantly concludes by affirming that she will sacrifice her other son as well.[21] Note here how this mother shares a common ideological terrain with the woman on the war poster and Vihara Maha Devi; all three women can speak of sending sons to war—with authority and moral righteousness—because it is they who gave them life in the first place.

Even though the majority of women in Sri Lanka may not wish to see their sons go to war—especially in today's context, when Sri Lankan soldiers have become mere cannon fodder—it is in such idealizations of a mother's love and sacrifice, of romanticized notions of patriotism, where they find solace and legitimation. In fact, images such as "warm tears" (*unu kandulu*), blood turned to milk (*le kiri kala*), and the dispatching of another son to take the place of the first are familiar and clichéd tropes that are harnessed in the writing of such poetry and other forms of public discourse such as war songs (*rana gi*),[22] political speeches, and statements to the press by bereaved parents. Similarly, many of the poems written by soldiers (or about soldiers)[23] draw upon romanticized codes such as equating the protection of one's mother with the protection of the motherland, the raising of the Lion flag (an abbreviated description of the Sri Lankan flag which draws attention to a symbol of Sinhalaness) in the land of the enemy, the admonishment to one's mother not to weep because one is fighting for one's country/race/religion (*rata daya samaya*), or following in the footsteps of that most heroic son of them all, Duttugemunu.

As a matter of fact, a recent advertisement calling for recruits to the Sri Lankan navy published in a leading Sinhala newspaper went so far as specifically to address the "brave sons of Duttugemunu's lineage." The fact that the English-language advertisement made no reference to Duttugemunu makes it very clear that the advertisers were aware of how they could best appeal to Sinhala youth from the lower and lower middle classes who are the chief audience of Sinhala newspapers. They were merely tapping into an available ideological field that I have already delineated in this chapter. However, such assertions of Sinhala hegemony were not allowed to pass unchallenged and were the subject of several heated articles of protest to the press by Tamil politicians (who also raised the issue in Parliament) and a multiethnic, feminist organization, Women for Peace. As these articles rightly pointed out, by specifically addressing those of Duttugemunu's lineage, that is the Sinhalese, the navy was denying all other minorities[24] the opportunity to enlist, and worse still, was blatantly attempting to arouse anti-Tamil sentiments.

Women Warriors

But how do we reconcile women soldiers within this binary of moral mothers and heroic sons? Consider this news report in an English newspaper. Entitled "STF women ready for battle," this is a rare piece of reporting about women in the Sri Lankan armed forces.[25] The occasion for the article is that twenty-nine women have joined the elite police commandos of the Special Task Force (STF) and have just completed their training in guerrilla warfare. However, the article concludes by noting that these women will be used in "crowd control, VIP security, Operations room and civil security in addition to the normal office work" (*Sunday Observer*, February 28, 1993). In fact, despite the fact that the new recruits describe their grueling training as a challenge they enjoyed and met, and assert their pride in being members of this elite force, the overall tone of the article conveys a contrary message epitomized in this excerpt: "Their acquired toughness has, however, not overcome their femininity as was evident when we caught them quietly freshening up when called to pose for a photograph. 'That is how it should be, because we don't want them to lose their feminine qualities,' said DIG [Deputy Inspector General] Karunasena" (ibid.). Earlier in the article, DIG Karunasena is bold enough to assert that the selection process entailed a search for "both beauty and brains" and that "very tall girls" were rejected as they would have been "too easily identifiable as police personnel when engaged in civil duties" (ibid.). It is very clear by the end of the article that despite these women's extensive training in guerrilla warfare, they will not be making use of it if their superiors can help it. It seems that the main purpose for recruiting women to the armed forces is to have them shoulder all civilian duties, thus freeing more of their male colleagues (in a context where fewer men are enlisting and vast numbers are deserting) for combat duty.

It is also interesting to note how differently women soldiers are portrayed in the English and Sinhala newspapers, even if they are published by the same company. A case in point is how the privately owned *Sunday Times*, which caters to a multi-ethnic, anglicized, city-based middle and upper class, presented a cover photograph of a very pregnant female soldier. The photograph, entitled "Mother Lanka," had a long caption that identified the woman and her battalion, where she was located, and what kind of work she did (she guarded a checkpoint). It further noted that this woman was fighting to "secure a future for the next generation, including the baby in her womb" and had not yet given up duties despite the fact that she was nine months pregnant, thus emphasizing her doubled identity as mother and patriot, a perfect embodiment of "Mother Lanka," as the photo title reminded us. The caption concluded with the statement that the "effect of armed conflicts on women and children is one of the many issues being discussed at the Fourth UN conference on Women in Beijing this week," thus cleverly tying the image to an international event and emphasizing the *victimization* of women and children in armed conflicts. This caption not only individualized and personalized the female soldier but also made it clear that if not for the terrible times in which we live, she would never have been reduced to this kind of work (*Sunday Times*, September 3, 1995).

The *Sunday Times*' sister paper, the *Lankadeepa*, on the other hand, which mainly caters to a Sinhala lower and lower middle class located in cities as well as rural areas, displayed a different photograph of the same woman on its front page. While the full-length photograph in the *Sunday Times* had highlighted the woman's pregnant condition by portraying her holding her rifle slackly from under her protruding belly, the *Lankadeepa* produced a more cropped photograph that gave more prominence to the soldier's rifle, which she now held cocked, over her stomach. This photograph was accompanied by a short poem:

> Her resolve to protect her country
> Increases her love for her son in her womb
> Tomorrow, her arms that cradled weapons will cradle her son
> Blessed is the country that has borne daughters like you
> (*Lankadeepa*, September 3, 1995)

The message is clear and simple, we are proud of you because you are doing a great service to your country, but now is the time for you to perform another kind of service (which because of her profession now takes on added significance—see second line of poem), that of nurturing your child. In my translation of the poem, I have glossed the word *puthu* (the poetic form of the word *putha*) as "son." However, this word can also be glossed in a broader sense to mean "child," i.e., someone gender neutral. The ambivalence inherent in this word, however, is what adds to the charge of this poem, which is framed in terms of motherhood and war. The relationship between protective mothers and heroic sons has been so naturalized that when we read the above poem, our instinctive reaction is to read *puthu* as son.

Even a brief exploration of the phenomenon of women soldiers makes it clear that their presence does disrupt the dominant Moral Mother/Stalwart Son binary that has been naturalized in Sri Lankan society. The fact that these women get such little publicity is a telling example. However, when these women are spotlighted in the media, great effort is expended to continuously encompass them within a gendered binary that may not necessarily be that of mother and son. In the first example I presented, the women were produced as sexual beings whose main responsibilities were to perform civilian, noncombative duties, thus keeping intact the Stalwart Son part of the binary. The article also constantly stressed the youthfulness of these women and the fact that they would not be allowed to marry for another five years (the common understanding being that one becomes pregnant soon after marriage), therefore seeming to suggest that the women's most productive time as warriors was before they became mothers. They thus straddle an interstitial space (which is nevertheless gendered—we are never allowed to forget that they are women) between that of the Stalwart Son and Moral Mother. But it is a space that is nevertheless part of one continuum, for once a woman soldier did become pregnant, as illustrated in my second example, she could be immediately incorporated into the Moral Mother part of the binary.

As the poem noted, her sensibility as a mother has been reinforced because of her participation in the protection of her country, but it is this sensibility that will also make her lay down her arms to tend to her newborn—after all, it is also to insure his security and the security of future generations that she continues to stand guard in the blazing sun even in her ninth month of pregnancy. It is an image of patience and alertness, of protection (and even of heroism, though this adjective is never used to describe her), but not of combativeness or valor, which continue to retain their connotations of masculinity.

Conclusion

The primary focus of this chapter has been the dissemination of a Sinhala (and more implicitly Buddhist) gendered binary among the majority community, the Sinhalese, and the subsequent mobilization of the dominant and condensed subject positions of Moral Mother and Stalwart Son (which simultaneously mark the two poles of the binary) in the context of a protracted civil war in Sri Lanka. Unfortunately, due to spatial limitations, I was unable to pursue a similar trajectory of inquiry regarding the dissemination of gendered Tamil subject positions.[26] However, as Sitralega Maunaguru (1995) has pointed out in her finely nuanced, historicized work on the construction of "woman" in Tamil nationalist projects, different constructions of womanhood came into play at different moments of Tamil nationalism and ethnic conflict. Her categorizations of "brave mother," "woman warrior," "new woman," and "social mother" describe the variety of subject positions that were made available to (as well as fashioned by) Tamil women during the past five decades. I would like to discuss briefly one convergence and one divergence between the Tamil stereotypes that Maunaguru presents and the Moral Mother/Stalwart Son binary that I have explicated above.

While I do not want to erase the subtle differences between the "brave mother" and "social mother" that are posited by Maunaguru, it is clear that both these subject positions can be encompassed within my formulation of Moral Mother, for as Maunaguru points out, one of the major differences between that of the "brave mother" and "social mother" is that the former speaks for war and the latter for peace (1995: 172–73).[27] Unlike the Sinhalese, who could look to historical sources such as the Pali Chronicles for role models of Moral Mothers and Stalwart Sons (this deployment is especially clear in Kamala Wijeratne's reference to "twenty hundred years of gold-inscribed history" in the poem quoted above), the Tamils did not possess such ancient records and had to look to literary sources such as Sangam poetry from the first century A.D., or to the seventh-century epic, *Silapathikaram*, to locate examples of brave mothers and loyal wives (Maunaguru, 1995: 161; cf. Hellmann-Rajanayagam, 1990).

While this has not enabled the emergence of a more consistent and historically continuous stereotype such as that of Vihara Maha Devi, it has nevertheless provided opportunities for the creation of more contemporary heroes and heroines from among the Tamil militants (de Alwis, 1994b; cf. Schalk, 1992). However, the convergence I see between the Sinhala examples I presented above and the Tamil models of "brave woman" and "social mother" is that the purchase of these ideal types arises from the authority and authenticity vested in the mother to speak either for peace or war, life or death.

Maunaguru's discussion of the subject positions of "woman warrior" and "new woman," on the other hand, illuminates a significant divergence from the Sinhala "woman warrior" I discussed above. The women warriors in the Liberation Tigers of Tamil Eelam (LTTE) have acquired almost as much notoriety as their male counterparts since a female suicide bomber killed the prime minister of India, Rajiv Gandhi, in 1993. The increased visibility of these women has also generated much discussion among feminists in Sri Lanka on the role of female militants in anti-state movements, a familiar question to those who have studied the positioning of female fighters in the Algerian, Eritrean, and Nicaraguan guerrilla forces. Much of this feminist debate is framed in terms of whether the women in the LTTE are liberated or subjugated (de Silva, 1994; Coomaraswamy, 1997), agents or victims (de Mel, 1996). Maunaguru's paper, on the other hand, is able to transcend such a dichotomizing debate by locating "women warriors" within the broader context of other male and female subject positions in Tamil society. Maunaguru also complicates the category of "woman warrior" by marking two distinctive phases of its mobilization by militant groups.

In the first phase, which was spearheaded by the LTTE—which "owed more to its militarism than to an ideological allegiance with feminism" (Maunaguru, 1995: 163)—the ideal Tamil woman was expected to be a mother as well as a fighter, thus integrating the subject position of "brave mother" with that of "woman warrior," that is, a "warrior mother."[28] The second phase, which was facilitated by the women's wings of the more progressive Tamil militant groups (which have since disbanded or been decimated by the LTTE) such as the Eelam People's Revolutionary Liberation Front (EPRLF), enabled a formulation of the "new woman" who contested "patriarchal aspects of Tamil cultural ideology" and insisted on linking national liberation with women's liberation (Maunaguru, 1995: 165–67).[29] A later phase of the "woman warrior," which Maunaguru does not discuss but which has been addressed in my earlier work (1993) as well as in the work of Mangalika de Silva (1994) and Radhika Coomaraswamy (1997), can be described as the "masculinized virgin warrior." In a context where the LTTE reigns supreme, having exiled, incorporated, or killed all dissenters and critics (including many feminists), it is this ideal of womanhood that now seems to be foregrounded within Tamil society (through LTTE propaganda). As Coomaraswamy points out, the "armed virgin" is a purely LTTE innovation having no precedence in Tamil literature or culture (1997: 9). However, while the LTTE woman's internal makeup is expected to be "pure," "chaste," and "virginal," her outer body is marked as masculine; her hair is cut short and she wears a beret, combat fatigues, boots, and a cyanide capsule around her neck[30] (just like her male counterparts) but no makeup or jewelry (cf. Coomaraswamy, 1997: 9). The poetry of Vanati, a female martyr of the LTTE, poignantly captures the female revolutionary's desire to transform her biologically as well as culturally marked body (as feminine) to that of "heroic" masculinity while simultaneously proclaiming her virginity and chastity—she refuses the red *kumkumum*[31] and *thali*[32] and embraces weapons, not men:

> The Ideal Woman of Tamil Eelam
> Her forehead shall be adorned not with red *kumkumam*
> but with blood
> All that is seen in her eyes is not the sweetness of youth
> but the tombs of the dead
> On her neck will lay no *tali*
> but a cyanide capsule
> She has embraced not men
> but weapons!
>
> (Quoted in Schalk, 1992: 95).

These three formulations of the "woman warrior" are especially interesting for the ways in which they can be read against the Moral Mother/Stalwart Son binary. Like the Sinhala women soldiers, they can be located at different points between the two poles that I have set up, with the "warrior mother" closer to that of the Moral Mother end and the "masculinized virgin warrior" closer to the Stalwart Son end. However, it is the category of the "new woman" that most forcefully disrupts this binary, for its very makeup contests the structures of power that produce and disseminate such binaries. However, it is also a subject position that has been effectively suppressed by the LTTE. While one can locate Sinhala parallels to the "new woman" within Sinhala society, thanks to a feminist movement that has its antecedents in the nationalist movements of the early twentieth century (Jayawardena, 1986: 109–36) as well as the youth insurrection of 1971, it is a subject position that is occupied by a minuscule part of the population and invigorated by an ideology that continues to be reviled and countered by those who control crucial ideological state apparatuses such as schools, the family, the media, and so forth. It is because of these reasons that we have been unable to "retire the Moral Mother [and the Stalwart Son] from the field" (di Leonardo, 1985: 615).

NOTES

1. This is the opening question in Micaela di Leonardo's thought-provoking article (1985).

2. For analyses of such articulations within Sri Lanka, see Tennekoon (1986), de Alwis (1994a), and de Mel (1996).

3. For the discussion of such an equation that exceeds all proportions, see Menon and Bhasin (1996), who analyze the state-organized "recovery" of Hindu and Muslim women who had been abducted during the partition of India in 1947. Cf. Maunaguru, 1994; Kannabiran, 1996.

4. The Sri Lankan state provides free education from the primary school to the university level.

5. See Jeganathan (1992) for a discussion of Independence Day celebrations in Sri Lanka that interpellate citizens as Sinhala Buddhists and de Alwis (1994b) for an engagement with this discussion and an exploration of counterhegemonic rituals produced by the Tamil militant group, the Liberation Tigers of Tamil Eelam (LTTE). See also de Alwis (1993) for a brief discussion of a public, antigovernment ritual performed by an opposition party (in 1960) that nevertheless invoked a similar formulation of Sinhala Buddhist motherhood that was also being disseminated by the government-in-power.

6. What is even more remarkable is that textbooks such as these have been endorsed by successive governments whose political orientations were extremely diverse, such as the "National Government" of 1965–70, the Socialist "United Front" government of 1970–77, and the right-wing, capitalist United National Party government from 1977 to 1994.

7. This is a common feature in Sinhala, English, and Tamil language textbooks but especially so in the Sinhala ones.

8. This claim continues to be celebrated by Sinhala nationalists even though it is contested on many fronts; for example, see Gunawardana (1984) and Walters (forthcoming).

9. Historical plays are a very popular genre in Sri Lanka. They are frequently performed at school functions such as drama contests and end-of-term concerts.

10. Kavantissa was the ruler of the Ruhunu Rata (the southeastern region of Lanka) in ancient times. He married Vihara Maha Devi, who was the daughter of Kelanitissa, who ruled Maya Rata (the southwestern region of Lanka).

11. This traditional concept of female beauty was especially popularized through the now much quoted fifteenth-century Sinhala text, the *Salalihini Sandesaya*, which was influenced by Sanskrit poetry. It describes the five ideal attributes: face like a full moon, teeth like pearls, blue-black hair reaching to the ground, hips like chariot wheels, and breasts like swans (quoted in Jayawardena, 1986: 114).

12. This echoes one of the best-known episodes of Gemunu's life. When Gemunu was twelve years old, King Kavantissa called his two sons—Prince Gemunu, the elder of the two, and Prince Saddhatissa, the younger—and, feeding them three mouthfuls of milk rice each, asked them to make three promises with each mouthful: the first, that they would not fight each other; the second, that they would not divide the *Sangha* (the order of Buddhist monks); and the third, that they would never fight the Tamils (invaders from South India who were

presently ruling in the north-central region of Lanka). The two boys happily accepted the first two mouthfuls but adamantly refused to accept the third. Queen Vihara Maha Devi, entering Gemunu's bedroom later on, discovered him curled up in bed like a fetus and asked him why he was lying so. Gemunu, comparing his bed to his country, replied: "Over there beyond the river are the Tamils; here on this side is the sea; how can I lie with outstretched limbs?" (Quoted in Siriweera, 1985: 111.)

13. This resonates with another familiar incident in Gemunu's life when he, incensed by his father's refusal for the third time to let him fight the Tamils, sends him female garments and jewelry and goes into exile to escape his wrath. Gemunu from then on became known as Duttugemunu, *dutta* meaning "disobedient." However, some Sinhala nationalists, including the late President Ranasinghe Premadasa, disliked even such a minor besmirchment of their hero and preferred to refer to him as Detugemunu meaning "Gemunu the Senior" (Premadasa, 1986: Preface).

14. Interestingly, here too he is not called Duttugemunu.

15. See American Heritage Dictionary (1985).

16. Bloch (1978) argues that the rise of the "Moral Mother" is a specifically nineteenth-century phenomenon that is connected with the rise of Protestant evangelicalism that sought to redefine women's maternal role by stressing their religiosity and domesticity.

17. I am also fully in agreement with di Leonardo's critique that the ideology of Moral Mother "glorifies the heterosexual, reproductive woman and implicitly depreciates the lives of childless women and lesbians" (1985: 613).

18. One could make a parallel argument in terms of the Buddhist monks' accompanying Gemunu's army—they are doing it to safeguard their country, race, and religion—despite the fact that they are in "blatant contradiction of Buddha's ruling forbidding [them] to witness army parades and reviews. Not only do they witness here but actually participate in the very activity of war" (Siriweera, 1985: 114). In fact, similar arguments have been made by monks who have been involved in recent youth insurrections in 1971 and 1987–90, though such participation continues to be a contentious issue for many Buddhist stalwarts and Sinhala nationalists.

19. This fortuitous reprieve of course enables her to give birth and to nurture the savior of the Sinhala race and religion and the first unifier of the entire country!

20. When the most famous park in the capital city of Colombo—named after Queen Victoria—was rededicated to Vihara Maha Devi after Sri Lanka gained Independence from Britain in 1948, the prime minister, SWRD Bandaranaike, used this occasion to berate the women of Sri Lanka for not taking sufficient interest in the affairs of the country, unlike their counterparts in India. He reminded them of Vihara Maha Devi's supreme sacrifice in her youth and hoped that the statue of the queen that was installed in the park "would be an inspiration to the younger generation" (*Times of Ceylon*, July 19, 1958).

21. There is an interesting juxtaposition of scarce commodities, such as rifles, against that of replaceable human bodies, such as sons, which reflects a sentiment that was concomitant with lifestyle in the 1960s and 1970s when Sri Lanka was governed by a socialist government and the import of foreign goods was restricted. I am grateful to Pradeep Jeganathan for pointing this out to me.

22. See Serena Tennekoon (1986) for an interesting discussion of the imagery and rhetoric in a music tape of battle songs issued by the National Youth Service Council (a state-funded institution) in 1985.

23. Many Sinhala newspapers and weekly magazines would devote an entire page once a week for the publication of poetry written by soldiers as well as civilians. Many of the poetry

would focus on patriotism, valor, death, despair and enmity, the tribulations of war, and the strength of spiritual, parental (mainly maternal,) and romantic love.

24. Such as Tamils, Moors, Malays, Burghers (descendants of Portuguese and Dutch colonizers), and minuscule numbers of Veddahs (indigenous peoples), Eurasians, Chinese, Kaffirs, etc.

25. Women make up only about 8 percent of the Sri Lankan armed forces and rarely engage in combat.

26. However, see de Alwis (1994b) for a discussion of the dissemination of a particular masculinized ideal among male and female cadres of the LTTE as a counterpoint to a similar Sinhala one. For more general discussions on gendered ideals among male and female cadres of the LTTE, see Balasingham (1983), Hoole et al. (1990), Schalk (1992, 1994), Ismail (1992), de Silva (1994), de Mel (1996), Coomaraswamy (1997), and Roberts (1996). For other accounts that do not provide specifically gendered readings, see Hellmann-Rajanayagam (1986), Jeyaraj (1993), Narayan Swamy (1994), de Silva (1995), and Manikkalingam (1995).

27. Note however, that the subject position of "social mother" while available within Tamil society, was one that was specifically mobilized by women. See de Alwis (1997) for a similar point that is made with regard to a Sinhala motherist movement that was mobilized in response to state atrocities during the Sinhala youth insurrection of 1987–90 in the south of Sri Lanka.

28. Such a model is exemplified in the now clichéd image that was used by national liberation movements in the Third World in the 1960s and 1970s (Maunaguru, 1995: 164; cf. di Leonardo, 1985: 602–3).

29. The "new woman" was not necessarily a "woman warrior." It was primarily a feminist subject position that enabled a critique of both the Sri Lankan state as well as many militant groups.

30. All members of the LTTE wear a cyanide capsule so that in the event of capture they can bite on it and die instantly without betraying their movement under subsequent interrogation.

31. Auspicious circular mark on forehead to signify a woman's married status.

32. Marriage band tied around the neck of the bride during the wedding ceremony.

REFERENCES

Althusser, Louis. 1971. "Ideology and the Ideological State Apparatus." In *Lenin and Philosophy and Other Essays*, 127–86. London: New Left Books.

Balasingham, Adele. 1983. *Women and Revolution: The Role of Women in Tamil Eelam National Liberation*. Madras.

Bloch, Ruth. 1978. "American Feminine Ideals in Transition: The Rise of the Moral Mother, 1785–1815." *Feminist Studies* 4 (June): 101–26.

Coomaraswamy, Radhika. 1997. "Tiger Women and the Question of Women's Emancipation." *Pravada* 4 (9): 8–10.

de Alwis, Malathi. 1993. "Seductive Scripts and Subversive Practices: Motherhood and Violence in Sri Lanka." Paper presented at the Senior Research Colloquium on *Violence, Suffering and Healing in South Asia*, Department of Sociology, University of Delhi, August 1993.

———. 1994a. "Toward a Feminist Historiography: Reading Gender in the Text of the

Nation." In Radhika Coomaraswamy and Nira Wickramasinghe (eds.), *Introduction to Social Theory*. Delhi: Konark Press.

———. 1994b. "Paternal States and Baby Brigades: Violence in the Name of the Nation." Paper presented at the international conference on Children and Nationalism, Centre for Child Research, Trondheim, Norway, May.

———. 1997. "Motherhood as a Space of Protest: Women's Political Participation in Contemporary Sri Lanka." In Amrita Basu and Patricia Jeffrey (eds.), *Appropriating Gender: Women's Activism and the Politicization of Religion in South Asia*. London/New York: Routledge.

de Mel, Neloufer. 1996. "Static Signifiers: Metaphors of Women in Sri Lankan War Poetry." In Kumari Jayawardena and Malathi de Alwis (eds.), *Embodied Violence: Communalising Women's Sexuality in South Asia*, 168–89. New Delhi: Kali for Women/London and New Jersey: Zed Books.

de Silva, Mangalika. 1994. "Women in the LTTE: Liberation or Subjugation?" *Pravada* 3(7): 27–31.

de Silva, P. L. 1995. "The Efficacy of 'Combat Mode': Organisation, Political Violence, Affect and Cognition in the Case of the Liberation Tigers of Tamil Eelam." In Pradeep Jeganathan and Qadri Ismail (eds.), *Unmaking the Nation: The Politics of Identity and History in Modern Sri Lanka*, 176–90. Colombo: Social Scientists' Association.

di Leonardo, Micaela. 1985. "Morals, Mothers and Militarism." *Feminist Studies* 11 (3): 599–617.

Enloe, Cynthia. 1989. *Bananas, Beaches and Bases: Making Feminist Sense of International Politics*. Berkeley: University of California Press.

Foucault, Michel. 1979. *Discipline and Punish: The Birth of the Prison*. New York: Vintage Books.

Gunawardana, R.A.L.H. 1984. " 'The People of the Lion': Sinhala Consciousness in History and Historiography." In *Ethnicity and Social Change*. Colombo: Social Scientists' Association.

Hellmann-Rajanayagam, Dagmar. 1986. "The Tamil Tigers in Northern Sri Lanka: Origins, Factions, Programmes." *Internationales Asienforum* 17: 63–85.

———. 1990. "The Politics of the Tamil Past." In Jonathan Spencer, ed., *Sri Lanka: History and the Roots of Conflict*. London: Routledge.

Hoole, Rajan, Daya Somasunderam, K. Sritharan, and Rajani Thiranagama. 1990. *The Broken Palmyrah*. Claremont, CA: Sri Lanka Studies Institute.

Ismail, Qadri. 1992. "Boys Will Be Boys: Gender and National Agency in Fanon and the LTTE." *Pravada* 1(7).

Jayawardena, Kumari. 1986. *Feminism and Nationalism in the Third World*. London: Zed Press.

Jeganathan, Pradeep. 1992. "Students, Soldiers, the Princess and the Tiger." *Pravada* 1(4).

Jeyaraj, D. B. S. 1993. "The Composition, Ideology and International Dimension of the Tamil Secessionist Movement in Sri Lanka: An Overview." In R. Premdas (ed.), *The Enigma of Ethnicity*, 282–308. St. Augustine, Trinidad, and Tobago: School of Continuing Studies, University of the West Indies.

Kannabiran, Kalpana. 1996. "Rape and the Construction of Communal Identity." In Kumari Jayawardena and Malathi de Alwis (eds.), *Embodied Violence: Communalising Women's Sexuality in South Asia*, 32–41. New Delhi: Kali for Women/London and New Jersey: Zed Books.

Kumarodaya (in Sinhala). 1965[1952]. Colombo: Government Printing Press.

Laclau, Ernesto, and Chantal Mouffe. 1985. *Hegemony and Socialist Strategy: Toward a Radical Democratic Politics*. London: Verso.

Manikkalingam, Ram. 1995. *Tigerism*. Colombo: Social Scientists' Association.

Maunaguru, Sitralega. 1995. "Gendering Tamil Nationalism: The Construction of 'woman' in Projects of Protest and Control." In Pradeep Jeganathan and Qadri Ismail (eds.) *Unmaking the Nation: The Politics of Identity and History in Modern Sri Lanka*, 158–75. Colombo: Social Scientists' Association.

Menon, Ritu, and Kamla Bhasin. 1996. "Abducted Women, the State and Questions of Honour: Three Perspectives on the Recovery Operation in Post-Partition India." In Kumari Jayawardena and Malathi de Alwis, eds., *Embodied Violence: Communalising Women's Sexuality in South Asia*. 1–31. New Delhi: Kali for Women/London and New Jersey: Zed Books.

Narayan Swamy, M. R. 1994. *Tigers of Lanka: From Boys to Guerrillas*. Delhi: Konark Press.

Obeyesekere, Gananath. 1963. "Pregnancy Cravings (Dola-Duka) in Relation to Social Structure and Personality in a Sinhalese Village." In *American Anthropologist* 65 (2): 323–43.

———. 1979. "The Vicissitudes of the Sinhala-Buddhist Identity through Time and Change." In Michael Roberts (ed.), *Collective Identities, Nationalisms and Protest in Modern Sri Lanka*. 279–313. Colombo: Marga Institute.

Premadasa, Ranasinghe. 1986. *The Silent Sea (Golu Muhda)*. Trans. Neil Sri Wijesinghe. Columbo: Dayawansa Jayakody.

Risseeuw, Carla. 1988. *The Fish Don't Talk about the Water: Gender Transformation, Power and Resistance among Women in Sri Lanka*. Leiden: E. J. Brill.

Roberts, Michael. 1996. "Filial Devotion in Tamil Culture and the Tiger Cult of Martyrdom." *Contributions to Indian Sociology* (n.s.) 30(2): 245–72.

Schalk, Peter. 1992. "Birds of Independence: On the Participation of Tamil Women in Armed Conflict." *Lanka* (December).

——— .1994. "Women Fighters of the Liberation Tigers in Tamil Ilam: The Martial Feminism of Atel Palacinkam." In *South Asia Research* 14: 163–83.

Schrijvers, Joke. 1985. *Mothers for Life: Motherhood and Marginalization in the North Central Province of Sri Lanka*. Delft: Eburon.

Seneviratne, Maureen. 1969. *Some Women of the Mahawamsa and Culawamsa*. Colombo: H. W. Cave.

Siriwardene, Reggie, K. Indrapala, Sunil Bastian, and Sepali Kottegoda. 1982. *School Textbooks and Communal Relations in Sri Lanka*, Part I. Colombo: Council for Communal Harmony through the Media.

Siriweera, W. I. 1985. "The Dutthagamani—Elara Episode: A Reassessment." In *Ethnicity and Social Change*. Colombo: Social Scientists' Association.

Tennekoon, Serena. 1986. "Macho Sons and Man-made Mothers." *Lanka Guardian* 8(15): 12–3.

Walters, Jonathan. Forthcoming. "Buddhist History: The Pali Vamsas of Sri Lanka." In Inden, Ronald, Jonathan Walters and Daud Ali (eds.), *Querying the Medieval*. New York: Oxford University Press.

Chapter Twenty-Eight

Parenting Troops
The Summons to Acquiescence

Rela Mazali

Said "My darlin' son I wish I was the one
Who spared you spared your precious life"
—(Joan Baez, from "Isaac and Abraham,"
Play Me Backwards, Virgin Records, 1992)

Dissent as Disloyalty

This paper has grown out of my emerging experience as a soldier's mother, as my oldest son has enlisted and performed his three-year term of mandatory military duty in Israel's Defense Force. As I began work on it, I found I was having an unexpectedly hard time organizing and recording my thoughts. Though I had already written and spoken on the emotionally and politically loaded subject of Jewish parents, their sons,[1] and the military, I had never run up against the type of difficulty I was encountering here. I kept drawing a blank.

Only after several attempts did it dawn on me that this was in fact my subject. My extreme difficulty in stating my views on the parent-soldier-army-society complex—or in even fully recognizing what they were—was not just a personal block, it was at the core of what I was trying to write about. What I was looking at was an aspect of what I might call "the summons to acquiescence" experienced by soldiers' parents.

To illustrate what I mean by this, I'll begin with a story. When Israel invaded the villages and towns of southern Lebanon in 1982, there was a fairly common feeling among respected members of Peace Now and some of their associates, that we (that is, the Israeli peace movement) shouldn't protest the invasion of Lebanon as long as the troops were still in there. While the actual combat was going on, we should keep our peace (instead of keeping the peace) and refrain from undermining the soldiers' sense of homefront support and belief in their goal. Clearly a contradiction—when do you protest a war, when it's over?—the message was nevertheless, "Not while our boys are at it, not while they're in danger."

So for some weeks at the beginning of the war, significant parts of the Israeli peace movement were advocating no protest for fear of avoidable losses caused by undermining the troops' determination and morale. The line, then, was to refrain from criticizing the government's step of unnecessarily endangering the troops, so as not to endanger the troops. An underlying assumption that was made by those who took this line was that our government meant what it said, and that consequently the invasion of Lebanon would be over in a matter of days or weeks as proclaimed. (All of this of course proved disastrously wrong.) Then, the reasoning went, when the troops were out of danger, we would be able to state our case. I didn't get it. And indeed the largely suspect edge of the peace movement went on to protest regardless, both in the media and at demonstrations.

The first demonstrations against the 1982 invasion of Lebanon were more colorful than the usual Peace Now kind. They were always attended by a relatively good number of Palestinians. For me this heightened the slight sense of danger and excitement and lawlessness. At the time I didn't know a single Arab personally, either from Israel or the Occupied Territories (or very many of the Jewish marchers, either), and the simple fact of Arabs and Jews present at a combined demonstration had for me the sharp, highly political taste of leaving familiar, safe terrain.

Looking back, I think it is fairly clear that I was struggling with the difficulty of separating myself from an inherited and formerly largely unquestioned social affiliation, a separation I experienced as an unfocused sense of guilt and defection. It was no coincidence that communists and Arabs—the traditional "others" of Israeli society—figured in these sensations. On the other hand, because it was a separation and, moreover, an ideologically motivated one, it also gave me a new sense of self and autonomy. And this dual, ambivalent sense of independence and freedom coupled with misgivings and unease has intermittently accompanied the entire course of my personal political biography. I identify these as the tracks of my Jewish, Israeli, and feminine socialization, attaching deeply internalized fears to the nonobservance of standard sociopolitical groupings, to the possibility of visibly standing apart. Step outside and there is literally no knowing what will happen to you. I find them interesting in the degree to which they pinpoint fear as a central agent in the process of socialization.

However, in the initial reactions of the peace movement to Israel's 1982 invasion of Lebanon, the tension between autonomy and unease surfaces as a public rather than private experience. While my personal sense of unnamed fear and guilt may provide one anecdotal illustration, the general "not while our boys are in there" impulses were precisely of the same kind. All of these were products of the fear of hurting oneself and one's own by voicing dissent. All of them cringed at distancing oneself too pointedly—too far and fundamentally—from the group.

While such fear may well be present and active to some extent in every society or culture, it occurs in a highly potent form in the Jewish society of Israel. Internalized firmly and universally through Israeli Jewish socialization is the belief that Israel faces an ever-present state of existential peril. This belief is still deeply entrenched today, after nearly half a century of independent sovereignty, three decades of essentially unthreatened occupation of close to two million Palestinian Arabs, and almost two decades of stable peace with Egypt, formerly Israel's most powerful and feared enemy. In the context of such a belief, dissociating oneself from the collective is almost automatically perceived and experienced as creating a threat to it—by the collective and often as not by the dissenter as well. For a person who would voice dissent, apprehensions of separating from the clan are magnified by the sense of imminent danger and transmuted into a fear of committing treason.

And this sense of possible treason is at its height when the direct object of one's dissent is military action performed by and endangering an identifiable group of individuals. In these instances, fear of hurting by dissent converges with fear for the lives of individual people (whom, I might add, it is difficult to view as abstract statistics in the small and obligatorily chummy Israeli Jewish community). In such instances, the equation of dissent with lethal disloyalty becomes almost unavoidable. The story I have been telling, then, is about the fearfulness of dissent "when the boys are in there" and the imperative of a silence that functions as support.

Think how much more forceful that imperative is when one's son is among the troops. How much more fearful it is to question the troops' acts or the fundamental assumptions underlying their deployment.

Moreover, dissent by parents of troops may be fearful in other ways. Besides increasing individuals' vulnerability by undermining military performance, publicly voicing dissent may (or may be believed to) jeopardize a son's placement, assignments, promotion, and so forth within the military, and result in his relegation to a relatively menial, humiliating job. On a different level, it may question the justness of the army's and thus a son's actions, implying a moral judgment of one's son, which might prove extremely difficult for a parent to face. Or one's taking issue with the necessity for the military actions might render the possible death or injury of one's son unnecessary and meaningless, an outcome that would seem unbearable to many. Finally, disbelieving the vital need for national self-defense and hence for general (Jewish) induction would introduce the option (albeit an illegal one at present) of refusing or dodging the draft. This, in turn, could shift the responsibility for a son's decision to enlist away from the assumedly uncontrollable circumstances, and toward the parents' education and acculturation of their children. In the event of a son's death or injury, such a sense of personal responsibility for his choice would again prove unbearable.[2] Consequently, the pressures are enormous on soldiers' parents to avoid or suppress dissent on such fundamental levels.

Dissent Licensed and Limited

Behind the phenomenon of sons-turned-troops lies the parents' participatory cohesion with the collective, strengthening the sons' socialization. Such parents tend to fulfill specific expectations and play predefined roles as mothers and fathers of soldiers, through which they provide de facto support for the social institutions of army, collective, and state. In sustaining their sons' adherence to mobilization laws, parents too are upholding what is arguably the most fundamental social contract in Israeli Jewish society. This, I believe, is the central insight that I am offering:

along with their military duty, soldier sons in Israel are also performing the task of resocializing their parents.[3]

In the existing social order, Jewish parents in Israel are subject to a state-imposed, temporal limit terminating their ability to prevent their sons' exposure to violence. As opposed to the gradual give and take of maturing and acquiring individual independence, this line is arbitrary, sudden, and dictated from above. Beyond it lies the boys' likely exposure to physical danger and to violence—both as perpetrators and victims. An acceptance of this violence contradicts the ongoing investment of parenting and caretaking. And yet, the vast majority of Jewish Israeli parents nevertheless feel duty-bound to accept this limit and support their sons' fulfillment of the military task. They view it as necessary for the survival of the collective and therefore as a justified sacrifice. This is a view they have accepted on faith from political leaders, from their own parents and teachers, from standard media formulas and general consensus. Almost all have done so without attempting to analyze, delineate, or delimit the necessity in question (Mazali, 1993).

Military service is accordingly internalized by members of the Israeli Jewish collective as essential to a boy's right to belong to this group and more specifically to the inner circle of adult males. Literally a rite of passage, it is related to and spoken of in fatalistic, quasi-religious terms, as an inevitable, inescapable, pseudo-biological phase of male maturation. Wish as they might to ensure their sons' well-being, Jewish Israeli parents are consequently required to silence any impulse to object to their sons' induction. Rather, they must raise sons to accept and revere military service. I believe that widespread among these parents, though largely suppressed or transformed (for instance, into heroic nationalism), are feelings of guilt, shame, and inadequacy arising from this act.

Perhaps even more important is that such acquiescence feeds a profound sense of individual powerlessness that erodes participatory democracy. While soldier sons are probably the most pronounced example, I view children in general as agents through which each society reinforces the social cohesion of its adult, parent members. As parents guide, support, and (more often than we might wish to believe) coerce their children through institutions such as schools, religious rituals, and national holidays, they themselves are continually reaffirming their participation in the society that operates and performs them. They are enacting their practical acceptance of the rules and the underlying principles implemented through such social constructs. Although children commonly bring home concepts, projects, and instructions which their parents find objectionable, most parents tend to overlook these and avoid "making a fuss," so that their child need not stand apart from the group. Their sense of the child's (and their own) vulnerability moves the parents to protect their children by keeping silently in line, practically valuing group affiliation over other objectives, beliefs, or tastes. In so doing, parents lend de facto support to what they have found objectionable and reinforce their own social training for silence, acceptance, and passivity.

The predicament of soldiers' parents is, however, uniquely subtle. Such parents participate in their own resocialization through actions that are commonly considered far more positive and commendable than stifling objections and, in addition, are even more mundane and habitual. All that these mothers and fathers have to do is be good, caring parents.

As a soldier, a member of the order of warriors, a son becomes maximally vulnerable—potentially sacrificing his life and health in the service of the collective to which the family belongs, and in most Israeli families he consequently becomes maximally privileged—commanding the utmost support, loyalty, and, in fact, subordination of his immediate family. The shift to privileged status is a very sharp and sudden one, occurring very swiftly along with the boy's process of induction. Following it, his needs begin to dominate the family in a way which, in some respects, is strangely analogous to the "reign" of an infant. Family scheduling and planning are largely suspended to make room for the unpredictable comings and goings of the young soldier, and assigning top priority to being available for him either at home (if he gets leave) or at the base (if visiting is permitted). Soldiers on leave are often given privileged access to family resources such as cars. Parents tend to invest concentrated physical service toward fulfilling the son's needs while exempting him totally from domestic responsibilities. This may constitute a total reversal of the pre-army family work-sharing that was gradually achieved as the son matured. Over weekends and leaves at home, especially during the first difficult period of acclimatization and basic training, many parents provide services such as doing the laundry, cooking favorite dishes, hosting the son's guests, running urgent errands, purchasing helpful accessories, chauffeuring, arranging and accompanying visits to doctors or dentists, and so on. When the young soldier can be visited on base, they make long weekend pilgrimages to see him, taking along picnic lunches, friends, girlfriends, clean underwear, and other necessities and luxuries.

The suspending of plans, the unpredictability, the servicing and the uncompromising placement of the son's needs first are accompanied by a continuous state of waiting, further intensifying the sense of suspension. Parents wait for telephone calls, for his arrival on weekends, often without knowing whether he'll get leave, stay on duty, or be "grounded" at base as punishment for one of many inevitable missteps. They wait for postcards, letters, calls from buddies who pass on the son's regards. They wait to hear he's all right. Family phone conversations are often limited in duration to ensure parents' accessibility should the soldier get a chance to call. Many parents tend to shorten or avoid trips abroad during a son's (three-year) term of active duty.

Parents of soldiers thus find themselves limiting mobility and autonomy in a variety of ways, as do parents of infants. Like many infants' parents, they often share experiences with other parents in their condition, exchanging information, humor, and support, together developing a discourse of acquiescence with the family's new circumstances. And like infants' parents, they too feel emotionally compensated in many cases, taking pride in the son's new and privileged status and his personal achievements. However, while the state of infancy and the conditions of caring it imposes consist in biological and developmental facts and needs, soldierhood and the conditions it imposes on parents are created entirely by social contract and law. Therefore, when parents care relatively selflessly for a soldier son, they also affirm and reinforce the social contract that makes him a soldier in the first

place. By following their parental impulse to serve the personal needs of their enlisted son, they also acknowledge and serve the interests of the state that enlists him.
Moreover, the majority of them override a powerful parental impulse to protect and
preserve their child, surrendering to the collective that which is most precious. It is
by no coincidence that the biblical tale of Isaac's near-sacrifice by Abraham was a
tale about ultimate obedience. A mother's obedience in sending off her child to the
army is indeed ultimate. And so too are the underlying sense of powerlessness, guilt,
and shame which, I believe, arise from this submission to the state. In serving the
state, she is necessarily betraying her son.

Paradoxical is the emergence over recent years of activism and protest among
parents of a number of soldiers killed in training accidents (currently estimated to
constitute 60 percent of the death rate in the Israeli Defense Force [IDF]). A look at
the contents of this activism, the justifications offered for it, and especially the
boundaries it sets itself provides a body of complex but sound evidence for the
thesis that soldier sons act as powerful resocializing agents, even and perhaps especially (cynical as this may sound) when they are dead.

One widely publicized accident occurred on November 5, 1992. An elite unit was
performing a live-ammunition drill at Tze'elim firing range in the Negev Desert,
allegedly preparing for a special top-secret mission, when a rocket fired in the wrong
direction hit and killed five soldiers on the spot. Coined "Tze'elim B" by the media
(an equally fatal accident had occurred at the same firing range about two years
earlier), the incident engendered a prolonged battle between the army and four of
the five bereaved families, who consistently demanded the resignation of the top-
ranking officers responsible for the planning and implementation of the drill. In the
upshot, two of the lower-ranking officers in direct command of the drill and the
firing were tried by a military court in Tel-Aviv.[4]

Previously censored in the press for many years, such accidents are now routinely
publicized by the media, giving rise to a context within which dissent seems legitimized. The consensually recognized, extreme pain and loss suffered by the bereaved
families, along with the explicit fact of avoidability and the absence of a sound
security-based justification for the deaths, make harsh criticism on the part of the
families legitimate and even expected. Immediately following the accident, the media solicited and reported the five families' reactions. Their opinions were subsequently reported extensively throughout the prolonged chain of events that has
followed: two military investigations, a decision by the Head Military Attorney to
initiate legal proceedings, the consequent resignation of a top officer responsible for
the mission, the head military attorney's retraction and amendment of his first decision, the return to post of the top officer, and the trial of two lower-ranking
officers fingered as directly responsible.

For the duration of this process, four of the five families have repeatedly expressed a great deal of anger, disillusionment, and severe criticism of the military.
As stated, they have consistently demanded the resignation of the top-ranking officers responsible. They have also lobbied for legislation that would place the investigation of fatal military accidents in the hands of an independent, nonmilitary
authority. One of these families has also petitioned the High Court of Justice for

permission to add a line of personal text to the standard inscription on their dead son's tombstone, subsequently leading to a motion for legislation.

And yet, evident in press coverage of these forcefully opinionated people is a deeply embedded perception of military service as presupposed and beyond their control. Moreover, nowhere in the course of their monologues do any of these parents offer evaluations of the objectives toward which the state is utilizing its army, the army to which they have unquestioningly sent their sons. Both of these fundamental levels are taken for granted, left outside of the critical discourse, firmly entrenched as areas in which the parents remain passive subjects.

Eran Wechselbaum, for instance, was nine years old when his parents emigrated to the United States. He had had the legal option of exemption from military service in the IDF but served and died. In an interview immediately following his death (Rosenbloom, 1992), his mother Chava said that his decision to return to Israel for his military service was received by her and his father with mixed feelings. And yet, she said, "We knew it would come some day. He had always wanted to serve in the army. . . . We let him decide for himself . . . I knew that with us, away from Israel, he wouldn't be happy" (Rosenbloom, 1992).[5]

Much later, four families—Shilo, Shifran, Cohen, and Wechselbaum—published a joint letter opposing a plea bargain for one of the lower-ranking officers on trial. Among other things, the letter stated, "We encouraged our sons to serve in this unit, where people take considerable responsibility, for better or for worse" (Levin, 1994). Military service remains a basic unquestionable premise. In addition, active parental encouragement toward service in a dangerous, difficult unit reveals a basic trust that the army is not being misused by the state. Such encouragement can only be taken to indicate these parents' confidence that even the most dangerous and daring missions are justified and responsibly decided on by the politicians directing the army.

Shlomo Cohen, father of Arie, eventually emerged as the most vocal of these activist parents. Some of his statements nearly break with the presupposition of army service as inevitable, but though sometimes self-contradictory, he finally upholds it. In an article published one week after the head military attorney's amended decision to try only two lower-rank officers, while merely reprimanding the two generals involved, he said,

> I used to think that the army was a privilege. Since the tragedy I've changed my mind. More and more I see military service not as a privilege but as a duty. If it's a duty, everyone will draw their own conclusions. . . . The attorney's decision was predictable due to the deep-rooted norm in the IDF since 1948 of cover-up, fudging and lying in order to keep on doing the same things. . . . They're conning us. We brought up children to love the country. There's a limit to lies and cover-up. . . . This is another generation. Not like the old one. The generation that knows and understands won't agree to the IDF norms. You have to think twice about sending a son to an unreliable system. They should tell parents something might happen to them. As things are now, the military system won't hold out for long. No one accepts responsibility. (Ifargan, 1994)

Cohen cites a long tradition (since 1948) of coverup, fudging, and lying with which he was well acquainted as a fighter in one of the first and most legendary commando units of the IDF (Unit 101). Nevertheless, he "used to think that the army was a privilege" and "brought up children to love the country," by which he clearly means serving its army faithfully. Though fully aware of them, he formerly failed to set "a limit to lies and cover-up," refusing to perform reserve military duty only after his son's death. The danger he foresees, the disaster his activism sets out to prevent, is the possibility that "the military system won't hold out for long." He is questioning the wisdom of sending a son to an unreliable system, not the need or justification for the system itself. These go without saying, they are taken for granted. As Yitzhak Laor has stated, "The political hegemony in Israel has, for a long time now, had at its disposal that which is nationally taken for granted, the security premise" (Laor, 1994).

Cohen's formulation, "They should tell parents something might happen to them," would be downright comical if not for the premise stated by Laor, automatically read into the text by almost any Israeli Jew and entailing a distinction between accidents and necessary, worthwhile, unavoidable injury in the military. Of course, something might happen to soldiers—that's what armies are all about. But the basic premises of the army's necessity and its reliable utilization by the government inform Cohen's account of his activism.

> We, the bereaved families, will fight for investigations to be taken out of the hands of the army. That every accident which occurs and ends in death, be investigated by an external team and not have the IDF investigate itself. We will fight for parents' involvement in the [investigation of the] deaths of their dear ones. . . . If I don't do anything and another tragedy happens, I'll feel guilty that I didn't do what I should have, especially for others. (Laor, 1994)

He and the other parents are earnestly working for the good of the system and the collective. They are thus reaffirming the validity and importance of this system.

Ayala Katz is the widow of Rami Katz, one of five soldiers killed in the 1990 "Ze'elim A" accident. Katz, too, has long been active in pressing for better safety measures in army drills and practice. In a recent press interview she explained, "In a few years my son will enter the army and I have to go on trying to keep them doing something about safety, I can't allow myself to keep quiet" (Meidan, 1994). Despite the futile waste of her husband's life, it is taken wholly for granted by Katz that her son will serve, indeed needs to serve, in the army. Any breach of Israel's basic social contract remains unthinkable.

Yael German, whose son, Eyal, was killed in a training accident in November 1987, wrote in memoriam, "Eyal was killed in a training accident. His death was in vain" (Meidan, 1994). German and her husband founded an association for the prevention of accidents in the military. In Meidan's article, German explains,

> We did it all quietly, with and not against the army, but it was clear both to us and the IDF representatives that if we weren't taken seriously we would stop being good little girls and boys and go public. We planned booths collecting signatures telling

mothers, "Beware, soldiers are killed not only in wars." . . . It was hugely important to me not to become a bitter woman so I chose the positive direction, going along with the army, not against it. (Meidan, 1994)

Despite planning that verges on a challenge to both the law and the social contract, German states her choice—not to become an outsider, or in her words "a bitter woman," to go along with the system rather than opposing it.

Lea Zuryano is mother of Gil, killed in a helicopter accident in 1992. She says, "We've discovered that all these years we lived blindly. I never imagined that this was how things were managed, that there's this kind of negligence in the army and then it's covered up" (Meidan, 1994). Conversely, she states, "We're not our parents' generation, we served in the IDF and know exactly what it is and we aren't afraid to be critical" (Meidan, 1994). But this criticism has its limits, reflected in her bottom line, "We're demanding that the investigation of training accidents be taken out of the hands of the army. It's obviously absurd for the army to investigate itself" (Meidan, 1994). Portrayed by Meidan as the opposition, who unlike German works against the army, Zuryano nevertheless views herself as acting for the good of the system whose fundamental validity she is not questioning.

At the very core of socialization is that which is taken for granted, that which remains unquestioned, accepted by the entire collective as reality, "the world, the way things are," and whose refutation is literally unthinkable. While sharply reformist in content, the protest and activism of these parents reiterate and strengthen the existing boundaries between what can legitimately be questioned and criticized (and hence reformed) and what there is no question about. To paraphrase a claim directed by Yitzhak Laor at David Ben-Gurion (Laor, 1994), these parents are very good at separating what should be discussed from what should stay silent. This is the very essence of socialization. The collective silence about what need never be questioned is vindicated especially forcefully where there is a seeming license to dissent.

Activism Muted

The realm of "what should stay silent" at the heart of Israeli socialization is, moreover, systematically extended by the secrecy imposed upon military matters. The security premise grants a sweeping and largely unquestioned blanket of silence to the military and almost everything associated with it, which in Israel means a huge portion of state and state-related activities. Questions about these are presented as potentially dangerous, information about them should be kept confidential, exposure to almost any degree is claimed and indeed felt to endanger one's son or one's neighbors' sons.[6] Parents of many soldiers acquire limited access to the secret inner security circle, gaining some amount of knowledge of military matters through their sons. They accordingly become partial secret sharers, supposedly privileged yet by the same token bound to withhold the privileged knowledge they may have. All of this feeds directly into habits of silence, of passive refrainment from information-seeking or spreading, of complying with (security) dictates—habits that maintain the unquestioned inner core of collective conduct and belief. A central component in the resocialization of many soldiers' parents, then, is their enlistment into this regular practice of silence, of habitually suppressing information, opinions, and inquiry.

Surprisingly, perhaps, this last point is evident in some of the attitudes and statements of radical political activists who have become soldiers' parents. These are parents who do not take the "security premise" for granted. Nevertheless, they do take for granted another related premise, according to which the alternative to belief in the former has to be belief in the army's abolition. For the most part, such parents too stop short at this point. They too (I might say, myself included) comply with the role of soldiers' parents, supporting and sustaining their sons through their term in the military, while most avoid explicitly suggesting that their sons choose to refuse or dodge this term of duty.[7] Similarly to Chava Wechselbaum, they state their reason as respect for these sons' autonomy and freedom. I will cite some of the instances I've encountered.

The first woman[8] has been a radical peace activist for quite a few years, despite her concurrent and persistent membership in the decidedly mainstream Labor Party. I met her through her activity in organizing Israeli-Palestinian meetings under the auspices of the "21st Year," a group that sought civil noncooperation with Israel's continuing occupation of the West Bank and Gaza. Later, while working on a film about the actions and reactions of Israeli soldiers involved in suppressing the Palestinian uprising of 1987 (Testimonies Group, 1993) I asked her, the mother of two soldiers, if she would agree to be interviewed for the film. She asked to delay her answer until she could consult her sons, one of whom was already a professional army officer. Her reply, when she got back to me, was that he had asked her not to do a film interview as they felt it might jeopardize his status. She did agree, however, to an unfilmed interview, viewing the film as a more potent, public, and therefore more endangering medium (which could, of course, have been seen by the same token as a promising means toward her political objectives). This was coming from a woman who had not hesitated to continue her political activism throughout her sons' terms of military service. However, a publicly visible interview, directly focusing on the connections between her opinions and her sons' roles as soldiers, seemed too frightening. In this case, she placed her sons' judgments and needs first, and through them upheld those of the army and the state.

Another soldier's mother who consented to an interview was an activist in the "Horim Neged Schika" (Parents against Erosion) group, which publicly protested the then government's policies. Her activities began and continued for two years concurrently with the military service of her son, during 1988–89. At a preliminary interview, she spoke explicitly of the "dissonance between the sons' military service and what they have to do there, and the parents' objection to the occupation." She told me, "For the first time I felt that I was a collaborator," but said that despite her son's extreme distress when he first took part in operations in the Occupied Territories, he was very frightened when she decided to take action. "He didn't want me to tell him to refuse [to serve in the territories]. I didn't feel I could tell him to. Refusing mandatory [as opposed to reserve] duty is extremely difficult," she said. "Quite early on I felt I had to dissociate my activism from my son. . . . I couldn't burden him with the whole complexity of my personal entanglement." On a few occasions she suggested citing his experiences in her protest activities but he refused. While bravely persistent in speaking out publicly against the government and the policies being implemented through the army, she felt bound to a silent acceptance of the personal choices of her soldier son. Here, the self-imposed silence clearly held at bay the possibility of a confrontation between mother and son on painful moral issues.

This mother reported that in a matter of months, her son, who had reacted with severe and fully verbalized shock and distress following his first encounter with army operations in the territories, stopped speaking of what he was seeing and doing. He developed the view that it was a job which had to be done and was better off being done by people like himself. Later on, she said, he acquired a sense of camaraderie, loyalty to and pride in his unit, and made his peace with the army. Eventually he also claimed that things in the territories were not so bad as before.

In this case, mother and son clearly seem to have reinforced each other's ability to live with the dictates of his military service. Despite a firm commitment to active dissent outside the home, the mother's acceptance of her son's silence, her own silence within the family, and her practical acquiescence with the social-military contract seem to undercut if not negate her own activism. Indeed, she referred to this activism apologetically, as deriving from her "personal entanglement," relegating it to the realm of individual psychology. Revealingly, she said: "I have a problem. What right do I have to undermine [his] very shaky mental balance, while I too am simply protecting my own?"

"I'm ashamed to tell this," said another mother, a central activist in a determined, highly visible group of parents who opposed Israel's presence in Lebanon and called themselves "Horim Neged Shtika"—Parents against Silence. The silence they were breaking was none other than the same refrainment from protest, "while our boys are in there." And yet, two years earlier when her son, then seventeen, had suggested that he might try for the military computer unit, "God forgive me," she told me, "I answered, 'So your friend Uri will bust his guts and you'll be sitting at a computer?' " or, in other words, shirking his duty. She was active in the peace movement before his induction and before Israel's invasion of Lebanon. "When the war [in Lebanon] broke out," she said, "I was the only one in my social circle who opposed it right from the outset. I felt terribly alienated." She "spent an entire summer outside the Prime Minister's [Menachem Begin's] house," or canvassing on streets and house to house. As she did so, her son told her, "I don't think the timing is right, but you do what you believe should be done and so will I."

At her son's request, this mother, divorced for many years and with no other children, had to sign an official form stating her consent to his service in a combat unit. This is standard procedure in the IDF in the case of only sons wishing to join combat units. "I very much disliked having to sign," she told me, "but I felt it wasn't his fault that he was an only son." Though she gave consent that she could have withheld (although probably at the cost of a severe crisis in relations with her son), she felt, as he neared his induction, increasingly afraid of any kind of intervention in the direction his service was to take. "Who knows what can happen in any job," she said, referring to the fatal collapse of an IDF administration building in Tyre, Lebanon. "If you intervene, I told myself, you will feel responsible." Signing consent, however, didn't register as taking responsibility. Because of the belief that no other choice existed, both her consent and her fear expressed fatalism. "At the time I still believed it a necessity," she said.

Despite her breach of the public silence, no analogous process occurred on the personal level. "During his mandatory term the possibility of his refusal simply never crossed my mind," she said, "even when I objected to the war and thought it absurd. I thought I'd go ahead and do what I could and he would just keep up what he was doing." When he "graduated" to a yearly month of reserve duty and was called up to the Occupied Territories, she swiftly developed a conscious wish that he would refuse and, as she put it, "conveyed the message to him repeatedly." Even then, however, she did not tell him explicitly that she wished he would refuse, "not wanting to dictate to him." She mused thoughtfully over my inquiry as to why openly stating an opinion should necessarily amount to dictating.

Finally, a similar account—"We didn't state our opinion, it was his own decision"—was given to me by a couple whose son was one of the few to resist service in the Occupied Territories in the course of their mandatory term of duty. These parents, both longtime and active ràdicals, nevertheless silenced any explicit assertion of their positions prior to his decision, although following their son's refusal and throughout his imprisonment they gave him their full support.

Resisting Resocialization — A Start

All these instances seem to suggest that the impetus of Jewish Israeli parents' resocialization through the soldierhood of their sons is extremely powerful. These parents' complicity with the summons to military duty is very deep-seated. Even in cases of sharply dissenting parents, it imposes limits either on the dissent itself or on the intimate, interpersonal dialogue between parents and sons (and usually on both). Limiting dissent on such an intensely personally important subject must certainly deepen the general disempowerment of parents as active citizens. In Israel, where the vast majority of Jewish sons are inducted, the significance of such an effect on the society may well be enormous.

As regards the military, parental complicity would seem to be crucial. The Israeli military operates in close geographical proximity to its civilian constituency and soldiers move regularly between civilian and military contexts, which potentially exposes them to severe incompatibilities between their identities as civilians, sons, husbands, fathers, and their identities as fighters. While working on *Testimonies,* I was continuously preoccupied with the human context enabling the military actions. Absent from our interviews and from the screen, and yet vital for the occurrence of the events being shown, was the normalcy maintained in the participant soldiers' homes by their mothers, fathers, siblings, wives, girlfriends. Worried about their welfare, glad to see them home safe on leave or following reserve duty, almost always uncritical of their actions as individuals (even in homes where the military as a whole was criticized), often unaware of their individual actions and content to keep these blanketed behind "security secrecy," their families went on accepting them, supporting them, reinforcing their sense of decency, of balanced, sensible, customary existence. While some of the men we interviewed remarked on the terrible loneliness and sadness they felt in these unquestioning homes, the family message was coming through clearly: "Go ahead and do what you have to, we trust you and don't want to know, so there will be no unpleasantness."

As I began to understand this over the years leading up to my two sons' inductions, I intentionally started transgressing the boundary between the public sphere and my home, between my children's (supposedly) insular, independent act of "deciding for themselves" and my political views and activism outside the home. As an attempt to offer some degree of resistance against my complicity as a soldier's mother, I purposely brought home parts of my public political activism, introducing it into the private interpersonal conversation and linking or confronting it with my sons' future/current soldierhood. Refusing the silence expected of me while my boys "are in there," I made and make a point of discussing with them my questions about the justification of both their military service per se and of its central components. This may sound simple and self-evident. It isn't. It is painful and frightening to question the value of my sons' efforts as soldiers, being fully aware of how excruciating these efforts are. These efforts are required of them by law and Jewish-Israeli socialization. Still, I try to talk openly about my doubts as to whether these efforts are really necessary. I try to listen honestly to their self-searching responses. The result is a fairly complicated mother-son configuration. To confront anyone, let alone a son or daughter, with a critical view of what they are doing, and to do this in a productive way, is always complicated. And it can't stay impersonal or abstract, because even though having to be soldiers may not be "their fault," the point of stating my views is to place responsibility for the decisions and actions they (and I) are taking.

Finally, I try to undercut some of the roles expected of me. This is no less complicated. Just as supporting and succoring a soldier son amounts to supporting the army, noncooperation with the army can conversely mean nonsupport of a son. One of the roles that I take particular care not to play is that of martyr-mother who can't sleep nights, who is incessantly aware of waiting in fear for her son to return but bears this bravely, who assumes and commands the respect and reverence of family, neighbors, and friends for her pain and courage. While there is no way of keeping out the fear, because it's real, I've usually been able to resist the halo. Instead of living out the required (addictive) tragic excitement and life-on-the-edgeness, I've tried to domesticate the fear and make it useful, to legitimize rather than fetishize it. I express it as I feel it, stating outright that I'm afraid and that I'm angry that I'm afraid, because I don't consider it necessary or inescapable, because I don't consider its causes worthwhile. Such, I think, are the nuances that comprise an individual's resistance to her (re-)socialization.

Not clear-cut endeavors, any of these. Not always carried out well or gracefully or tactfully. Not always carried out, period. Sometimes it's simply too scary and I stay silent. But I try to keep pushing the limit.

NOTES

1. While secular Jewish women also serve terms of mandatory military duty in Israel, the content and structure of their service is vastly different from that of men, embodying and implementing a very different social dynamic (see, for instance, Izraeli [1994]; Mazali [1993]). Thus, this article deals with relations between parents and inducted sons only. Also, male members of some minority groups (Druze, Bedouin, and Circassian) in Israel are inducted into or may volunteer for military service. While a good deal of the social and family conduct surrounding their induction and terms of duty may bear similarities to those prevalent in Jewish society, this article restricts itself to the latter, as I have not researched the characteristics of sons' military service in minority group families.

2. The recurring phenomenon of suicides committed by parents whose sons have been killed in the military may suggest that some parents do retain a sense of personal responsibility for their son's choices and death despite the rationale of a national, existential imperative.

3. It may be contended that this is true only of a fairly recent period, during which the immediacy of possible collective peril and the tangible need for self-defense have lessened in Israel and become increasingly debatable. However, popular folklore and literature include numerous stories of high school boys stealing away from home, against their parents' will, to fight in pre-state Jewish military organizations. It is significant that such tales have been widely disseminated and applauded.

4. Each of these officers has been sentenced to three months suspended imprisonment and demotion by one rank.

5. I find it interesting that although Ms. Wechslebaum states, "We let him decide for himself," she implicitly associates herself with the soldiers directly responsible for Eran's accidental killing, saying, "I pity the soldiers who fired the rocket at least as much as I pity myself but someone in the higher ranks is to blame."

6. It is on this point that the above parents' activism is indeed significantly, perhaps even radically, reformist. With the active and crucial partnership of the media, they have, to some extent, broken (at least part of) the seal of silence imposed on all military matters in Israel. Without detracting from the personal courage required to take such action, it should be noted that their position is unique in that they can no longer endanger their (dead) sons by doing so.

7. There is currently no provision in Israeli mobilization laws for conscientious objection among secular Jewish men. (Orthodox men can defer army service indefinitely to study religious texts.) A Jewish boy eligible for army service and refusing to serve theoretically risks years of imprisonment in military jails, though in reality the few men who have refused to serve their mandatory term of duty were discharged on grounds of unfitness after up to about a year's imprisonment.

8. While the former examples are all based on published interviews from which I can of course quote freely, the activist parents I am quoting in the following examples were not interviewed for the express purpose of the present article, aside from one who requested anonymity. I have accordingly refrained from their identification in this article.

REFERENCES

Ifargan, Shimon. 1994. "The Death of the Sacred Cows or Ze'elim 2 as Allegory." *Kol Hangegv*, Friday, March 11.

Izraeli, Daphna. 1994. "On Women's Status. in Israel: Women in the Army." *International Problems — State and Society* 33, no. 63.

Laor, Yitzhak. 1994. "The Torn Tongue." *Ha'aretz*, Monday, September 19.

Levin, Ron. 1994. "Parents of the Dead in Tze'elim B Tragedy: 'Where is the Commander's Courage?' " *Ma'ariv*, Wednesday, March 2.

Mazali, Rela. 1993. "Military Service as Initiation Rite." *Challenge* 4, no. 4: 36–37.

Meidan, Anat. 1994. "I So Much Wanted to Save Him." *Yediot Aharonot*, Wednesday, July 13. (The article was written as a preview for the film *Raising a Child Who's Gone* [1994], directed by Chaim Tal, on the activism of bereaved parents [especially mothers].)

Rosenbloom, Sarit. 1992. "The Tze'elim Tragedy: The Pain." *Yediot Aharonot*, Sunday, November 11.

Testimonies Group. 1993. *Testimonies*. Director: Ido Sela. [English subtitles.]

Part VI

Peace Culture and Peace Action

Chapter Twenty-Nine

Women or Weapons?

Betty A. Reardon

This is a time of crises and opportunities, a time of crucial choices for all human societies. No more critical choices must be made than those of either endorsing or rejecting state violence as a mechanism of political policy, and of either maintaining authoritarian inequality or instead promoting universal human dignity. Women can play a role central to both choices.

Women have been the largest group to be oppressed by doctrines of inequality. Their exclusion from political power has left them with virtually no part in making decisions to use violence in the name of their societies. Thus, women have been less able to mitigate violence in public affairs, and have only recently been able to publicize the "private" violence they suffer. Thus, we should consider the possibilities for overcoming violence that might result from women's growing political empowerment. Women's political participation constitutes the best hope for achieving a culture of peace. The choices of nonviolence over militarism and equality over sexism underlie the broader choice of a democratic peace culture over a weapons-dependent patriarchy.

In recent decades women have become more politically active than ever before. Many hold public office, and some very few hold the highest national positions. Nonetheless, women are still a minority, shockingly underrepresented in the halls of power. In most practical senses, patriarchy prevails in all states and thus still painfully manifests itself in the international system. Most palpably, this occurs at the United Nations, especially in the highest levels of the Secretariat, and in the ambassador delegations. With the notable exception of the Security Council, women cannot be found in the ministries of defense, security, and international offices. The male-dominated state system has largely rejected women's overtures toward a truly equal political partnership.

The state system governing world politics is a creature of patriarchy. For nearly five centuries it has presumed that women were inferior to men. It has never benefited women nor does it promise to do so. Indeed, the patriarchal power structures that control the state system fear women's full political participation. They seem to believe that equitable and democratic politics would undermine the system. Governments claim that peace is not a woman's issue, and they have blocked, for example, the international disarmament action plans that have emerged from the world conferences on women. This reflects their opposition to women's participation in security matters, their deliberate avoidance of the possibilities for demilitarization and disarmament, and their arrogant disregard of equity and democracy.

Most women, particularly feminist peace activists, view as transformational the inevitable changes that will result from greater equity and democracy. Even more than to achieve their own equality, women seek full political partnership with men to realize these broader transformations. Women have long envisioned transformations such as those that have inspired UNESCO's Culture of Peace Program and *Our Global Neighborhood* (U.N. Division for the Advancement of Women, 1995)— a report on the requirements for the survival of Earth and humanity. The state system still shows little sign of comprehending our situation as one humanity, dependent upon one fragile planet. It has not amended its behavior to address the undeniable threats to survival posed by the war system and its weapons dependency.

Given the reciprocal relationship feminists discern between patriarchy and the institution of war, and the peace movement's growing focus on the urgency of disarmament, we must more deeply reflect on weapons—the tools and icons of the war system. We must consider the functions of weaponry, the pragmatic rationales for their continued development, and their psychosocial and symbolic impact.

Weaponry is the main determinant of power in the international state system. Nations believe that "adequate" quantities of "advanced" weapons and "weapons systems" will determine their global position, and how other nations deal with them. Vast resources are spent on weapons, perhaps more for status and national pride than for defense or "security." Only states may legally acquire such weaponry and maintain organized armed forces. They have the exclusive legal power to exercise violence, a power legitimated by the state's responsibility to preserve social order and protect the national interest.

Preserving order and providing protection, however, have legitimated force other than state violence. The culture of war encourages violence by actors other than the state. When states use violence to serve their purposes, they legitimize the use of violence by others for other purposes. If states used more nonviolent approaches to achieving their policy goals, societies would also do so. But such a shift would require an authentic commitment to democracy and equality. States hold fast to their dependence on violence largely to avoid this commitment and to maintain present power arrangements. Armed force perpetuates existing power structures while purporting to protect the society.

The patriarchy has as much of an interest in legitimating state violence as it has in avoiding gender equality. The claim to the lawful use of lethal force maintains the patriarchal state, and limits challenges to that system, including the challenges of democracy and of women's equality.

The patriarchy's control of legitimate state violence also maintains social and economic systems of dominance that preclude the equitable and democratic relations essential to a culture of peace. Indeed, a greater access to superior force and a sophisticated range of weaponry have maintained the public authority's monopoly over violence and the primacy of dominant/subservient relationships that accounts for most violence against women. This profoundly affects all human affairs, and has produced the most agonizing experiences of human history.

No greater evidence exists for the need for women to participate in determining if, when, and how weaponry are used than the frequent, ineffective, and unbalanced (in all senses of the word) way armed force is applied. More than any other manifestation of patriarchy, the compulsive use and acquisition of weaponry illustrates the male-dominated state system's abuse of power. Indeed, it seems to be a destructive addiction.

We must confront that addiction by reconsidering the aforementioned crucial choices: between human dignity and authoritarian inequality; between coercive force and authentic democracy. We must do so while recognizing the interrelationship between violence and inequality, and particularly between the war system and women's oppression. And we must consider weapons as emblematic of a culture of war.

Of course, we all experience the cultures of war from the perspective of our own cultures, and thus the conditions cited here must be regarded as at least somewhat culturally specific. Nevertheless, most of these issues pertain to most world cultures, and thus we can pursue a cross-cultural inquiry into women's contributions to a global culture of peace. The most significant contribution women can now make would be to illuminate the relationships between the culture of war—or a "weapons culture," as Alva Myrdal called it—and the systematic violation of the human rights of women. Power elites must be convinced to undo the exclusion of women from high-level policymaking on matters of peace and security.

The culture Myrdal decried has been shaped by an addiction to weaponry that has profoundly influenced all public policy and the daily lives of most citizens. For women, the impact has been decidedly negative. Extensive research shows that the limits arms spending imposes on social expenditures explain the inability of societies to meet human needs. When human needs are denied, women (and through them, their children) most frequently experience the greatest deprivation. As Ruth Sivard—an economist, peace advocate, and UNESCO Peace Education Peace Prize laureate—has documented for over two decades in her *World Military and Social Expenditures* (Sivard, 1995), policymakers have chosen weaponry over welfare, denying fundamental economic security to tens of millions of people.

We must also document other ways militarism erodes fundamental security and debases the quality of life by its effects on the environment, human rights, and the possibilities for nonviolent conflict resolution. These effects constitute a net security deficit. War and war preparation, especially weapons design, development, deployment, and traffic, make all societies less secure. These conditions have instigated women's peace movements and much public discussion, yet military expenditures have not declined. Even less consideration has been given to using alternatives to weapons for defense or alternatives to armed conflict for resolving disputes. A reluctance to consider alternatives to destructive habits constitutes addictive behavior.

Addicts frequently "need" ever larger quantities of that to which they are addicted. Thus, in 1996 the United States Congress budgeted even more than the president requested for weapons systems while imposing further cuts in social expenditures. And peacekeeping operations have become more dependent on armed forces, and thus more costly.

Weapons still constitute the primary instruments of political power, whether used by states or their challengers. Weapons are seen as the only reliable source of defense in a world of intense power conflicts. The addiction to weapons survives, and the dependency remains, even though arms accumulation promotes dire dangers and no real security. Thus, a culture of peace requires us to reconceptualize security, and even more importantly, power. We must transcend everything symbolized by weapons, and confront the weaponry addiction. Above all, it requires "breaking the habit."

Women have greatly influenced recent trends toward redefining security. Their mobilization against the arms race, military spending, and nuclear testing reflects their long-held view that military security does not equal human security; in fact, it undermines it. Real human security lies in the well-being we experience when we're protected against harm of all kinds: when our basic needs are met, when we experience human dignity and human rights, and when we have a healthy, natural environment capable of sustaining life. Yet the fixation on weapons and military security undermines all these sources of human security. Since women typically have more comprehensive perspectives on security, their participation in policymaking is essential to redefining both security and power.

The patriarchal state system conceptualizes power as the ability to coerce or enforce. But as suggested by the *Power Handbook* of the National Federation of Social Democratic Women of Sweden, many women who seek political power see it very differently: "Power enables us to exercise influence and to effect change, at the same time as we must be prepared to accept responsibility for the decisions which we help to push through" (*Power Handbook*, n.d.).

Women thus seek power to make change. They're willing to face the responsibilities of their choices in ways male power elites have avoided. But those elites have tried to dissuade women from seeking power. According to the *Power Handbook*, they'd rather keep women politically subservient by making women invisible or ridiculous, by withholding information from them, or by burdening women with guilt and shame for pursuing public careers.

Nevertheless, women still seek a power partnership to transform the culture of war. They want to transform power into a medium for exercising responsibility rather than privilege. They are pursuing what Riane Eisler and David Loye have called a "partnership society" (Eisler and Loye, 1990). The notion of power as not merely capacity but also responsibility underlies the drive to replace dominance with partnership. Responsible partnership should apply to all our relationships: earth-human, governments-citizens, North-South, and women-men. But responsibility cannot be exercised by agents who suffer the kinds of addictions now held by current elites.

Like all addictions, weaponry addiction negatively affects one's whole environment. But the addicts themselves may suffer the most destructive effects. For example, second-hand smoke may disturb or even hurt bystanders, but smokers themselves are even more likely to suffer, often dying from destroyed lungs and impaired hearts. They are victimized by instruments of pleasure that instead act more like weapons. And weapons are frequently turned on those whose well-being they are supposed to serve.

Weapons are instruments to incapacitate, injure, and, especially, to kill. Any object used or intended for such purposes is a weapon. A knife can be a kitchen implement or a murder weapon. The mind of the user makes all the difference. A mind conditioned by a culture of war views weapons as essential for dealing with those who are identified as threatening. As in the case of smoking and drugs, even though addicts might understand the harmful effects of their addictions, they cannot function without those things that ensure their sense of well-being. Addicts are generally insecure persons who have difficulty confronting reality. Contemporary societies "depend" on weapons for their sense of security, even though they often realize the detrimental effects. The intersection between drug trafficking and arms trafficking makes this chillingly clear. Thus, when we consider the effects of weaponry generally, we should recognize the link between drug addiction and the social violence inflicted by weapons.

Women's peace groups and other organizations have tried to publicize these detrimental effects. But since the media typically ignore the weapons culture and the policies that intensify it, most citizens remain ignorant of these realities. In many ways, women peace activists play a social role similar to the way spouses, families, and friends try to make addicts see the negative effects of their behaviors.

In the case of weapons addiction, these effects go beyond economic deprivation. Having arms always exacerbates the threat of armed conflict. Few nations have escaped terrorist threats and random attacks on their citizens. Yet this violence often results from the weapons governments have developed to promote their "national security." Some governments have turned these weapons on their own citizens, ostensibly to protect national security from internal threats. Some terrorists have also used these weapons, which they've received from governments who believe they're supporting "freedom fighters."

In the United States, private citizens have acquired a proliferation of handguns and other weapons to protect themselves, their businesses and their families from others who have acquired still more weapons, sometimes for criminal purposes. Because many crimes involve weapons, they impose far more devastating consequences than merely lost property. Ironically, the weapons bought to defend homes have killed and injured more family members than intruders. Visitors have also been killed or injured when mistaken for prowlers. While weapons are seen as the effective tools of security, such lethal force is more often turned on itself. Yet like their governments, many citizens feel insecure without the capacity to threaten, injure, or kill others.

Lethal weapons have become commonplace in many communities ostensibly at peace. Yet a form of perpetual social warfare continues to destroy communities and undermine the essential security of daily life. The culture of war and weaponry manifests itself at all levels of society. Women's peace organizations have challenged the cultural acceptance of the violence that occurs at each of these levels. As the

U.N. experts meeting on Gender and the Agenda for Peace observed, "The myth of the efficacy of violence must be challenged" (U.N. Division for the Advancement for Women, 1994:6).

Even among those who organize against "war toys" and violent games, little has been said about the legitimacy of lethal tools for any social purpose. Activists correctly lament the way war toys socialize children into militarism, desensitize them to violence, and close their minds to nonviolent alternatives for defense and conflict resolution. Critics are concerned about how sports and popular games emphasize competition over cooperation. Yet much less discussed has been the "weapons mentality"—the way of thinking where weaponry pervades human discourse and human affairs.

The weapons culture constitutes our art, literature, and entertainment, and dominates our languages and metaphors. We often celebrate national holidays with parades of our largest, most fearful weapons to demonstrate the nation's power and pride. In public places, cannons, tanks, and old fighter-plane skeletons serve as monuments to national heroism. In my mother tongue, we repeatedly use a weaponry vocabulary. We "shoot down" ideas we disagree with or "go gunning" for persons with whom we wish to argue. Our unreflective acceptance of weaponry holds us in thrall to the weapons culture. To counteract this culture, and to convey the specific skills of peacemaking, many women have become the main advocates of peace education.

Of course, war constitutes the most devastating consequence of the weapons addiction. "Armed conflict" inevitably results from serious conflicts when weapons are at hand. Recent events have shown that the more weapons are available, the more likely a conflict will escalate into violence. Conflict may be inevitable, but armed conflict depends on arms.

In the 1960s, students asked, "What if they gave a war and no one came?" I ask now, "What if there were a serious conflict, but there were no arms?" It would pose great difficulties but none that humans could not overcome. In contrast, the lethal consequences of weapons can never be overcome. They must be avoided. The struggle by many women to institutionalize that avoidance may be their greatest contribution to a culture of peace.

Weaponry constitutes a destructive addiction that has been perpetuated by the war system the same as drug addiction in pre-revolutionary China was perpetuated by European colonials and imperial authorities. The addiction slowly undermines the general well-being, providing immediate harm to the addicts and preventing them from understanding authentic human security. Addictions fill a void, real or perceived, in the sources of well-being. As drug addicts "shoot" heroin into their veins, the culture of war "shoots" weaponry into our minds and politics, poisoning both. Both must be cured.

Curing an addiction takes considerable strength of mind, courage, and love, qualities women are socialized to develop on behalf of others. Their contributions to a culture of peace come considerably from this socialization and the skills they've acquired to fulfill it. But women's potential contribution to a culture of peace cannot be fully realized as along as male elites maintain our current weapons-dependent state systems. Liberating the human family from the culture of war requires the transformation of that system.

This transformation can be achieved only through a genuine partnership between men and women where they share power equally. The perspectives, concerns, insights, and experiences of both men and women must be constructively combined to overcome the weapons addiction. Together they must devise a global order so committed to fulfilling human needs and to developing a just and equitable interdependence that the need for weapons will ultimately disappear. As the experts group of the Gender and the Agenda for Peace conference concluded, "Lethal weaponry has no place in a culture of peace" (U.N. Division for the Advancement of Women, 1994:4). That place can only be filled by real human security. This will require big changes in all aspects of our lives. Only then will the weapons culture be uprooted from our minds and violent force purged from our relationships.

REFERENCES

Eisler, Riane, and David Loye. 1990. *The Partnership Way*. San Francisco: HarperCollins.

Myrdal, Alva. 1978. *The Game of Disarmament*. New York: Pantheon.

National Federation of Social Democratic Women in Sweden. N.d. *Power Handbook*. Stockholm.

Reardon, Betty. 1993. *Women and Peace*. Albany, NY: SUNY Press.

Sivard, Ruth. 1995. *World Military and Social Expenditures*. Washington, DC: World Priorities.

United Nations Division for the Advancement of Women. 1995. *Our Global Neighborhood*. London: Oxford University Press.

———. 1994. Report of an Expert Group Meeting on Gender and the Agenda for Peace, GAP/199/1, United Nations, New York, December 9, 1994.

An expanded version of this chapter will appear in *Toward a Women's Agenda for Peace*, to be published by UNESCO in 1998.

Chapter Thirty

Dissension in the Ranks
The New York Branch of WILPF vs. the National Board, 1914–1955

Harriet Hyman Alonso

The Woman's Peace Party (WPP) was created as a direct response to the European conflict of 1914. It was, in fact, both the suffrage wing of the U.S. peace movement and the pacifist wing of the U.S. suffrage movement. Unbeknownst to most people, its origins lay within the New York City suffragist community. A look at the relationship between this local group, formed in November 1914, and its mother organization, formed the following January 15, throws new light onto the history of the Women's International League for Peace and Freedom (WILPF), which up to now has been largely concerned only with the national and international leadership.

The dominant force behind the Woman's Peace Party of New York City was Crystal Eastman, a self-proclaimed socialist-feminist who held a Master's degree from Columbia University and a law degree from New York University. In organizing the New York City branch of the Woman's Peace Party, Eastman was joined by such activists as Margaret Lane, Anne Herendeen, Freda Kirchwey, Katherine Anthony, Jessie Wallace Hughan, and Madeline Doty, all of whom took an assertive stand not only on suffrage but on reproductive rights, labor organizing, anti-imperialism, and other issues as well.

Throughout the World War I era, tension existed between the Woman's Peace Party's national board and the New York branch. The differences were rooted primarily in the women's preference for one of the two philosophies of organizing within the suffrage movement: the local aligned with the militant Congressional Union, the national with the more conservative National American Woman Suffrage Association. However, until the United States actually entered the war in April 1917, the two factions managed to tolerate each other.

They experienced a rupture following U.S. war participation. The Woman's Peace Party's national board did not immediately respond to the war declaration. When it finally addressed the issue, its approach was to avoid confrontation with the government by solely proposing plans for a postwar peace. The New Yorkers, however, were assertive in their response. They immediately demanded that the president explain to the public exactly what the U.S. troops were supposed to be fighting for and on what terms the Wilson administration would accept peace.

The national board also took no official stand on conscientious objection and did not provide adequate leadership for the branches. In the New York branch, the women took conscientious objection very much to heart, especially after Governor Charles S. Whitman ordered a "Census and Inventory of the Military Resources of the State." According to his decree, every woman in the state between the ages of sixteen and fifty was required to report to the government her educational background, training, and availability for war service. In a letter to the members, the New York executive board protested that the census neglected to ask whether a woman was *willing* to lend her energies to the prosecution of the war." The board suggested that each woman, to avoid possible arrest and imprisonment, give the information but insert a phrase like, "But I object to aiding war" or "As a conscientious objector to this war, I claim exemption from either direct or indirect war service" (Dear Member 1917). In addition, several New York City members helped young men who did not believe in war to pursue conscientious objector status.

Another point of contention was the national organization's ambiguous stand on relief work. Jane Addams personally supported the idea of relief work and in early 1918 became very much involved in Herbert Hoover's Food Administration. Addams felt that feeding the hungry would help to unleash a positive force in the world that could lead to peaceful coexistence among nations. WPP branches differed on their feelings about this issue. The Massachusetts branch, for example, took up relief work for the remainder of the war, while the New York branch did not. On July 14, 1917, an article entitled "The 'Sister Susie' Peril" by Katherine Anthony appeared in the branch's newsletter, *Four Lights*. It directly attacked the women on the national board and those in Massachusetts who had taken up relief work, specifically the knitting of woolen stockings for soldiers. Anthony accused these "Sister Susies" of taking jobs away from self-supporting working women in the knitting mills and garment factories. Relief work, she said, was "a peculiarly infantile form of patriotism" (Anthony 1917). Needless to say, the article angered both the national board and Massachusetts members.

The war officially ended on November 11, 1918, with the signing of the armistice. The next year, in Zurich, the international women's peace network became the Women's International League for Peace and Freedom (WILPF). The Woman's Peace Party became the U.S. section of WILPF, and the New Yorkers became the New York branch. Jane Addams was named international chair. Anna Garlin Spencer, a minister, suffragist, and founding member of the organization, became the new national chair. Her job was not easy. World War I and the "red scare" of the postwar era left United States-WILPF decimated. Membership had fallen to below one hundred. Spencer began the difficult task of rebuilding the organization. Under her leadership, it began to revive, reaching five hundred in 1920 and over two thousand in 1922.

The New York branch, however, was in disarray, many of its members disillusioned with the terms of peace settled upon in Versailles. As a result, in 1918, the branch issued a scathing statement against the men in power, who they felt dominated and oppressed all women. At the same time, they recognized their own need to act responsibly and assertively now that they had the vote. Their statement read:

> War to end war has proved a failure. The war is won, yet nowhere is there peace, security or happiness. Hate, fear and greed still rule the world. . . . The control of the world is still in the hands of men who have no respect for human life, or for the counsel and needs of women. . . . In the struggle for our own emancipation we have not destroyed a single life. By aiding men to release themselves from their bondage to violence and bloodshed, we shall also free ourselves, for women can never know true liberty in a society dominated by force. (Statement 1918).

A certain discontent had surfaced in the branch. Several of the members felt that the group had moved away from its truly pacifist position. By late 1921, the branch's struggle over the definition of "pacifism" and the strategies needed to achieve peace resulted in its division into three separate organizations: WILPF, the Women's Peace Society (WPS) and the Women's Peace Union (WPU) (a result of a split within the Women's Peace Society). Both the Women's Peace Society and the Women's Peace Union followed a philosophy of nonresistance. Under the leadership of Fanny Garrison Villard, the daughter of the abolitionist William Lloyd Garrison, members of the WPS signed a pledge avowing their belief in the sanctity of human life. WPU members went even further, promising not to cooperate with war in any way, including refusing to purchase war bonds, participate in relief work or in honoring the draft. The WPU devoted its efforts to campaigning for an amendment to the U.S. Constitution making war illegal. WILPF members, on the other hand, approved of any worldwide move toward peace, whether by treaty, disarmament, international law, or diplomatic conferences.

The year 1924, however, proved to be a turning point for WILPF as its head-quarters were moved to Philadelphia and Washington, D.C., under the leadership of Mildred Scott Olmsted, Hannah Clothier Hull, Emily Greene Balch, and Dorothy Detzer. The New York branch was most affected by the work of former suffragist Katherine Devereux Blake. For thirty-four years the principal of Public School 6, Blake was eventually responsible for recruiting large numbers of public school teachers into the New York City branch. In 1925, out of 144 new members, 118 were teachers and principals; in 1928, she signed up 233 more teachers. In 1930, the New York membership list included 766 teachers.

In addition, Blake and Margaret Loring Thomas, another Woman's Peace Party alumna, made a concerted effort to bring women of color into WILPF. In February 1929, the two sponsored the branch's first interracial meeting, attracting about thirty African American women. In 1930, the New Yorkers were successful in having Helen Curtis, one of the first members of color, make a citywide speaking tour on their behalf. Throughout the 1930s and the World War II years, all the New York City branches held meetings specifically designed to recruit women of color. Women, such as Addie Hunton of Manhattan, were asked to be on the local boards so that more diverse perspectives could be incorporated into all branch affairs. The local group did not approve of the special "Intra-American" committees recommended by the national board. According to Caroline Singer, the New York board member in charge of such matters, it was discriminatory to have special committees for recruitment. The less racist path was to incorporate all kinds of women on the regular membership committee.

While the efforts to attract women of color were never as successful as the organizers had hoped, the attraction of WILPF to ethnic, especially Jewish, women in New York proved to be a boon. By 1927, for example, active WILPF groups were operating in Brooklyn and the Bronx. Although these two new groups were autonomous, they also operated as part of the New York City branch, based in Manhattan.

The diverse nature of the New York membership proved to be a challenge both to the national's White Anglo-Saxon Protestant heritage and also to the local's white suffrage roots. For example, in 1934 the New York branch members squabbled over whether to pass a resolution suggested by Addie Hunton supporting the proposed United States Senate Anti-Lynching Bill. The resolution was approved by the branch but not without a battle. Sadie A. Cohen, a member of the group, was outraged by the very fact of disagreement. She wrote to Dorothy Detzer that the New York City branch chair, former suffragist Grace Hoffman White, suffered from a "Mayflower complex" and would fare better in the DAR than in WILPF. "Among other things," wrote Cohen, "the name 'Sirovich' came up and she said, 'Why don't those people get some real American names?'" Cohen went on to relate the tale of the resolution to support the Anti-Lynching Bill, then added, "But what a tragic illustration that each group must fight for their own lives! . . . Surely there is no greater blot on American life than our southern justice." Going on, Cohen included her Jewish self in this anger against the white tradition in WILPF.

> Must we Jewish women speak for ourselves when our souls are so burdened? Can we not expect those by whose side we have labored in the cause of World Peace to speak for us in our direst need? . . . I'm afraid that many of those who profess to be internationalists really have very little feeling for minority groups. They do only lip service to Peace and that doesn't quite satisfy us. (Cohen 1934)

And, indeed, it did not satisfy Addie Hunton either. A year later, she wrote to Dorothy Detzer, "For a year or so I have felt less and less sure of the fact that the organization was really ready for an inter-racial program" (Hunton 1935). With hesitancy, she gradually withdrew from WILPF in order to devote her time to the anti-lynching campaign and attend to her seriously ill daughter.

The New Yorkers' frustration with the national board reached a peak during the 1930s. One of the most controversial issues was the neutrality legislation passed during the administration of Franklin D. Roosevelt to keep the United States out of foreign wars while also allowing for trade. Particularly troublesome for the New York women was the 1937 version, which prevented support of the elected Spanish Republican government in its war with Francisco Franco's fascist forces. While the national board agreed with Roosevelt's neutrality stance in Spain, the New Yorkers supported U.S.-led mediation between the warring parties. However, they opposed the mandatory embargo of war materials unless that embargo was placed on *all* belligerents. This included the banning of oil sales to Italy, which relied on the fuel to carry on its wars against Ethiopia and later, Albania. Furthermore, the New York women felt that unless the United States pulled all of its own military personnel and ships out of Asia and Latin America, neutrality was a hypocritical policy. In 1938, Dorothy Detzer changed her view and agreed that, in the case of Spain, where Italian and German military support had insured Franco's victory, the Neutrality Acts had been unjust. That same year, the Bronx branch decided to withdraw from WILPF after seven years of active organizing. In a letter to Hannah Clothier Hull, three Bronx women stated, "Specifically we find ourselves at variance with the Women's International League for Peace and Freedom policy on neutrality, since we believe that taking neither side in a conflict is analogous to helping the stronger side, namely the aggressor" (Cohen, Antin, and Sellinger 1938).

In the case of Germany, the New Yorkers felt even stronger that neutrality was wrong. Hitler's persecution of the Jews was a particularly emotional issue. Although the national board would later lament the effects of Nazism, at first it tried to avoid a strong stand by claiming that Hitler's policies were simply a European matter. The New York City WILPF did not take kindly to this view, especially since so many of its members were Jewish. Taking matters into their own hands, in 1936 the New York women supported a boycott sponsored by the American Jewish Congress against the buying of German goods or the use of German services. However, because such an action was frowned upon by the national board, the women were prevented from officially endorsing it. The Bronx branch firmly voiced its feeling that there could be "no peace unless this greatest threat to peace [Germany] were eliminated or at least checked." Although military action was not the preferred approach, "the mere effort to keep America out of war [was] not enough" (Cohen, Antin, and Sellinger 1938). By 1939, the leaders of the Brooklyn branch had also resigned, citing the national board's views on neutrality as the reason. In 1972, Mildred Scott Olmsted lamented the loss of members that WILPF suffered because of the neutrality issue:

> At the time of the Spanish Civil War many of the liberals pulled out . . . because we wouldn't support the shipment of arms to the Spaniards. We said we were against the shipment of arms at any time to anybody. During the Second World War we lost many of our Jewish members. . . . During the Italian conquest of Ethiopia, we lost black members who felt that we should go into active support of Ethiopia . . . [but] we steadily opposed the war. (Randall 1972)

The price of neutrality was high, for as U.S. involvement in the war drew closer and woman power became more necessary, membership declined.

By December 1941, the United States was engaged in the Second World War. The WILPF national board announced it would not oppose the constitutionally made declaration of war. However, it promised to continue its search for peaceful solutions to conflict. Even though national and local membership decreased rapidly, the New York City branch maintained an active program throughout the war, emphasizing refugee work, reaching out to women of color and educating themselves on the politics and philosophy of both war and peace.

Once again, WILPF survived a major world war, and once again, its ranks were decimated. However, both the national board and local branches began rebuilding. The New York branch was slow to reorganize. In 1950, however, Mildred Scott Olmsted convinced Orlie Pell, a wealthy New Jersey woman affiliated with the War Resisters League, to reorganize the group. The national board needed local women to carry out WILPF's U.N. NGO work, including attending U.N. sessions and hosting WILPF's national and international visitors to New York. Ironically, the local branch had become central to its operation.

Pell set to work amid a myriad of resignations exaccerbated by the growing threat of McCarthyism. At this time, the branch not only had trouble finding members, but it also could not easily find a meeting place. No one was willing to rent a room to the group until the Carnegie Endowment for International Peace offered them office space in its new building located opposite the United Nations. By 1953, the group had once again become an active component of WILPF, but from this time the national board and local branch functioned more like allies than adversaries, with several New York City women sitting on national committees and participating actively in U.N. work.

Internal disruption caused by McCarthyism also hit a personal note within the Metropolitan New York branch. During the 1950s, New York WILPF members, frightened by the concept of communism and the possibility of what they perceived as Communist Party infiltration of their organization, began to look suspiciously at their closest allies. By 1953, the New York leaders were visiting prospective members in their homes to assure themselves that they were not filling their ranks with die-hard members of the Communist Party. As one woman reported, when most members of the Chelsea Women's Committee for Peace wanted to join up with the Metropolitan New York branch, the women were visited informally by representatives of the group (Anonymous). Another member complained that Orlie Pell, then president of the branch, was "violently anti-Communist" and therefore made it close to impossible for New York Communist members to move freely within the group. At one point during the 1950s, Pell had actually recommended that the branch cease having meetings and simply use its efforts to raise money for the national so as to limit the activities of Communist members (Anonymous). When asked for help, however, the national board did not reply with a clear position, therefore leaving the local women to sort out internal distrust, accusations, and hysteria by themselves. Somehow, the Metropolitan New York branch managed to survive the period, although to this day older members do not like to speak about the fifties. Even though some members still have hard feelings, the branch as a whole was able to heal its wounds and carry on.

This study of the tensions between the New York City women of WILPF and their national leadership raises many questions about the ideal of a consensus which WILPF leaders often touted. Obviously, there was no such thing as peace within the organization. From 1915 on, the New York City women expressed their discontent. Whether the differences in political approaches were caused by age, ethnicity, class, or race, the fact is that they were very real. However, at times the national board chose to turn a deaf ear to these local voices. During World War I, the national board viewed the New York City women as troublemakers from the bohemian left.

During the interwar years, they saw them as primarily Jewish women too emotion-ally involved with the situation in Europe. During the McCarthy era, they left the New Yorkers to sort out their political differences on their own.

However, the rocky road the New York City women of WILPF traveled in order to assert their unique multicultural identity smoothed out after the 1950s. The national board came to rely on this local branch to maintain its presence as a nongovernmental consultative organization within the United Nations, and several New York women were elected to the national board. In addition, the civil rights, anti-Vietnam War, and feminist movements of the 1960s and 1970s attracted many different types of women to national WILPF. The Metropolitan New York branch became just one of many that reflected class, race, and ethnic diversity.

Historical accounts of WILPF (and other women's peace organizations) generally emphasize national leaders. These women tended to be educated, white, Protestant, and monied. The local branch histories—the stories of average women from all backgrounds—are just starting to be heard. This short account hopes to open ques-tions in other historians' minds so that, together, we can reconstruct a more accu-rate and complete history of the women's peace movement, one which seeks to address the issues of difference and dissension as well as consensus.

ACKNOWLEDGMENTS

A different version of this paper, entitled "Seventy-Five and Going Strong: A Brief History of the Metropolitan New York Branch of WILPF," was presented at the Eighth Berkshire Con-ference on the History of Women, June 1990, at Douglass College/Rutgers. I would like to thank Frances Early, Martin Dubin, Eileen Dubin, Brenda Parnes, Yvette Tomlinson, and the women of the Metropolitan New York branch of WILPF for their support and suggestions.

REFERENCES

Anonymous. Comment to member of Metropolitan New York Branch History Project. Henceforth cited as NYHP.

Anthony, Katherine. "The 'Sister Susie' Peril." *Four Lights*, July 14, 1917, WPP:SCPC.

Cohen, Sadie A,. to Dorothy Detzer. March 15, 1934. Reel 60, Women's International League for Peace and Freedom—U.S. Section, 1919–1959. Swarthmore College Peace Collection, Scholarly Resources Microfilm Edition. (Henceforth cited as WILPFF/US: SCPC-mf.)

Cohen, Sadie, Eva Antin, and Rachel Sellinger of the Bronx Branch to Hannah Clothier Hull, November 21, 1938. Reel 66, WILPF/US: SCPC-mf.

Dear Member. Letter from Executive Board, June 12, 1917. Woman's Peace Party Papers, Swarthmore College Peace Collection. (Henceforth cited as WPP:SCPC.)

Hunton, Addie, to Dorothy Detzer, January 8, 1935. Reel 59, WILPF/US: SCPC-mf.

Randall, Mercedes. 1972. Interview with Mildred Scott Olmsted, February 1972, New York City. Mildred Scott Olmsted Papers: Swarthmore Colege Peace Collection.

Statement. 1918. WPP:SCPC.

Chapter Thirty-One

Solidarity and Wartime Violence against Women

Leila J. Rupp

At the Non-Governmental Organization Forum of the United Nations Fourth World Conference on Women in Beijing in September 1995, women from around the world came together and decried the diverse and gender-specific violence that afflicts women everywhere. From systematic rape as a weapon of war to culturally sanctioned forms of domestic violence, women suffer from gendered violence that increasingly dominates discussions of women's solidarity across national and cultural borders. Yet violence against women is not new nor is the recognition that such violence might promote women's international solidarity. In fact, when we explore the first wave of the international women's movement, from its origins in the late nineteenth century through the ebb of the Second World War, we can detect the early murmurings of women against the rape of women in wartime.

These subdued voices emerged from the three major transnational bodies of the international women's movement: the International Council of Women (1888), the International Woman Suffrage Alliance (1904), and the Women's International League for Peace and Freedom (1915). Distinguishable from others that arose in the years surrounding the First World War by their theoretical openness to all women and their (admittedly limited) success in organizing beyond the Euro-American arena, these three groups might be seen as grandmother, mother, and daughter, as one gave birth to another.

The International Council of Women (ICW) grew from seeds planted during a transatlantic trip in 1882–1883 by United States suffragists Elizabeth Cady Stanton and Susan B. Anthony. The shoots surfaced at the 1888 convention of the United States National Woman Suffrage Association, where international representatives joined United States suffragists to found the ICW. Despite its suffragist origins, the ICW adopted a broad and uncontroversial program that would appeal to the largest number of women. As German secretary Alice Salomon put it, the ICW was "bound to be cautious, as it included women from the most outlying villages as well as from those regions better prepared for an energetic policy in favor of the franchise" (Salomon n.d., 77).

When the Council leadership insisted that anti-suffragists deserved a hearing at the 1899 congress session on women's political rights, German suffragists Lida Gustava Heymann and Anita Augspurg called an alternate meeting that called for an international women's suffrage organization. After a preliminary get-together in conjunction with the United States National American Woman Suffrage Association convention in 1902, the International Woman Suffrage Alliance (IWSA) came into being in 1904.

Just as differences over suffrage hastened what the ICW considered the "hiving off" of the IWSA, disagreement about peace activism in the Alliance helped create the Women's International League for Peace and Freedom. The Alliance's 1915 congress, scheduled for Berlin, was scuttled when war broke out. Nonetheless, some still wanted an international meeting. "Day and night I trouble my brains what we can do to stop this scandalous bloodshed" (Jacobs 1914) wrote Dutch suffrage leader Aletta Jacobs to other Alliance members. But opposition to meeting in wartime, especially from British suffrage leader Millicent Garrett Fawcett, axed the idea of Alliance sponsorship. As a result, a group of members from the Netherlands, Belgium, Britain, and Germany met in Amsterdam "in warm sympathy and the best harmony" (Augspurg 1915) in February 1915 and called for an International Congress of Women in April in The Hague. The famous congress established an International Committee of Women for Permanent Peace, which at war's end took on the name of the Women's International League for Peace and Freedom, prompting Aletta Jacobs to exclaim, "What an awful name!" (Jacobs 1919).

Through international organizations such as these, individuals began to break away from—or branched out from—national thinking to imagine the world sliced up differently. The ICW, Alliance, and WILPF offered regular congresses, formed substantive and administrative international committees, opened international headquarters in various European cities, and published journals that served as the structural basis for the face-to-face and more impersonal interactions that built international solidarity.

The League of Nations opened up new opportunities for internationally minded women to converge on Geneva and lobby delegates on issues that concerned them. But very few women could actively pursue this most focused international work. In some ways, the greatest contribution of the transnational organizations was to generate internationalism, an amorphous process that occurred through the interaction promoted by meetings-in-the-flesh and by encounters, as one WILPF member put it, with "Unmet Friends" on the written page (Sheepshanks 1918).

Although theoretically open to women worldwide, the organizations were not as diverse as they often claimed. Until after the First World War, all but one of the national sections were in Europe or what have been called the "neo-Europes"—countries such as the United States, Canada, Australia, and South Africa that had been European settler colonies. Patterns of leadership, the establishment of English, French, and German as official languages, the custom of holding conferences primarily in Europe (with a few excursions to North America), and the costs of international travel limited who could truly participate.

Nevertheless, women from different, even sometimes from warring, countries did gather in international solidarity. What held them together? Perhaps the central bond was the ideological conviction that women were fundamentally different than men, as manifested in women's penchant for peace and men's for war. Of the First

World War, British WILPF member Mary Sheepshanks wrote: "Men have made this war; let women make peace—a real and lasting peace" (Sheepshanks 1918). Between the wars, Egyptian feminist Huda Sha'rawi proclaimed that "if men's ambition has created war, the sentiment of equity, innate in women, will further the construction of peace" (Sha'rawi 1935). Putting it more bluntly, United States suffrage leader Carrie Chapman Catt insisted: "All wars are men's wars. Peace has been made by women but war never" (Catt, 1931).

Hatred of war unleashed a veritable barrage of anti-male sentiment, already implicit in the hierarchy of female and male values. Hungarian Paula Pogány, during the First World War, had never in her life "felt more aversion against everything that carries the character of manhood" (Pogány 1915). United States suffragist Anna Howard Shaw found their "war madness and barbarism" "unthinkable" and claimed, despite her already low opinion of men, that "I have not half the respect for man's judgment or common sense that I used to have, that they are such fools as to go out and kill and be killed without knowing why" (Shaw 1915, 1916). Kathleen Innes of England wrote to a colleague on a sunny November day when she could smell the grass and the newly turned black earth, noting, "What fools men are to make such a mess of a lovely world" (Innes 1938). Catt ventured that men had never wanted to end war: "They like to fight, they like the adventure, they like the prestige, and they certainly love conquest" (Catt 1942).

Such a polarized vision of women's ways and men's ways had a strong basis in women's potential or actual motherhood. But another powerful argument for women's difference claimed that wartime sexual violence provided a stark boundary separating women from men. The ICW Peace Committee protested in 1913 against "the horrible violation of womanhood that attends all war," and the quinquennial congress the following year appealed to the next international peace congress to take up the protection of women from rape in wartime (ICW 1914).

During the First World War, such protests increased in intensity. In their petition to Woodrow Wilson, the women of twelve nations lobbied the United States president to mediate, not only to save the lives of men, but also to avoid making women "victims of the unspeakable horrors which inevitably accompany the bloody game of war!" (Schwimmer 1914a). Emphasizing the violence theme, the flyer announcing the upcoming Hague congress referred circumspectly to rape as one reason women must unite internationally: "The moral and physical sufferings of many women are beyond description and are often of such a nature that by the tacit consent of men the least possible is reported. Women raise their voices in commiseration with those women wounded in their deepest sense of womanhood and powerless to defend themselves" (WILPF Papers 1915). Quoting German pacifist Lida Gustava Heymann, Jane Addams, presiding at the Hague Congress, proclaimed: "Worse than death, yes, worse than hellish, is the defenselessness of women in warfare and their violation by the invading soldier!" (Addams 1915).

According to Carrie Chapman Catt, who here revealed her Euro-American vision of civilization, the "conditions of war subvert the natural instincts of many men of all races, who temporarily return to the brutal practices of the most savage primitive races" (Catt 1914). Expressing a gloomier view of "civilized" men's peacetime behavior, Rosika Schwimmer protested that the "victimizing of children, young girls, and women of all ages so common in peaceful times, because under the double standard of morals men are not outlawed for sexual crimes, is multiplied in war time" (Schwimmer 1914a).

Violence against women, like motherhood, had the potential to unite women across cultures, since all women were fair game, especially in war. Catt pressured Mary Sheepshanks to collect evidence of "wrongs done to women" by the belligerents during the First World War (Sheepshanks 1914a). The reports that surfaced followed predictable patterns. Catt mentioned rapes by Bulgarian and Greek soldiers in the Balkan war; Rosika Schwimmer learned of the rape of Hungarian women by Russian soldiers and the violation of French women by German troops; WILPF took up the issue of the rape and imprisonment of Armenian women by the Turks after the First World War; and a Western woman living in Japan told of the rape of women in China.

WILPF provoked a protest from African American women when the organization called for the removal of African soldiers serving in the French army of occupation because they were raping German women. Mary Church Terrell, head of the United States National Association of Colored Women, as a member of "a race whose women have been the victims of assaults committed upon them by white men and men of all other races" (Terrell 1921), sympathized with any violated woman, but she did not believe that black men were any different than white men in their propensity to rape. The potential universality of wartime rape, as powerful a bond among women as it might be, could also be undercut by assumptions about superior civilizations and by wartime animosities.

This whispered dialogue about violence against women in wartime represents an important precedent for the contemporary international women's movement. On the global scene, unity based on political powerlessness declined after 1920 as women's fundamental difference from men was increasingly questioned, and after women's suffrage and political party participation increasingly divided women into "haves" and "have-nots." Yet women's economic disadvantage relative to men and their vulnerability to violence remained powerful potential bonds.

Thus the bold proclamations against global violence that issued from Beijing have roots that go back to the First World War. In both the similarity of the experience and the possibility that some societies will be viewed as less civilized, this is a history we ignore at our own peril.

REFERENCES

Augspurg, Anita, to Rosika Schwimmer. February 23, 1915. Schimmer-Lloyd collection, box A-40, Rare Books and Manuscripts Division, New York Public Library (NYPL). Astor, Lenox, and Tilden Foundations, New York.

Bosch, Mineke, with Annemarie Kloosterman. 1990. *Politics and Friendship: Letters from the International Woman Suffrage Alliance*. Columbus: Ohio State University Press.

Catt, Carrie Chapman. 1914. "The Atrocities of War." *Jus Suffragii* 9, no. 11 (October 1, 1914).

———. 1931. "Man Made Wars." *Pax* 6, no. 6 (May).

Catt, Carrie Chapman, to Margery Corbett Ashby and Katherine Bompas. June 16, 1942. Catt Papers, box 3, NYPL.

Innes, K. E., to Gertrud Baer. November 10, 1938. WILPF Papers, reel 3.

International Council of Women (ICW). 1913. "Memorandum of the Meeting of the Executive and Standing Committees." *Annual Report.*

———. 1914. "Resolutions Adopted at the Quinquennial Council Meeting of the ICW." ICW Papers, box 1, Sophia Smith Collection (SSC), Smith College, Northampton, MA.

———. 1915. "An International Conference of Women." WILPF Papers, reel 16.

Jacobs, Aletta, to Miss Macmillan, Miss Sheepshanks, Rosika, and other suffrage friends. August 16, 1914. New York: Schwimmer-Lloyd Collection, box A-40.

Jacobs, Aletta, to Emily Greene Balch. June 22, 1919. WILPF Papers, reel 36.

Peters, Julie, and Andrea Wolper. 1995. *Women's Rights, Human Rights: International Feminist Perspectives.* New York: Routledge.

Pogány, Paula, to Mary Sheepshanks. February 8, 1915. Schwimmer-Lloyd Collection, box A-54, NYPL.

Salomon, Alice. N.d. "Character Is Destiny." Salomon Papers, Leo Baeck Institute, New York.

Schwimmer, Rosika. 1914a. "The Women of the World Demand Peace." Schwimmer-Lloyd Collection, box A-42, NYPL.

———. 1914b. "The Atrocities of War." Catt Papers, box 3, NYPL.

Shaw, Anna Howard, to Aletta Jacobs. August 22, 1915 and April 18, 1916. Aletta Jacobs Papers, Internationaal Informatienncentrum en Archief voor de Vrouwenbeweging (IIAV), Amsterdam.

Sha'rawi, Huda. 1935. "L'Orient et l'Occident en coopération." *La République.* Margery Corbett Ashby Papers, box 484, Fawcett Library (FL), London, Guildhall University.

Sheepshanks, Mary. 1918. "Peace." *Jus Suffragii* 13, no. 3 (December).

Sheepshanks, Mary, to Rosika Schwimmer. December. 15, 1914. Schwimmer-Lloyd Collection, box A-50, NYPL.

Sterritt, Annie B. 1927. "Unmet Friends." *Pax* 3, no. 2 (December).

Terrell, Mary Church, to Jane Addams. March 18, 1921. Jane Addams Papers, reel 13.

Vellacott, Jo. 1987. "Feminist Consciousness and the First World War." *History Workshop* 23: 81–101.

WILPF Papers. 1915. Microfilming Corporation of America.

Wiltsher, Anne. 1985. *Most Dangerous Women: Feminist Peace Campaigners of the Great War.* London: Pandora.

"Women in Earnest, Says Jane Addams." *New York Times*, April 29, 1915.

Chapter Thirty-Two

Making Connections

Building an East Asia–U.S. Women's Network against U.S. Militarism

Gwyn Kirk and Margo Okazawa-Rey

In May 1997, some forty women activists and researchers from mainland Japan, Korea, Okinawa, the Philippines, and the U.S. gathered in Okinawa to talk and strategize about the effects of U.S. military bases in each of these countries, especially on women and children, and on the environment. This four-day meeting was a new step in the ongoing process of building international links among women around such issues. It owed much to prior connections and networks. In July 1988, for example, a women's conference in Okinawa also brought together women from the same countries, with a focus on "the sale of women's sexual labor outside U.S. military bases in the region" (Sturdevant and Stoltzfus, 1992: vii). In 1989, the National Disarmament Program of the American Friends Service Committee organized a speaking tour in the United States entitled "Voices of Hope and Anger: Women Speak Out for Sovereignty and Self-Determination," with speakers from many countries that house U.S. military bases. Some of the participants at the recent meeting were involved in the 1993 United Nations Tribunal on Human Rights in Vienna, or the NGO Forum of the Fourth U.N. Conference on Women in Hairou, China, in 1995. Some had worked together locally or regionally, but this whole group had never come together before. The inspiration for this meeting came from our hearing women from Korea, Okinawa, and the Philippines talking to North American audiences about the terrible effects of U.S. military bases in their countries, and our wanting to create a forum where they could also talk to each other as well as to women from the United States. Carolyn Francis, Suzuyo Takazato, and other members of Okinawa Women Act Against Military Violence were also involved in the core planning group. In this chapter we outline the main issues and perspectives that participants brought to the meeting in Okinawa, and we also discusses the importance and the challenge of building anti-militarist alliances of women across boundaries of culture, class, race, age, and nation.[1]

U.S. Bases Overseas: Protecting American Interests

Participants shared the view that, at root, the purpose of U.S. military bases in Asia is to maintain the political, economic, and cultural dominance of the United States in the world, and to support U.S. corporate investments in Asia. The host governments are also complicit in this process, though many local people see the presence of U.S. bases as an outrageous encroachment on their sovereignty and self-determination. The presence of U.S. companies, U.S. popular culture and TV, fast-food outlets like Wendy's and McDonald's, have all eroded traditional local cultures. Young people in South Korea and Okinawa, for example, are wearing old U.S. military uniforms and paraphernalia; some young people are keen to go onto the bases to learn English and hang out with young U.S. military personnel.

These understandings emerged during our four days of discussion as we reviewed the justifications that our governments have given us for maintaining high levels of U.S. military spending and the complex network of U.S. bases, troops, ships, submarines, and aircraft around the world. During the Cold War, one justification for U.S. military policy and intervention was to stop the spread of communism, and specifically to "contain" the Soviet Union. In the Asia-Pacific region, dozens of U.S. bases in Okinawa, mainland Japan, and the Philippines were used as forward bases during the Korean and Vietnam wars. U.S. troops lived there, training and resting while they waited to be sent into combat. The bases were refueling and repair depots for warships and planes. Military personnel were also "refueled" by local women and girls, through officially sanctioned "Rest and Recreation" in the many bars, clubs, and massage parlors just outside the bases.

Since the fall of the Berlin Wall in 1989 and the dramatic changes in the political economy of the former Soviet Union, the Pentagon has sought to relegitimize the military in the eyes of U.S. taxpayers and politicians by mobilizing public opinion in support of the Persian Gulf War, and by emphasizing a new international "policing" role for the military. In the latest review, a 1997 Pentagon report reiterated the view that the world is still a dangerous place. Its continued objective is to be able to fight and win two regional wars at the same time. For planning purposes these are assumed to be in the Middle East and Korea. This scenario justifies the need for ongoing war games and maneuvers at U.S. bases around the world, on ships at sea, and across large tracts of land belonging to local people. It assumes that 100,000 U.S. troops will continue to be based in East Asia, and that the military budget will remain steady at around $250 billion per year (*Japan Times*, May 14, 1997: 6).

In the mid-1990s a steady trickle of news reports of "war-mongering" attitudes and "uncompromising" or "belligerent" postures on the part of North Korea, China, and even Taiwan have appeared in the U.S. media, serving to keep alive the notion that there are serious military threats to U.S. interests in Asia. Other reasons for the continued justification of overseas bases are rooted in U.S. colonial history, where military interventions led to the appropriation of land and property and the opening up of new markets for U.S. goods. Racist contempt for "uncivilized savages" reinforced attitudes of U.S. superiority. Currently, the United States is number one in the world in terms of military bases, military technology, the training of foreign forces, and military aid to foreign countries. Many people in the United States believe that America is simply Number One and entitled to intervene in other countries' affairs if this is in "American interests."

Negative Effects of U.S. Military Bases, Budgets, Policies, and Practices

Participants at the Okinawa meeting worked in small groups on four related themes: women and children, the environment, legal agreements between the U.S. and host countries, and base conversion, with economic development that will benefit local people, especially women. We had much more information concerning women and children compared to the other issues, as this has been the focus of much women's organizing to date.

Women and Children

Participants shared the view that violence against women is an integral part of U.S. military attitudes, training, and culture. It is not random, but systemic, and cannot simply be attributed to "a few bad apples" as the military authorities often try to do. We noted the many reports of rape, assault, and sexual harassment within the U.S. military that have come to light over the past few years. We also noted that U.S. military families experience higher rates of domestic violence compared to nonmilitary families. But the main emphasis of our discussion concerned crimes of violence committed by U.S. military personnel against civilians in Korea, Japan, and the Philippines, especially violence against women, and the institutionalization of military prostitution.

Crimes of Violence

Women from all countries represented, including the United States, reported crimes of violence committed by U.S. military personnel against local women. Okinawan women emphasized violent attacks of women and girls by U.S. military personnel, especially the marines who are in Okinawa in large numbers. In May 1995, for example, a 24-year old Okinawan woman was beaten to death by a G.I. with a hammer in the doorway of her house. On their return from the Beijing Conference in September 1995, Okinawan women immediately organized around the rape of a twelve-year old girl, which had occurred while they were away. This revitalized opposition to the U.S. military presence in Okinawa and drew worldwide attention to violence against women on the part of U.S. military personnel. The National Coalition for the Eradication of Crimes by U.S. Troops in Korea, which comprises human rights activists, religious groups, feminists, and labor activists, was galvanized into action by a particularly brutal rape and murder of a bar woman, Yoon Kum E, in 1992. Korean participants commented that pimps and G.I.s try to intimidate the women against speaking out; women are also afraid of public humiliation. Drawing public attention to such crimes is embarrassing to the U.S. military. They are usually denied and covered up.

Militarized Prostitution

The governments of the three host countries have all made explicit agreements with the U.S. military concerning R and R (or I and I—intoxication and intercourse—as it is sometimes called), including arrangements for regular health checkups for women who service the men, assuming that they are the cause of sexually transmitted diseases. At the height of U.S. activity in the Philippines, as many as 60,000 women and children were estimated to have worked in bars, night-clubs, and massage parlors servicing U.S. troops. Participants noted many similarities concerning militarized prostitution in Asia, especially during the Vietnam War. U.S. military personnel returning from battle were angry, fearful, and frustrated, and took it out on Okinawan and Filipino women. In Okinawa there are many stories of women being beaten, choked, and killed. Many survived, are now in their fifties and sixties, but their scars remain. Currently it is Filipinas who work in the clubs around U.S. bases in Okinawa, because the strength of the Japanese economy has given Okinawan women other opportunities and reduced the buying power of G.I.s' dollars. Military prostitution serves the interests of patriarchal politics. It divides so-called "good" from "bad" women; moreover, separate bars for white G.I.s and African Americans also divide bar women into two categories. This work is highly stigmatized, and marrying a foreigner is thought by many bar women to be the only way out. Militarized prostitution has had very serious effects on women's health, including HIV/AIDs, sexually transmitted diseases, unwanted pregnancies and unsafe abortions, drug and alcohol dependency, malnutrition, respiratory diseases, and psychological problems related to the trauma and violence of this work.

In the Philippines, WEDPRO, BUKLOD, GABRIELA, and the Coalition against Trafficking in Women (Asia) are tackling this very difficult issue in several ways through public education and advocacy and political activism: providing support to women and Amerasian children through counseling, day care, legal and medical services, and referrals to other agencies; and training women in business skills, especially to set up microenterprises, get access to loans, and help establish women's co-ops. The Philippines constitution enshrines the ideals of a peaceful, just, and humane society; a self-reliant national economy; social justice in all phases of national development; respect for the rights of people and organizations at all levels of decision-making; and the protection of people's rights to a balanced and healthful ecology. It is now nearly seven years since the U.S. military withdrew from the Philippines, but there have been no government programs to address the needs of women and children. Women who worked in the bars were faced with how to survive. Some went to South Korea or Guam to service G.I.s, others moved to Filipino bars and clubs, and still others tried to make a go of small businesses. Many are still working in the bars around Olongapo City and Angeles, servicing G.I.s on shore leave as well as tourists, mainly from Australia and Europe. In March

1996 some 2,500 to 3,000 G.I.s took shore leave in the Philippines, creating such a high demand that the mayors of Angeles and Olongapo quickly got together to work on the problem of getting more women.

In Korea, military prostitution has deep roots in Japanese imperialism, and continues under the U.S. military. Prostituted women in G.I. towns (*kijichon*) outside the bases work in deplorable conditions and earn roughly $170 per month. They are allowed one rest day per month; if they take an additional rest day they are fined half a month's wages. Among the older women who draw in customers to bars and clubs are "comfort women" who survived the Japanese military. Two Korean NGOs, Du Rae Bang, and Sae Woom Tuh, work with bar women and women who date U.S. military personnel. They focus on counseling, education, and providing shelter and alternative employment. A bakery at Du Rae Bang has been running for nine years and has led the way for some bar women to learn new skills and become self-reliant. Similarly, Sae Woom Tuh women have started a herb-growing project. Both these organizations seek to empower bar women to make demands of the Korean and U.S. governments concerning their situation, and to educate the wider society on this issue.

Korean participants also reported that in the past few years G.I. towns have undergone changes, becoming international prostitution zones for foreign men, with foreign women workers coming to Korea from the Philippines, China, Taiwan, and Russia, some of them illegally. They noted links between militarized prostitution and sex tourism; many problems are similar to those in the Philippines and there is much to learn from that experience. Korean participants emphasized the exploitation and violence of *kijichon* women and also included powerful stories of their strength. There are examples of women clubbing together to buy each other out of the bar, for example. In the case of Yoon Kum E, another bar woman who knew the murderer waited outside the base for him and forced military police to arrest him. He still had blood on his white pants.

Amerasian Children

Amerasian children are a particularly stigmatized group in all three Asian countries represented. They suffer great discrimination due to their physical appearance and the stigma of their mothers' work. Those with African American fathers face worse treatment than those with white fathers. Most Amerasians grow up poor, with no regular income in their families. They are discriminated against in employment due to stigma, a lack of training and education, and the absence of credit and other supports for poor families. The average age of Amerasians in the Philippines is twelve years. Two-thirds are raised by single mothers; others by relatives and nonrelatives; 6 percent live on their own or in institutions. Ninety percent are born to single mothers. A lawsuit filed in the United States in 1993 on behalf of Amerasian children in the Philippines was not considered in any serious way. Six basic needs identified by Amerasians in the Philippines are education, employment, housing, livelihood, skills, and U.S. citizenship, the latter so they are able to find their fathers.

Similarly, in Korea Amerasians are thought of as "half persons" who can only half-belong to Korean or to U.S. society. Most older Amerasian people have menial jobs; some are stateless persons who have never been officially registered and, as a result, could not attend Korean schools. There is no government support for Amerasian children from either the Korean or U.S. governments. The 1982 Amerasian Immigration Act, passed mainly with Vietnamese Amerasian children in mind, is of little help to many Amerasians in Korea, Japan, or the Philippines due to its stringent conditions. It applies only to people born between 1951 and 1982; applicants need documentation that their father is a U.S. citizen, as well as a financial sponsor in the United States. In each country, limited support to Amerasian children is provided by local NGOs and the U.S.-based Pearl Buck Foundation. In Korea, Du Rae Bang and Sae Woom Tuh have educational programs for Amerasian children that seek to educate Korean society about their situation. The women of Sae Woom Tuh demanded that every Amerasian be given U.S. citizenship and educational opportunities, with visas for their mothers. The Korean government should also provide education, job training, basic livelihood, and medical care.

Environmental Hazards

Militaries cause more pollution than any other institution. Participants from all countries represented talked about the environmental contamination of base lands, ground water, and the ocean as a result of military activities, and the possible effects of toxic pollution on communities near the bases. The land has been used for weapons storage (including chemical and nuclear weapons in some cases), and the repair of ships and planes and military equipment. Major air force bases store large quantities of fuel, oil, solvents, and other chemicals. Some areas, like Iejima island in Okinawa and small islands off the coast of Korea, have been used as bombing ranges for many years. There are unexploded shells in places used for live ammunition drills. In Korea and Okinawa, U.S. marines have fired depleted uranium shells. Participants from all the countries represented knew stories of particular incidents of accidents or sickness affecting people living near U.S. military bases. In the Philippines, water from wells near Clark Air Force Base has left a golden yellow stain on plastic water buckets, suggesting contamination. There seems to be a high incidence of breast cancer and cervical cancer in women living near the former bases, and hearing problems and other health conditions in children. In 1996 an interim report on babies born to women living near Kadena Air Force Base in Okinawa showed that these babies have significantly lower birth weights than those in other parts of Okinawa, which local people attribute to the severe noise generated by the base.

In general, little information about the environmental effects of military operations is available to local people, though there are active environmental groups in all our countries, some of whom are working on the need for the cleanup of contamination caused by U.S. military operations. If the experience of bases in the United States is any guide, military records of contaminants, if available, may not be complete. The Korean government, for example, denies reports of environmental contamination caused by U.S. military activities because it fears this will fuel anti-bases sentiment in the country. In any case, under the Status of Forces Act, the Korean government cannot release information about environmental contamination without agreement of the U.S. military. The Philippines government is also unwilling to pursue this matter for fear that it will deter prospective investors in baseland redevelopment. The Japanese government, similarly, does not release information about contamination of U.S. bases in Japan. There is a great deal of research to be done on this issue in all countries. This may start with anecdotal information, noting patterns gathered by local people who have worked on the bases or who live nearby, followed by more formal research. It is notoriously difficult to pinpoint environmental causes because of the difficulty of controlling for all variables. It is also a slow process. The U.S. government has finally accepted responsibility for some cancers in military personnel who were exposed to radiation during atomic tests in the Pacific in the 1950s, and in residents of St. George, Utah, who live "downwind" of the Nevada Test Site. In the United States, contamination attributable to military programs also includes the contamination of land and water around military bases, nuclear power plants, nuclear weapons plants, uranium mines, and radioactive waste dumps. In base conversion in the San Francisco Bay Area, for example, it has been determined that human beings cannot live on the former bases for at least twenty years, and that fish caught locally should not be eaten.

Current negotiations between the U.S. military and Japan over bases in Okinawa could also have a serious environmental impact. Okinawans are demanding the return of Futenma Marine Corps Air Station, which takes up acres of land in Ginowan City. In return, the U.S. military is insisting that a new floating heliport should be built off the coast, with clear implications for the ocean environment. Other proposals for military use of areas in the north of Okinawa would destroy fertile agricultural land and likely affect the island's main water supply reservoirs.

Limited Legal Protection

Provisions governing the use of land for overseas bases, and details of required conduct for U.S. military personnel are found in the Japanese Status of Forces Act, the Korean Status of Forces Act, and the Philippines Access and Cross-Servicing Agreement (ACSA). These provisions vary considerably from one host country to another. We noted that this was probably a historic moment, where women looked at these agreements from a gender perspective for the first time. Comparing the different Status of Forces acts, one of the working groups at the Okinawa meeting found that the German Status of Forces Act is some three hundred pages long (in English translation) including detailed provisions for the protection of Amerasian children and environmental cleanup that hold the U.S. military accountable to standards set down in German environmental law. The Status of Forces acts for Japan and Korea are some fifty pages long (English translations), with no provisions for environmental cleanup. This may be because Japan and Korea have not developed sufficiently detailed environmental-law standards, because these governments did not push for such provisions, or because the United States ignored their concerns. Japanese participants commented that Japanese law is inadequate for the protection of either women or the environment. In Korea, the U.S. military can use land for bases forever, for no payment. Land belonging to private landowners was simply confiscated, so there are no Korean anti-war landowners as there are in Okinawa. Clearly, the various host governments are in relatively different power positions in relation to the United States, though none of them come to negotiations as equal partners. The Philippines ACSA is written on one page.

One area of concern for participants is what happens to U.S. servicemen who commit crimes against local people. The National Campaign for the Eradication of Crimes by U.S. Troops in Korea cites a Korean Congress report that estimates 39,542 crimes committed against Korean civilians by U.S. military personnel between 1967 and 1987. These include murders, brutal rapes and sexual abuse, arson, theft, smuggling, fraud, traffic offenses, and an outflow of PX merchandise and a black market in U.S. goods. The Japanese and Korean Status of Forces acts protect such military personnel from Korean or Japanese law. In many cases, if they are disciplined, it is by U.S. military authorities. Often they are simply moved to another posting, perhaps back to the United States. Thus, military personnel who have injured or, in some cases, killed local people through negligent driving, for example, are usually not brought to trial in local courts. This situation incenses local people who see it as a daily manifestation of U.S. insensitivity and high-handedness. In both Japan and Korea there are current pressures for changes in the Status of Forces acts to give more protection to local people. The case of the twelve-year-old girl who was raped in Okinawa was unusual in that the U.S. authorities handed over the three military personnel responsible (two Marines and a sailor) to Japanese civilian authorities in view of the enormous popular outcry this incident generated in Okinawa and internationally. The young men stood trial in a Japanese court, were found guilty, and are serving seven-year sentences in the Japanese prison system.

Base Conversion

The Philippines experience of base conversion provided important data for women from Korea and Japan, perhaps especially those from Okinawa, where a strong anti-bases campaign is pushing the issue of the future use of land currently occupied by U.S. bases. Participants from the Philippines emphasized that the overall economic, social, and cultural impact of the bases has been to strengthen neo-colonial relations. In the Philippines, Korea, and Okinawa, U.S. goods from PX stores, military surplus, or U.S. military families are in high demand by local people. Korean participants reported that this is a serious problem in Korea. There is an outflow of PX goods from U.S. bases and a black market in U.S. goods. Under the Status of Forces Act, U.S. military personnel in Korea do not pay customs duty for imports and can sell U.S. goods to local people at a big profit. This reinforces the view that the best goods and services come from the United States. Duty-free stores in the former base lands in the Philippines sell U.S. goods, continuing the "PX culture." Canned foods from Del Monte and Hormel, for example, are available there, undercutting local grocery stores and tying people into the export economy. More food could be grown locally, but in the interests of earning hard currency, much of the best land in the Philippines is not used for local food production but to grow cash crops or for industrial development.

Subic Bay Navy base and Clark Air Force Base were very large (Subic Bay took up some 70,000 acres), and their closure presented a major opportunity for new development, especially in a country like the Philippines where 70 percent of the people live below the poverty line. Several plans that would benefit local people were put forward, including recommendations by WEDPRO. But the government preferred to attract foreign investment from Japan, Taiwan, Korea, the United States, and Europe, using local people as cheap labor. Both bases now have duty-free shops, new hotels, private casinos, and golf courses. Their very large airfields are international airports, bringing tourists and businessmen directly to these development areas. Some military buildings have been freshly painted and converted into hotels. Others provide housing for the Philippines air force, or industrial space for factories making electronic products and hospital supplies. Federal Express now uses Subic Bay as its Asia hub. This kind of development was justified on the argument that it would create jobs. So far most jobs are part-time or temporary, and low paid, sometimes below the minimum wage of 143 pesos a day. As mayor of Olongapo City, Richard Gordon initiated a project called "People Power" (appropriating the slogan of the 1980s pro-democracy movement), where people volunteer to work on the base for a year, clearing trash or planting and weeding flower beds. There is no guarantee that they will get paid employment after doing this free work, though this is implied. As mentioned above, there has been no government help for the many women who used to work in bars and clubs near the base, or for their Amerasian children.

Women from Okinawa talked of their concerns about future redevelopment of the bases, especially with the Philippines experience in mind. Given the political situation in Korea, this discussion is not yet on the horizon there. In the United States, the process of base conversion has generally involved more consultation with citizen groups than has happened in the Philippines, and the authorities have taken responsibility for toxic cleanup, though it is debatable whether sufficient funds have been devoted to this. But base conversion in the United States is another form of privatization, as formerly public land passes to private investors. Participants suggested compiling a women's budget, comparing current military spending with socially useful expenditures, and a women's Status of Forces agreement.

Building International Alliances among Women

During the meeting, both in formal sessions and in informal conversations, we talked about the importance of acknowledging the complex inequalities among participants, and the relationships of domination and oppression that exist among our countries. This includes the dominant position of the United States, economically, politically, and culturally in many Asian countries, and specifically the colonization of the Philippines. At the same time, there are many people in the United States who are also hurt by U.S. military policies, and much current military recruitment can be seen in terms of a "poverty draft." Then there is the imperial history of Japan, which sought to control eastern Asia from the central Pacific to India. Japan colonized Okinawa in 1865, Korea in 1910, and the Philippines from 1942 to 1945. Koreans were profoundly affected by thirty-five years of Japanese colonization. Korean names, language, newspapers, and political parties were all banned by the Japanese. There was discrimination in education and employment, and raw materials and agricultural produce were extracted for use in Japan. Many thousands of Koreans were forcibly drafted to work in the Japanese war effort—men in factories and mines, women to sexually service the Japanese Imperial Army. Filipinas, too, were forced to be "comfort women."

Now Korea's staggering postwar economic growth means that Korean companies are in the Philippines alongside companies from Japan, Taiwan, and the United States, making money out of a much poorer country. For Okinawans there is a clear distinction between Okinawa and mainland Japan and a long-standing resentment of Japan's colonization of Okinawa. Okinawa was used as a shield in World War II, protecting mainland Japan from direct U.S. invasion. Okinawan participants commented that some of the Okinawans who lost their lives in the Battle of Okinawa were killed by Japanese. Korean participants visiting Japan for the first time were surprised to learn of the similarities between the annexation of Korea and Okinawa. They had initially lumped Okinawans together with other Japanese because they had not known this history.

Such differences are reflected in participants' knowledge and perspectives. They are also reflected in something as mundane as needing a visa to attend the meeting. Those of us with European or U.S. passports did not need a visa to enter Japan. The Korean women had to fill in lengthy forms and attend an interview at the Japanese Embassy in Seoul. Those with Philippine passports had to queue for hours at the Japanese Embassy in Manila which is only open from 2 until 4 P.M., four days a week. They had to show a return ticket and an invitation letter from a Japanese organization. They had to explain their circumstances and answer any questions put to them by embassy staff, if successful, they had to return three working days later to collect the visa in person. Another difference is the buying power of our various currencies. Dollars go a long way in the Philippines; but in Japan many everyday things are very expensive for Americans. For Filipinas, who had to change pesos into hard currency, Japanese prices are astronomical. A third difference concerns the risks we take in speaking out on these issues. For example, it is officially illegal for Koreans to publicly oppose U.S. military policy in South Korea. They risk being labeled communist or unpatriotic, a serious charge in a context where many social activists have served jail sentences for opposing the government. Other participants are not constrained in the same way.

These histories and inequalities may make it difficult for women to sit down together, to really hear what each is saying, or to trust that women with relative privilege will be their allies. We tried to acknowledge these differences and inequalities and to frame issues and questions so as to be able to make connections. An example is the connection between U.S. domestic and foreign policy. These are often treated separately, but the military budget is a helpful way to link them. Not only does military spending harm women overseas, it also harms poor women and children in the United States. In addition, we needed to know something of one another's personal and national history, the economic and political conditions that obtain in our respective countries, and the constraints we experience as activists. Throughout the meeting the group emphasized the importance of listening carefully to our various perspectives and opinions. This is no small task under any circumstances. Here it required careful translation into four languages (English, Japanese, Korean, and Tagalog), and we needed translators who not only knew the technicalities of language but also something of the conceptual vocabulary and context assumed by different speakers. Many of the participants spoke Japanese and a number spoke English, with the result that these (imperial) languages were often dominant. This process is slow and sometimes cumbersome, requiring patience and concentration as well as skilled translators.

The purposes of this network are to learn from one another; to deepen our understandings of our own situations and how these common issues play out in other places; to strategize together; and to work out practical ways we can help one another. The meeting generated a range of strategies including education and information sharing, research, media campaigns in each country, support for community-based organizations and coalition building, lobbying and networking at local, national, regional, and international levels, and direct action. The local and regional organizations represented will work on these issues according to their own needs and circumstances. The following suggestions and plans for future projects emerged from our discussions:

- We should all distribute the final statement (see below) as widely as possible to government officials, NGOs, and members of the public.
- The four working groups should continue to work together and share information through the mail, e-mail, Websites, and personal visits.
- A new young people's group in Okinawa called DOVE (Deactivating Our Violent Establishments) will hold a day conference in June 1997 for young people to discuss these issues.
- Women from the Philippines would like to go to Korea to find out more about Filipinas working in G.I. towns.
- Women in the United States undertook to try to initiate research into what happens to Korean women and Filipinas who marry G.I.s, where they live, and what their lives are like. So far there is only anecdotal evidence that many end up in bars, clubs, and massage parlors in the United States.
- We should continue to analyze and compare the different Status of Forces Agreements and other legal agreements between host governments and the United States.

- We should compile information concerning environmental hazards, find out what evidence to look for, and how to go about this.
- We should meet again, hopefully in 1998 in Washington, D.C., to liaise with relevant U.S. organizations, and to lobby members of Congress and their aides.

Security and Sustainability

Throughout the meeting the question of what constitutes true security kept coming up. In Japan, for example, the Japan-U.S. Security Treaty officially defines security. But this treaty in no way protected the twelve-year-old Okinawan girl who was raped, or others who have been harmed and abused by U.S. military personnel. Women's lack of security is directly linked to this Security Treaty. Participants agreed that the U.S. military presence does not protect local people but endangers them, and that we need to redefine security for our communities. We do not need 100,000 U.S. troops in Asia. Implicit throughout our discussion is the realization that true security requires respect for land, air, water, and the oceans, and a very different economy with an emphasis on ecological and economic sustainability, not the pursuit of profit. The increasing globalization of the economy will create a world market where many countries cannot control their own resources or provide for their people. We recognized that environmental concerns and economic development are often currently in conflict. Thinking in terms of sustainability removes such conflicts.

Our vision is for a sustainable, life-affirming future focusing on small-scale projects, local autonomy, and self-determination, with an emphasis on community land-use systems rather than private property. It includes the creation of true local democracies, the empowerment of local people, and the inclusion of women and children in decision-making. It will involve base conversion as well as nonmilitary approaches to resolving conflicts. It means promoting the value of socially responsible work, and the elimination of weapons-making industries. We agreed that we need a deeper understanding of demilitarization that goes beyond bases, land, and weapons, to include cultures, consciousness, and national identities. Given that masculinity in many countries, including the United States, is defined in military terms, it will also involve a redefinition of masculinity, strength, power, and adventure. It will involve more harmonious ways of living among people, and between people and the nonhuman world that sustains us. It will need appropriate learning and education, cultural activities, and values moving away from consumerism to sustainable living, where people can discover what it means to be more truly human.

Final Statement

WOMEN AND CHILDREN, MILITARISM, AND HUMAN RIGHTS: INTERNATIONAL WOMEN'S WORKING CONFERENCE

NAHA CITY, OKINAWA

MAY 1–4, 1997

We are a group of women activists, policy-makers, and scholars from Okinawa, mainland Japan, Korea, the Philippines, and the U.S. who share a deep concern for the impact of the U.S. military presence on women and children in all our countries.

For four days we have exchanged information and strategized together about the situation of victims of violence committed by U.S. military personnel against civilians, especially women and children. We have shared information about the plight of Amerasian children who are abandoned by their G.I. fathers, and the effects of U.S. military bases on the social environment, in particular on women who are absorbed into the dehumanizing and exploitive system of prostitution around U.S. bases. We have considered the current status of the various official agreements governing U.S. bases and military personnel; also the effects of high rates of military spending on women and children in the U.S. We see militarism as a system of structural violence which turns its members into war machines and creates victims among women and children in our local communities. Underlying our discussions this week is the clear conviction that the U.S. military presence is a threat to our security, not a protection. We recognize that the governments of Japan, South Korea, and the Philippines are also complicit in this.

This is the first time that women have sat down together to discuss these issues which are usually marginalized in discussions concerning U.S. military operations. As a result of our work this week, we see the many striking similarities in our various situations more clearly than ever before. As women activists, policy-makers, advocates, and scholars, we have strengthened our commitment to work together toward a world with true security based on justice, respect for each other across national boundaries, and economic planning based on local people's needs, especially the needs of women and children. We will continue to support women and children affected by U.S. militarism in all our countries, and to create alternative economic systems based on local people's needs. We will establish new guidelines to prevent military violence against women that are quite separate from existing official agreements.

In addition we demand the following:

- that the Status of Forces Agreements between the United States and the governments of Japan and South Korea be significantly revised to protect the human rights of women and children, and to include firm environmental guidelines for the clean-up of toxic contamination to restore our land and water and to protect the health of our communities;
- that the U.S. government cease circumventing constitutional provisions and national laws in imposing their continued military access or presence;
- that our governments pursue sincere efforts to support the democratization and reunification of Korea;
- that our governments take full responsibility for violence against women perpetrated by U.S. military personnel;

- that all military "R and R," which has meant widespread sexual abuse and exploitation of local women and children, be banned;
- that all military personnel receive training aimed at preventing the sexual exploitation, harassment, and abuse of women and children who live and work around bases;
- that our governments provide substantial funding for the health care, education, training, and self-reliance of women who service GIs, and their children, including Amerasian children;
- that the U.S. government and the governments of Japan, South Korea, and the Philippines take full financial responsibility for Amerasian children, and that the U.S. government introduce immigration law that provides for all Amerasians in these three countries;
- that all U.S. bases, weapons, and military personnel be removed from Japan and South Korea;
- that our governments fund detailed, independent research on health conditions due to military activities and operations (e.g., the incidence of low birth-weight babies in the vicinity of Kadena Air Base in Okinawa), as is being done in the U.S.;
- that our governments take full financial responsibility for environmental clean-up of U.S. military bases in a way that meets local people's needs;
- that our governments and public agencies recognize the central importance of women's issues in all base conversion projects, and include women in all levels of base-conversion decision-making;
- that money currently spent on the U.S. military by taxpayers in the U.S., Japan, and Korea be devoted to socially useful programs that benefit women and children;
- that the lands currently in U.S. military use be developed to benefit local people rather than investors and transnational corporations as has happened at the former Subic Bay Naval Base and Clark Air Force Base in the Philippines;
- that local, national, and international media investigate and report the issues and concerns referred to here, and educate people on the effects of the U.S. military presence in our countries.

We have committed ourselves to establishing an international network to hold our governments accountable on these issues, and to build a broad base of support to create a secure and sustainable world for future generations.

REFERENCES

Associated Press, "Cohen announces intention to keep U.S. military near present strength." *Japan Times*, May 14, 1997, 6.

Brock, Rita Nakashima, and Susan Brooks Thistlethwaite. 1996. *Casting Stones: Prostitution and Liberation in Asia and the United States.* Minneapolis: Fortress Press.

Conversion Leadership Project. 1995. *Transforming the Military Economy: Grassroots Strategies for Change.* Mountain View, CA: Center for Economic Conversion.

Enloe, Cynthia. 1990. *Bananas, Beaches and Bases: Making Feminist Sense of International Politics.* Berkeley: University of California Press.

Enloe, Cynthia. 1993. *The Morning After: Sexual Politics at the End of the Cold War.* Berkeley: University of California Press.

Gerson, Joseph, and Bruce Birchard (eds.). 1991. *The Sun Never Sets: Confronting the Network of Foreign U.S. Military Bases.* Boston: South End Press.

Matsuoka, Martha. 1995. *Reintegrating the Flatlands: A Regional Framework for Military Base Conversion in the San Francisco Bay Area.* San Francisco: Urban Habitat Program, Earth Island Institute.

Seager, Joni. 1993. *Earth Follies: Coming to Feminist Terms with the Global Environmental Crisis.* New York: Routledge.

Sivard, Ruth Leger. 1996. *World Military and Social Expenditures.* 15th ed. Washington, DC: World Priorities Institute.

Sturdevant, Saundra, and Brenda Stoltzfus. 1992. *Let the Good Times Roll: Prostitution and the U.S. Military in Asia.* New York: The New Press.

Zinn, Howard. 1995. *People's History of the United States: 1492–Present.* Rev. and updated ed. New York: HarperPerennial.

FURTHER RESOURCES

For more information about the organizations mentioned here please contact them directly:

Du Rae Bang (My Sister's Place), 129 Suyu-5-Dong, Dobong-gu, Seoul, South Korea 132-791.

Sae Woom Tuh, 483-034 Kyunggi-do, Dongduchon City, Saeng-yun 4 dong 541-39 11/4, South Korea.

Korean Church Women United, Korean Ecumenical Building, Room 1110, 136-56 Yunchi-Dong, Chongno-Ku, Seoul, Korea 110-470.

Korean Women's Hot Line, Women's House for Peace, third floor, 38-84 Jangchung-dong 1-Ga, Jung-ku, Seoul, South Korea.

National Campaign to Eradicate Crimes by U.S. Troops in Korea, room 307, Christian Building, 136-46, Yunchi-Dong, Chongno-Ku, Seoul, South Korea, 110-470.

BUKLOD Center, 23 Rodriquez St., Mabayuan, Olongapo City 2200, Philippines.

WEDPRO (Women's Education, Development, Productivity and Research Organization), Box 44-43 U.P. Shopping Center, UP Diliman, Quezon City, Philippines.

Coalition Against Trafficking in Women (Asia-Pacific), suite 406, Victoria Plaza, 41 Annapolis, Greenhills, Metro Manila, Philippines.

Okinawa Women Act Against Military Violence, 405, 3-29-41, Kumoji, Naha, Okinawa, Japan.

Bay Area Okinawa Peace Network, 353- 30th Street, San Francisco, CA 94131.

Asia Pacific Center for Justice and Peace, 110 Maryland Ave. NE, Washington, DC 20002

Chapter Thirty-Three

Afghan Women in the Peace Process

Pamela Collett

> I know what is a mine, or tank, or *kalashnikov* but I
> don't know what does peace look like. Because I have
> not seen it. I have just heard of it from others.
> —(Afghan third-grade students at Khorasan School,
> Islamabad, Pakistan)

Young Afghans have never known peace. Many of the students who wrote this prose poem have never even seen Afghanistan. They have grown up as refugees in Iran or Pakistan. Seventeen years of war have erased nearly every Afghan's memory of what peace looks like. Nonetheless, a few Afghan women are trying to reconstruct a vision of peace for themselves, their children, their families, and their communities.

Afghan women working for peace do so within a society composed of traditional, predominantly tribal cultures that do not accept women as decision-makers or leaders. The Soviet occupation of Afghanistan was resisted in part because the Communist-backed Afghan regime was pushing rural Afghan women out of *purdah* (seclusion) and into literacy classes. Rural male societies saw this as a threat to their identity, since they define honor as having complete control over the women in their families.

Inside Afghanistan, in the southern and western regions, the situation has worsened for women during the past year, thanks to the increasing control held by the Taliban military faction. The Taliban have forbidden women—except for some health workers—to work outside the home and have closed all girls' schools. Female teachers have also been forbidden to work in the boys' schools.

Under Taliban rule, women are forbidden the freedom of mobility, study, or employment. A woman who went to the market alone in Kandahar was beaten by Taliban supporters and later died from her injuries. A nurse who was ordered to operate on a woman refused because she was unqualified; she was then beaten for trying to consult a male doctor.

Taliban, most of whom come from the Pashtun ethnic group and have received religious and military training in Pakistan, claim that all contact between men and women—except near relatives—is forbidden in Islam. Their "fundamentalist" interpretation of Islam has rationalized their disregard for human rights and their direct use of force. Many claim that rather than "fundamentalist," a more appropriate term to describe the Taliban would be "fascist," since they do not represent an authentic interpretation of Islam based on the Qu'ran nor do they represent traditional patriarchal Afghan culture.

As noted in the September 1994 Special Rapporteur's report to the United Nations, Afghanistan has no effective central government: not in the army, the police, the judiciary, or in the rule of law. Instead, the nation is governed by regional administrative units, led by commanders or councils (*shuras*); Afghans have no personal security because the armed militia are a law unto themselves.

In Kabul and in Mazar-i-Sharif—located in northern Afghanistan—women still have some mobility and work in offices, schools, and government agencies (although they're rarely consulted in internal decision-making or in the U.N.'s external peacemaking process). They do not have to wear the *hijab* but can walk down the street wearing a thin head scarf, a long skirt, and high heeled shoes. In Jalalabad, which is governed by a *shura* that opposes women's human rights, a woman dressed this way would likely be stoned.

Three principal groups now control Afghanistan: those led by Rashid Dostum in the north, by the Taliban in the south and west, and by Burhanuddin Rabbani in Kabul. For several months, the Taliban, who control more territory than the other two rival factions, have been trying to capture the capital city, Kabul. Almost daily, the Taliban lob rockets on civilians in Kabul. Every day a few more are killed—people walking down the street, working in offices, or riding in buses. Every day a dozen or more men, women, and children are brought to the hospitals, maimed or killed by land mines planted through many sections of the city.

Although the situation seems outwardly calm, people are frightened by the Taliban attacks. Many remember what happened in 1992, after the Soviets withdrew and the Afghan factions fought among themselves, destroying large sections of Kabul. Women and girls were not safe. Militias in Kabul would rape, torture, and kill any woman from a tribe or ethnic group other than their own. Young women were abducted by commanders and forced into "marriage" (that is, raped). Commanders had as many as ten "wives." If the girls or their families resisted, they were often killed. Many families sent their girls and women away to Pakistan to protect them.

This was a very repressive time for women. Among other things, they had no reproductive rights. All contraceptive drugs had been destroyed by the *mujahadin*, because they were "un-Islamic." If any women or girls were seen on the streets in clothing that the *mujahadin* considered "improper," they were threatened with punishment if it happened again. Guards were posted in every office to watch how women dressed, and how they behaved. Women were told they must wear *hijab* (veil) and no makeup.

Some families in Kabul fear a repeat of the rapes, tortures, and murders of 1992. One woman described the women in Kabul as "like the living dead, with no hope for tomorrow. They are not sure what may happen in the next hour" (personal interview). Many, especially educated women and widows, fear that if the Taliban overrun Kabul, they won't let the women leave their homes.

Women have suffered the effects of war in Afghanistan differently than have men. While men were off fighting, women suffered the loss of family protection, the loss of physical and economic security, the loss of home, and the loss of health and education services in their daily lives. Although children, husbands, brothers, and other relatives were killed and wounded, women continued to carry out their familial responsibilities.

Most of the Afghan refugees are women and children. Up to one-third of Afghan women are widows. Many must care for their children alone, and somehow provide them with food, housing, health care, and education despite the ongoing war (and a limited ability to work). Refugee women living in Pakistan are often the sole supporters of extended families. One woman working for a U.N. agency in Islamabad supports twenty family members: "I have never married, because if I did, who would support all of my family?" she asks. Due to war, many women are playing a key economic role in their families, yet they still lack a decision-making role in their society.

Female refugees, especially widows, have no right of safe return to Afghanistan. Traditionally, all women are supposed to be protected by a male family member. Because they now lack this, widows have no protection, no right to employment, no benefits or guarantees of security. Women are sometimes targeted for revenge killings by particular factional groups or tribes. As a result, widows living in Pakistan whose husbands were members of the former Communist-backed regime fear they will be executed if they try to return to Afghanistan.

The story of one woman illustrates these problems. After suffering through a year of constant bombing and fighting by rival *mujahadin* groups, a university professor fled from Kabul in 1993 with her husband and three children. They took only one bag filled with clothes for their children. When a militia man snatched the bag from her, she challenged him, demanding to know what her children should wear if he took their clothes. He returned the bag. On a bus heading for Pakistan, they disguised their eleven-year-old daughter because they feared she might be kidnapped. After a long journey with several stops by armed militia searching for valuables, young women, or members of rival factions, the family was ordered off the bus. They walked into the dark night, stumbling over rocks, urging their children to walk faster, frightened by every sound. Not knowing where they were going, they somehow found their way across the border into Pakistan.

The family came to Peshawar, where the professor's sister was working with the United Nations. Her husband had to return to Kabul when he heard that two of his brother's children had been killed when a rocket hit their home. The professor never saw her husband again. She heard that he was murdered by the *mujahadin* upon his return to Kabul. She works as a translator, living with her mother (who is sick), her sister, her three children, and her two nieces in two rooms above a shop in a bazaar. Her two nieces have been sent from Kabul so that they can continue their education since most schools are closed in Kabul.

The professor has nightmares that cause her to wail in an eerie whining voice. In her dreams, rockets fly through the air and she can see her family's house being destroyed. The walls of the family home collapse, and everything is gone. She is plagued by constant anxiety. Where can she go? What can she do to support her family if educated women have no right to work outside the home?

She loves her country, and hopes to return someday. But she also wonders whether she should try to emigrate to Canada. Where can she be safe? Where can she see her children receive an education? She cannot answer these questions right now, but to help create answers for herself and other women in similar situations, she has joined a group of women who are working for peace in Afghanistan.

Despite the limitations placed on women, a few educated Afghan women—many of them displaced persons or refugees from Kabul—have decided to work for peace. Traditionally, even educated women have not played a major decision-making role in their families, communities, or countries. The shredding of their culture and the devastation of their country have pushed them to take steps for peace.

The few Afghan women who attended the NGO Forum on Women in Hairou, China, in September 1995, as part of the United Nations' Fourth World Conference on Women, were exposed to the international peace movement. Upon their return to Pakistan, they organized a follow-up meeting in Islamabad. This produced the Afghan Women's Network, formed to work for peace and women's human rights in Afghanistan. Because they lack a tradition of civil society, where individuals voluntarily pursue projects to improve their society, Afghan women involved in peace activities lack organizational skills. But they are learning very quickly.

In October 1995, Equality Now, the New York-based international NGO for women's human rights, passed on a report on women's human rights in Afghanistan to the U.N. Human Rights Committee and to the *New York Times*. It noted that among other violations of women's human rights, U.N. agencies in Jalalabad had themselves suspended Afghan women staff in response to a religious *shura* decree that women were forbidden to work outside the home.

The report and the media response focused international attention on the human rights of women and girls in Afghanistan. In accord with the Convention on the Rights of the Child and its own charter—which forbids discrimination—UNICEF suspended its educational programs in areas of Afghanistan where girls were denied access to education. This decision has provoked a debate within U.N. agencies and NGOs about whether women's human rights should be a precondition for humanitarian assistance. To provide a forum to discuss gender and development, the Advisory Group on Gender Issues in Afghanistan—comprised of U.N. agencies and NGOs working in Afghanistan—was established in Islamabad, Pakistan, in December 1995.

But even the Advisory Group refused to endorse the idea that Afghan women should be involved in the peace process. Some members noted that the warring factions would never allow women's participation and that only military groups were relevant. The Afghan Women's Network disagreed, claiming there would be no lasting peace without women's participation. They quietly took action to try to include women in the peace process.

In January 1996, the Afghan Women's Network wrote to Ambassador Mahmoud Mestiri—the special envoy of the U.N. Secretary-General responsible for establishing peace in Afghanistan. It explained the importance of including women in the peace process. The Network explained their view of peace, as something built up slowly in communities, based on mutual respect, cooperation, and human rights. It advocated this as complementary to the political process of stopping the fighting. But stopping the fighting does not equal peace. Peace will take time and effort to develop. All U.N., NGO, and Afghan groups and individuals interested in peace must cooperate to build a truly lasting peace.

The Network explained to Mestiri and his male advisors that war has affected women differently than men. Women do not profit from the war: they get no power, money, or positions from it. Women only experience war's deprivations. Afghan women are not corrupted by war the same way as men. Most women are not involved with the Afghan factions. Women are better positioned to work for peace in Afghanistan than are most men, who are more directly involved with fighting and power games. As one woman noted, "Why is the U.N. talking to the warlords about peace? Their lives are based on making money and getting power from war. They don't want peace" (personal interview).

To hear women's views on peace, Mestiri must add a woman to his team. Otherwise, he cannot hear the voices of women, because in traditional Afghan communities, women cannot meet with strange men. Without any women on Mestiri's peacemaking team, the U.N. has effectively ruled out the participation of Afghan women. A female representative of the U.N. Special Mission, with the help of U.N. and NGO agencies, could arrange a series of meetings with women to discuss their views on peace. This could be part of organizing women's *shuras* for peace and human rights throughout Afghanistan, and among refugees in Iran and Pakistan.

The Afghan Women's Network has urged Mestiri to consult regularly with women and women's organizations. He has encouraged the Network to contact other U.N. officials, including the Secretary-General Boutros Boutros-Ghali to discuss the importance of including women in the peace process in Afghanistan.

But Afghan women are not waiting for the U.N. to act. Instead, they have started a series of their own activities in Afghanistan and Pakistan to promote peace. In March 1996, a group of women in Mazar-i-sharif gathered in a circle in front of one of Afghanistan's most famous shrines to pray for peace. Traditionally, even women in *purdah* (seclusion) can visit shrines with other women to pray.

To stimulate discussion within the Afghan community, the Afghan Women's Network started a peace questionnaire that is being circulated among the Afghan community in Pakistan and Afghanistan. The Network hopes individuals and organizations will spontaneously spread the idea of the peace questionnaire among Afghans to help initiate grassroots discussion about peace. The questionnaire invites people to give their ideas on "What is peace?" and "What can women, men, and children do for peace?" Responses are published in the Network's newsletter.

Several members of the Afghan Women's Network work as teachers. They have asked their students to write and to make drawings about peace. A group of teachers and parents will select some of the writings and drawings, and put them in a booklet. They are also organizing an exhibit of student posters for peace. The prose poem that begins this essay illustrates the student writing about peace. The students remain hopeful, as expressed in their words: "When peace comes, I will see what does it look like. I am sure I will then forget the names of all the weapons I know."

Chapter Thirty-Four

The Impact of Women in Black in Israel

Gila Svirsky

Never doubt that a small group of thoughtful, committed citizens can change the world. Indeed, it's the only thing that ever has.

These words from Margaret Mead have been facing me across my desk for many years and have often given me heart when change seemed hopeless. Women in Black as a movement seems to have been sustained by this thought, or by one like it. But how did the change actually come about, and what role did Women in Black play in making it happen?

Making Peace an Option

What turned the situation around—from Palestinians and Israelis trying to clobber each other into submission to the same groups negotiating peace?

I believe the dynamics were as follows. The Palestinians in the territories, crushed under the burden of the occupation, began their popular uprising, the *intifada*. The violence of the *intifada* woke up the Israeli people to the evils of the occupation. Not only did it send a message of Palestinian suffering, it also brought suffering into the homes of the Israelis. Since, with several exceptions, army service is compulsory for all Israeli Jewish young men and women, almost every household began to feel the effects of the violence—death, injury, or the terror of being killed or injured. Simultaneously, the Israeli peace movement began to flourish, motivated both by (a) a sincere desire to end the repression of another people, and (b) a desire to stop the violence turned against Israel. The years of *intifada* created an intolerable situation inside Israel, and the Israeli government was searching for a way to end it. Force had proven ineffectual. Meanwhile, the peace movement was continuously bombarding the government and the public with its message that holding on to the territories was a liability and that the Palestine Liberation Organization (PLO) was an acceptable partner for negotiations. It fomented discontent within the status quo and the Greater Israel policy, and created a climate of legitimacy for compromise with the PLO.

The final factor that made peace possible began with the Gulf War. Yassar Arafat took the side of Saddam Hussein, who lost the war, and as a result Arafat lost considerable financial support from the wealthy Arab Gulf states that had rallied against Saddam. Arafat was about to lose power to his rivals within the PLO when Yitzak Rabin won the election in Israel and offered him a way out—making peace. Rabin and Shimon Peres knew that Arafat was in a vulnerable position and they could strike a good bargain with him at this moment. Arafat had no choice. Either he made peace, hoping to mobilize support for this from the Palestinians and the wealthy Gulf states—or he would lose his power base. The Palestinians had by then had their fill of *intifada*. Arafat chose peace.

What was the role of the peace movement? It legitimized the options out of the quandary, options that previously had been unpalatable to Israelis: it maintained that compromise was fine. It said that Arafat was no hero, but he was the one with whom to negotiate. It agreed that a Palestinian state is a viable option. In short, the peace movement guaranteed support to the government for entering into negotiations with Arafat. It was, thus, one critical component in a chain of factors.

Impact Wears Many Faces

The Women in Black vigil was one part of the tidal wave of seventy-four peace organizations that mobilized Israelis to demand peace. Singers sang peace songs, writers wrote books, lobbyists leaned on Knesset members, organizations documented human rights violations, some soldiers refused to serve in the territories, and many others went to demonstrations, marches, teach-ins, civil disobedience actions, and vigils, week after week after week. All of us together made the difference. All the protest work during this period contributed to creating the public climate that made possible the choice of peace by the politicians and countered the message of a Greater Israel that had dominated the Israeli agenda until then.

In the discouraging old days, before Oslo became a concept, not just a city, it was easy to disparage the effect that any of us were having. But now with the hindsight of the peace process we can be more realistic about our impact and we can ask ourselves, more usefully: What was the contribution that each group made to the tidal wave of protest? Specifically, what was the unique contribution of Women in Black to creating the climate for peace? The place to begin is with the woman herself.

Impact: Personal Transformation

Some of the founding Women in Black were already highly political women who had been involved in organizing for years. For most of us, however, donning black and standing on the vigil brought about a profound personal transformation. You could not stand on this intense vigil for six, seven, or eight weeks—not to mention six, seven, or eight years—without being significantly altered. In what ways?

First, standing on the vigil politicized women who had not previously been politically involved. Reactions to our vigil (by bystanders, friends, or family) made it incumbent upon us to have a more informed response ready for them. Now we were educating ourselves about the issues, reading about and discussing them, attending political lectures, giving political activity a higher priority in our lives than activities that had previously consumed our attention and devotion. Second, participation in the vigil radicalized our thinking. It made us more critical of the comfortable views of the liberal camp, more skeptical of official positions, leading us to shift our votes from the centrist Labor Party to the liberal Meretz, or from liberal Meretz to progressive Hadash. Discussions among ourselves—and communication with women peace activists from other countries—raised our consciousness to more progressive solutions, leading us to eschew military and violent solutions to political problems, to adopt a more human rights perspective, and to repudiate the glorification of the army, one of Israel's holiest cows. And, third, participating in the vigil was a tremendously empowering experience. A woman who continued to stand through the anger and fear we evoked, through the bitter cold and broiling sun, through the seeming hopelessness of change—had to have honed the strength inside her. It increased a sense of determination, of belief in self, of powerfulness.

Related to these changes was the increased appreciation for feminist formats and values—cooperative decision-making, power-sharing, support for the weaker links in social networks. Not every woman on the vigil would agree to be labeled "feminist," but all were persuaded by the feminist process and moved closer to a feminist perspective.

Once you have several thousand women feeling politicized, radicalized, and empowered, it is not surprising to find them having an effect on others. The following categories suggest some audiences where the impact of Women in Black was—and was not—absorbed.

Impact: Immediate Circles

Inevitably, women who are more politicized and more radicalized will have an impact on their immediate environment away from the vigil, and so we did. Women as mothers, teachers, nurses, social workers, secretaries, doctors, librarians—all the many audiences we encountered in our personal lives were exposed to our thinking. We, the great army of nurturers, now served up politics with your dinner. My two daughters became Women in Black. Some of our mothers started coming to the vigil. Our schoolchildren were captive listeners to our message of ending political violence (couched within more neutral material). The ripple effect of our presence, thousands of secret agents who refused to sit still for inhumanity and violence, could only be felt in ever-widening circles.

Impact: Jewish Constituents in Israel

Although there was a flowering of peace organizations in Israel following the outbreak of the *intifada*, it subsided as the initial shock of the violence wore off and burnout took its toll. Throughout the period of the Likud government and even more so during the Labor government, the right wing dominated the streets—posters, stickers, flyers, buttons, demonstrations, marches. You could barely find a major intersection in the main cities without a few right-wing activists holding their favorite slogans aloft. Throughout this period, Women in Black was the only group that made a consistent effort to counter the pro-occupation barrage, to keep the message of peace out on the streets. Peace Now held rallies, some with very large turnouts, but they were few and far between. Women in Black were "the most persistently visible of campaigners" (Silver, 1991:16). We did not let the public slip into inattention. "Their constant presence is a clear and unavoidable reminder of the issues at stake" (Schrag, 1990:10). We were there to remind other Israelis who were discouraged by the visibility of the right wing that the voices for peace had not been silenced.

Peace groups also had dynamic effects on one another. The radical groups kept nipping at the heels of the more centrist organizations, pushing them to keep up, to assume more daring postures, to take greater risks. Women in Black was itself urged into more courageous positions by the seasoned radicals of the Women and Peace Coalition, and by reactions to us from the authorities and outsiders. Peace Now was the largest mixed-gender peace organization, and its reputation for moderation gave it credibility. When the PLO (in December 1988 at a conference in Algeria) declared its renunciation of terrorism and, implicitly, its acceptance of a Jewish state beside the Palestinian state-in-the-making, Peace Now was free to espouse the positions of negotiating with the PLO and two states for two peoples. Peace Now's approval now gave the seal of *kashruth* to these former taboos, and won over many more mainstream supporters than the radical groups ever could.

One odd offspring of Women in Black that must be mentioned is the "Women in Green" movement. At some point during the *intifada* when the nationalist right was dominating the streets, a group of extremist right wing women became the focus of considerable media attention. Dubbed "Women in Green" by the media in reference to their green hats and frank allusion to us, these women hardly resembled Women in Black in other ways. They espoused a religiously fundamentalist vision of Israel and pursued it by staging unruly demonstrations against peace, occasionally ending in arrests on charges of disturbing the peace or violating police orders, and once for squatting on Palestinian land. Not surprisingly, most members of Women in Green deny any connection to feminism, though they are not beyond a cynical use of feminist slogans to achieve the desired effect: "This junta [the Labor government] is raping the Jewish people" (Sugarman, Zacharia, and Grynberg, 1995:15). Thus, Women in Black begot a rebellious "daughter movement" to counter our effect.

A more natural and friendly successor to Women in Black is the organization Bat Shalom, which opened its doors in March 1994 in an effort to devise new strategies for the women's peace movement in Israel. We can only wish them success. Bat Shalom is further evidence that women realize the crucial role they can play in advocating for peace.

Impact: International

Long before the Madrid peace conference and very long before the current peace negotiations, Palestinian and Israeli women were taking part in international conferences for peace, including the "peace tent" at the Nairobi Women's Conference. Detailed peace treaties were hammered out between Israeli and Palestinian women in Jerusalem, Brussels, New York, Italy, Malta, and Geneva years before the men figured out how to do it in Oslo. True, these women did not have the weighty burdens of office to consider, but the question still arises: Why were "enemy women" sitting together to negotiate years before the men?

First, it should be said that during the years of the *intifada*, this was not the work of the vigil, but of the larger Women and Peace Coalition. In this body, the more radical women set the tone. It was the Coalition that maintained contacts with the European organizations of women for peace, signed international peace agreements with the Palestinians, held aloft slogans that were light years ahead of "End the Occupation," and staged demonstrations that left more moderate women, sometimes literally, gasping for air: "With the first joint Palestinian-Israeli women's march in December 1989—in which both groups were tear-gassed by Israeli soldiers and police—the movement secured its place in the avant-garde of the Left" (Katz, 1995: 20). Virtually all members of the Women and Peace Coalition were also Women in Black, and it often suited the drama of the occasion to dress in black for these events.

The internationalist feminist approach of these women made it possible—and quite natural—to reach across borders and even across so-called enemy lines. This was not a woman's natural predilection for peacemaking, but the ideological commitment of women to a vision of international peace. It did not come from instinct, but from socializing and educating each other over the years. Being outside establishment politics was an asset in taking a more critical perspective.

Whether through the Coalition or directly, the links of Women in Black with women's peace organizations around the world were a two-way street of support and sustenance. We drew inspiration from each other. "Women in Black gained prestige as its name spread; it became a model for the international women's movement for peace" (Katz, 1995: 20). And the international women's movement for peace become a model for us: "Belonging to the circles of feminist women throughout the world who struggle against violence and who work to promote a political-cultural alternative which will include the experience of women gives me the strength to continue in work that is often perceived as hopeless" (Deutsch, 1994: 6). The impact of our activity in Israel was amplified by the dozens of Women in Black vigils that formed all over the world, some in solidarity with our cause and others taking a stand about their local issues. From the brochure of the Asian Women's Human Rights Council based in Manila:

> We are the Women in Black—a movement that has inspired groups of women in different parts of the world to stand in their own towns and cities, at street corners, in market squares and other public places—for one hour every week—dressed in black—

silently protesting the many forms of violence which are increasingly becoming intrinsic to our everyday realities in our different cultures and communities. (Asian Women's Human Rights Council, 1995: 1)

And one more testimony to our impact from an international source:

It is clear that there is a particular power to this quite simple gesture. Just the intensity of response that it can provoke—to say nothing of the way it has spread among women internationally, or the effect it can have on participants—is enough of an indication of that. Probably the effectiveness of any symbolic protest action depends on the extent to which it can shake our traditional mental categories. The Women in Black phenomenon does that . . . these Women in Black were standing, blatantly, in the middle of the public world—visible, unavoidable, inescapably political. (Helwig, 1993: 8–9)

Impact: Palestinians

One of the important audiences for Women in Black was the Palestinians. It was important for them to know that there are Israelis with whom a real peace can be made. This was as important for the Palestinian trucker who delivered a crate of cucumbers to the vigil at Kibbutz Nahshon so that his son could learn "that not all Israelis are border guards, soldiers, police, or tax collectors" as it was for Arab political leaders. President Mubarak of Egypt and Hanan Ashrawi, the former spokesperson of the PLO, have both mentioned Women in Black in the context of taking heart from the peace camp in Israel. It was important for us to tell the Palestinians, to tell Arabs in general, and to tell the world at large that not all Israelis support the occupation policies of the Israeli government, and that some of us also yearn for a just peace.

Impact: Passersby

And finally, the angry passersby. Here, of course, we had no impact at all. I have no illusions that there was a single person who disagreed with us who became convinced of our views by seeing us stand there. They were not our target audience. We did not stand on the vigil to convince Likud voters to vote Labor, nor did we hope to convince Shamir to forfeit his vision of a Greater Israel. These were obviously impossible tasks.

What we did attempt to do was create a constant sound of peace, a *soprano continuo* demanding reconciliation. Women in Black and other peace organizations together encouraged and gave voice to the growing body of Israelis who had enough of war and suffering. We were the voice of the silent public who would rather sit at home than be on the streets holding up signs. We represented the Israelis who wanted peace but were too well mannered (or constrained by jobs or family) to raise their own voice. Our silent protest served as their voice, demanding peace on behalf of us all.

Women in Black were the conscience of Jerusalem and Tel-Aviv and Kibbutz Nahshon and the thirty-six other places in Israel where we stood. We were not Cassandras, wailing our prophecies of doom to an inattentive public. We were heard, though it wasn't always pleasant for those listening. Week in and week out, year in and year out, Women in Black did not allow the Israeli public to forget the occupation and its brutal consequences. And ultimately, the impact was felt through all these ripples, our personal and our public lives, pulsing through Israeli society and the world at large.

Peace. Peace?

And, finally, the question of peace. If you walk through the streets of modern post-Oslo Israel, particularly through the streets of Jerusalem, that beautiful but cursed town seething with intensity and suffering, you will see a variety of stickers on the cars. Bumper stickers are where the silent majority and the silent minority express themselves best. During the days of the *intifada*, the only stickers extant were "Greater Israel," "Hebron Forever," "The Nation is with the Golan," and the like. Peace stickers were rare, as their presence would invite a passing political adversary to slash the tires, "fold" the wipers, or simply "key" the paint job. Not anymore. Today, you can gauge the climate that favors peace by a long line of blue squares, sun clouds passing through a clear blue sky, with one word only on them: "Peace." A beautiful production of the Peace Now movement. And there are stickers saying "Yes to Peace, No to Violence," a sad allusion to the many terrorist incidents that continue to plague both Israelis and Palestinians by extremist forces. I saw a picture of Rabin on one sticker: "In his death, he left us a legacy of peace." I wish a legacy of peace—one even deeper than Rabin's—really were on the doorstep: not a state of nonbelligerence, but a peace that fuses the concepts of shared land, shared destiny, and shared struggle for a better life. But we still seem to be some way off from this.

The conflict in the Middle East, while rooted in conflicting claims to the same territory by two nations, is fueled by the many parties who have an interest in keeping the enmity alive. In Israel and the Arab countries, these parties include religious fundamentalists, right-wing politicians, liberal governments with reactionary policies, the military establishments, and the international arms industry. Some of these parties foment violence deliberately, while others don't realize that their actions in the interests of "security" foster the kind of fear that leads to aggression. Developing, testing, and carrying a big stick is an invitation to get hit.

I wish I could end this story by saying, "And now there is peace and we are living happily ever after," but I cannot. No matter when I stop this story, it will not have an unequivocally happy ending. A true reconciliation of hearts and minds is still distant in the Middle East, battered and scarred by years of hostility. Open borders and a "new Middle East" will not come about in my lifetime. As an optimist, I am hoping that it will come about in my children's lifetimes, but as a realist, I think of ill-will between two otherwise wonderful nations. Now in their twenties, my daughters have already lived through (though not all their friends have made it) the scuds of Saddam, the bus bombs of Hamas, and, as I finish this writing, *katyushas* of the Hezbollah in Lebanon exploding on my younger daughter's kibbutz. My Palestinian friends have lived through much suffering as well.

The price of war and violence is fierce and often irreversible. I can only pray that my daughters and all our children have absorbed the lessons of hope, the will to persist, and a sense of the power of committed citizens. Efforts to make peace can exact a very high price, but their rewards are immeasurable.

REFERENCES

Asian Women's Human Rights Council. 1995. *Women in Black: A Gathering of Spirit*. Bangalore, India.

Deutsch, Yvonne. 1994. "And Peace Shall Multiply Like Mushrooms." Unpublished essay.

Helwig, Maggie. 1993. "Wearing Black for the Enemy." *Peace News*, November, 8–9.

Katz, Shira. 1995. "New Agendas of the Women's Movement for Peace: To Be or How To Be?" *Challenge*, May–June, 21.

Schrag, Carl. 1990. "Staking a Claim for Peace: Grassroots Peace Movements in Israel." *Israel Scene*, April/May, 8–12.

Silver, Eric. 1991. "What Now for Peace Now?" *The Jerusalem Report*, March 7, 16–17.

Sugarman, Margo Lipschitz, Janine Zacharia, and Daniel Grynberg. 1995. "A Chronology of Hate." *The Jerusalem Report*, November 30, 15.

Chapter Thirty-Five

Israeli and Palestinian Women Working for Peace

Ronit Lentin

> Peace? I don't remember a time of peace during my life. My father used to speak of the 'time of peace' before World War I, but since I was born in 1921, there was always either war or a war looming.
> —(Lia Tsabar, seventy-six-year-old Israeli woman, personal communication, December 1994)

> For me, as a Palestinian and a woman, peace means being equal to Israeli women; and equal to my brother, a Palestinian man. If this does not exist, it is not peace.
> —(Manar Hassan, member of Al Fanar, the Israeli-based Palestinian Feminist Organization, personal communication, December 1994)

Although peace in the Middle East has been negotiated by military men, Israeli and Palestinian women have played a central, though unsung, role in the peace process since the 1967 war. Like war, peace in the Middle East is gendered. A direct link exists between the Israeli-Arab conflict and women's position in both societies, and between militarism and sexism. We must ask whether the current vision of peace, negotiated by military men, is what women really want. Israeli and Palestinian women, aware of the link between the patriarchal nature of war and the position of women, increasingly try to tie together the national and the feminist agendas.

Societies with a national liberation struggle high on their agenda tend to treat women's emancipation as marginal to the national question. But in recent years, Israeli feminists have challenged this notion, realizing that the Arab-Israeli conflict has influenced the construction of Israeli women as ethnic subjects. New trends in interpretive Israeli sociology portray Israel as a settler-colonial society, and thus current Israeli feminism has been shifting the debate from looking at the status of Israeli women to analyzing Israel as a masculine-military society.

New analyses of the Occupied Palestinian Territories examine women who work for national liberation or for women's liberation, or for some combination of the two. Souad Dajani, a Palestinian lecturer at Antioch College in Ohio, argues that the fundamentalist backlash against women who assumed public roles during the *intifada* warned women about the discrimination they could face in a future Palestinian state. Dajani argues that as Palestinian women explore the implications of living in a future Palestinian state, "perhaps the next *intifada* will be the women's *intifada*" (Dajani, 1994: 54).

Simona Sharoni, an Israeli professor at American University in Washington, D.C., examines the relationship between militarism and sexism within broader feminist debates. Sharoni rejects equity feminism, which encourages women to serve in the military so they can transform it and also gain greater social power. She also rejects essentialist feminism, which argues that women, because of their mothering qualities, are more peaceful than men. Instead, Sharoni argues that military power itself must be understood as gendered. Thus, only social feminism can explain the link between militarism and sexism, and between violence against women and the general violence of Israeli-Palestinian relations (Sharoni, 1994).

Indeed, violence against women in both Israeli and Palestinian societies increases when military violence escalates. During the 1991 Gulf War more complaints of violence against women were recorded than at any other time. During the *intifada*, violence against Palestinian women by Palestinian men also increased. Israel—like many colonized nations once they assume independence—privileges national security above all else. The Palestinians, colonized for centuries, also elevate the national agenda above all else, and thus maintain rigid gender divisions.

The difference between the peace activism practiced by Israeli women compared to Palestinian women stems from the difference between occupier and occupied. Like their male counterparts, Israeli women peace activists are largely motivated by their moral revulsion against the occupation and its "corruptive" influences on Israeli society, and by their solidarity with the Palestinians. Palestinian women are motivated more by their national aspirations for statehood and their recognition that this can be achieved only through peace.

If Palestinian peace activism is linked to Palestinian nationalism, Israeli nationalism is the antithesis of peace activism. This Israeli left-right split divides Israeli society between those favoring "national" goals, such as a strong and often "greater" Israel, and those favoring Palestinian political self-determination side-by-side with Israel.

The distinctive styles of Israeli women's peace efforts suggests a continuing tension between women's quest for equality within the existing political system and their search for more fundamental changes in Israeli politics and society. According to Knesset member and Hebrew University political science professor Naomi Israeli, women's reasons for being involved in peace activities are diverse and contradictory. The limited political opportunities open to women have pushed them to create their own informal networks. Some women became involved because of their heightened identification as Israelis and Zionists. Other women responded to the specifically feminist themes of the Israeli-Palestinian conflict: oppression, self-determination, human dignity, justice, and security. This led to their willingness to trade territories for peace, and to their greater openness toward the PLO than that shown by Israeli men. The growing awareness of gender inequalities in Israeli society highlighted the connections among women (in both communities), the ongoing conflict, and the growing militarization of Israeli society. Finally, symbols of motherhood were used to explain both women's involvement in peace activism and increasing female right-wing extremism.

Israeli women's peace activism has had three main phases. The first emphasized solidarity-motivated protests and vigils, and work with Palestinian women political prisoners. The second phase promoted a dialogue between Palestinian and Israeli women. The third and current phase combines solidarity-inspired protests, dialogue and uninational feminist consciousness raising.

By the end of 1989 there were some 180 Israeli and Israeli-Palestinian mixed and women-only peace groups. Women's peace work has followed four main paths. First, there was women's peace activism in formal (mostly left) political parties committed to peace, including the coalition partners in the Labor Party and the left-alignment, Merez. Eight of the eleven female Knesset members (who constitute 9.2 percent of the legislature) are drawn from these parties. Second, there were peace activities within established women's associations. Third, there was work in mixed extra-parliamentary peace movements, where women, although the majority, were often relegated to answering phones and taking notes at meetings. Because peace groups such as "Peace Now" are headed by former high-ranking officers who "dared put their bodies on the line" to defend Israel and who control the terms of the peace discourse, women have been prevented from offering a serious feminist challenge to the national security rhetoric.

Finally, there has been peace activism in women-only peace organizations. Very soon after the *intifada* began in December 1987, women-only peace groups were formed around projects such as "The Peace Cloth" (devoted to stitching together 200 meters of peace messages to cover the negotiating table), and various Israeli-Palestinian women's dialogue groups. At the same time, several women's coalitions for peace, such as the Women's Organization for Political Prisoners, and Shani— Israeli Women Against the Occupation, were formed.

The best-known Israeli women's peace organization is Women in Black, founded in January 1988 when ten women from the radical left began to stand in vigils in a central Jerusalem square between 1 and 2 P.M. each Friday to protest the occupation and its attendant violence. After two years, there were between two thousand and three thousand Women in Black throughout Israel. Often they became targets of verbal and physical violence by passersby who told the women, among other things, to "go home and wash the floor" or called them "whores of Arafat." Some male passersby claimed the women were sexually frustrated and volunteered their "weapons" to cure the women's "protest disease." Sharoni sees this as another example of the intertwined cultures of militarism and sexism (Sharoni, 1994: 125).

Erella Shadmi, a Woman in Black member and sociology lecturer at Bet Berl Institute, claims that Women in Black redefined traditional images of femininity. Members used their bodies to express their protest; they dressed in black, ridiculing the image of woman as "pure" and the traditional "white" of peace; they broke the public/private dichotomy and entered politics through the back door, creating new spaces for women in society and thus a new political discourse (Shadmi, 1992:9).

Women in Black vigils stopped after the Declaration of Principles was signed in September 1993, but they resumed again in March 1995 with more explicit slogans: "Connection and Openness Instead of Segregation and Closure;" "Dismantle the Settlements"; "End the Closure"; and "Jerusalem: Two Capitals for Two States."

In December 1988 the national coalition Women and Peace was established, and in May 1989, after an Israeli-Palestinian Women's Conference in Brussels, a broad women's peace coalition, The Israel Women's Peace Net (Reshet), committed to dialogue with Palestinian women, was founded. Reshet hosted home meetings in Israel with Palestinian women and visits by Israeli women to the Occupied Territories.

Some feminists criticized Reshet and Women in Black as nonfeminist, but Israeli women from the political center were now working on an agenda hitherto supported by the left, advocating Palestinian rights and a two-states solution. At the same time, a new feminist agenda was being formed within the Women and Peace coalition, linking violence against women to the Israeli occupation.

Formal peace activities came to a halt with the 1991 Gulf War when Israeli and Palestinian women found themselves on opposite sides. According to Yvonne Deutsch, director of the Jerusalem feminist center Kol Haisha, Israeli women's political responses during the Gulf War stemmed from deep fears of Iraqi threats—even though they sided with the West, while the Palestinian women's point of reference was the Third World. Although some Women in Black vigils resumed during the war's fourth and fifth weeks, the growing gap between the reality of war and their aspirations for peace frustrated the Israeli women. Palestinian women, meanwhile, were disappointed by the failure to break through the political barriers of Jewish society.

While Israeli women peace activists emphasize peace, Palestinian women peace activists are more inclined to put the gender issue onto the Palestinian national agenda. Ghada Zughayar, director of Jerusalem Link, a joint Israeli-Palestian women's peace movement, attributes this to a reaction against Islamic fundamentalism—whether Hamas or jihad el Islami—and against the national movement's collusion in constructing a Palestinian womanhood that portrays women predominantly as mothers and as protectors of Palestinian, Moslem, and Arab identity (Zughayer, pers. comm., December 1994).

Despite their differences on social issues, most Palestinian women seem committed to a feminist vision of a future Palestinian state. While the Israeli women's peace movement lacks the support of the majority of women, the Palestinian women's movement owes its very existence to the women's organizations that began appearing in the late 1970s and early 1980s.

Palestinian women challenge existing patriarchal priorities. They don't debate their efficacy as peace activists the same way Israeli women do; instead, they concentrate on the national campaign's effect on the feminist agenda. Palestinian women activists, particularly during the *intifada*, took every opportunity to challenge the definitions of the acceptable roles for women. Souad Dajani claims that women's growing involvement in the *intifada* and the backlash against them from traditional religious circles strengthened their conviction that national liberation is insufficient without equality for women and democratization throughout Palestinian society (Dajani, 1994:51).

Women's peace activism in Israel, on the other hand, which uses multiple strategies and which tries to connect feminism, political radicalism, and peace activism, seems inapplicable to the Israeli context, where women's roles have been shaped mostly by the immediacy of the conflict. Naomi Chazan argues that Israeli women's peace activism reflects the polarization and uncertainty inherent in Israeli politics. Its contribution lies precisely in its divergence and its ability to encompass a broad range of concerns (Chazan, 1991:160).

Yvonne Deutsch calls on women to link the recent awareness of violence in Israeli society to the centrality of the Israeli army, and to link militarism to the status of women. Deutsch urges the Israeli women's peace movement to keep crucial issues, such as Jerusalem's fate and the Palestinian right to return, on the political agenda, since only a "confrontation of the meaning of the differences between the two societies will bring about reconciliation between the two peoples." Deutsch advocates the creation of "a feminist political peace culture . . . (which will) challenge the existing patriarchal priorities" (Deutsch, 1994:103).

During the long history of the Israeli-Palestinian conflict the national agendas have eclipsed all others. War, a way of life for decades, is gendered, and when peace is made by military men, peace processes are also gendered. Too many Israeli and Palestinian women peace activists believe that once peace is achieved, "there will be time" to deal with other issues, such as the status of women. But only if peace is ungendered and removed from the jurisdiction of fighting men, and only if women can play a central role in shaping the peace, will peace cease being a masculine enterprise.

In Israel, a man's identity is often his military role and a woman's identity is her support for a military male. Zionism has collapsed the citizen-soldier-man and offered Jewish males a new and unfortunate gender identity based on their military role. In response, women must challenge this very Israeli concept of citizenship, and assure their men that their identities depend on far more than their military role.

The identity of Palestinian men has also been determined by the ongoing conflict. It is defined by their role in resisting or cooperating with the occupation on the one hand, and by the humiliation they suffer under occupation, which often divests them of their very manhood, on the other hand. Palestinian women have traditionally derived their identity from their supportive role in the national struggle. But Palestinian women must challenge this traditional definition of the national struggle and promote a new women's agenda as part of the vision of the future Palestinian state.

Finally, Israeli and Palestinian women should work together to create an alternative, ungendered peace plan, one conceived not by military men but rather by noncombative women, a peace plan that will not privilege security as the only issue at stake but that will take into account the lives of real people.

REFERENCES

Chazan, Naomi. 1991. "Israeli Women and Peace Activism." In Barbara Swirski and Mary-lin Safir (eds.), *Calling the Equality Bluff: Women in Israel*. New York: Pergamon Press.

Dajani, Souad. 1994. "Between National and Social Liberation: The Palestinian Women's Movement in the Israeli Occupied West Bank and Gaza Strip." In Tamar Mayer (ed.), *Women and the Israeli Occupation*. London and New York: Routledge.

Deutsch, Yvonne. 1994. "Israeli Women against the Occupation: Political Growth and the Persistence of Ideology." In Tamar Mayer (ed.), *Women and the Israeli Occupation*. London: Routledge.

Hassan, Manar. 1991. "Growing Up Palestinian and Female in Israel." In Barbara Swirski and Marylin Safir (eds.), *Calling the Equality Bluff: Women in Israel*. New York: Pergamon Press.

Lentin, Ronit. 1996. "A *Yiddishe Mame* Desperately Seeking a *Mame Loshn*: Toward a Theory of the Feminization of Stigma in the Relations between Israel and Holocaust Survivors." *Women's Studies International Forum* 19, no. 1–2: 87–97.

Shadmi, Erella. 1992. "Women, Palestinians, Zionism: A Personal View." *News from Within* 8/10–11:13–16.

Sharoni, Simona. 1994. "Homefront as Battlefront: Gender, Military Occupation and Violence against Women." In Tamar Mayer (ed.), *Women and the Israeli Occupation: The Politics of Change*. London and New York: Routledge.

Chapter Thirty-Six

Silent or Silenced?

Lynne M. Woehrle

As international war grows less popular as a means of confronting differences, what agenda emerges for peace studies? We can consider one approach, built on feminist principles, for designing a pro-active curriculum for peace studies in preparation for the twenty-first century. Several issues must be addressed. First, what do we mean by a "feminist perspective," and why is it important? Second, how would the infusion of feminism affect peace studies: what would be the curriculum's agenda? Third, what are the problems with claiming a feminist standpoint for peace studies? Finally, how can we integrate this new agenda into peace studies programs around the world?

But before we can answer, we must ask: What do we mean by feminism and by peace? Feminism is a method of social and political analysis and action that regards gender and its social construction as essential for assessing the systems that shape human relationships. Here, we're mostly concerned with socialist feminism, radical feminism, poststructuralist feminism, and womanist (women of color) feminism. Peace, on the other hand, may be positive or negative. It is not merely the absence of war or violence, and it represents more than some utopian trek into an alternative future. Peace constitutes a system comprised of a variety of interdependent ingredients.

Several themes dominate a feminist analysis of peace studies: how gender shapes issues of war, peace, and justice; how to form an agenda where the personal is political; how to make connections from the individual to the transnational and vice versa; and how to integrate theory and action. The three latter themes already exist in the peace studies curriculum. But the first theme, the role of gender, can help expand peace studies by providing a more sophisticated understanding of politics, by clarifying what we mean by thinking globally and acting locally, and by helping us devise a workable praxis.

Peace studies must recognize the experiences of women as important, and often as different, from those of men. Yet women themselves are diverse, not homogeneous, and thus peace studies must also consider the impact of race, class, and sexual orientation. The lens we now need to frame the traditional questions of peace studies is a kaleidoscope that adjusts depending on one's social location.

Considering the impact of gender, as well as race, class, and sexual orientation, on one's experience of war and peace or of justice and injustice, would allow peace studies to be examined from women's perspectives and not merely men's. In response to the critiques of feminist peace researchers, the peace studies curriculum has become increasingly open to feminist methodology.

Through a feminist methodology, peace studies can make its curriculum more applicable to our daily lives. It can concretely recognize the personal as political, and make connections among the individual, national, international, and transnational. According to George Lopez (1985), a personal or "nonviolent values and life styles approach" has been the least emphasized in most United States peace studies programs. This frustrates women in peace studies courses when they realize that most of their personal experiences with injustice, violence, and insecurity are absent from the central theories or practical examples they are taught. Nor does peace studies very often teach skills for one's daily life or for creating alternative structures for changing the world.

In contrast, by listening to women we can understand more clearly the difference between mere survival and living in a just and peaceful world. Women's life experiences expand our definition of violence to the personal: to rape and the fear of rape, to battering—crimes that should be public yet still remain primarily in the private or so-called domestic sphere. Understanding the feminist outrage at misogyny illustrates yet another example of the militarization of our lives. Concerns women raise each day about the increasing difficulty of getting access to fuel, food, water, and shelter remind us that ending war is not enough when our lifestyles themselves are killing this planet.

If we better understand the functioning of our ecosystem, then perhaps we can more successfully pursue a pro-active peace project. But we must beware of essentialism: we are not all the same in our experiences, our goals, and our means. We each must learn to define peace in relation to others, but we must not define peace for others. Peace studies could be improved by incorporating current debates on feminism over essentialism and difference, and by creating more space for diversity and coalitions.

Peace studies must also reconsider the praxis of peace and its effects on both those who teach and take the courses. George Lopez has shown that despite the rhetoric favoring the practical experience of activism and internships, peace studies degrees generally do not require active participation. Peace studies and feminist studies share a similar split between academia and activism. This stems partly from the division that often occurs between many university communities and surrounding local communities. Also, activists often condemn theorists for preaching without movement experience, while theorists often view activists as "hot-headed" or "irrational." Only a few straddle both theory and practice, but the creation of a peace system requires that we better nurture these connections.

While feminism itself still searches for a workable approach to participation, and a way to teach it, it may nevertheless offer peace studies an eventual way out of the academic-activist divide. Feminism emphasizes the personal as political. This validates experience as essential to understanding. Experientially based theory is fundamental to effective peace action. In other words, both what and how we teach are important. What structures, for example, do we reinforce in the classroom when we encourage competitiveness, individuality, and ownership of ideas? How can we integrate political actions into the classroom that actively involve our students? What tools do our classes provide the student body? Are we developing a foundation for the alternative society we teach about?

We must help empower students. We can teach them about social change, about nonviolent action, and about a world without weapons, but we must also encourage them to participate in projects such as helping the poor and oppressed. Peace studies should enable us not merely to talk about differences but also to experience them and appreciate cultural diversity. Thus, our education should include multicultural living and working experiences.

Moreover, our curriculum must include issues and theories that speak to the lives of women, of people of color, and of all the dispossessed. Incorporating diversity and daily experiences with peace, conflict, and justice should guide the development of the peace studies curriculum in the 1990s.

We must also better integrate a feminist framework into the classroom and into the research components of peace studies. First, we should revise the list of issues analyzed by peace studies, and the methods for understanding them. Second, we should incorporate the insights feminism offers for new peace research and peace studies. The curriculum must become much more receptive to gender analysis.

Feminism requires us to renegotiate the meaning of several phenomena. For example, feminism expands the traditional definition of the violence studied in peace research to include personal violence and structures of violence that affect women in particular. Feminism alters our traditional understanding of power as the ability to control, and to have or own. Rather than focusing on the tangible accumulation of the symbols of wealth, such as money, women, land, industry, food, shelter, slaves, and employees, we can instead redefine power as something based on competence, ability, and self-determination. We can emphasize power as "power-with" rather than as "power-over." We can transform power into a creative force for empowerment and self-esteem.

Feminists also force us to reconsider our concepts of justice. For example, Carol Gilligan (1982) has described how women, as compared to men, learn to make moral decisions. In the female world, justice and morality are contextualized within relationships. Justice is not simply the codes of law or a matter of rights. One's understanding of justice and morality comes from his or her gender, race, class, sexual orientation, and other factors that define her identity. This might question, for example, whether universal norms or human rights really exist throughout the world.

Feminism could also change how peace studies considers questions of difference and diversity. Peace studies might learn from the contemporary debate within feminism about how diversity is influenced by racism, classism, and imperialism. It might also help peace studies revise its curriculum accordingly. For example, social movement theory has evolved beyond the Eurocentric/Western tradition of the Enlightenment. But besides accounting for other cultures, social movement theory must also be made more relevant to women's experiences and the feminist movement.

We should heed three cautions in our attempt to infuse feminism into peace studies. First, as Christine Sylvester suggests, the "marriage dilemma" questions whether feminists are comfortable with the integration of peace studies and women's studies—how far do we go? Merging the two may sublimate women's specific experiences into humanism: in our present world that will probably mean "man-ism." Rather than completely overlapping, perhaps we need instead to merely recognize how the separate circles of peace studies and feminist studies intersect.

Second, we should be cautious of certain kinds of essentialism or the creation of a mythical homogeneous category of "women." In fact, the relationship between women and war varies cross-culturally. Nor can there be any one feminist agenda; people have a diversity of needs. To curb essentialism, we must include in our curriculum the voices of women from many cultures, classes, and experiences.

Third, we should beware of "ghettoization." How can we study the experiences and contributions of women to war, peace, and justice without being relegated to a token course or to a particular week in the semester? Also, if only feminists teach feminist approaches to peace studies, the discipline will likely not change very much. Instead, everyone teaching peace studies must be encouraged to adopt a feminist perspective.

This might be accomplished, for example, by emphasizing feminist approaches to peace studies as a necessary theme in an introductory course. This could be followed with an upper-level seminar that explores these approaches more thoroughly. Feminist perspectives on peace studies should inform syllabi and scholarship across each program.

So far, feminist peace studies has more readily found a voice through women's studies than through peace studies. When I recently began collecting entries for a bibliography on women's contributions to thinking about peace, war, conflict, and justice, I quickly learned that women's studies rather than peace studies publications were much more likely to produce references.

Why has this happened? Perhaps peace studies has remained associated primarily with arms control and disarmament. Perhaps fears of "watering down" the definition of peace studies has blocked the peace and justice concerns of women and other traditionally marginalized groups. Getting published, staying in print, and being recognized seem to be as hard for feminists working in peace studies as it is in any other field.

Which texts do we use in our classrooms? Some core textbooks in peace studies leave out women completely. Perhaps peace research has been unable to undo its strategy of offering alternatives to the way we organize the world and to traditionally male-dominated disciplines such as political science and international relations by merely substituting an alternative male paradigm.

Developing a feminist peace studies does not rely on studying women's participation in movements as a static feature of social life. Nor should it claim women are somehow "more peaceful" than men. Instead, bringing feminism into peace studies means rethinking how we teach war, peace, conflict, justice, nonviolence, and conflict resolution. We must learn to approach these topics in a way that makes the personal political, that challenges the essentialism of Western theory, that reconsiders conventional peace studies paradigms, and that asks what these issues mean to real and diverse peoples living on this planet at the end of the twentieth century.

We peace educators must reevaluate what we teach, how we teach, and the purpose of our teaching. We must similarly reevaluate our research agendas, which could do more to promote peaceful and just societies. But to do so, peace studies need a wider base of knowledge from which to draw. Feminist scholarship and action can broaden that base, and help peace studies devise a curriculum that will better promote the social transformations of the twenty-first century.

REFERENCES

Boulding, Elise. 1981. "Focus On: The Gender Gap." *Journal of Peace Research* 21, 1:1–3.

Brock-Utne, Birgit. 1989. *Feminist Perspectives on Peace and Peace Education.* New York: Pergamon.

Gilligan, Carol. 1982. *In a Different Voice: Psychological Theory and Women's Development.* Cambridge, MA: Harvard University Press.

hooks, bell. 1984. *Feminist Theory from Margin to Center.* Boston: South End Press.

Lopez, George. 1985. "A University Peace Studies Curriculum for the 1990s." *Journal of Peace Research* 22, 2:117–128.

Roberts, Barbara. 1988. "The Death of Machothink: Feminist Research and the Transformation of Peace Studies." *Women's Studies International Forum* 7, 4:195–200.

Sylvester, Christine. 1987. "Some Dangers in Merging Feminist and Peace Projects." *Alternatives* 12:493–509.

Woehrle, Lynne. 1995. "Teachings about Women from a Peace Studies Perspective: An Annotated Bibliography of Resources on Conflict, Peace, and Justice." *Women's Studies Quarterly* 23, 3/4 (December):214–48.

Chapter Thirty-Seven

The Psychology of Societal Reconstruction and Peace
A Gendered Perspective

Susan R. McKay

When societies are assailed by wars, state-sanctioned violence, revolutionary struggles, or nonviolent social movements, women have historically been actors in these conflicts. Consequently, women's roles are often radically altered because they are compelled to shed constraints of gendered traditions and respond to demands of profound social upheaval.

> During violent conflicts, both gender relations and opinions about the way they should be, change. Women take up new responsibilities and, at the same time, take on heavier duties. In the aftermath of conflicts, tensions may rise if the newly-acquired lifestyle of women is not accepted by the new society. During the process of reconstruction, women may easily be marginalized again. (National Committee for Development Education, 1994: 6)

For peace psychologists, concerned with the emergence of cultures of peace, peace building, and reconstruction, the inclusion of women in its discourse, analysis, and praxis is essential.

Feminists argue that global visions emphasize women's active involvement in structural transformation and the importance of deep commitment to self-reliance. It is proposed (Enloe, 1993) that because feminists start from the conditions of women's lives and because they see how many forms violence and oppression can take, peace is more likely to be defined as women's achievement of control over their own lives. Are they able to regain their rights or acquire new ones postconflict? How is self reliance of women made possible through changed economic, political, and social structures? Fogelberg spoke to the importance of the issue of the role and position of women with respect to peacekeeping and reconstruction: "Not simply because equal opportunities for women constitutes a universal, fundamental right, but also because societies have a greater chance of developing and of achieving social cohesion if the entire population, rather than only half of it is involved in reconstruction."

The purpose of this chapter is to assemble a compilation of disparate resources and to build thematic concepts in attempting to construct knowledge about women and societal reconstruction. As evidenced by searching psychology, sociology and women's studies databases, several indexes, and literature published by both governmental and nongovernmental agencies, issues facing women during periods of reconstruction—including their specific psychosocial concerns—are rarely discussed. There are many ways in which the content of this chapter could have evolved—for example, an in-depth discussion of women, human rights, and violence is very appropriate to discuss in terms of societal reconstruction. However, I chose to focus on broad themes and to raise feminist questions about gendered reconstruction.

For the purposes here, I use Reardon's definition of feminism as a strand of the human rights movement that insists on women's equality so that "women are of equal social and human value with men and that the differences between men and women, whether biologically based or culturally derived, do not and should not constitute grounds for discrimination against women" (1985: 20). Further, as discussed by Reardon, there is no one feminism but many feminisms, since contemporary feminism is a global and highly varied phenomenon.

The Centrality of Violence in Feminist Analysis

For feminists, violence is the central problem for peace—in all its forms and at all levels of society. Addressing the fundamental issue of violence, from personal to political, is necessary if women are to move toward gender equality and self-reliance during societal reconstruction. Violence, much of which results from lack of equity on multiple levels, represents a failure of humanity, manifests limited social skills, and shows a lack of imagination and creativity (Reardon, 1993). The mode of thinking that allows us to think of others as unequal also makes it possible to perpetuate acts of violence against those perceived as less important.

Violence can be conceived as structural or indirect violence or direct violence (Brock-Utne, 1989). It is essential that *both* indirect and direct violence toward women are understood as fundamental phenomena that maintain inequality. Structural violence incorporates inequitable social and economic structures and processes from the local to the global level that pose serious obstacles to a decent quality of life and to full development of the human person. Examples are hunger, disease, unemployment, illiteracy, racism, and sexism. Direct violence occurs as in assault, war, torture, and rape. Men are more apt to experience the direct violence of armed combat, make up the majority of perpetrators of violent crimes, and participate in interpersonal violence. Women, in contrast, are more likely to be helpless to save loved ones and those in their care in times of armed conflict, to experience deprivation related to economic structures, and to know gendered violence in the form of sexual abuse, rape, and lack of control over their bodies—including becoming prostitutes or being victimized by sexual slavery that often accompanies militarism (Brock-Utne, 1989). Also, women have suffered direct violence as political prisoners because men in their lives were underground, and women were convenient hostages (C. Montiel, personal communication, February 20, 1995).

Violence, Reconstruction, and Gender

Light (1992) has discussed the psychological scars of gender-specific abuse experienced by Guatemalan peasant women, pointing out that these special abuses do not constitute the whole of women's trauma but rather compound the general traumas of war in which life and livelihood are under constant attack, and loss of children, spouses and parents, and/or the witnessing of brutality against these loved ones is commonplace. With reference to refugee women, Light emphasized the importance of community in reestablishing group and individual identity. In many—if not most—cultures, community is essential to the identities of both men and women, although the relative importance of individual versus community needs varies widely.

Others have also identified the key importance of community building and its special significance to women's lives and healing. Utting observed, in relation to the Cambodian peace process, that "many women lament the fact that there is no longer a sense of solidarity in their communities and that certain traditional support systems no longer exist" (1994: 101). *Rebuilding Wartorn Societies*, a document from the United Nations Research Institute for Social Development (UNRISD), cautioned, "The construction of relationships between people, the establishing of accountability and trust between neighbors, will take time" (UNRISD, 1993: 14–15). Collective healing of a community and of psychological rehabilitation were identified in this UNRISD report as areas where little research has been carried out on local experiences of social upheaval.

Taylor viewed South Africa's culture of violence as a key influencing factor in the efforts of social and community development practitioners or agencies to become part of the social change process. She identified community development as the essential element in social reconstruction and cited the importance of communities being empowered to overcome the effects of violence and renewing their faith and trust in "fellow patriots" (Taylor, 1994: 130). Although Taylor's discussion is not a gendered one, her discussion reiterates the importance of community in overcoming the effects of violence and in reconstructing both men's and women's lives.

Gibbs, in discussing postwar social reconstruction in Mozambique, emphasized the importance of moving beyond the Western ideal of healing individuals through psycho-social processes, with reconstruction conceived as arising from *both* individual and community actions. "It was this latter area to which people consistently referred as being the most significant factor in the remaking of their worlds" (Gibbs, 1994: 275). Gibbs painted a picture of "true peace" for the community, which is in celebration of its harvest, the rekindling of community and individual lives.

Psychosocial healing of the individual must not replace a concern for broader social and economic reconstruction, but neither should community approaches be designed in exclusion of individual approaches when culturally appropriate.

For example, Montiel (personal communication, February 20, 1989), in citing the example of women in the Philippines, stated that women's emotional needs require attention as part of psychological reconstruction after a war, protracted struggle, or otherwise. Women have been required to protect themselves and their children against invading forces while their husbands were out fighting elsewhere.

> It is the women who care for children in times of war, and this can be traumatic for both mother and children, especially when there is no food, no physical safety, no protection from tropical storms or winter winds. Also the women may tend to forget themselves in favor of their husbands' or children's needs during war. Reconstruction would involve going through and rebuilding the self that she may have forgotten. (C. Montiel, personal communication, February 20, 1995)

Broader psychosocial reconstruction processes can address issues of structural violence, whereas multiple community and psychosocial approaches toward individual healing of sexually traumatized women need to be both culture and gender-specific in design.

Reconstruction: Traditional and Gendered Meanings

The Oxford English Dictionary defined reconstruction as "the rebuilding of an area devastated by war" (Simpson and Weiner, 1989: 357). This is consistent with a description from a U.S. Committee for Refugees issue paper discussing Liberian reconstruction: "The economy will have to be revived, industry and foreign investment encouraged. Basic services such as electricity and communication will need to be fully operative. More schools and institutions of higher learning must reopen" (Ruiz, 1992: 31). Other reconstruction efforts, such as in Afghanistan, also focus on mine clearance, shelter for displaced populations, food and agricultural production, and the physical environment (Christensen, 1990). Psychosocial aspects of reconstruction appear to be infrequently discussed and are seemingly rare if nonexistent as a priority.

As psychologists we have particular concerns that linkages be made between the physical and psychosocial reconstruction processes. For feminist psychologists, the gender dimension is important as well, not an "add on" but an integral part of psychologists' thinking about their contributions to societal reconstruction. There is, however, scant discussion in reconstruction literature about psychosocial aspects, and essentially none about gender.

Deconstructing Societal Reconstruction Processes

Important questions exist about how reconstruction is conceptualized. These generic questions are also profoundly gendered:

- What is societal reconstruction and who defines its values and priorities?
- Who and what institutions are reconstructed? Is there concern for people's lives and the devastation that has been unleashed on the human psyche?
- Is it concrete and literal, such as in the reconstruction of the physical infrastructure, or does it more expansively relate to community building and healing, to include social and psychological reconstruction?

From my search of the literature, it appears that gendered concerns about societal reconstruction have not been discussed. Some essential questions follow:

- In what ways are gender relationships maintained or re-created in peace accords, in the legal system including the Constitution, in landrights, and in political participation?
- What is peace from the perspective of women, and how does this relate to reconstruction?
- How are women affected by gendered power arrangements of reconstruction?
- How does postconflict reconstruction address the gender-specific traumas women have experienced on individual, family, and societal levels, such as rape and sexual torture?
- What psychological processes affect the ability of women to play full, equal, and effective roles in societal reconstruction? (For example, power arrangements, social identity processes, gender role stereotyping.)
- Are women's rights recognized as human rights, and how are these rights actualized in societal rehabilitation and reconstruction processes?
- How are conflict resolution processes gendered?

Integral to the discussion of these questions is an appreciation of the interactive elements of equality, development, and peace. Equality requires support mechanisms such as legal protection, literacy, education and training, day care and health care. Development is required for equality, which in turn requires peace (Urdang, 1989). The absence of peace makes elusive the potential for equality and development.

Women as Actors during Conflicts

Gilbert, in describing European women during World War II, argued that "women seemed to become, as if by some uncanny swing of history's pendulum, ever more powerful" (1987: 200). Stories abound of the self-sufficiency and courage that women developed as they dealt with situations of profound deprivation and personal threat, for example during World War II in Japanese (Brouwers, 1981; Brooks, 1987) and Nazi (Rittner and Roth, 1991) concentration camps, revolutionary struggles in Latin America (Agosin, 1993; Burgos-DeBray, 1984), and in the establishment of women's associations during the Palestinian *intifada* (Strum, 1992; Young, 1992). In Chechnya, soldiers' mothers marched en masse in the war zone to take back their sons: "The fact that dozens of mothers have walked onto military bases and taken their sons home without interference from officers is perhaps a sign of the confusion in the military. But it also is a sign of their [women's] fierce determinism" (Stanley, 1995: 4). Ferris (1993) noted the generations of silence surrounding the telling of stories about women's efforts for social change and peace and cited some of these struggles: protesting the violence in Northern Ireland, Palestinian and Israeli women trying to overcome barriers of distrust and enmity, the mothers of the Plaza de Mayo in Argentina, the Mothers of the Disappeared in El Salvador, the Mothers Front in Sri Lanka, Japanese women demonstrating against racism and nuclearism, and South African women with their long history of nonviolent resistance, which has been central to the country's struggle.

Contrary to these examples, Enloe observed that "in the torrents of media images that accompany an international crisis, women are typically made visible only as symbols, victims, or dependents. 'Womenandchildren' rolls easily off network tongues because, in network minds, women are family members rather than independent actors" (1993: 166). The media are not alone in their perception.

Women's Post-Conflict Expectations and the Global Reality

Movement toward greater gender equality during times of conflict may establish a presumption of women's involvement during postconflict reconstruction—whether at state, community, family, or individual levels. According to Osman (1993), women who are ready to shape the reconstruction of their country are facing the consequences of breaking tradition. In fact, women are inevitably deeply involved in reconstruction processes, although within circumscribed areas. Boulding observed that

> at the close of every war, destroyed communities have been rebuilt and much of the physical labour of rebuilding has been women's work. Further, . . . women have been called to a ceaseless reconstruction of the social infrastructure that provides the health, education and human services required for society not to fall apart, as well as a ceaseless tending of the rural resources of the land in order that there be an uninterrupted supply of food. (Boulding, 1988: 228, 229)

During the postconflict period, following women's involvement in nationalistic struggles in such diverse parts of the world as Zimbabwe, Nicaragua, and China, women have rarely achieved visible leadership roles, and the reinforcement of existing household relations has meant women have usually remained in, or even returned to, subordinate positions (Seidman, 1993). Many international examples convey analogous scenarios—that during reconstruction, women's place is at home. Another way women are marginalized is in the conflict resolution process: in the reconstruction period, conflicts and how to deal with them remain male-dominated issues (National Committee for Development Education, 1994).

In El Salvador, women ex-guerrillas are being pressured to remove their IUD's in the name of peace (Enloe, 1993). "Polish women are being urged to worry less about unemployment . . . and to take more satisfaction in bearing children for the sake of nationalist revival. Angolan women are being urged to put their own needs as women on the political back burner for the sake of keeping afloat the fragile boat of post-Cold War Angolan democratization" (Enloe, 1993: 257). When Namibia gained independence from South Africa in 1990, hopes for improvements in women's status were high, given the constitution's recognition that women have "suffered special discrimination" and need affirmative action policies so that they are "enabled to play a full, equal and effective role in the nation" ("Namibia, Empty Words?" 1995: 17).

Edwards observed that women who participated in Marxist liberation movements in Central America reported that dedication and sacrifice on behalf of the movement did not translate into leadership in postwar civil institutions. "Nicaraguan women warn Salvadorian and Guatemalan women not to equate participation in the armed struggle with gender equality" (1994: 52). Discussing Mozambique, Urdang (1989) observed how little change has taken place in the household, although the liberation of women is integrated into the ideological perspective on the need for building a new society; women have been actively called upon to leave aside gender struggles and to wait. In Somalia, women who desired to help shape the reconstruction of their country were faced with the consequences of breaking tradition when men felt threatened by women's new roles in the economy. The most active women community workers were shut out of negotiations toward peace and reconstruction, and women were excluded from nearly every formal meeting where Somalia's future was being determined (Osman, 1993). During early Kuwaiti societal reconstruction after the Gulf War, "Many Kuwaiti women active in the wartime resistance in the movement for women's suffrage . . . were concerned less with postwar militarization, however, than with reconstructing Kuwaiti womanhood so that it incorporated a sense of self-reliance" (Enloe, 1993: 185).

According to Seidman, post-apartheid South Africa may present a different situation because women's demands will likely be articulated by an urban popular movement, and women may not be willing to subsume questions of gender subordination under appeals to national unity. Further, the conditions of social reproduction have undermined male-dominated household patterns that have been reinforced in other nationalistic movements. "Especially in the labor movement and within community groups, there is clear evidence that many Black women believe a post-apartheid state should respond to gender-specific concerns" (1993: 293).

Mathabane cited the significance of women's involvement in South Africa's national freedom struggle and stated that their agenda must no longer be ignored, postponed, or compromised "They are insisting that their emancipation not be regarded as incidental to the overall liberation from apartheid. The two struggles are indivisibly linked" (1994: 346). She observed: "They want to ensure that South Africa doesn't go the way of many independent states in Africa where women contributed as much as men to the overthrow of colonialism and yet find themselves still oppressed, discriminated against, and treated as second-class citizens" (ibid.).

Peace Accords and Gendered Realities

In a recent United Nations publication about the reconciliation, reconstruction, and long-term human development processes in the postconflict period in El Salvador, Boutros Boutros-Ghali titled a section of his discourse about the peace accords in El Salvador as "The Birth of the Peace Process" (United Nations, 1995: 6). This gendered nomenclature, which some feminists would argue represents cooptation by men of women's functions (Cohn, 1989; Spretnak, 1989), highlights a discussion in which Boutros-Ghali's only mention of women occurred when describing a "womenandchildren"-focused cease-fire sponsored by the United Nations Children's Fund (UNICEF), an initiative intended to provide a break of a day or two at a time in the hostilities so that children could be immunized. In turn, related concepts of "peace corridors," "corridors of tranquility" and "zones of tranquility," have been developed during other global conflicts; according to Boutros-Ghali, "Most importantly, it underscored the humanitarian needs and rights of women and children during times of conflict" (United Nations, 1995: 9).

Interesting and feminist questions arise from Boutros-Ghali's choice of words: "Who gives birth to the peace process?" And where do these actors "give birth to peace"—in a public forum, within political arenas, or within the confines of home and community? Are women's rights written into peace accords? The answer, according to Ferris (personal communication, February 23, 1995), is "I don't know of *any* peace agreements that have incorporated gender perspectives. The typical pattern . . . is for women's particular concerns to be ignored—even when they played important roles in the struggle." It is noteworthy, however, that some newly crafted constitutions—such as South Africa's—have incorporated women's rights, even if their actualization has been indifferent.

Utting (1994) observed that "a peace process should not be seen simply as a mechanism that will enable a society to end hostilities and return to 'normal.' Rather, the very nature of that process may transform an economy and society in unexpected ways and *engender* [emphasis author's] new forms of economic, social and physical insecurity." Enloe has advocated reading peace agreements with a feminist lens to interpret whether the intent of the agreements is to demasculinize or remasculinize public life, to ask what has changed postwar. "Have the changes witnessed in Eastern Europe, the Persian Gulf, Central America, Southeast Asia and Southern Africa demilitarized masculinity? If so, then a principle ingredient of patriarchal culture will have been eliminated. If so, then women will relate to men differently, and the state will expect new attitudes from both. If so, the state itself and international diplomacy between states won't look the same" (Enloe, 1993: 252). Instead, as the Cambodian peace process has demonstrated (Utting, 1994), the peace process may not only fail to bring about a cessation of hostilities and reduce militarism, but possibly shape a particular style of development that will prolong the suffering and insecurities of the country's people.

Nationalism and Gender Inequality

Enloe (1993) argued that the war-ending process is a profoundly gendered event, far more complex than the signing of a peace accord or the decommissioning of a missile. During times of societal restructuring, conflict exists between the exigencies of nationalism and achievement of women's equality. The reality usually proves that, regardless of culture and place, women's roles revert to traditional ones, and nationalistic loyalties are more highly valued than is gender equality. Enloe, in her insightful analysis of post-Cold War sexual politics, observed that "in each country someone will be making calculations about how masculinity and femininity can best serve national security. This someone may be casual, confused, or ambivalent, but he or she will be making those decisions. This is a postwar period crowded with gendered decisions" (1993: 261).

Seidman stated that "since at least the turn of the century, nationalistic movements have regularly promised to improve the status of women; before taking power, they have pledged to end gender-based subordination. Just as regularly, however, most of these promises have gone unfulfilled" (1993: 291). Seidman attributed several causes to this maintenance of the gender status quo, including fear of dividing the "imagined community" on which nationalist ideologies are built and emphasis on national unity instead of gender equality.

Further, Seidman described the dilemma faced regularly by nationalistic leaders so that

> even when they sincerely hope to challenge the subordination of women, their efforts to maintain a popular base requires them to respond to supporters' demands, articulated primarily by men who generally have little immediate interest in challenging gender subordination. These demands frequently involve the reconstruction of beleaguered peasant households, even when that means reconstructing gender inequality. (1993: 292)

Back to the Family?

A tension exists between cultural values and Western views about gender equality and how it is to be enacted. An important recognition is that gendered analyses vary in their priorities across cultures and socioeconomic status (M. Roe, personal communication, February 17, 1995). Western feminists have been reproached for exporting their ethnocentrism, which decries the return of women to families and homes and, by implication, to oppression (MacDonald, 1987). Global feminist perspectives advocate that developmental processes occur within the context of non-Western indigenous cultural values (Bunch and Carrillo, 1990); further, gendered cultural relativism is conceptualized as a methodological and theoretical perspective that puts women at the center of knowledge but also contextualizes women's experiences to their culture. This approach recognizes the overly individualistic orientation of Western feminism as compared with collective notions of social interactions that dominate other social groups (West, 1992).

Whether postconflict reversion to traditional gender roles, especially in the household, is desirable will be contingent upon both ethnocentric and gendered perspectives. MacDonald has noted the very real and practical value of family life after a conflict in reestablishing stability and the promise of a future for people but that "what is crucial in this reordering of social values is whether women *also* retain a presence and voice in public politics" (1987: 10).

Young's (1992) feminist analysis described the patriarchal imperative in the Gaza Strip to maintain the family structure within the new socioeconomic system. Maintaining family structure, Young asserted, ensures women's position and therefore the support and social services that women provide. The implication is that gender equality cannot support male-dominated reconstruction processes.

Women from an El Salvadoran feminist organization, Movement of Women for Dignity and Life, described reconstruction as an extension of domestic work—health care, services, food. Literacy was named as an important aspect of reconstruction, as was women's active role in economic development, legal assistance, and women's rights (Lundoff, 1992). This perspective appears to be a curiously limited one for a feminist group since there is no discussion of women's political power and the strongest linkages are with traditional women's work.

White (1993) observed that, in South Africa, the argument runs this way: The African family is not a site of oppression but a much desired and rarely achieved haven from the racist world outside and that African women want the reconstitution and nurturing of family and marital structures. White's thesis has, however, promoted much debate in South Africa (C. de la Rey, personal communication, June 2, 1995). A glimpse of reality occurs in *African Women* (Mathabane, 1994), a biographic narrative of the lives of three generations of women from the same family. Any sense of romanticism one might have about "nurturing families" is quickly dispelled and, instead, a portrait is painted of cross-generational male abuse, poverty, and unceasing struggle by black women to provide for themselves and their children.

Gendered Solutions

Solutions to gendered marginalization within social reconstruction processes will not follow easily. According to Ferris (personal communication, February 23, 1995), the tendency has been to see women's issues in terms of "maternal health clinics" or additional support for widows who have lost male relatives in war, and sometimes to include women in income-generating projects of postwar credit schemes. Ferris, who directs the Church World Service's Immigration and Refugee Program, remarked that she is unaware of deliberate attempts to sit down with representative groups of women and ask them how reconstruction *should* take place. She noted the work of the Life and Peace Institute (LPI) of Sweden in Somalia, where the LPI works with the United Nations to establish local democratic councils at the village and provincial levels throughout the country, with the insistence that these councils have at least one female representative. This was a real change from "business as usual" in Somalia, and the Somalian women "have really taken this opening and run with it." Ferris cited several examples: (1) organizing representative groups of women to work with them to make sure the single female Council member is really representing the women, and (2) for Somali women from different clans to meet with each other around issues of common concern, most notably how to stop the fighting. She noted how striking this is because men in their families won't even talk to people in other clans, whereas their wives and mothers are "plotting peace with their opponents." Young (1992) and Ashrawi (1995) described similar intercommunal relationships within women's associations between Jews, Christians, and Muslims in the Arab world.

Montiel observed that

> women may contribute positively in post-conflict reconstruction because often (1) they were not involved directly in the fighting and killing so they have fewer politico-military enemies, and (2) they are used to fixing up squabbles/fights among their children, wanting to produce win-win outcomes because of their love for both children involved in the domestic conflict. And to the extent that win-win outcomes and "loving both parties" are needed in reconstruction, mothers (or maternal tendencies?) may contribute creatively to the social reconstruction process. (C. Montiel, pers. comm., February 20, 1995)

As has been argued, women's special role and needs are usually ignored, as in the recent example of social reconstruction in Afghanistan (Christensen, 1990), whereby vulnerable groups were identified for special programs but no mention was made of the needs of Afghan women specifically—or of their potential for participating in the rehabilitation efforts. A step toward remedying this lack was the organization of a UNICEF/UNIFEM (United Nations Development Fund for Women) workshop held in 1989 to construct recommendations for planning of reconstruction that involved Afghan women. Some concrete strategies were (1) a focus on women in the context of their homes and communities; (2) involvement of men in development projects of women to gain men's support; and (3) meeting women's needs through kinship-based networks (Christensen, 1990).

Women's organizations are central in social reconstruction efforts. Bunch and Carrillo recognized the long history of women's organizing at every level from caucuses within existing male institutions to autonomous groups. Although the role of independent organizing is crucial, it is not in itself sufficient to bring about deep structural transformation. "Women must also work with other sectors across race and class lines, build strong coalitions, and demand that our perspectives be included in all political platforms" (1990: 81–82). Fogelberg (1994) recommended actions toward this goal of including women in reconstruction, which include (1) promoting a dialogue on the position of women in the new civil society—both at government levels and in all ranks of society; (2) supporting local and regional women's organizations to enable them to work on consciousness-raising and structural change; such organizations can be found in countries which have recently experienced conflict, such as South Africa and Ethiopia, and in countries such as Zambia and Mali that are in the process of democratization; (3) giving aid to consciousness-raising campaigns aimed at increasing knowledge of women's statutory and fundamental rights within government bodies, the police, the army, and the criminal justice system; (4) reviewing and amending parts of the constitution and the legal system that are gender-related, with the aid of the Conference on Elimination of Discrimination Against Women (CEDAW); (5) increasing women's political participation through provision of aid for electoral training of female voters and for coaching female candidates.

All of the above recommendations speak to changing power relationships as an essential core of social reconstruction efforts. In a recent United Nations report on "Gender and the Agenda for Peace" (Division for the Advancement of Women, 1994), an expert group examined women's peace agenda and cited women's definitions of security as involving a preference for constructive rather than destructive power. Power was conceptualized as being used for the benefit of all. Peterson and Runyon (1993) highlighted the importance of the task of ungendering power so that women are added to the existing world politics power structures, resulting in these very power structures thereby being transformed ideologically and materially.

The Role of Peace Psychology

Many of the processes of reconstruction are intimately familiar to psychologists, in that they involve social learning. Boulding eloquently described the commitment to peaceful reconstruction of the social order as a continuous process of "social learning-cum-action. Nonviolent change is only possible when oppression is met by noncompliance and a refusal to cooperate with traditional dominance behavior. This requires an egalitarian spirit, and a transformation of leadership between the more and the less articulate members of a group" (1988: 235).

For change to follow, we will need to be aware of opportunities to facilitate constructive action. "Psychology is probably the most appropriate science to develop that awareness. In exposing the mechanisms of the prevalent ideology, psychology can make a meaningful contribution to the course of social change. This project would have to be complemented by deliberations on what constitutes the "good society" that is most likely to promote human welfare. Otherwise, psychologists will merely engage in denunciation without annunciation" (Prilleltensky, 1989: 799).

Prilleltensky advocated that constructive action be preceded by reflection, and that a commitment to social change must begin with conscientization and annunciation. "Conscientization refers to the process whereby people achieve an illuminating awareness both of the socioeconomic and cultural circumstances that shape their lives and their capacity to transform that reality. Annunciation [is] the act of conceiving a just social arrangement in which the well-being of the population is fostered" (1989: 800), such as in developing cultures of peace. Prilleltensky noted that women's groups have started to capitalize on the proposition of conscientization in attempting to analyze and modify male-oriented cultural practices, that their participation in consciousness-raising groups has advanced their social interests, and that beneficial psychological changes have occurred such as increased autonomy and self-esteem. Peace psychology, too, must begin the processes of annunciation and conscientization in order to bring to consciousness the realities of how gender constructs the process of societal reconstruction and, thereby, work toward social change based upon principles of equality of men and women. As elegantly stated by Martín-Baró, in speaking about what psychology can do in making a contribution to solving the crucial problems of our communities, "The principle holds that the concern of the social scientist should not be so much to explain the world as to transform it" (in Aron and Corne, 1994: 19).

REFERENCES

Agosin, M. 1993. *Surviving beyond Fear: Women, Children and Human Rights in Latin America*. New York: White Pine Press.

Aron, A. and Corne, S. (eds.). 1994. *Writings for a Liberation Psychology*. Cambridge, MA: Harvard University Press.

Ashrawi, H. 1995. *This Side of Peace: A Personal Account*. New York: Simon and Schuster.

Boulding, E. 1988. "Warriors and Saints: Dilemmas in the History of Men, Women and War." In E. Isaksson (ed.), *Women and the Military System*. New York: St. Martin's.

Brock-Utne, B. 1989. *Feminist Perspectives on Peace and Peace Education*. New York: Pergamon.

Brooks, M. 1987. "Passive in War: Women Internees in the Far East." In S. MacDonald, P. Holden, and S. Ardener (eds.), *Images of Women in Peace and War: Cross-Cultural and Historical Perspectives*. London: Macmillan.

Brouwers, J. 1981. *Sunken Red*. New York: New Amsterdam Books.

Bunch, C., and Carrillo, R. 1990. "Feminist perspectives on Women in Development." In I. Tinker (ed.), *Persistent Inequalities: Women and World Development*. New York: Oxford University Press.

Burgos-Debray, E. (ed.). 1984. *I, Rigoberta Menchú: An Indian Woman in Guatemala*. New York: Verso.

Christensen, H. 1990. *The Reconstruction of Afghanistan: A Chance for Rural Women*. Geneva: United Nations Research Institute for Social Development.

Cohn, C. 1989. "Emasculating America's linguistic deterrent." In A. Harris and Y. King, eds., *Rocking the Ship of State: Toward a Feminist Peace Politics*. Boulder, CO: Westview.

de la Rey, C. June 2, 1995. Personal communication.

Division for the Advancement of Women/Secretariat for the Fourth World Conference on Women. December 5-9, 1994. *Gender and the Agenda for Peace*. New York: United Nations.

Edwards, B. 1994. "Women, Work and Democracy in Latin America." *Convergence* 27 (2/3): 51–57.

Enloe, C. 1993. *The Morning After: Sexual Politics at the End of the Cold War*. Berkeley: University of California Press.

Ferris, E. February 23, 1994. Personal communication.

———. 1993. *Women, War and Peace*. Uppsala, Sweden: Life and Peace Institute.

Fogelberg, T. 1994. "Settling Differences: Conflict and Development from Women's Vantage Points." Paper presented at NGO Conference on Conflict and Development, The Hague, The Netherlands, February.

Gibbs, W. 1994. "Post-war Social Reconstruction in Mozambique: Re-framing Children's Experience of Trauma and Healing." *Disasters* 18 (3): 2268–76.

Gilbert, S. 1987. "Soldier's Heart: Literary Men, Literary Women, and the Great War." In M. R. Higonnet and J. Jenson (eds.), *Behind the Lines: Gender in the Two World Wars*. New Haven: Yale University Press.

Light, D. 1992. "Healing Their Wounds: Guatemalan Refugee Women as Political Activists." *Women and Therapy* 13 (4): 297–308.

Lundoff, C. 1992. "Feminists Reconstruct El Salvador." *Off Our Backs* 22 (4) (April): 8, 24.

MacDonald, S. 1987. "Drawing the Lines—Gender, Peace, and War: An Introduction." In S. Macdonald, P. Holden, and S. Ardener (eds.), *Images of Women in Peace and War: Cross-Cultural and Historical Perspectives*. London: Macmillan.

Mathabane, M. 1994. *African Women: Three Generations*. New York: HarperCollins.

Montiel, C. February 20, 1995. Personal communication.

"Namibia, Empty Words?" 1995. *MS* (March/April):17.

National Committee for Development Education. February 28, 1994. *Development and Conflict: Report NCO Congress*. Amsterdam: Author.

Osman, H. 1993. "Somalia: Will reconstruction threaten women's progress?" *MS* (March/April):12–13.

Peterson, V., and Runyon, A. 1993. *Global Gender Issues*. Boulder, CO: Westview.

Prilleltensky, I. 1989. "Psychology and the Status Quo." *American Psychologist* 44: 795–802.

Reardon, B. 1985. *Sexism and the War System*. New York: Columbia University Press.

———. 1993. *Women and Peace: Feminist Visions of Global Security*. Albany: State University of New York Press.

Rittner, C., and Roth, J. (eds.). 1991. *Different Voices: Women and the Holocaust*. New York: Paragon House.

Roe, M. February 17, 1995. Personal communication.

Ruiz, A. 1992, Feb. *Uprooted Liberians: Casualties of a Brutal War*. Issue paper. U.S. Committee for Refugees: American Council for Nationalities Services.

Seidman, G. 1993. "No Freedom without the Women: Mobilization and Gender in South Africa, 1970–1992." *Signs: Journal of Women in Culture and Society* 18 (Winter): 291–320.

Simpson, J. A., and Weiner, S., eds., 1989. *Oxford English Dictionary*, vol. 13, 2d ed. Oxford: Clarendon Press.

Spretnak, C. 1989. "Naming the Cultural Forces that Push Us toward War." In D. Russell (ed.), *Exposing Nuclear Phallacies*. New York: Pergamon.

Stanley, A. 1995. "Mothers Act to Save Their Sons from War." *The New York Times*, February 11, p. 4.

Strum, P. 1992. *The Women Are Marching: The Second Sex and the Palestinian Revolution*. Brooklyn, NY: Lawrence Hill Books.

Taylor, V. 1994. "Social Reconstruction and Community Development in the Face of Violence and Conflict in South Africa." *Community Development Journal* 29: 123–31.

United Nations. 1995. *The United Nations and El Salvador, 1990–1995*. New York.

United Nations Research Institute for Social Development. 1993. *Rebuilding Wartorn Societies*. Geneva.

Urdang, S. 1989. *And Still They Dance: Women, War and the Struggle for Change in Mozambique*. New York: Monthly Review Press.

Utting, P. 1994. *Between Hope and Insecurity: The Social Consequences of the Cambodian Peace Process*. Geneva: UNRISD.

West, L. 1992. "Feminist Nationalist Social Movements: Beyond Universalism and toward a Gendered Cultural Relativism." *Women's Studies International Forum* 15: 563–79.

White, C. 1993. " 'Close to Home' in Johannesburg: Gender Oppression in Township Households." *Women's Studies International Forum* 16 (2): 149–63.

Young, E. 1992. *Keepers of the History: Women and the Israeli-Palestinian Conflict*. New York: Teachers College Press.

Contributors

Harriet Hyman Alonso teaches at Fitchburg State College in Fitchburg, Massachusetts. She is the author of *Peace as a Women's Issue* (Syracuse: Syracuse University Press, 1993).

Lorraine Bayard de Volo is an assistant professor of political science at Franklin Pierce College. Her research interests include gender hegemony and resistance, and she is currently working on a manuscript on maternal identity politics in revolutionary Nicaragua.

Janet Beilstein works for the United Nations Division for the Advancement of Women. She is the author of a 1995 United Nations report on women in peacekeeping.

April Carter teaches in the Department of Government, University of Queensland in Australia. Her books include *The Politics of Women's Rights* (Longman, 1988), *Success and Failure in Arms Control* (Oxford University Press, 1989), and *Peace Movements* (Longman, 1992).

Anuradha M. Chenoy is associate professor at the School of International Studies, Jawaharlal Nehru University, New Delhi. She has written widely in journals and books on international politics, Russia and Central Asia, and on women's issues.

Pamela Collett works as an education consultant in informal education for Save the Children (USA) in Islamabad, Pakistan.

Rhonda Copelon is a professor of law and the codirector of the International Women's Human Rights Law Clinic of the City University of New York School of Law. She is the coauthor with Babcock et al. of *Sex Discrimination and the Law*.

Francine D'Amico teaches political science at Hobart and William Smith Colleges. She is a coeditor of *Women, Gender and World Politics* (Westport, CT: Greenwood Press, 1994), and *Women in World Politics: An Introduction* (Westport, CT: Bergin and Garvey, 1995).

Malathi de Alwis is a research fellow at the International Centre for Ethnic Studies, Colombo, and a lecturer in the Master's Program in Women's Studies at the University of Colombo, Sri Lanka. She is the coeditor, with Kumari Jayawardena, of *Embodied Violence: Communalising Women's Sexuality in South Asia* (New Delhi: Kali for Women; London and New Jersey: Zed Books, 1996).

Cynthia Enloe is professor of government at Clark University in Worcester, Massachusetts. Among her recent books are *Bananas, Beaches and Bases: Making Feminist Sense of International Politics* (London: Pandora), and *The Morning after: Sexual Politics After the Cold War* (Berkeley: University of California Press, 1993). Her new book is the forthcoming *Maneuvers: Militarizing Women's Lives*.

Ilene Rose Feinman teaches U.S. history and politics at the recently converted Fort Ord, the California State University, Monterey Bay. Her research centers on questions of gender and citizenship in the United States, and especially the relationships between feminism, antimilitarism, and women in the armed forces.

Gwyn Kirk is a teacher, writer, a member of the Bay Area Peace Network, and a founder-member of the East Asia–United States Women's Anti-Militarist Network formed in May 1997. She is coauthor with Alice Cook of *Greenham Women Everywhere* (Boston: South End Press, 1983), and coeditor with Margo Okazawa-Rey of *Women's Lives: Multicultural Perspectives* (Mayfield, 1997).

Uta Klein teaches Sociology and Gender Studies at the University of Muenster in Germany.

Ronit Lentin is course coordinator of the M.Phil. in Ethnic and Racial Studies, Department of Sociology, Trinity College, University of Dublin. She is editor of *Gender and Catastrophe*, a book on Palestinian women (Jerusalem: Mifras, 1981), the novel *Songs on the Death of Children* (Dublin: Poolbeg Press, 1996), and has written academic articles on feminist research methodologies, the gendered relations between Israel and the Holocaust, women's peace activism, and citizenship and minority Irish women.

Lois Ann Lorentzen teaches in the Theology and Religious Studies Department at the University of San Francisco. She is coeditor (with Jennifer Turpin) of *The Gendered New World Order: Militarism, Development and the Environment* (New York: Routledge, 1996), coeditor (with David Batstone, Eduardo Mendieta, and Dwight N. Hopkins) of *Liberation Theologies: Postmodernity and the Americas* (Routledge, 1997), forthcoming *Global Ethics: Theories and Issues* (Wadsworth) and *Gods in Question: Religion and Globalization* (Duke University Press).

Irene Matthews teaches comparative literature at Northern Arizona University, specializing in women writers of Latin America, feminist theory, postcolonialism, and film theory. She is the author of *Nellie Campobello: La Centaura del Norte* (Cal Y Arena, Mexico).

Rela Mazali is a feminist writer-activist. She is coinitiator of a film, *Testimonies*, on the actions and experiences of Israeli soldiers suppressing the Palestinian uprising of 1987. She is currently completing *Else Where*, a book about women's spatial im/mobility.

Susan R. McKay is professor of nursing and women's studies at the University of Wyoming and a psychologist in private practice. She is past president of the Division of Peace Psychology of the American Psychological Association and teaches and researches on gender and peace.

Seungsook Moon is assistant professor of sociology at Vassar College, where she also works with the women's studies program. She has published articles on masculinity, the state and gender politics, and Eurocentrism and social theory. She is completing work on her book *Modernizing Gender Hierarchy: Militarism, the State and Industrialization in South Korea, 1963–1992*.

Mariana Mora is from Mexico City and graduated from the University of California at Berkeley in conservation and resource studies. She is currently working in Chiapas on regional development projects.

Diana Mulinari is a Latin American feminist sociologist who currently teaches sociology at the University of Lund in Sweden. Her theoretical interest is to understand the interlocation of gender with other forms of oppression. She has conducted research on Nicaraguan women during the Sandinista revolution and on gender and racism in Nordic countries.

Monica E. Neugebauer is a Ph.D. candidate at the School of International Relations, University of Southern California. She has served as a publications intern for the *Middle East Journal*. Her research interests include ethnic politics, nationalism, women and politics, social movements, and Third World developments.

Vesna Nikolić-Ristanović is a researcher at the Institute for Criminological and Sociological Research and teaches at the Center for Women's Studies in Belgrade (Serbia, former Yugoslavia). She has written widely on women and war, violence against women, and women's criminality.

Carolyn Nordstrom teaches peace and conflict studies at the University of California, Berkeley. She is completing a research project on "Girls and Warzones" for the Life and Peace Institute of Sweden. She is the author of *A Different Kind of War Story* (Philadelphia: University of Pennsylvania Press, 1997), and coeditor of *Fieldwork under Fire* (Berkeley: University of California Press, 1995).

Elaine R. Ognibene teaches English at Siena College and has published several articles on multicultural literatures, especially as they illustrate peace and justice issues. She is a founding member of Siena's Martin Luther King, Jr., and Coretta Scott King Lecture Series on Race and Nonviolent Social Change, and she serves on the Advisory Committee for Siena's Peace Studies Program.

Margo Okazawa-Rey is professor of social work at San Francisco State University, a member of the Bay Area Okinawa Peace Network, and a founder-member of the East Asia–United States Women's Anti-Militarist Network. Related publications include "Amerasian Children in GI Town: A Legacy of U.S. Militarism in South Korea," *Asian Journal of Women's Studies* 3 (1) 1997; and, with Gwyn Kirk, "Military Security: Confronting the Oxymoron," *Crossroads* (60) (1996).

V. Spike Peterson teaches government at the University of Arizona. She is the author of *Global Gender Issues* (with Anne Sisson Runyon) (Boulder, CO: Westview Press, 1994), and the editor of *Gendered States: Feminist (Re)Visioning of International Relations Theory* (Boulder, CO: Lynne Rienner, 1992).

Ninetta Pourou-Kazantzis is a psychologist and political activist who has worked on women's issues for more than twenty years. She is vice president of the Women's Section of the Free Democrats in Cyprus and has been general secretary of the Association of Women of the Mediterranean Region since 1996.

Betty A. Reardon is the director of peace education at Teacher's College, Columbia University. She is the author of *Sexism and the War System* (New York: Teachers College Press, 1985), and *Women and Peace* (Albany: State University of New York Press, 1993).

Darius M. Rejali teaches comparative politics and political philosophy at Reed College. He is the author of *Torture and Modernity: Self, Society and State in Modern Iran* (Boulder: Westview Press, 1994), and he is currently working, among other things, on the history of electric torture.

Sara Ruddick teaches at the New School for Social Research in New York. She is the author of *Maternal Thinking: Toward a Politics of Peace* (London: Women's Press, 1990).

Leila J. Rupp teaches history at Ohio State University. She is the author of *Worlds of Women: The Making of an International Women's Movement* (Princeton, N.J., Princeton University Press, 1997).

Nancy Scheper-Hughes teaches anthropology at the University of California, Berkeley. She is the author of *Death without Weeping: The Violence of Everyday Life in Brazil* (Berkeley: University of California Press, 1992), and *Saints, Scholars and Schizophrenics: Mental Illness in Rural Ireland* (Berkeley: University of California Press, 1979).

Gila Svirsky has been an activist in Israel's Women in Black movement since its inception and edited their international newsletter. She has played a key role in many peace and human rights efforts in the Middle East and is currently acting director of Bat Shalom, the Israeli partner to Jerusalem Link—the joint Israeli-Palestinian women's peace movement.

Jennifer Turpin is associate dean for arts, humanities, and social sciences at the University of San Francisco and past chair of the American Sociological Association's Section on Peace and War. She is the author of *Reinventing the Soviet Self* (Westport, CT: Praeger, 1995), and coeditor of *Rethinking Peace* (Boulder: Lynne Rienner, 1994), *The Web of Violence* (Urbana: University of Illinois Press,

1997), *The Gendered New World Order* (Routledge, 1996), and *The Encyclopedia of Violence, Peace and Conflict* (San Diego: Academic Press, forthcoming).

Lynne M. Woehrle is an assistant professor of sociology at Wilson College in Chambersburg, Pennsylvania. She is a teacher and community activist interested in women's issues, environmental concerns, social inequality, and community economic development. She has published several pieces on feminist peace studies and women's contributions to social change.

Angela Woollacott teaches history at Case Western Reserve University in Cleveland. She is the author of *On Her Their Lives Depend: Munitions in the Great War* (Berkeley: University of California Press, 1992).

Jodi York is a graduate of the University of San Francisco in politics, women's studies, and peace and justice studies. She is the former managing editor of *Peace Review,* a transnational peace studies journal.

Index